The Tale of the Outcasts

4

story & art by
Makoto Hoshino

The tale of outcasts

4

Contents

⚜Night 28⚜ In a Split Second

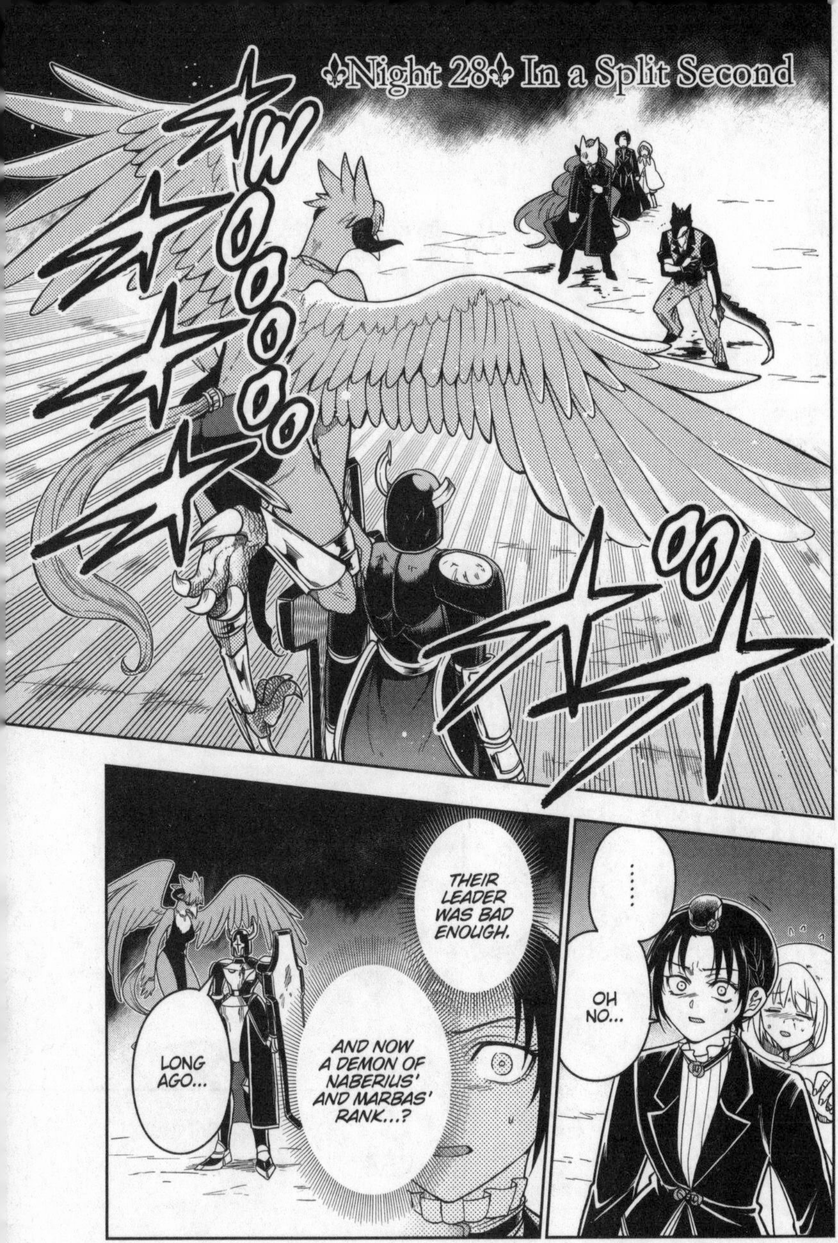
......
OH NO...
THEIR LEADER WAS BAD ENOUGH.
AND NOW A DEMON OF NABERIUS' AND MARBAS' RANK...?
LONG AGO...

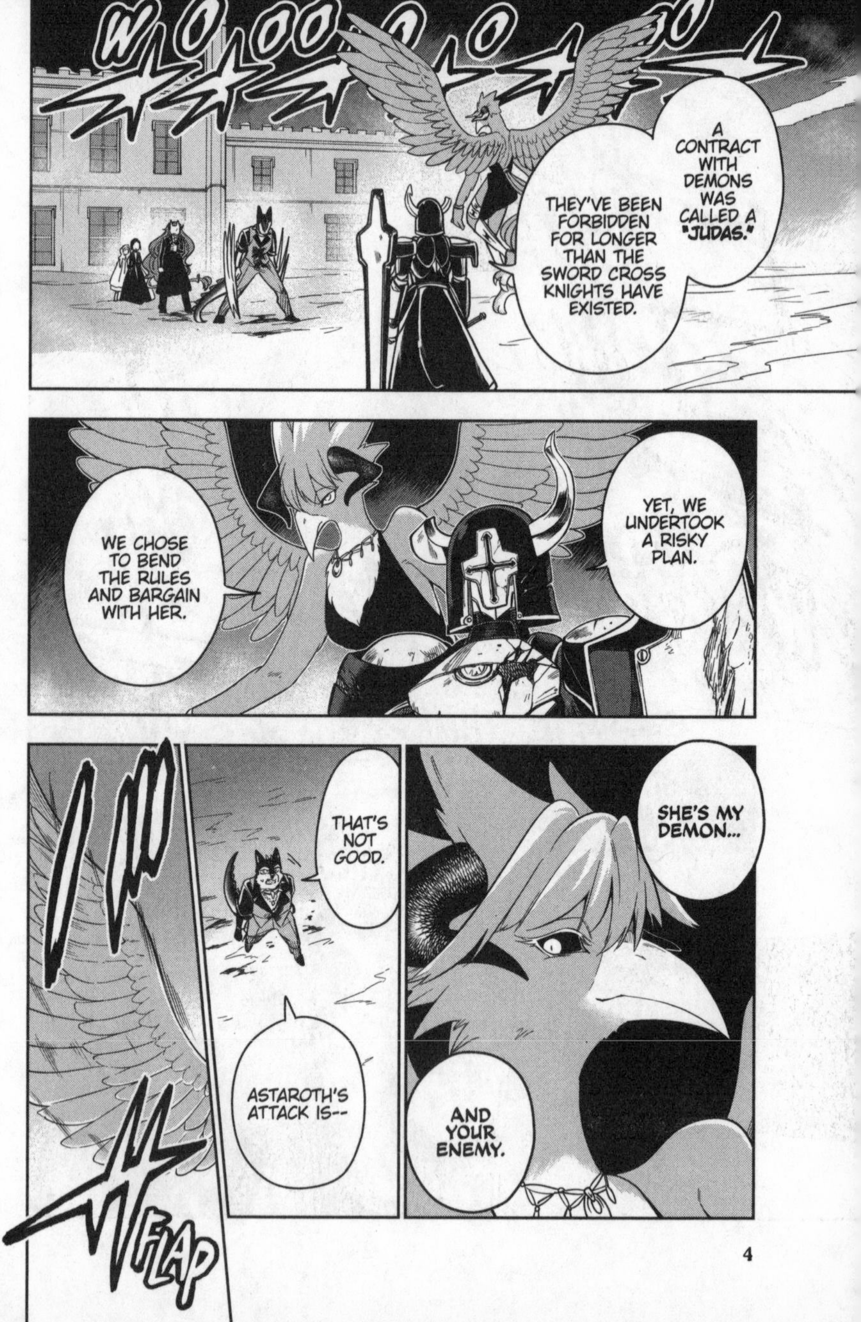
A CONTRACT WITH DEMONS WAS CALLED A "JUDAS."
THEY'VE BEEN FORBIDDEN FOR LONGER THAN THE SWORD CROSS KNIGHTS HAVE EXISTED.
YET, WE UNDERTOOK A RISKY PLAN.
WE CHOSE TO BEND THE RULES AND BARGAIN WITH HER.
SHE'S MY DEMON...
AND YOUR ENEMY.
THAT'S NOT GOOD.
ASTAROTH'S ATTACK IS--
FLAP

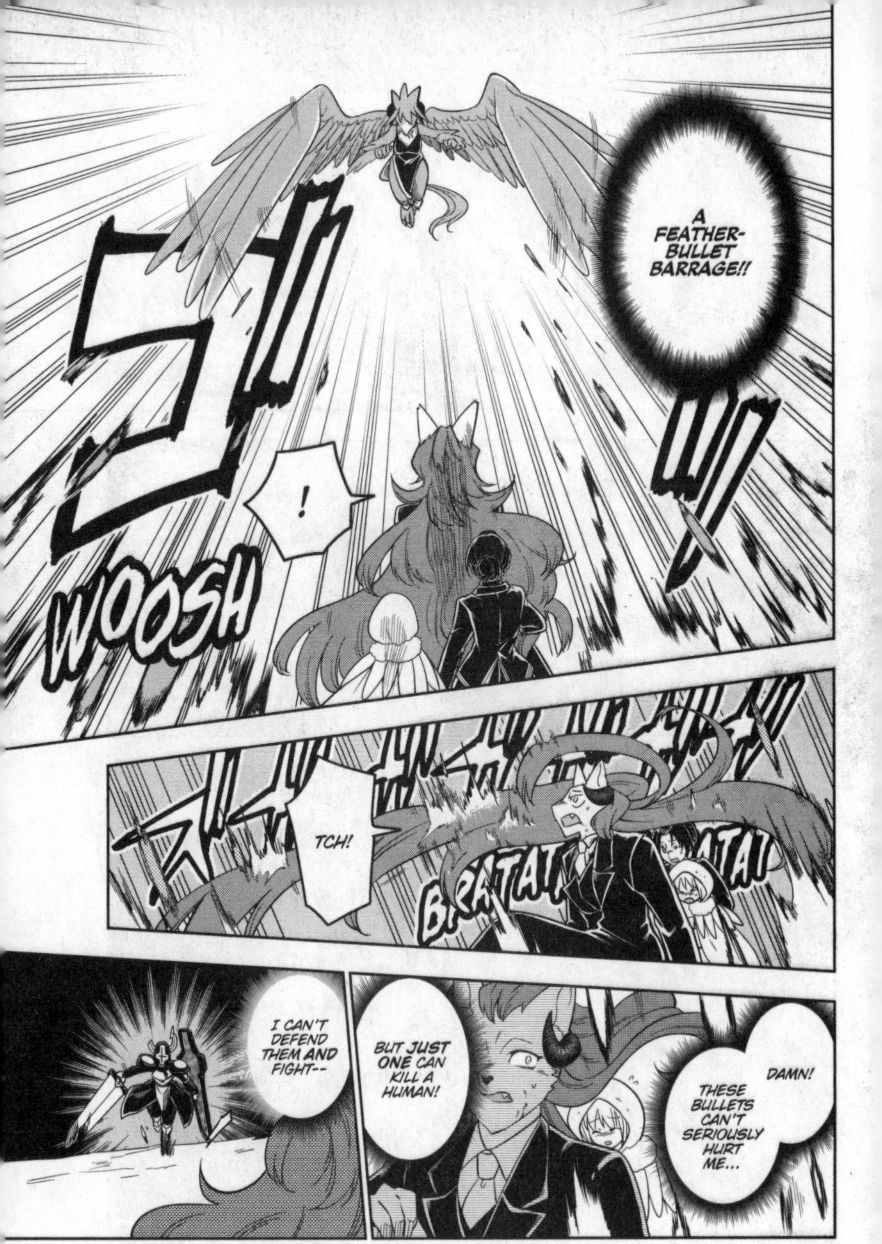
A FEATHER-BULLET BARRAGE!!
!
WOOSH
TCH!
DAMN!
THESE BULLETS CAN'T SERIOUSLY HURT ME...
BUT JUST ONE CAN KILL A HUMAN!
I CAN'T DEFEND THEM AND FIGHT--

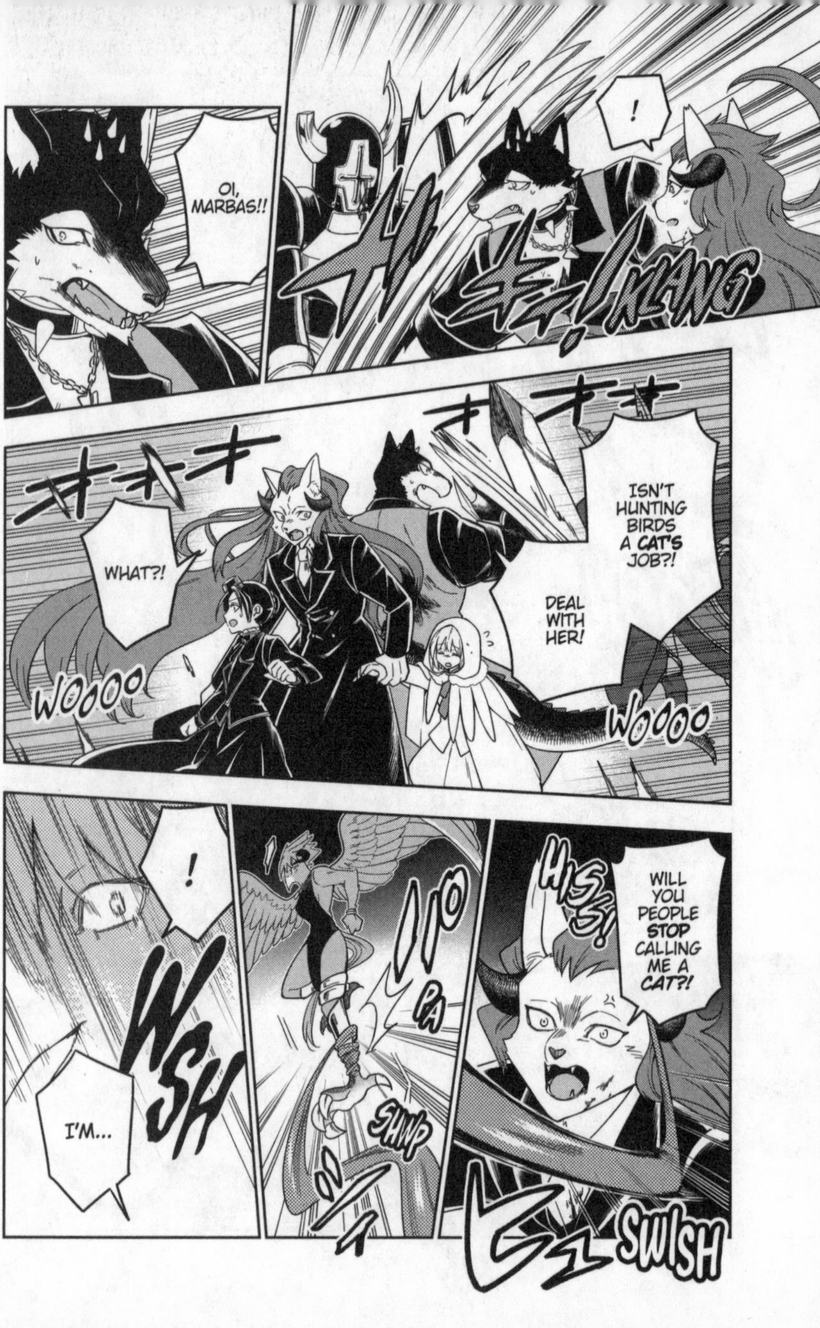
!
KLANG
OI, MARBAS!!
ISN'T HUNTING BIRDS A CAT'S JOB?!
DEAL WITH HER!
WOOOO
WHAT?!
WOOOO
HISS!
WILL YOU PEOPLE STOP CALLING ME A CAT?!
SWISH
PA
SHWP
!
WSH
I'M...

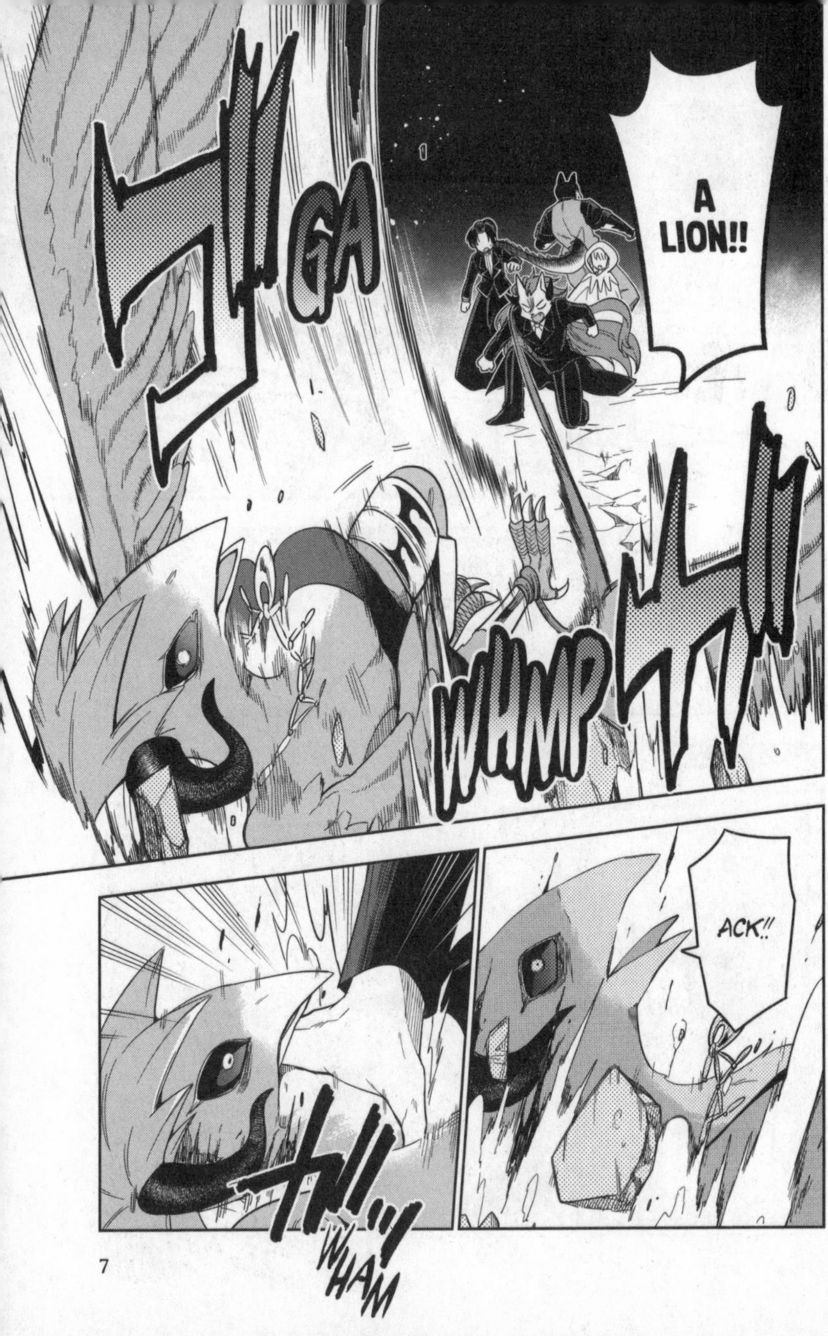
A LION!!
GA
WHMP
ACK!!
WHAM

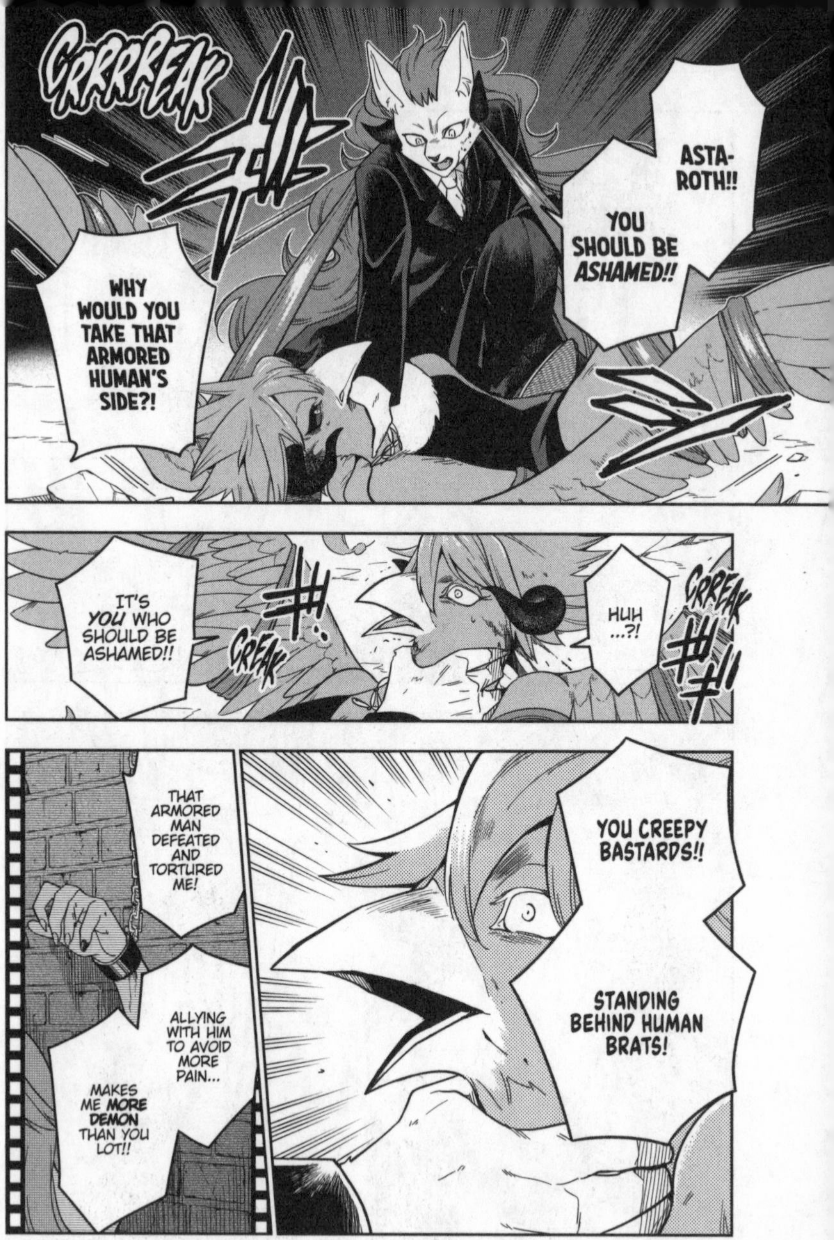

ASTA-ROTH!!
YOU SHOULD BE ASHAMED!!
CRRRREAK
WHY WOULD YOU TAKE THAT ARMORED HUMAN'S SIDE?!
CRREAK
HUH ...?!
CREAK
IT'S YOU WHO SHOULD BE ASHAMED!!
YOU CREEPY BASTARDS!!
STANDING BEHIND HUMAN BRATS!
THAT ARMORED MAN DEFEATED AND TORTURED ME!
ALLYING WITH HIM TO AVOID MORE PAIN...
MAKES ME MORE DEMON THAN YOU LOT!!

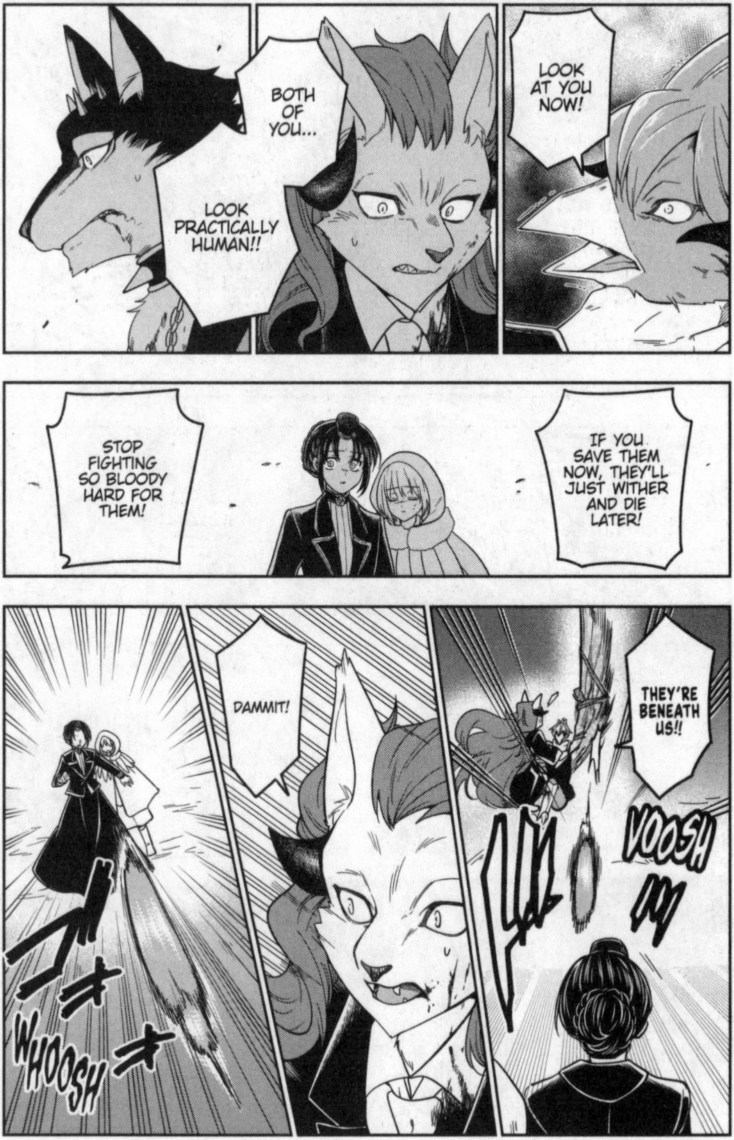
LOOK AT YOU NOW!
BOTH OF YOU...
LOOK PRACTICALLY HUMAN!!
IF YOU SAVE THEM NOW, THEY'LL JUST WITHER AND DIE LATER!
STOP FIGHTING SO BLOODY HARD FOR THEM!
THEY'RE BENEATH US!!
VOOSH!!
DAMMIT!
WHOOSH

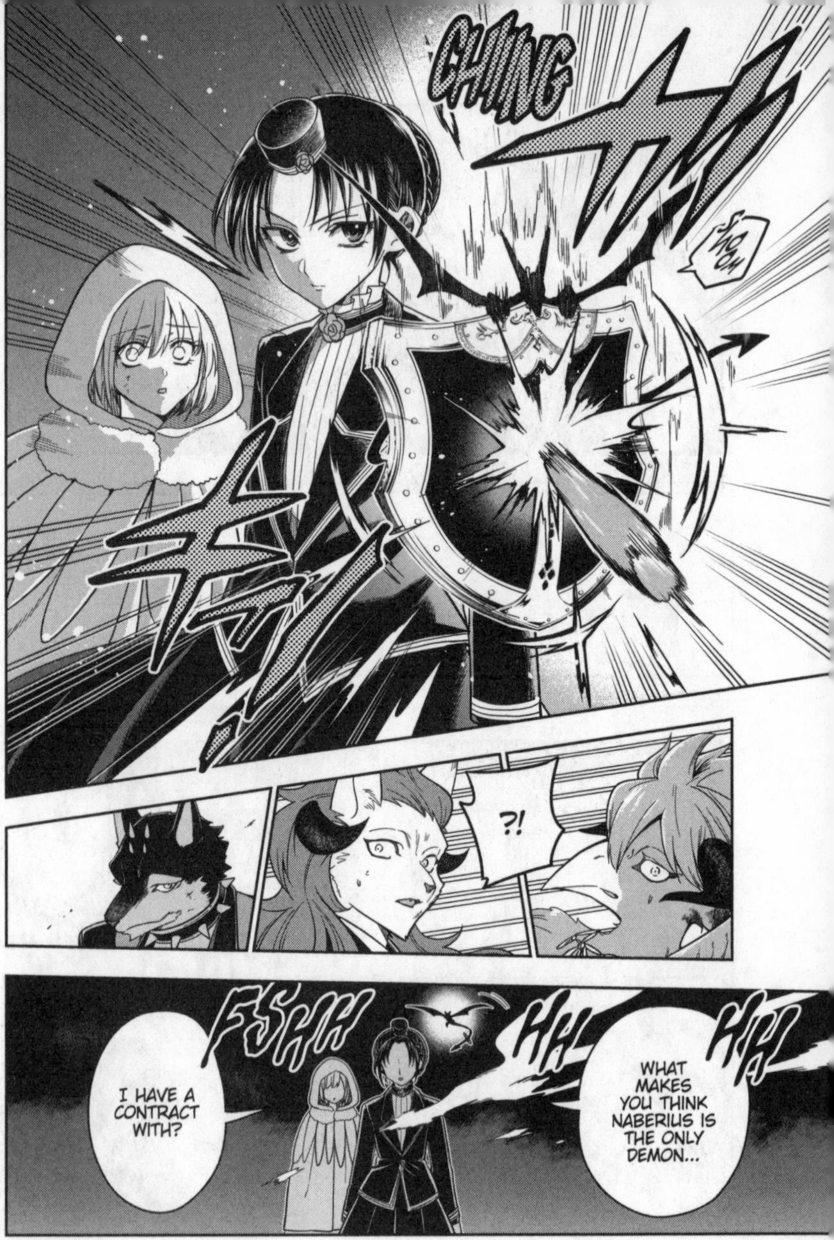
CHING
SHOW
?!
HA HA
WHAT MAKES YOU THINK NABERIUS IS THE ONLY DEMON...
I HAVE A CONTRACT WITH?
FSHH

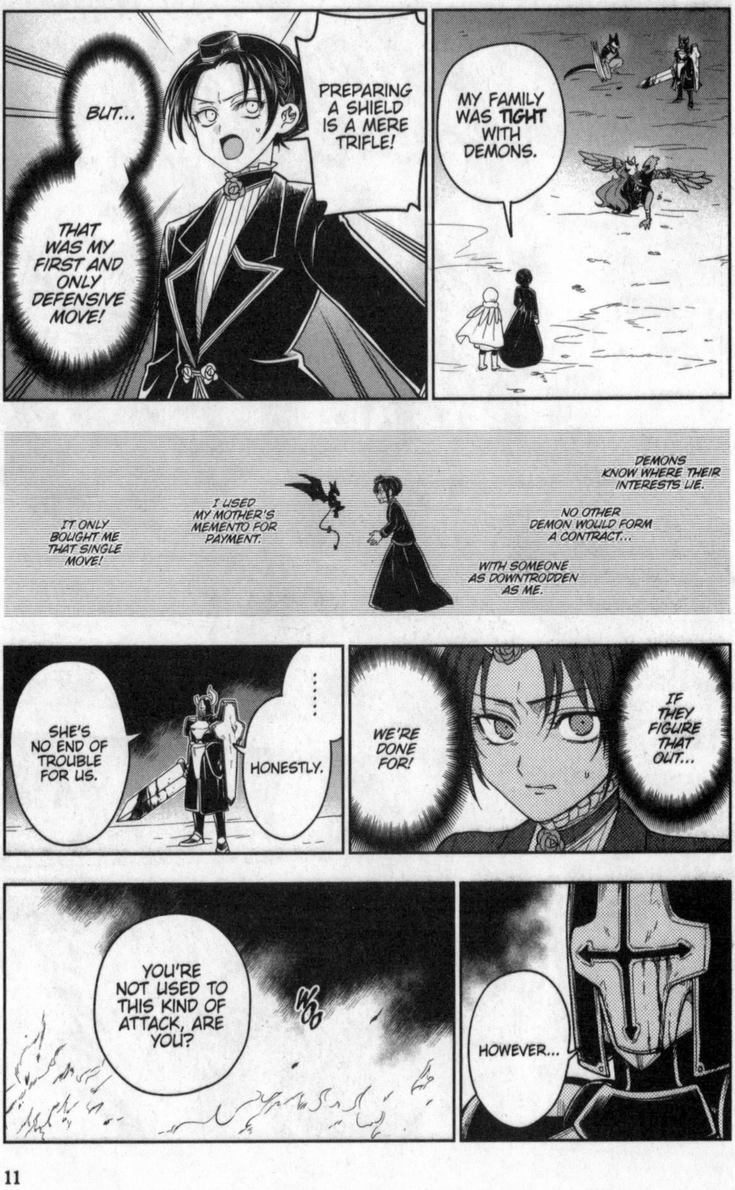
MY FAMILY WAS **TIGHT** WITH DEMONS.
PREPARING A SHIELD IS A MERE TRIFLE!
BUT...
THAT WAS MY FIRST AND ONLY DEFENSIVE MOVE!
DEMONS KNOW WHERE THEIR INTERESTS LIE.
NO OTHER DEMON WOULD FORM A CONTRACT...
WITH SOMEONE AS DOWNTRODDEN AS ME.
I USED MY MOTHER'S MEMENTO FOR PAYMENT.
IT ONLY BOUGHT ME THAT SINGLE MOVE!
IF THEY FIGURE THAT OUT...
WE'RE DONE FOR!
......
HONESTLY.
SHE'S NO END OF TROUBLE FOR US.
HOWEVER...
WOO
YOU'RE NOT USED TO THIS KIND OF ATTACK, ARE YOU?

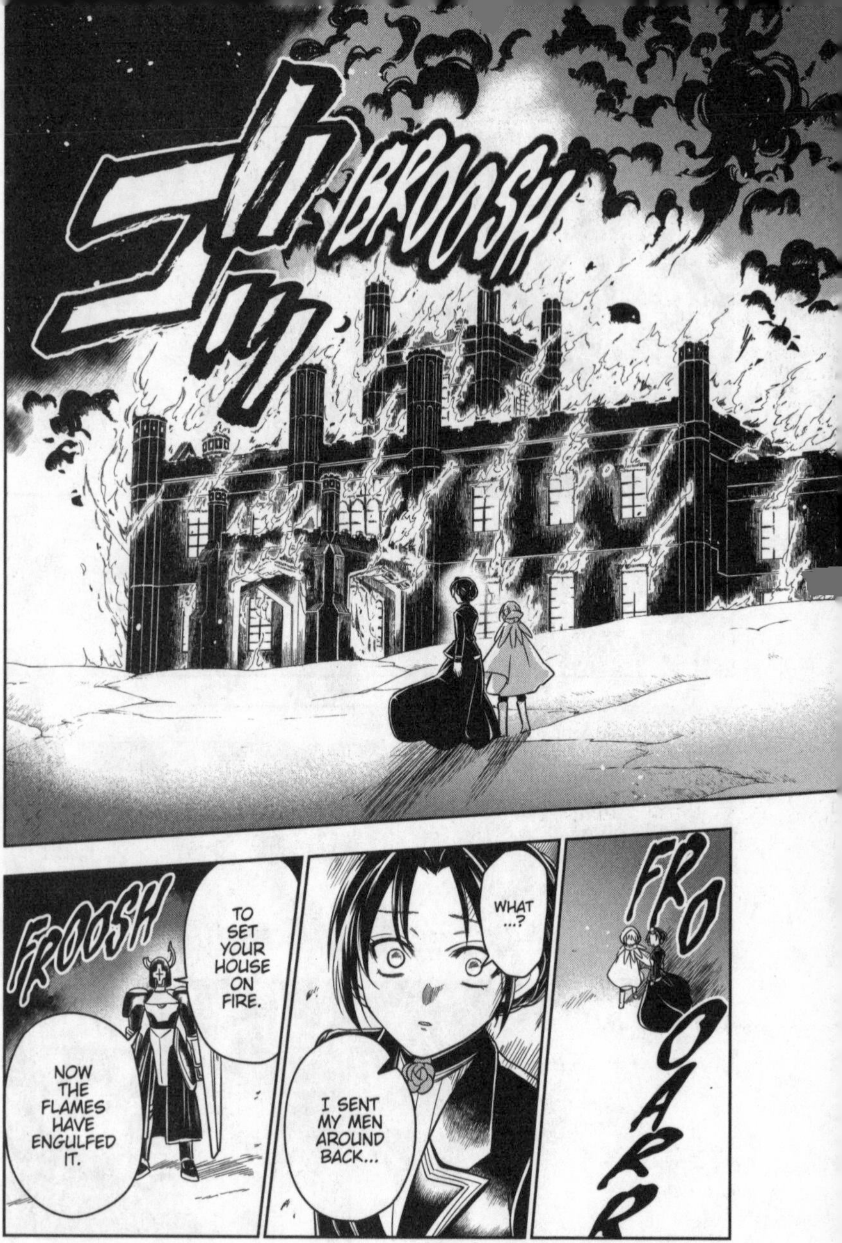
BROOSH
FROOARR
WHAT ...?
I SENT MY MEN AROUND BACK...
TO SET YOUR HOUSE ON FIRE.
NOW THE FLAMES HAVE ENGULFED IT.
FROOSH

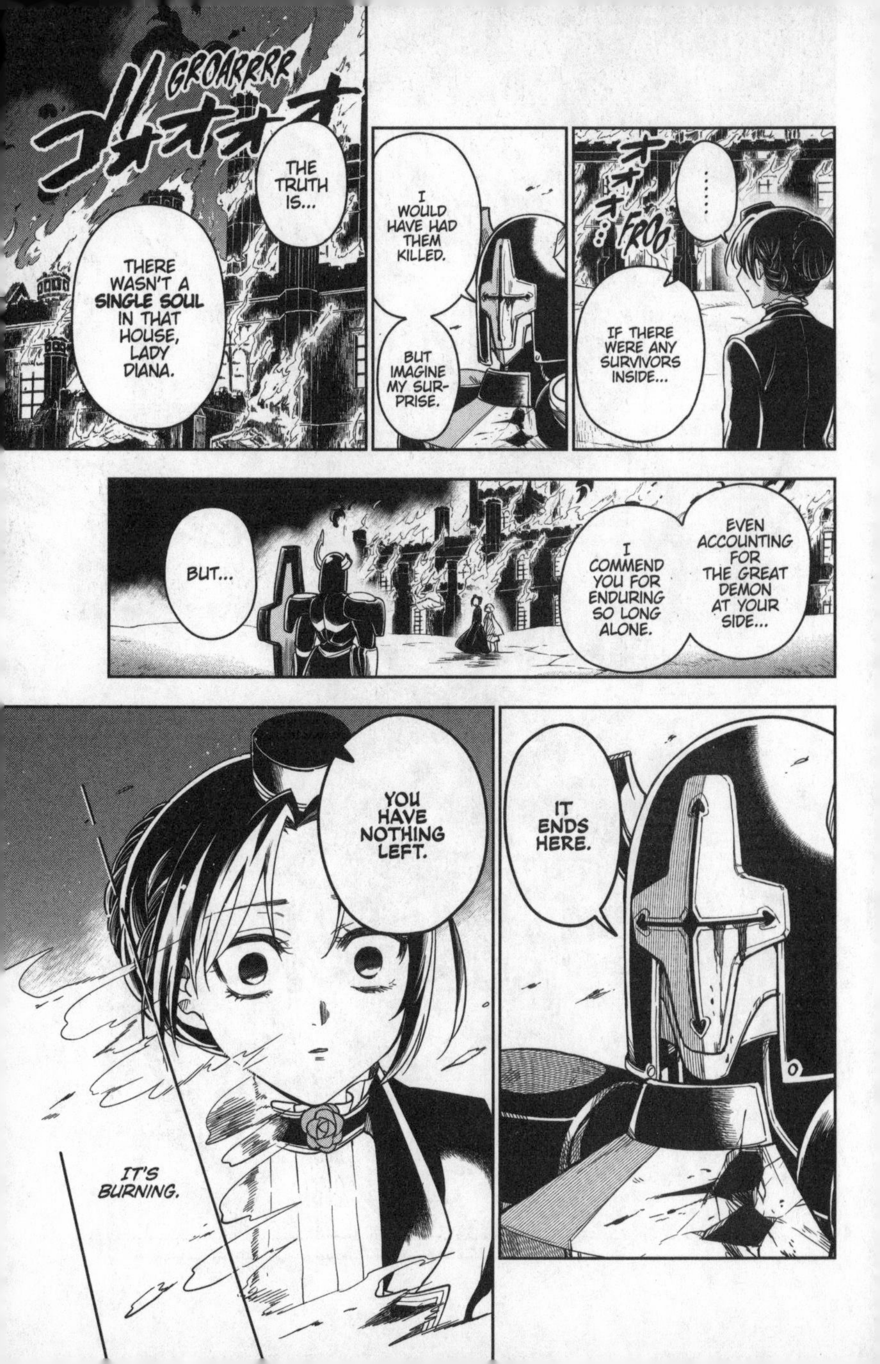
......
FROO
IF THERE WERE ANY SURVIVORS INSIDE...
I WOULD HAVE HAD THEM KILLED.
BUT IMAGINE MY SURPRISE.
GROARRRR
THE TRUTH IS...
THERE WASN'T A SINGLE SOUL IN THAT HOUSE, LADY DIANA.
EVEN ACCOUNTING FOR THE GREAT DEMON AT YOUR SIDE...
I COMMEND YOU FOR ENDURING SO LONG ALONE.
BUT...
IT ENDS HERE.
YOU HAVE NOTHING LEFT.
IT'S BURNING.

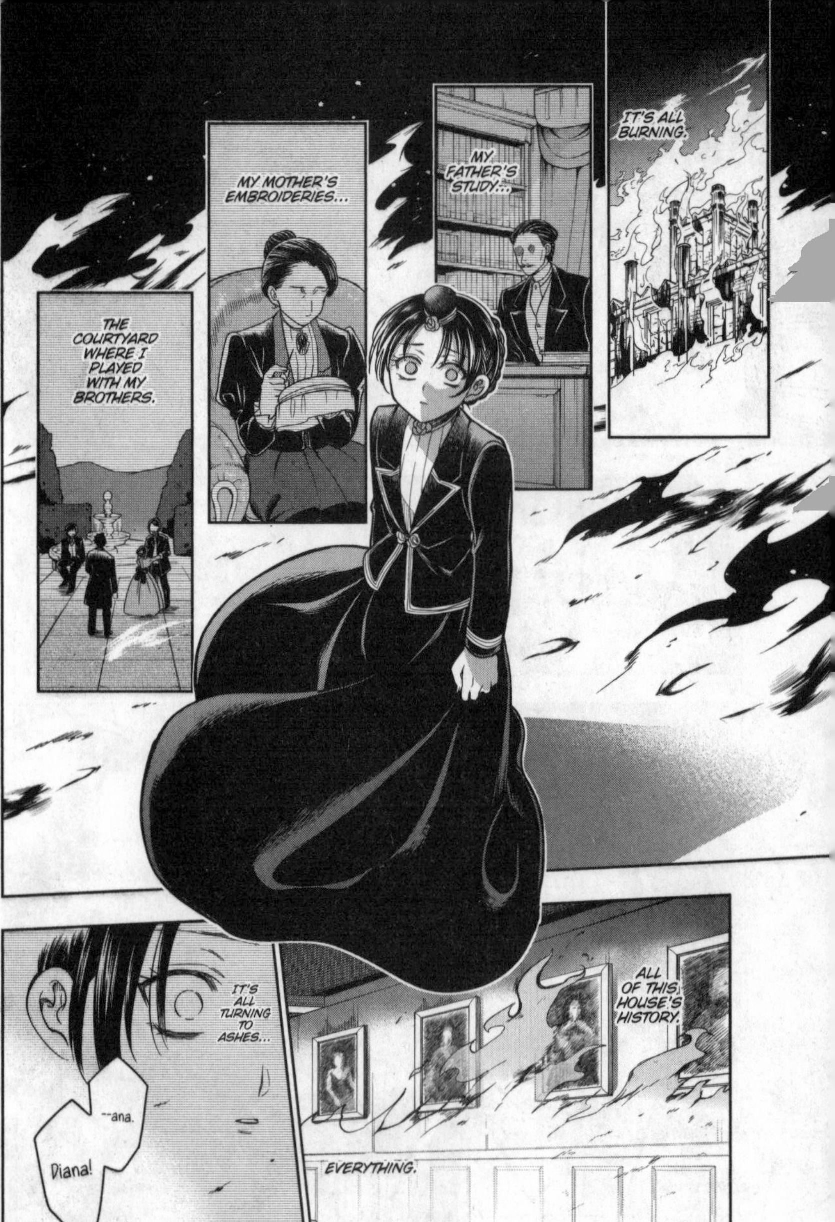
IT'S ALL BURNING.
MY FATHER'S STUDY...
MY MOTHER'S EMBROIDERIES...
THE COURTYARD WHERE I PLAYED WITH MY BROTHERS.
ALL OF THIS HOUSE'S HISTORY.
EVERYTHING.
IT'S ALL TURNING TO ASHES...
--ana.
Diana!

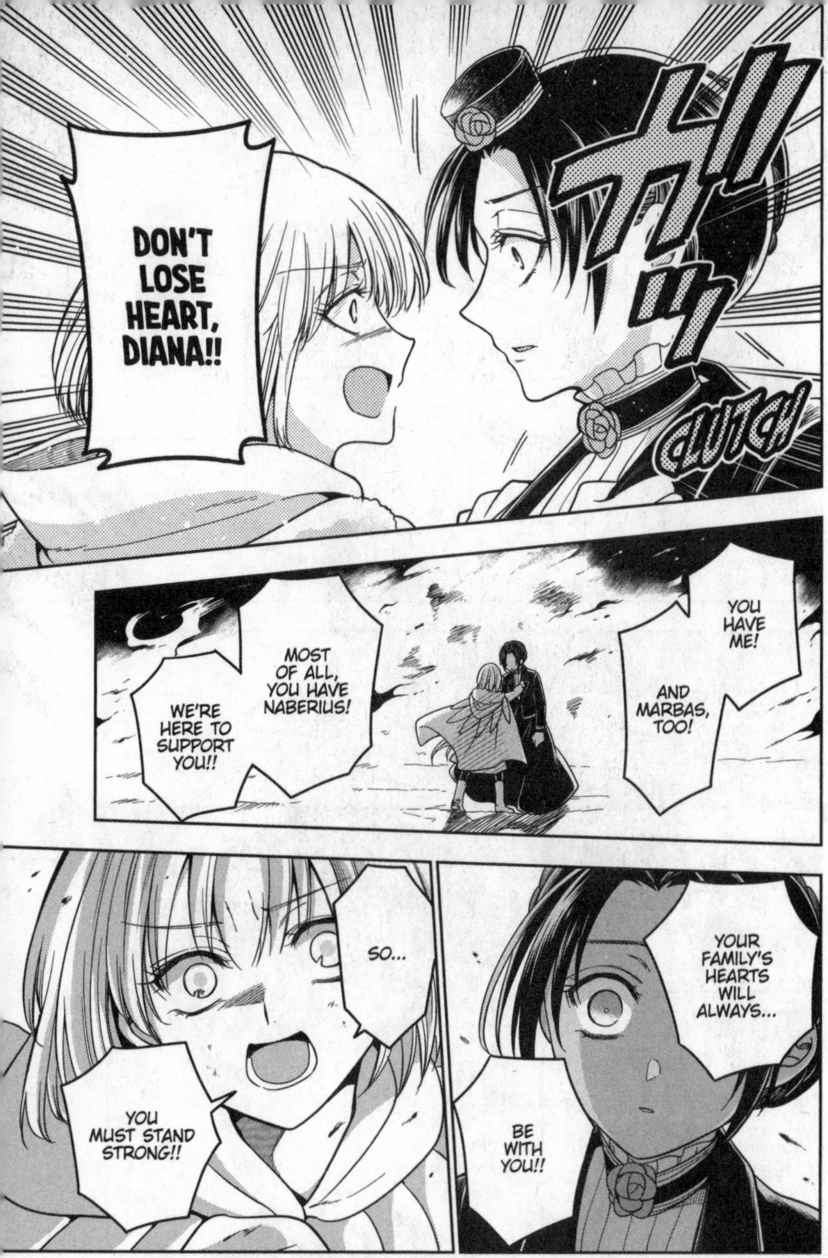

DON'T LOSE HEART, DIANA!!
CLUTCH!!
YOU HAVE ME!
AND MARBAS, TOO!
MOST OF ALL, YOU HAVE NABERIUS!
WE'RE HERE TO SUPPORT YOU!!
YOUR FAMILY'S HEARTS WILL ALWAYS...
BE WITH YOU!!
SO...
YOU MUST STAND STRONG!!

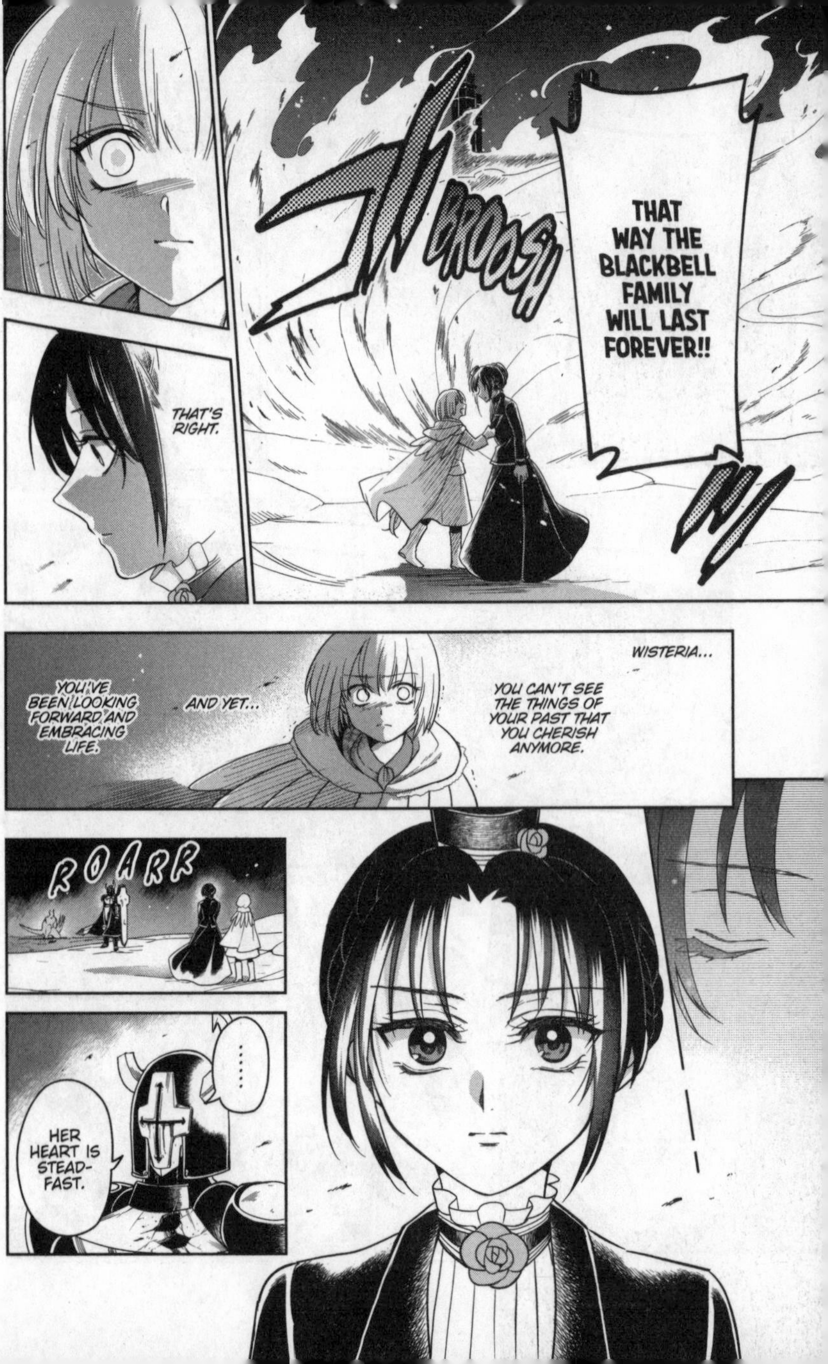
THAT WAY THE BLACKBELL FAMILY WILL LAST FOREVER!!
THAT'S RIGHT.
WISTERIA...
YOU CAN'T SEE THE THINGS OF YOUR PAST THAT YOU CHERISH ANYMORE.
AND YET...
YOU'VE BEEN LOOKING FORWARD AND EMBRACING LIFE.
ROARR
......
HER HEART IS STEAD-FAST.

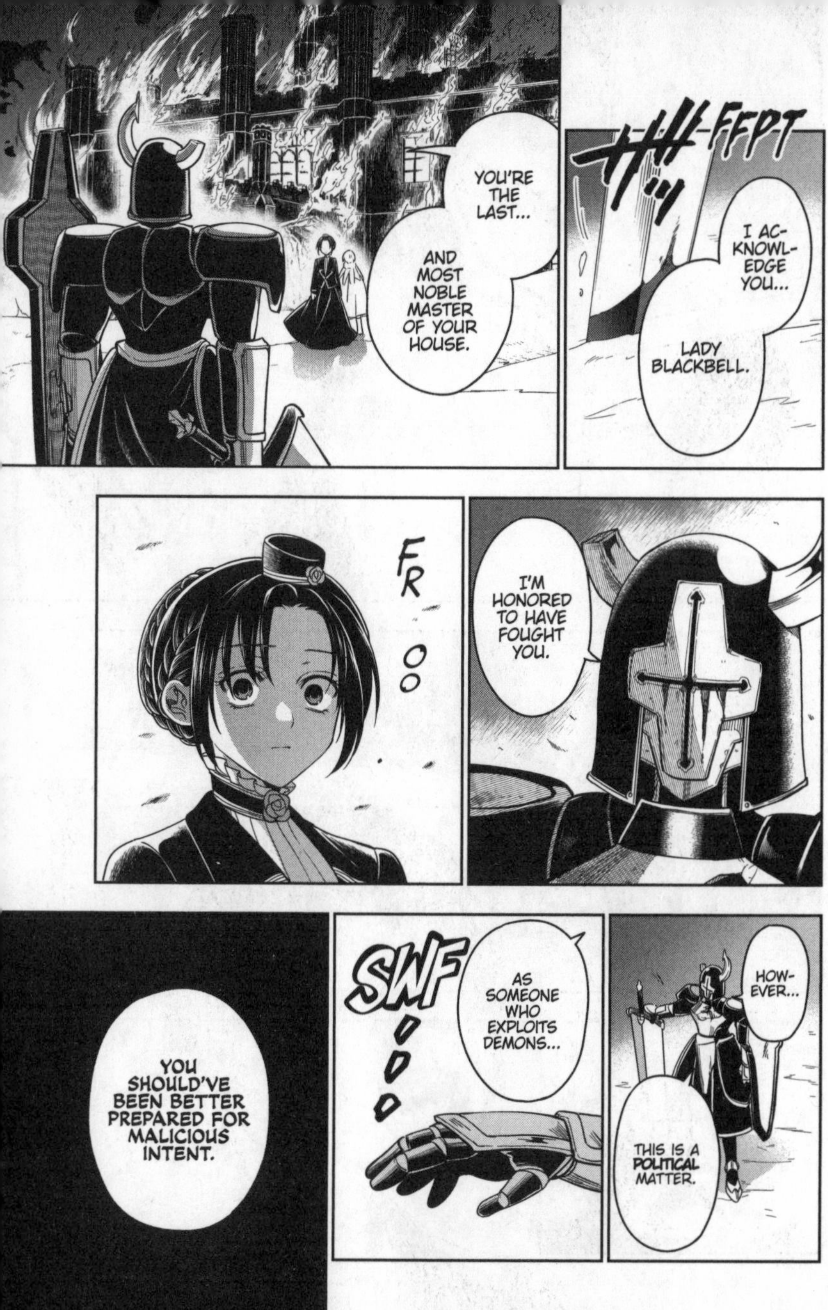
HH-FFPT
I ACKNOWLEDGE YOU...
LADY BLACKBELL.
YOU'RE THE LAST...
AND MOST NOBLE MASTER OF YOUR HOUSE.
I'M HONORED TO HAVE FOUGHT YOU.
FROO
HOWEVER...
THIS IS A POLITICAL MATTER.
SWF
AS SOMEONE WHO EXPLOITS DEMONS...
YOU SHOULD'VE BEEN BETTER PREPARED FOR MALICIOUS INTENT.

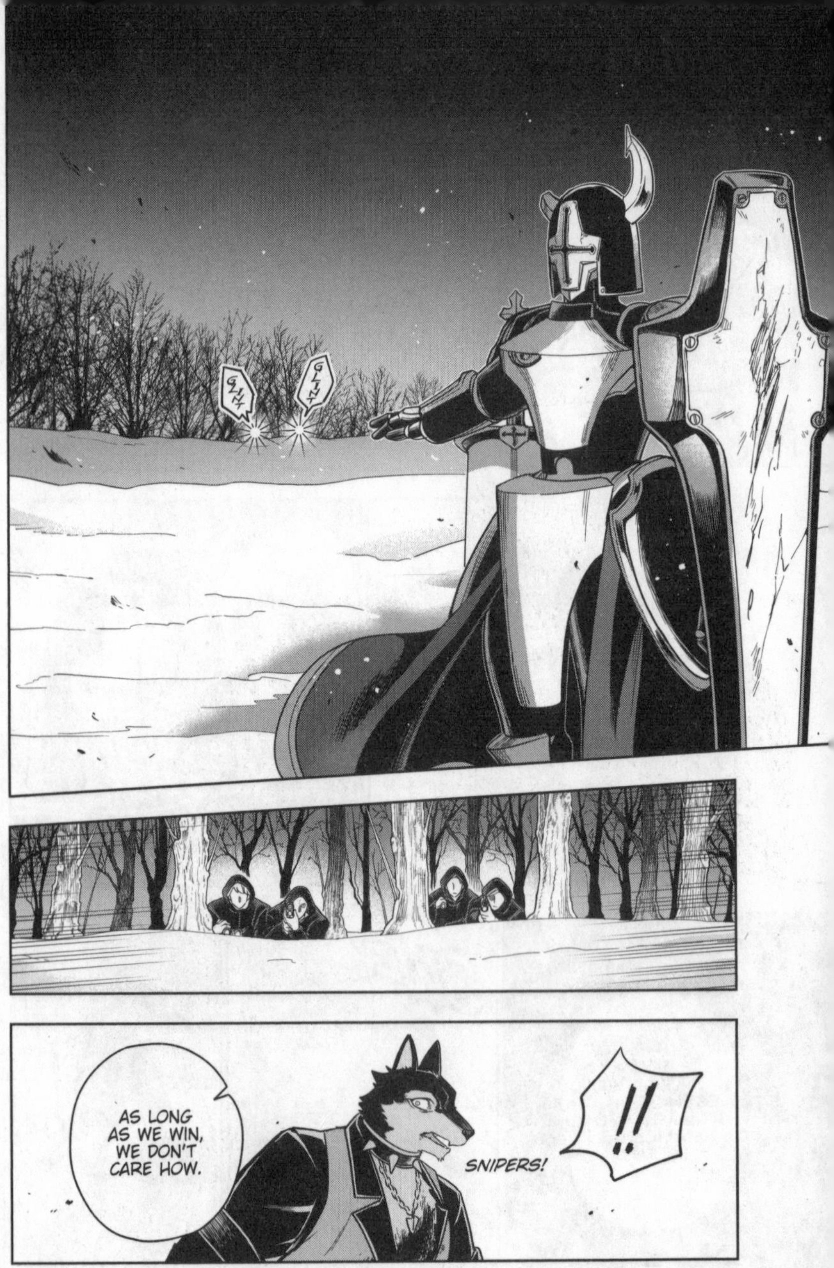
GLINT
GLINT
!!
SNIPERS!
AS LONG AS WE WIN, WE DON'T CARE HOW.

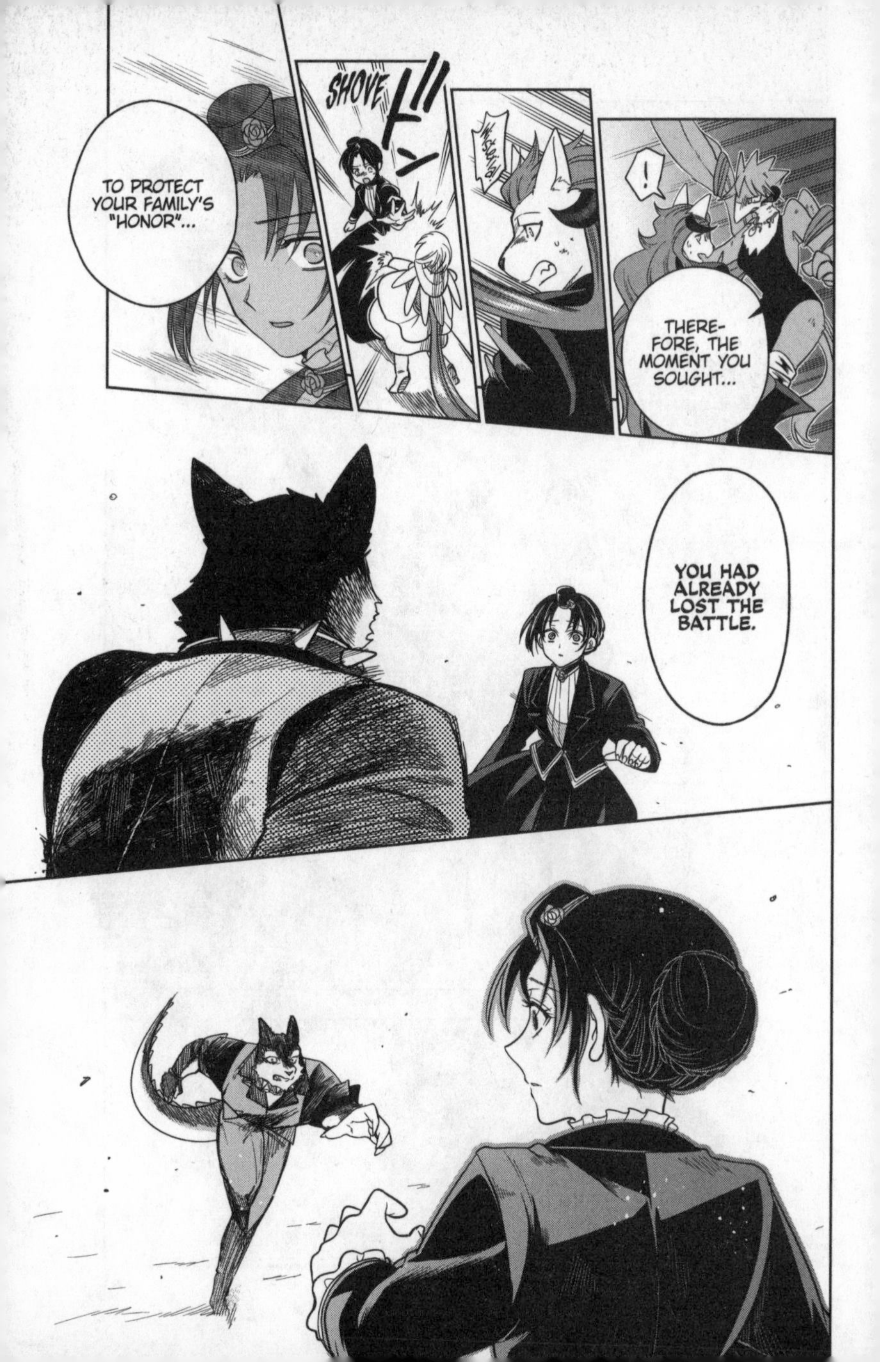
!
THERE-FORE, THE MOMENT YOU SOUGHT...
M-Stella!
SHOVE
ドン
TO PROTECT YOUR FAMILY'S "HONOR"...
YOU HAD ALREADY LOST THE BATTLE.

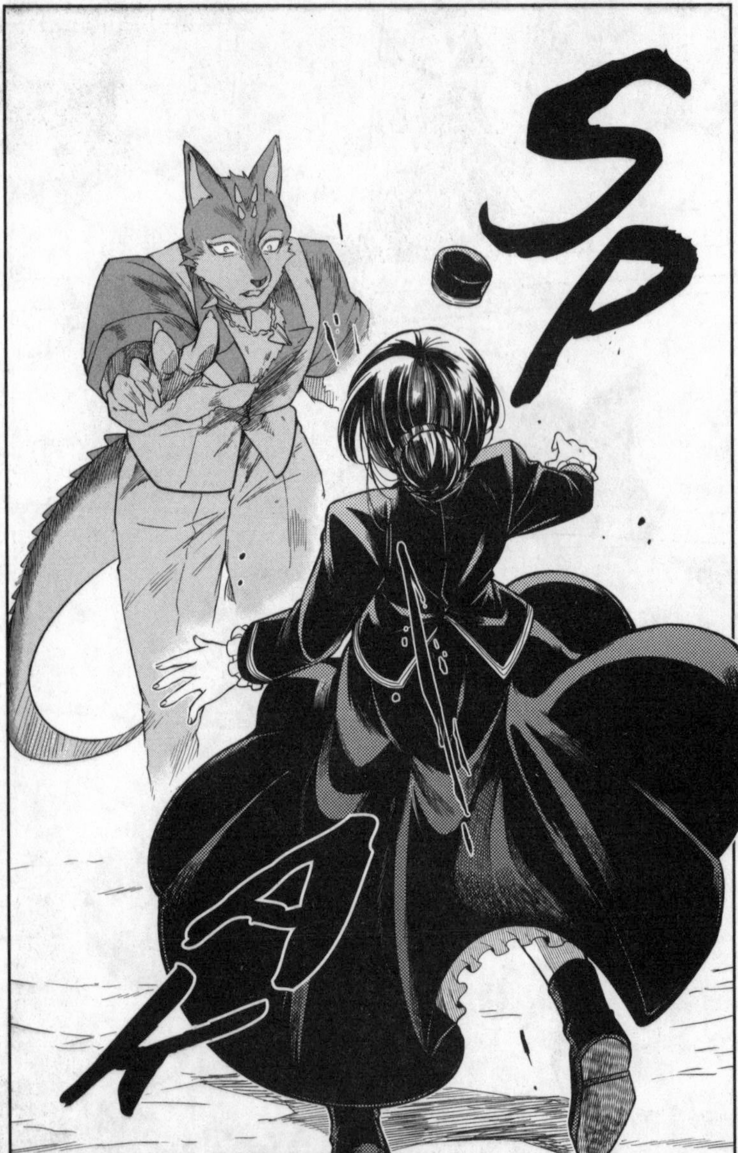
SPAK

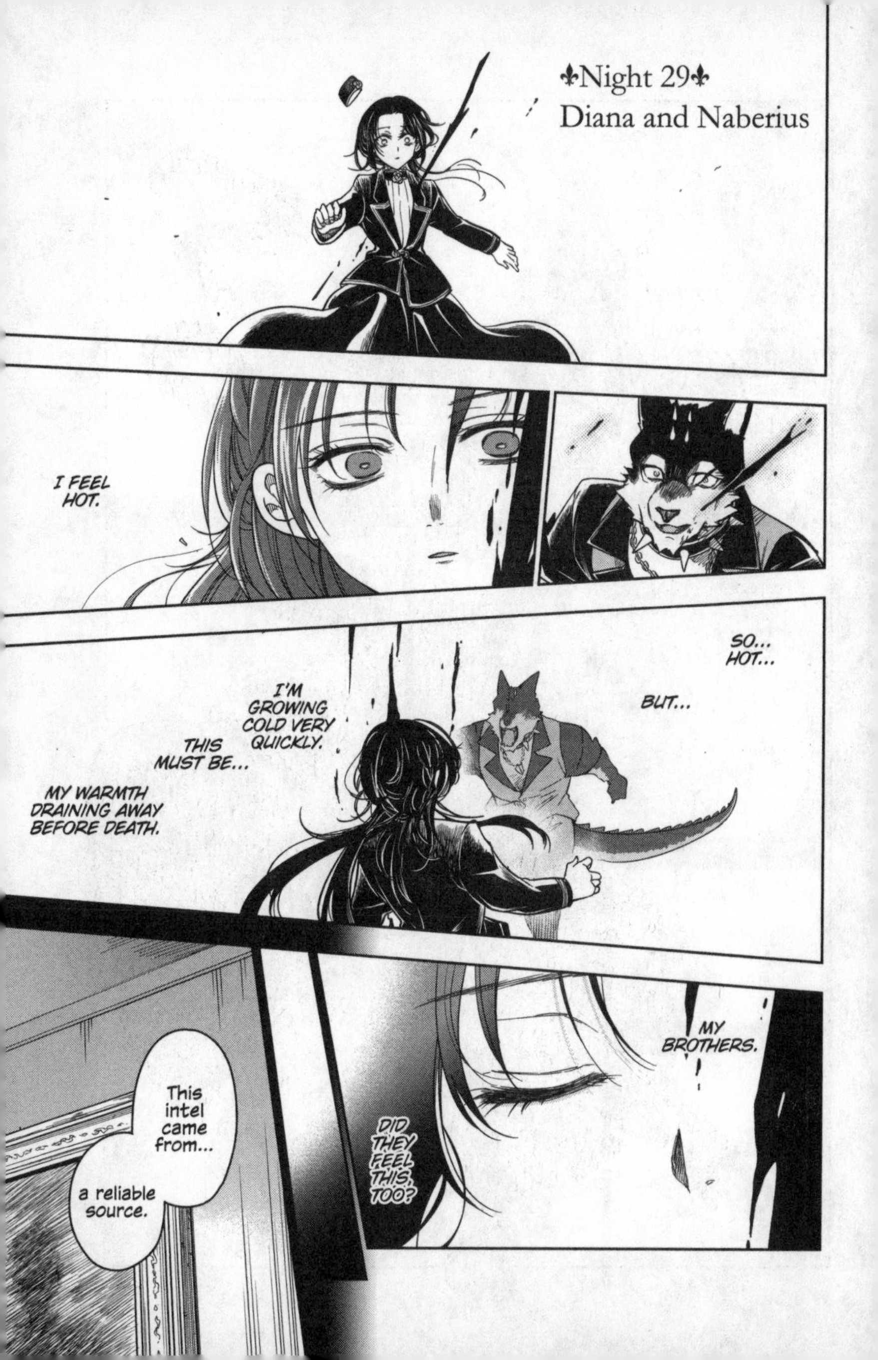
⚜Night 29⚜
Diana and Naberius
I FEEL HOT.
SO... HOT...
BUT...
I'M GROWING COLD VERY QUICKLY.
THIS MUST BE...
MY WARMTH DRAINING AWAY BEFORE DEATH.
MY BROTHERS.
DID THEY FEEL THIS, TOO?
This intel came from...
a reliable source.

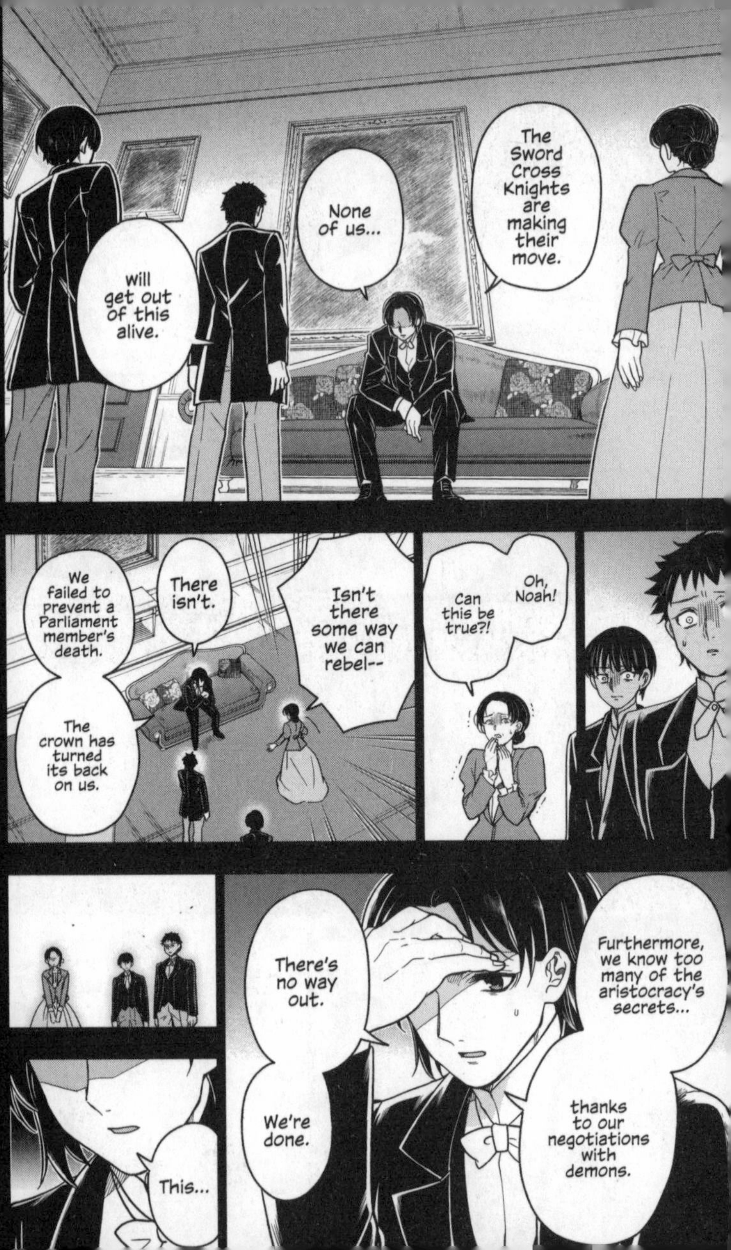
The Sword Cross Knights are making their move.
None of us...
will get out of this alive.
Oh, Noah!
Can this be true?!
Isn't there some way we can rebel--
There isn't.
We failed to prevent a Parliament member's death.
The crown has turned its back on us.
Furthermore, we know too many of the aristocracy's secrets...
thanks to our negotiations with demons.
There's no way out.
We're done.
This...

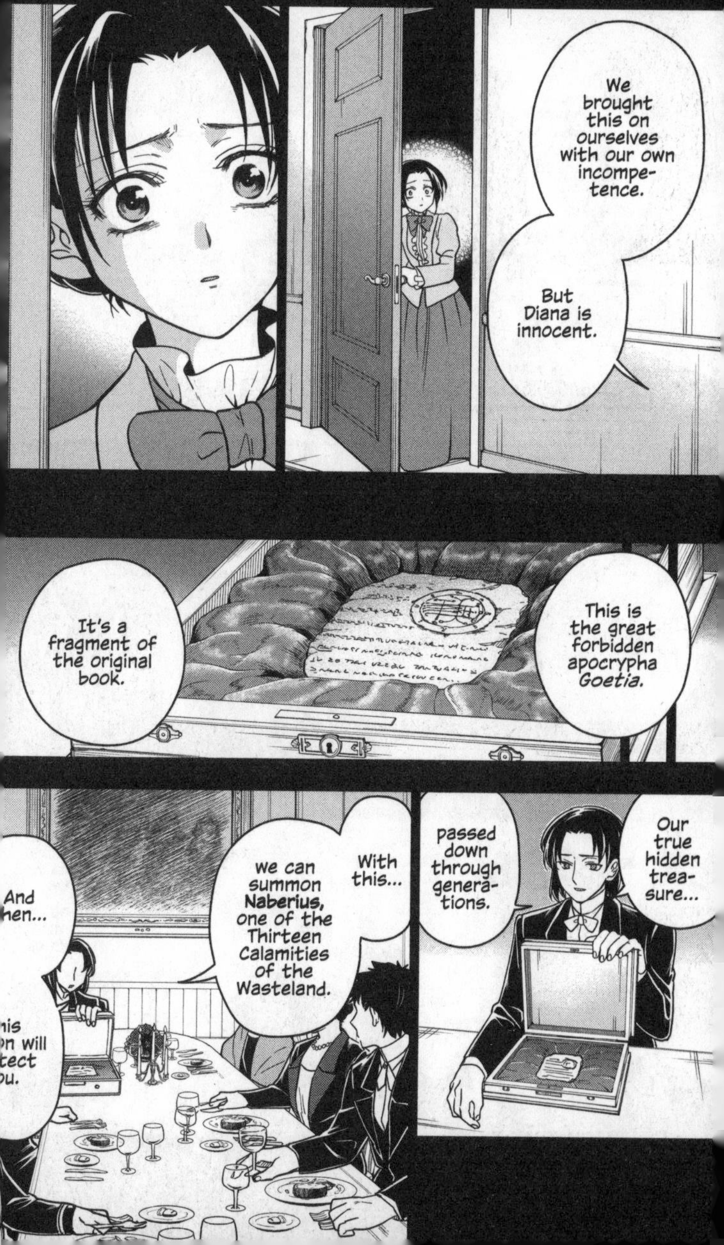
We brought this on ourselves with our own incompetence.
But Diana is innocent.
This is the great forbidden apocrypha *Goetia.*
It's a fragment of the original book.
Our true hidden treasure...
passed down through generations.
With this...
we can summon **Naberius,** one of the Thirteen Calamities of the Wasteland.
And hen...
his on will tect ou.

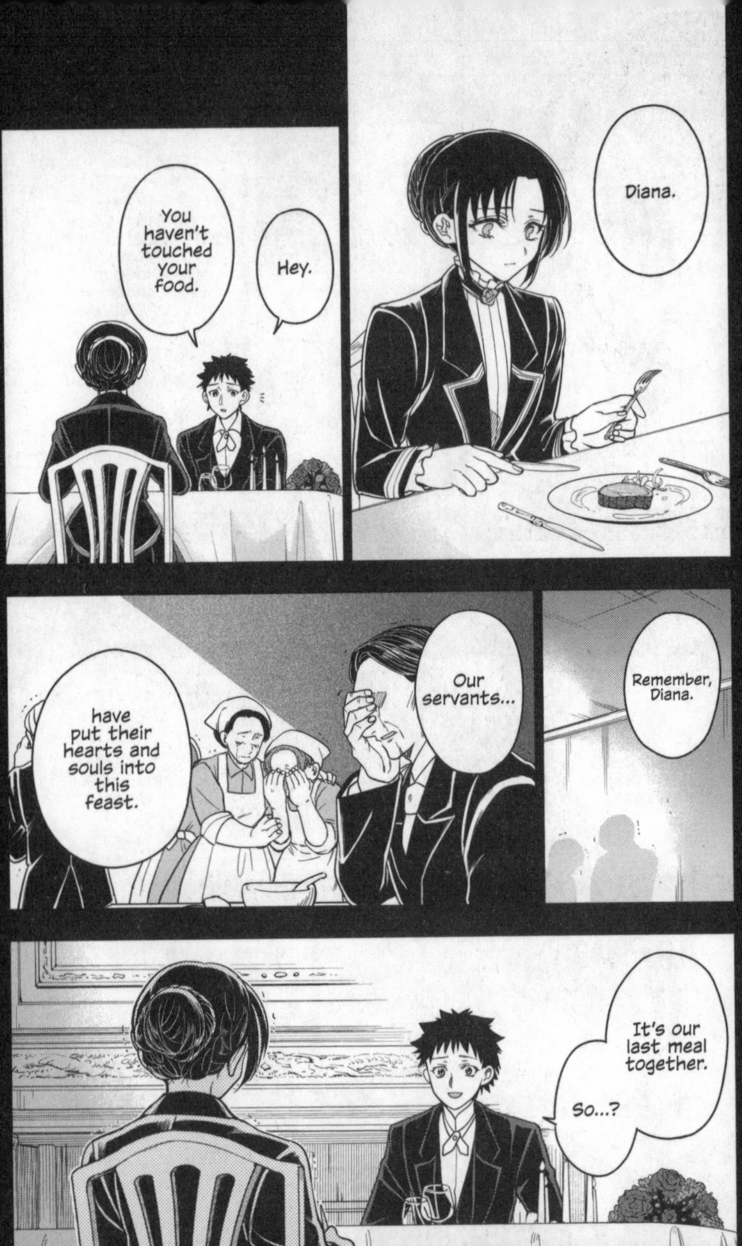
Diana.
Hey.
You haven't touched your food.
Remember, Diana.
Our servants...
have put their hearts and souls into this feast.
It's our last meal together.
So...?

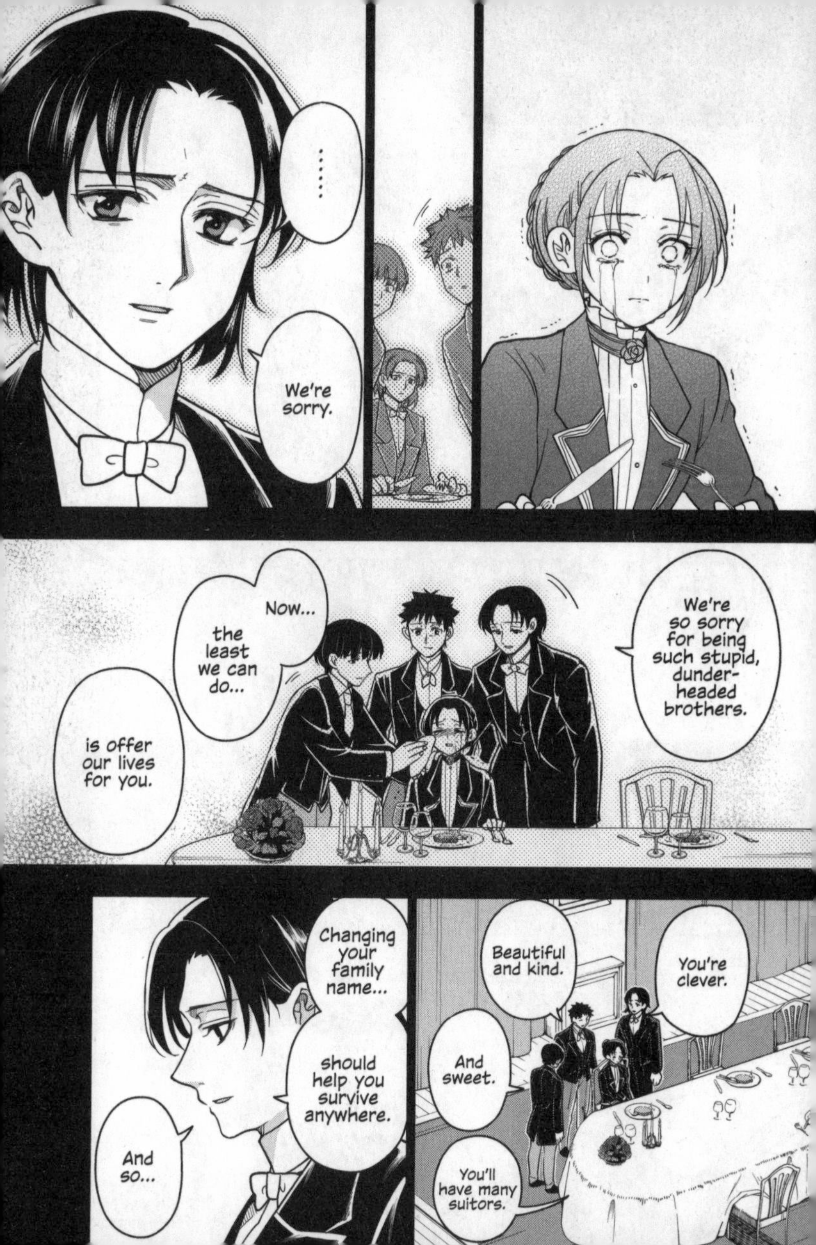
......
We're sorry.
We're so sorry for being such stupid, dunder-headed brothers.
Now...
the least we can do...
is offer our lives for you.
You're clever.
Beautiful and kind.
And sweet.
You'll have many suitors.
Changing your family name...
should help you survive anywhere.
And so...

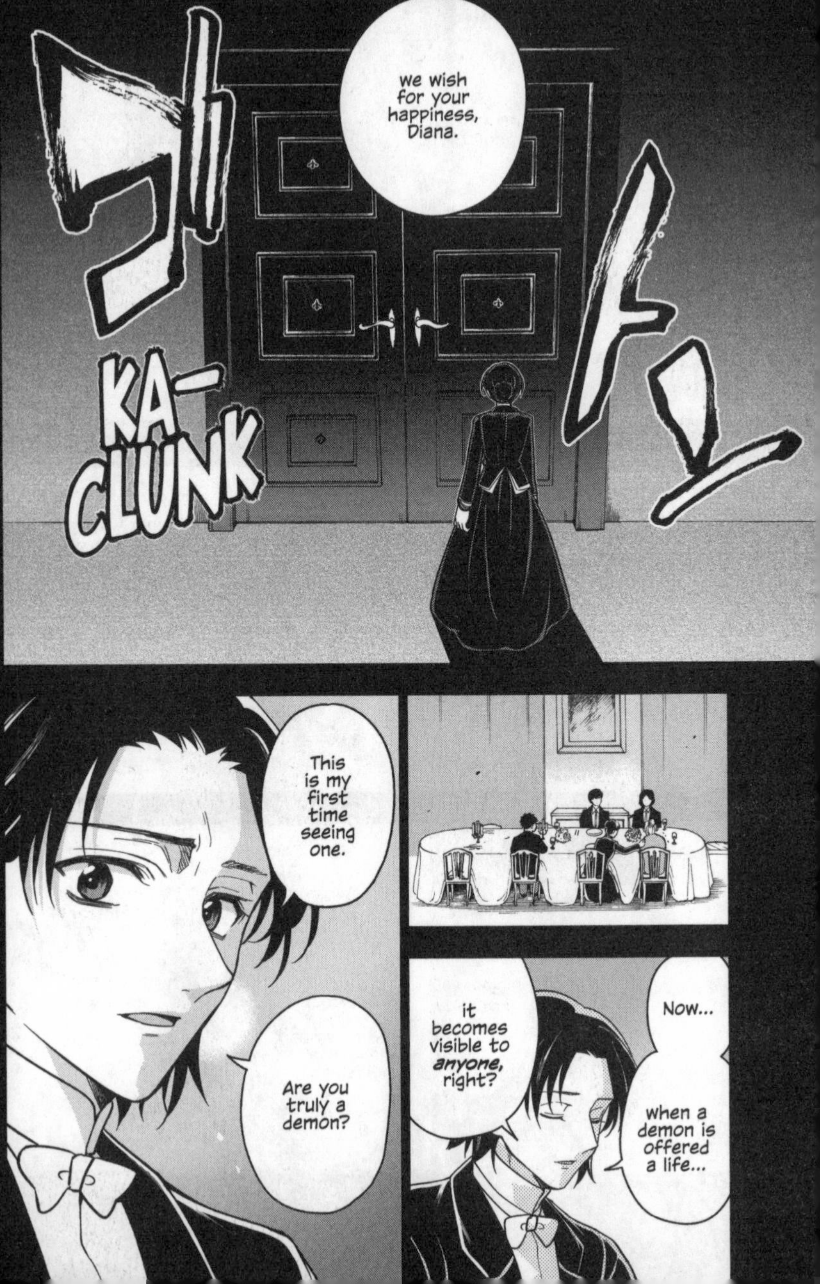
we wish for your happiness, Diana.
KA-CLUNK
Now...
when a demon is offered a life...
it becomes visible to *anyone*, right?
This is my first time seeing one.
Are you truly a demon?

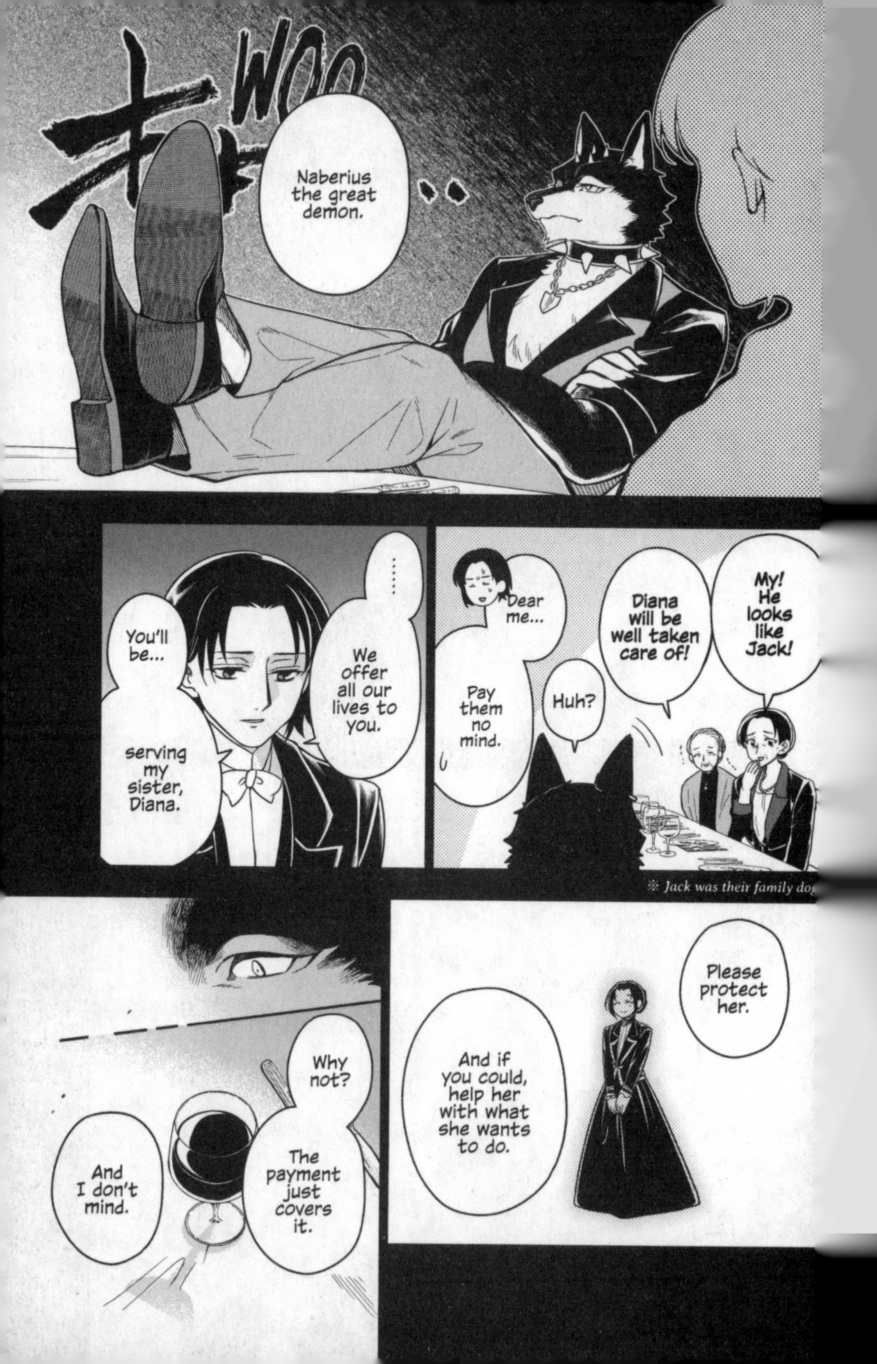
WOO
Naberius the great demon.
My! He looks like Jack!
Diana will be well taken care of!
Huh?
Dear me...
Pay them no mind.
......
We offer all our lives to you.
You'll be...
serving my sister, Diana.
Please protect her.
And if you could, help her with what she wants to do.
Why not?
The payment just covers it.
And I don't mind.

※ Jack was their family dog

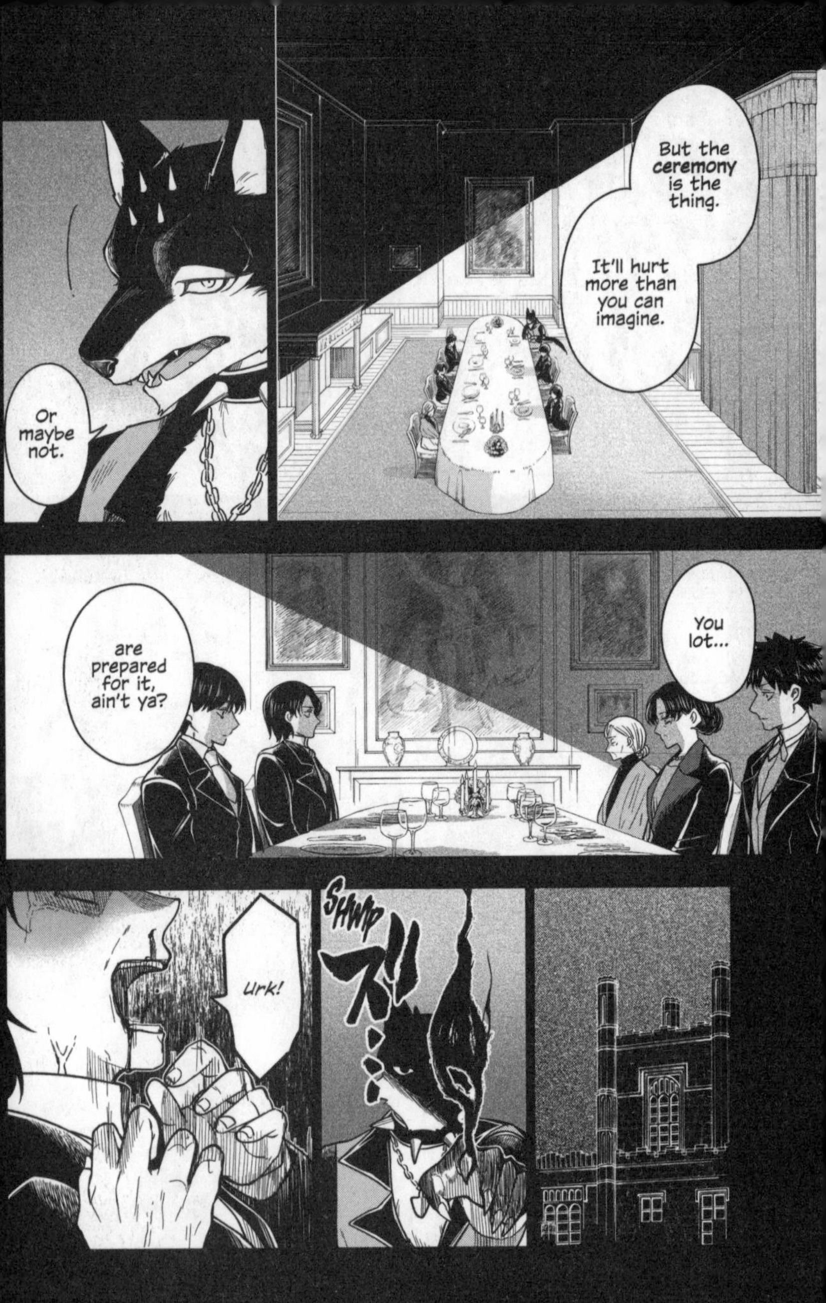
But the ceremony is the thing.
It'll hurt more than you can imagine.
Or maybe not.
You lot...
are prepared for it, ain't ya?
SHWIP
Urk!

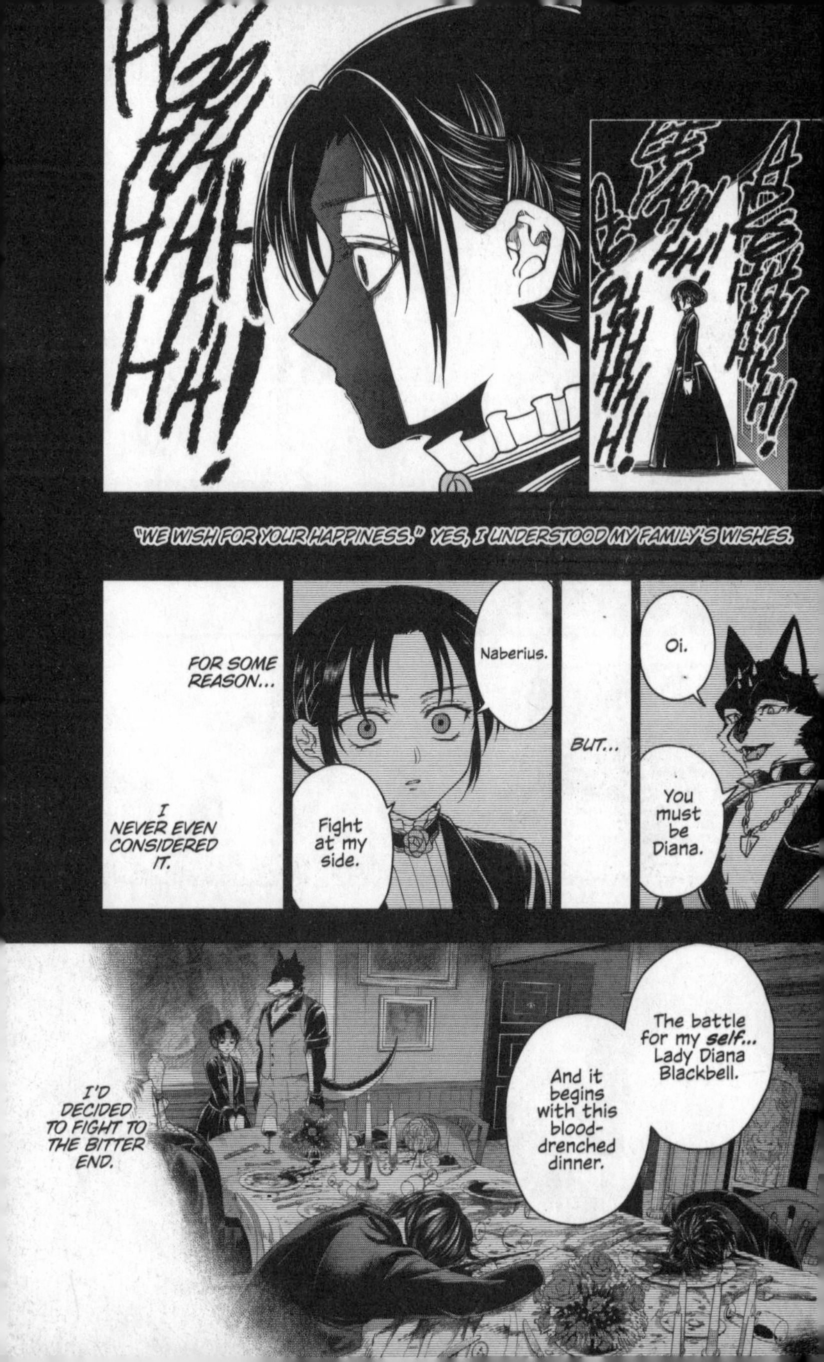
HAHAHAHAHA!
"WE WISH FOR YOUR HAPPINESS." YES, I UNDERSTOOD MY FAMILY'S WISHES.
Oi.
You must be Diana.
BUT...
Naberius.
Fight at my side.
FOR SOME REASON...
I NEVER EVEN CONSIDERED IT.
The battle for my *self*... Lady Diana Blackbell.
And it begins with this blood-drenched dinner.
I'D DECIDED TO FIGHT TO THE BITTER END.

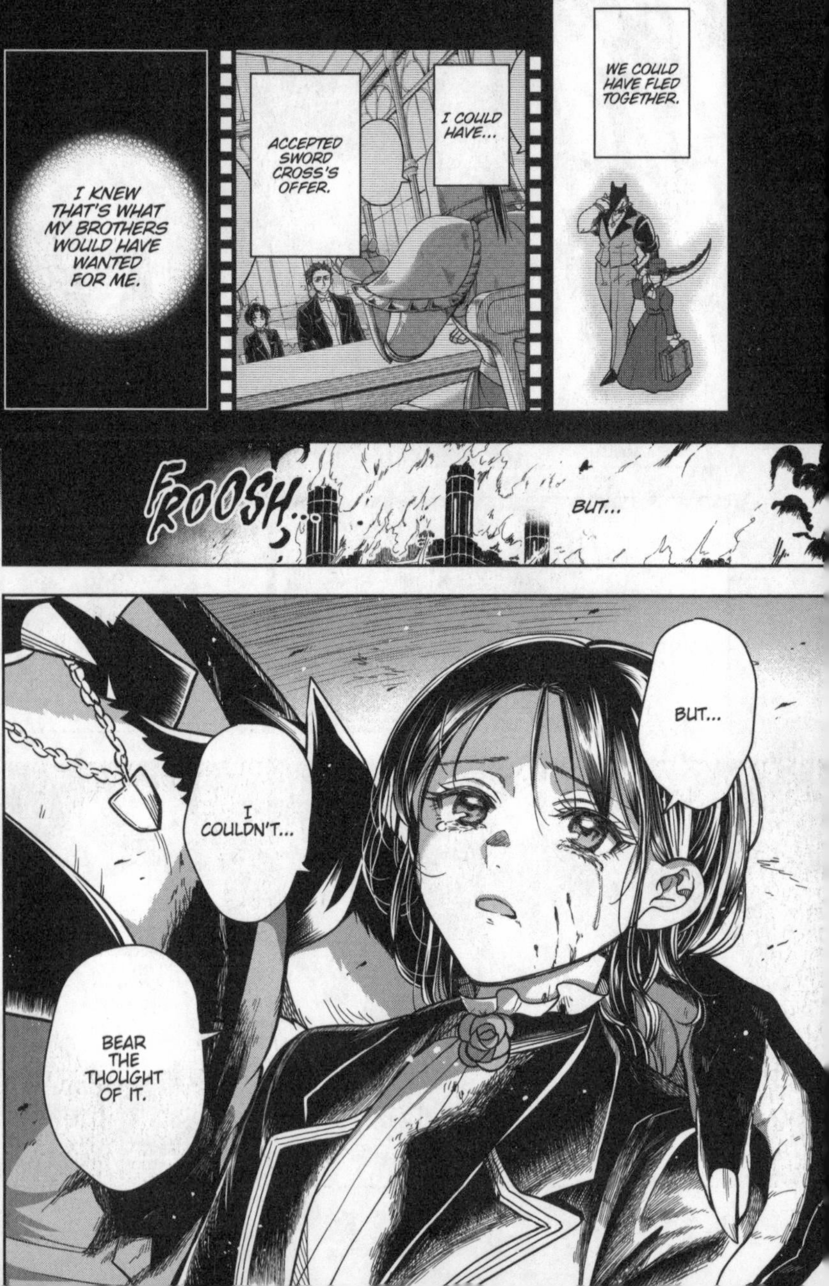
WE COULD HAVE FLED TOGETHER.
I COULD HAVE...
ACCEPTED SWORD CROSS'S OFFER.
I KNEW THAT'S WHAT MY BROTHERS WOULD HAVE WANTED FOR ME.
BUT...
FROOSH...
BUT...
I COULDN'T...
BEAR THE THOUGHT OF IT.

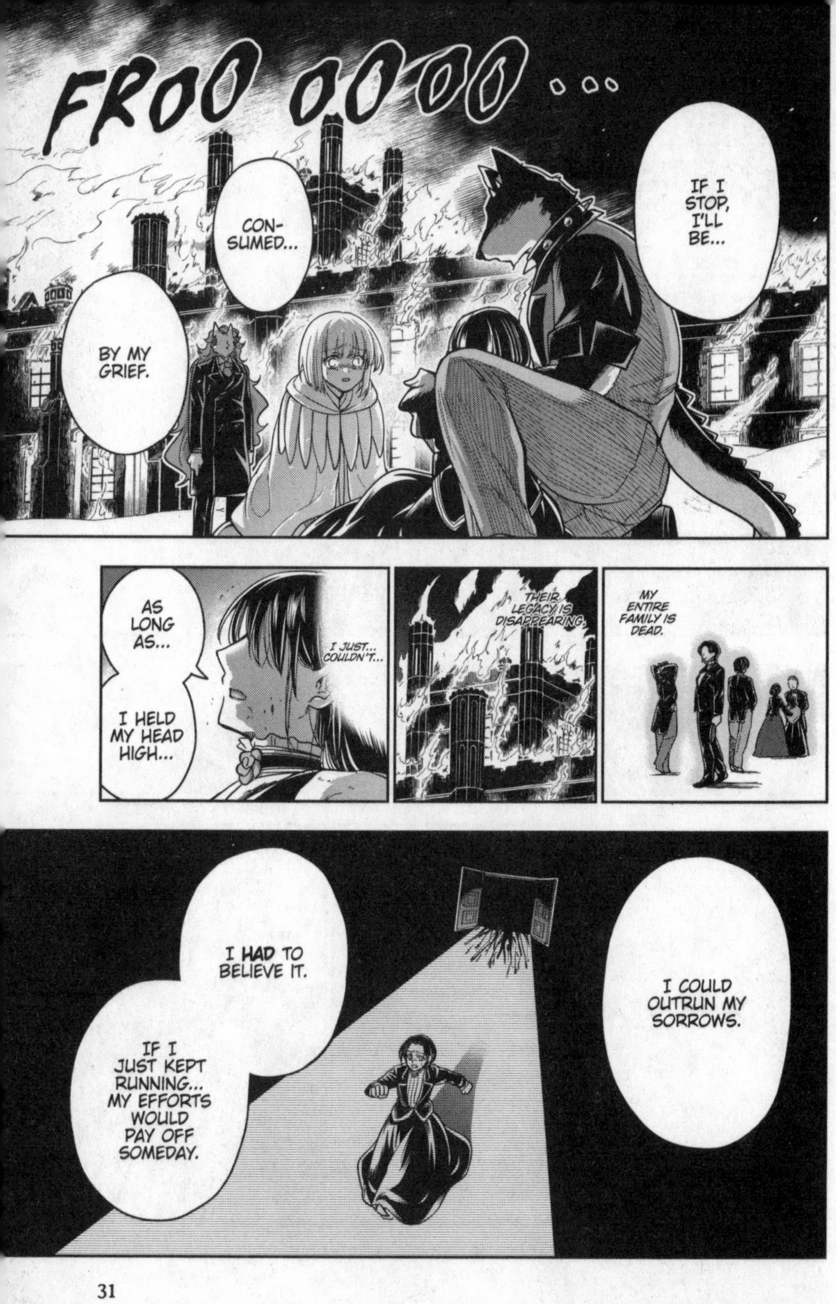
FROO OOOO...
IF I STOP, I'LL BE...
CON-SUMED...
BY MY GRIEF.
MY ENTIRE FAMILY IS DEAD.
THEIR LEGACY IS DISAPPEARING.
I JUST... COULDN'T...
AS LONG AS...
I HELD MY HEAD HIGH...
I COULD OUTRUN MY SORROWS.
I HAD to BELIEVE IT.
IF I JUST KEPT RUNNING... MY EFFORTS WOULD PAY OFF SOMEDAY.

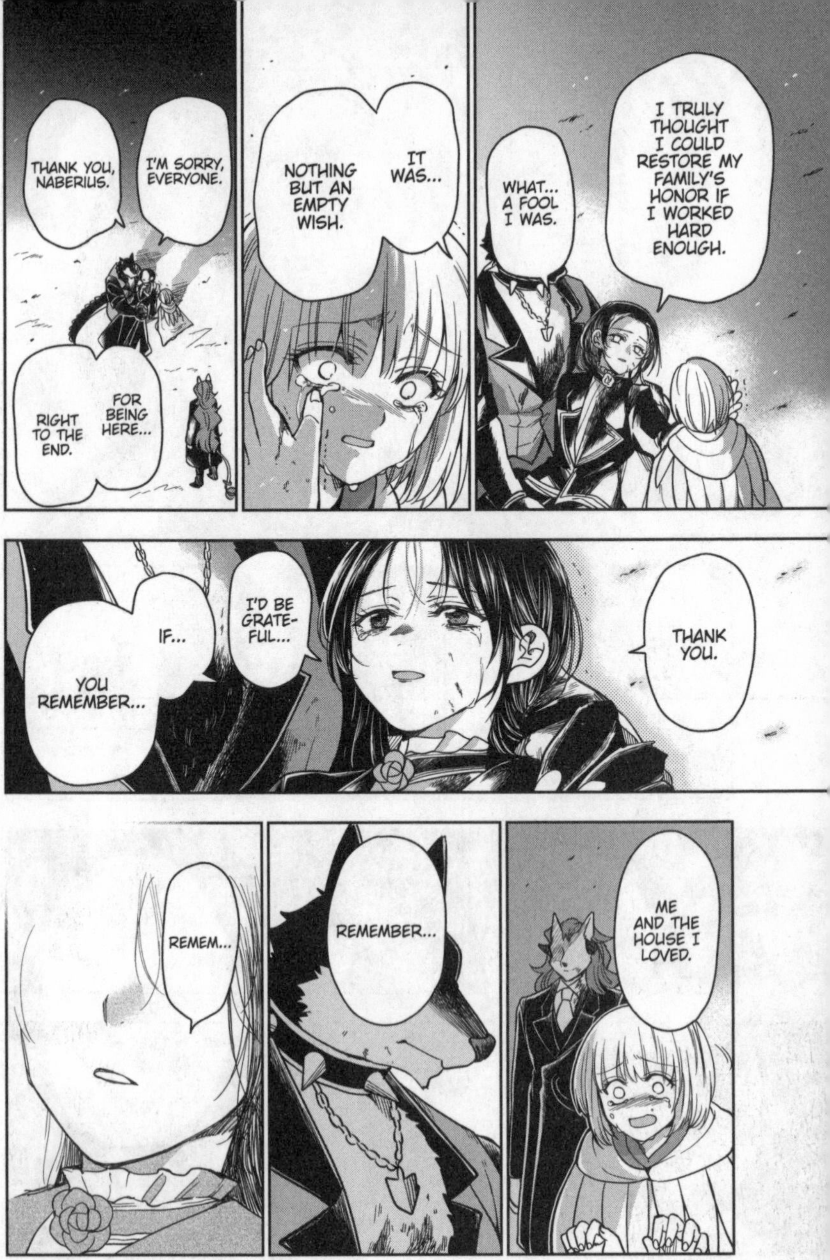
I TRULY THOUGHT I COULD RESTORE MY FAMILY'S HONOR IF I WORKED HARD ENOUGH.
WHAT... A FOOL I WAS.
IT WAS...
NOTHING BUT AN EMPTY WISH.
I'M SORRY, EVERYONE.
THANK YOU, NABERIUS.
FOR BEING HERE...
RIGHT TO THE END.
THANK YOU.
I'D BE GRATE-FUL...
IF...
YOU REMEMBER...
ME AND THE HOUSE I LOVED.
REMEMBER...
REMEM...

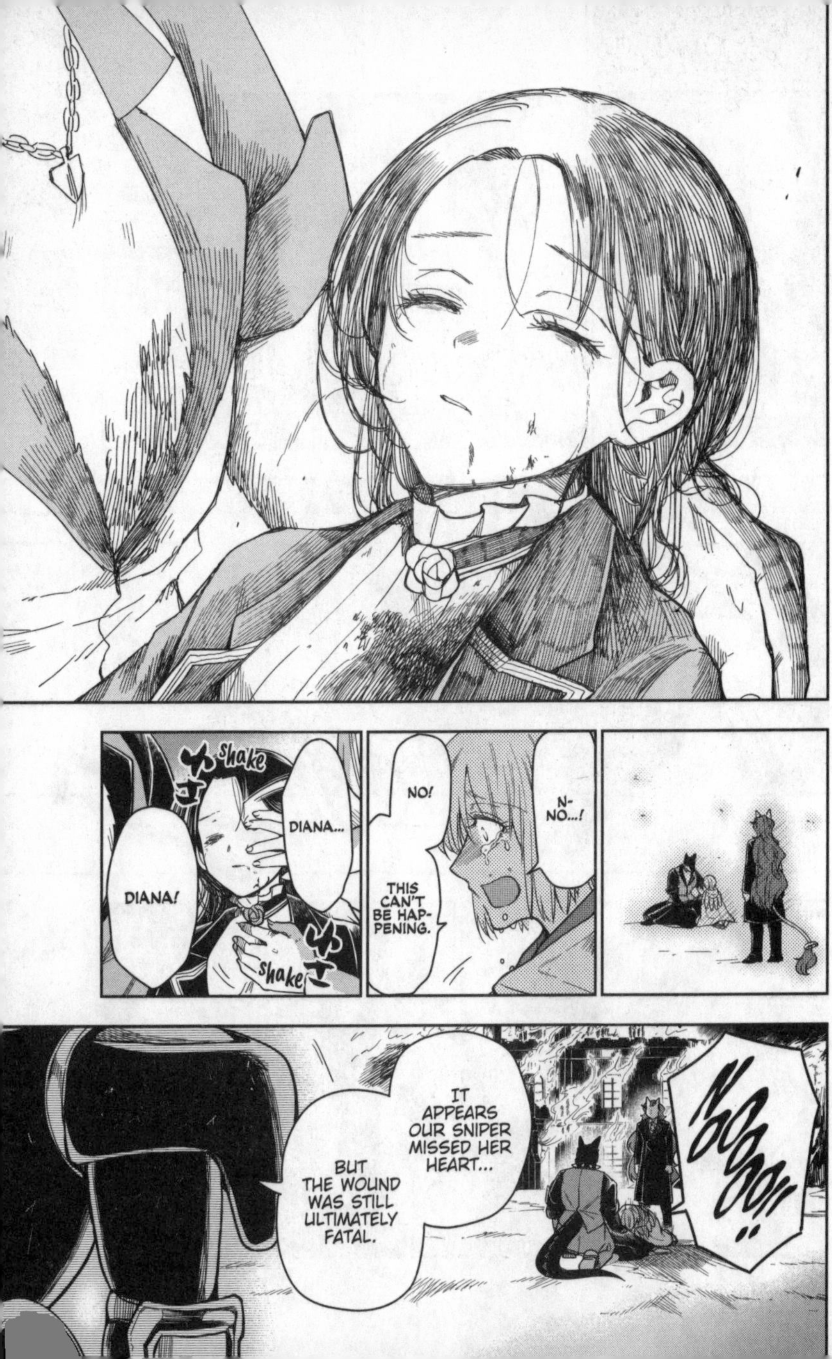
N-NO...!
NO!
THIS CAN'T BE HAP-PENING.
shake
DIANA...
DIANA!
shake
NOOOO!!
IT APPEARS OUR SNIPER MISSED HER HEART...
BUT THE WOUND WAS STILL ULTIMATELY FATAL.

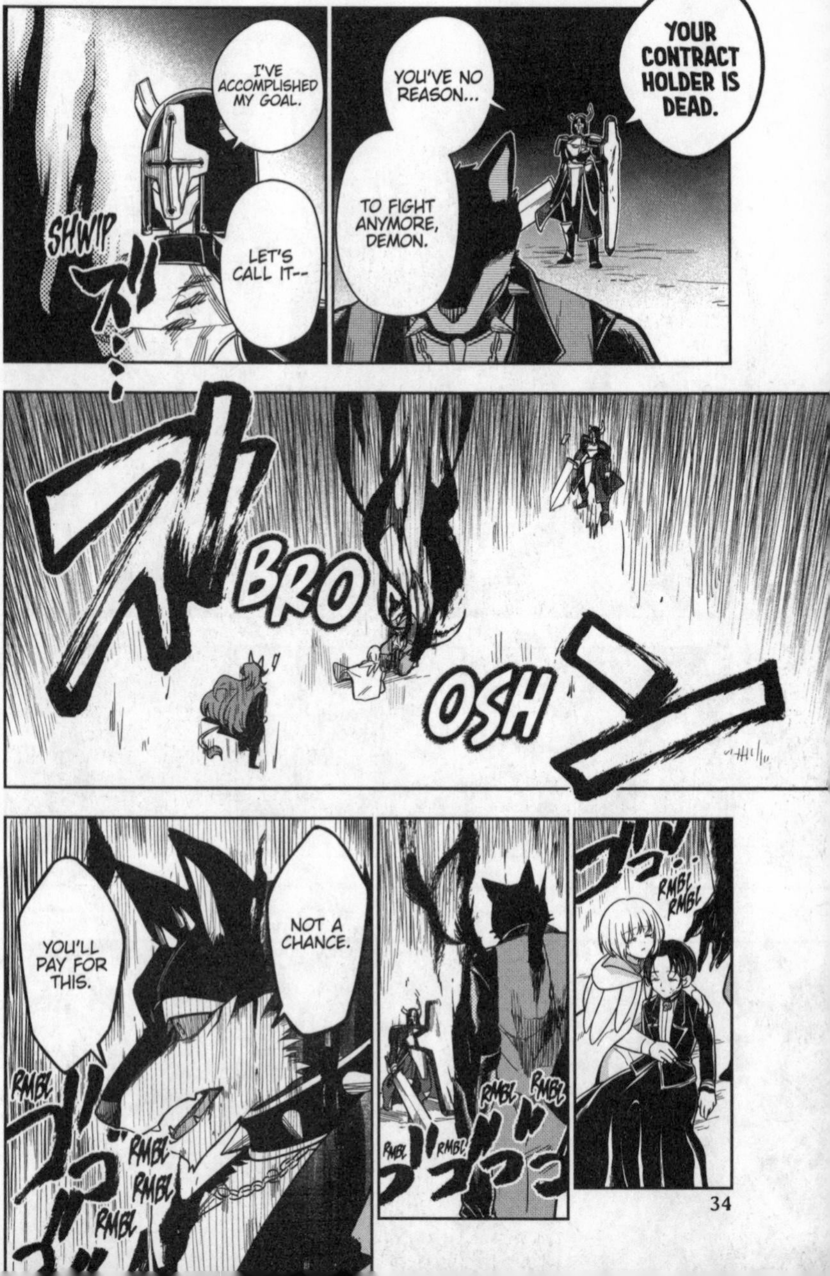
YOUR CONTRACT HOLDER IS DEAD.
YOU'VE NO REASON...
TO FIGHT ANYMORE, DEMON.
I'VE ACCOMPLISHED MY GOAL.
LET'S CALL IT--
SHWIP
BRO
OSH
RMBL RMBL
RMBL
RMBL
RMBL
RMBL
NOT A CHANCE.
YOU'LL PAY FOR THIS.
RMBL
RMBL
RMBL
RMBL

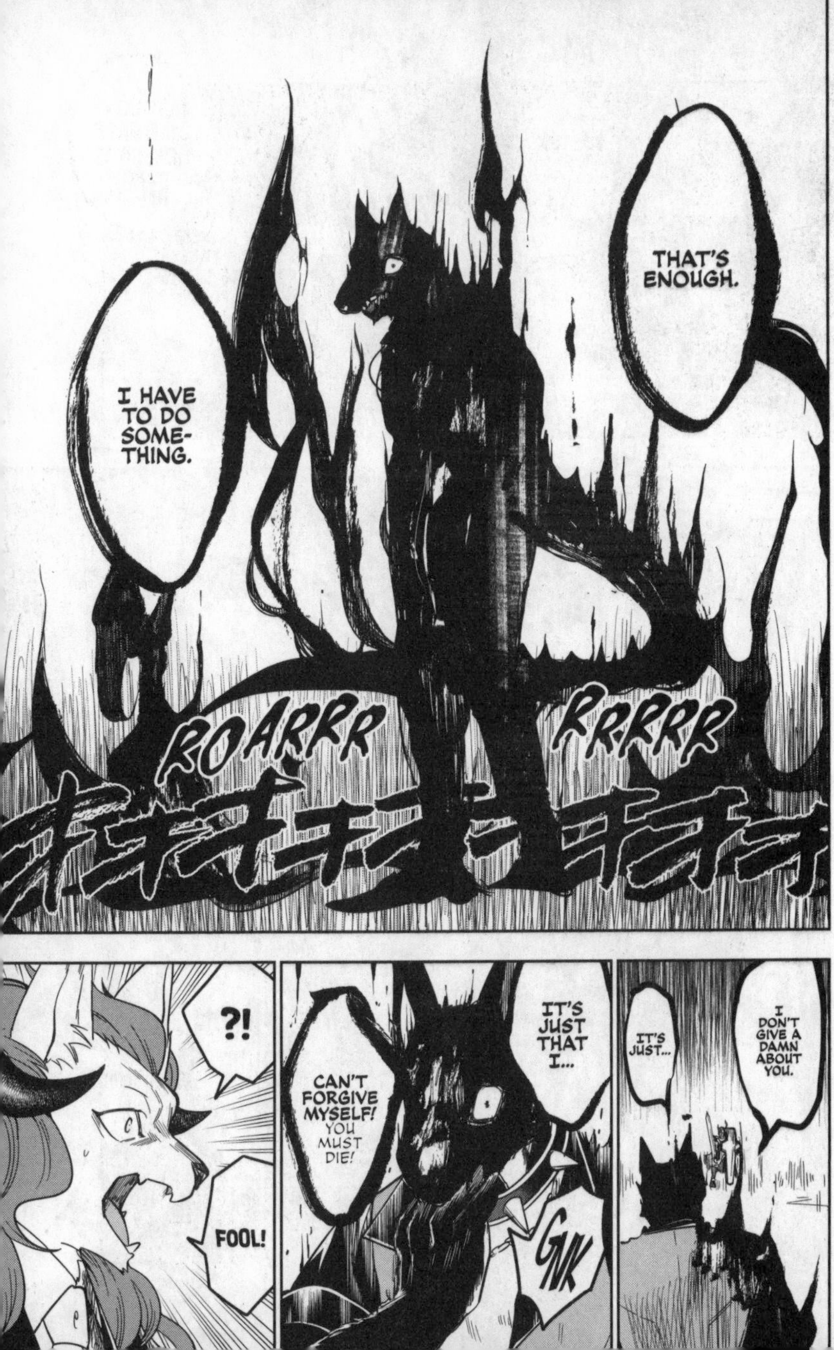
THAT'S ENOUGH.
I HAVE TO DO SOME-THING.
ROARRR RRRRR
I DON'T GIVE A DAMN ABOUT YOU.
IT'S JUST...
IT'S JUST THAT I...
CAN'T FORGIVE MYSELF! YOU MUST DIE!
GNK
?!
FOOL!

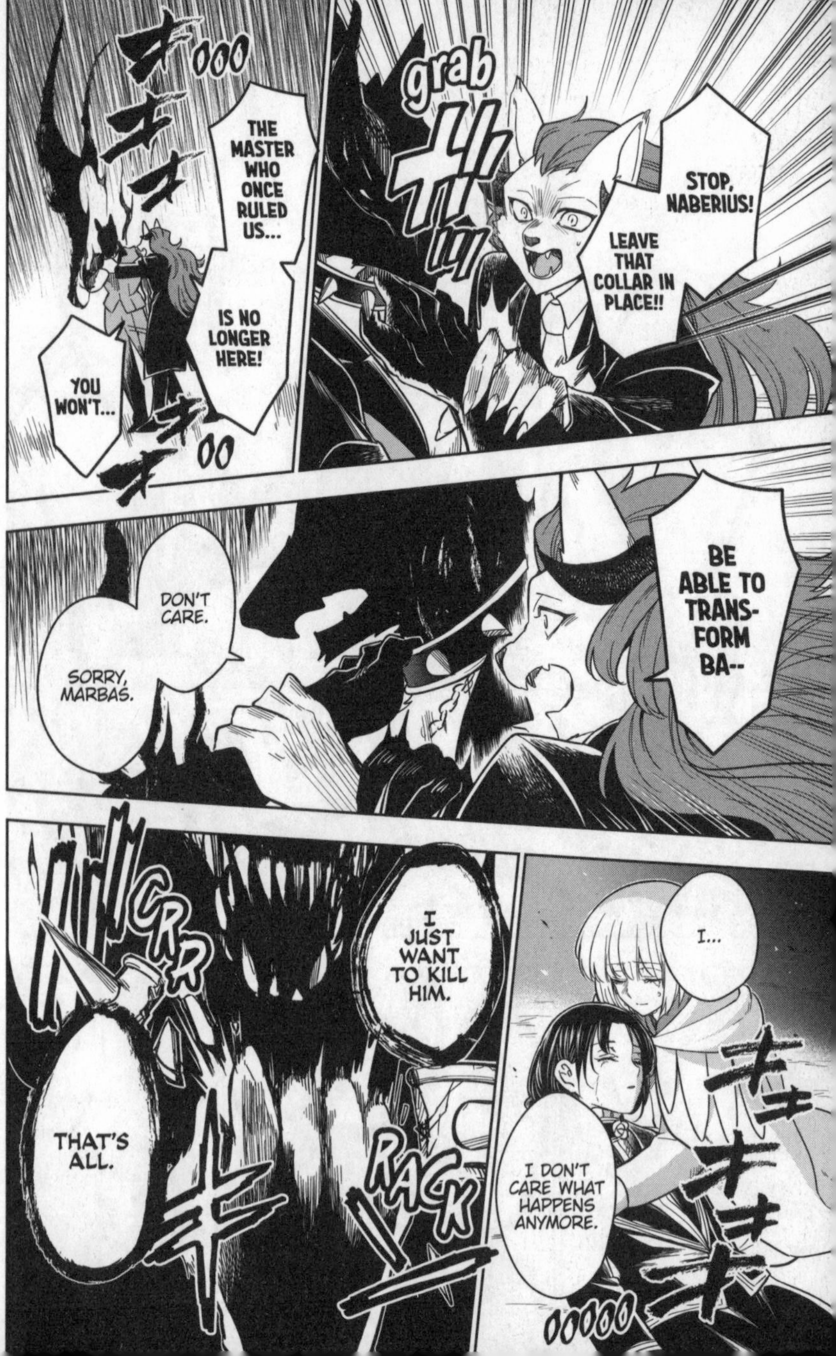
grab
STOP, NABERIUS!
LEAVE THAT COLLAR IN PLACE!!
OOO
THE MASTER WHO ONCE RULED US...
IS NO LONGER HERE!
YOU WON'T...
OO
BE ABLE TO TRANS-FORM BA--
DON'T CARE.
SORRY, MARBAS.
I...
I DON'T CARE WHAT HAPPENS ANYMORE.
OOOOO
I JUST WANT TO KILL HIM.
CRR
RACK
THAT'S ALL.

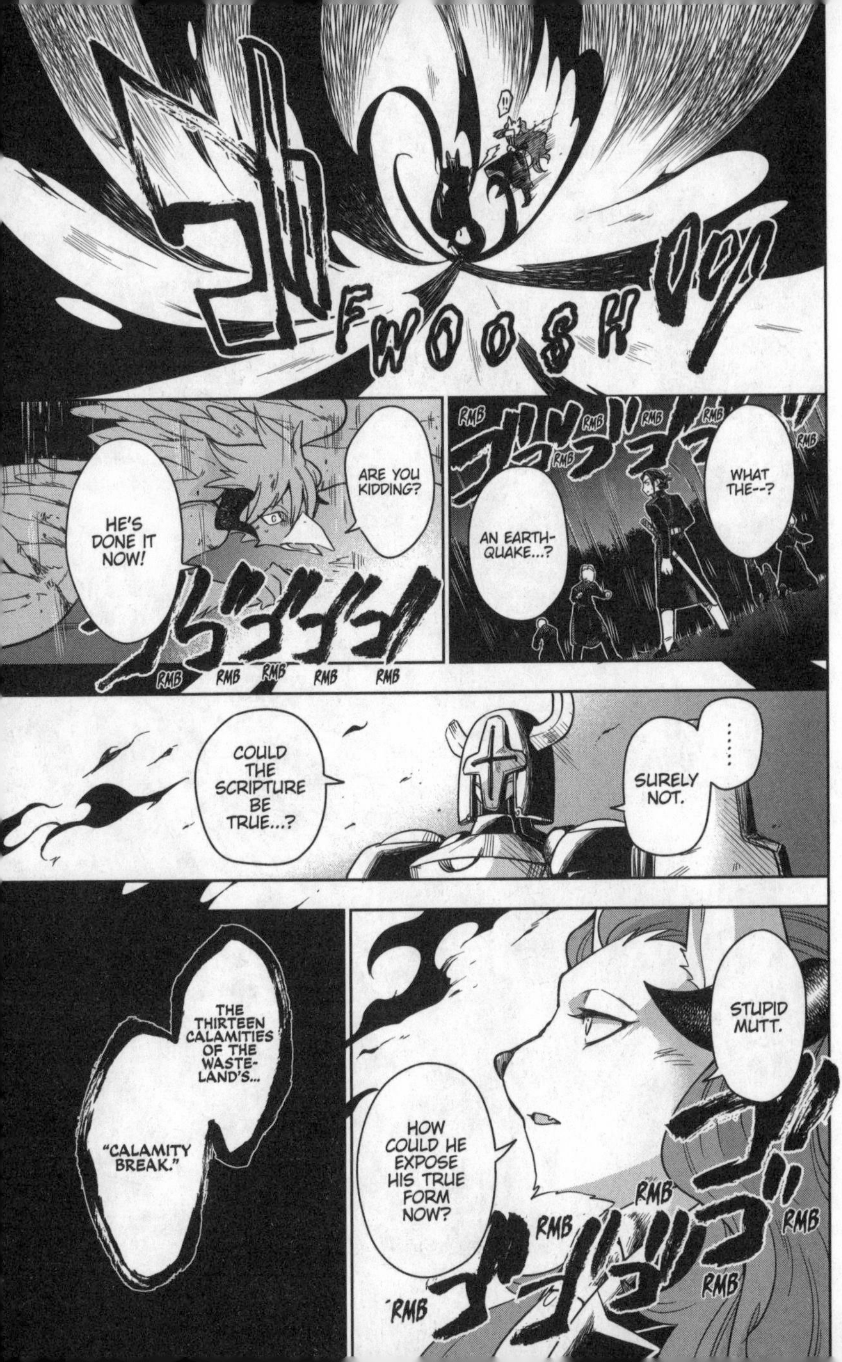
!
FWOOSH
RMB RMB RMB RMB RMB RMB
WHAT THE--?
AN EARTH-QUAKE...?
ARE YOU KIDDING?
HE'S DONE IT NOW!
RMB RMB RMB RMB RMB
......
SURELY NOT.
COULD THE SCRIPTURE BE TRUE...?
STUPID MUTT.
HOW COULD HE EXPOSE HIS TRUE FORM NOW?
RMB RMB RMB RMB RMB
THE THIRTEEN CALAMITIES OF THE WASTE-LAND'S...
“CALAMITY BREAK.”

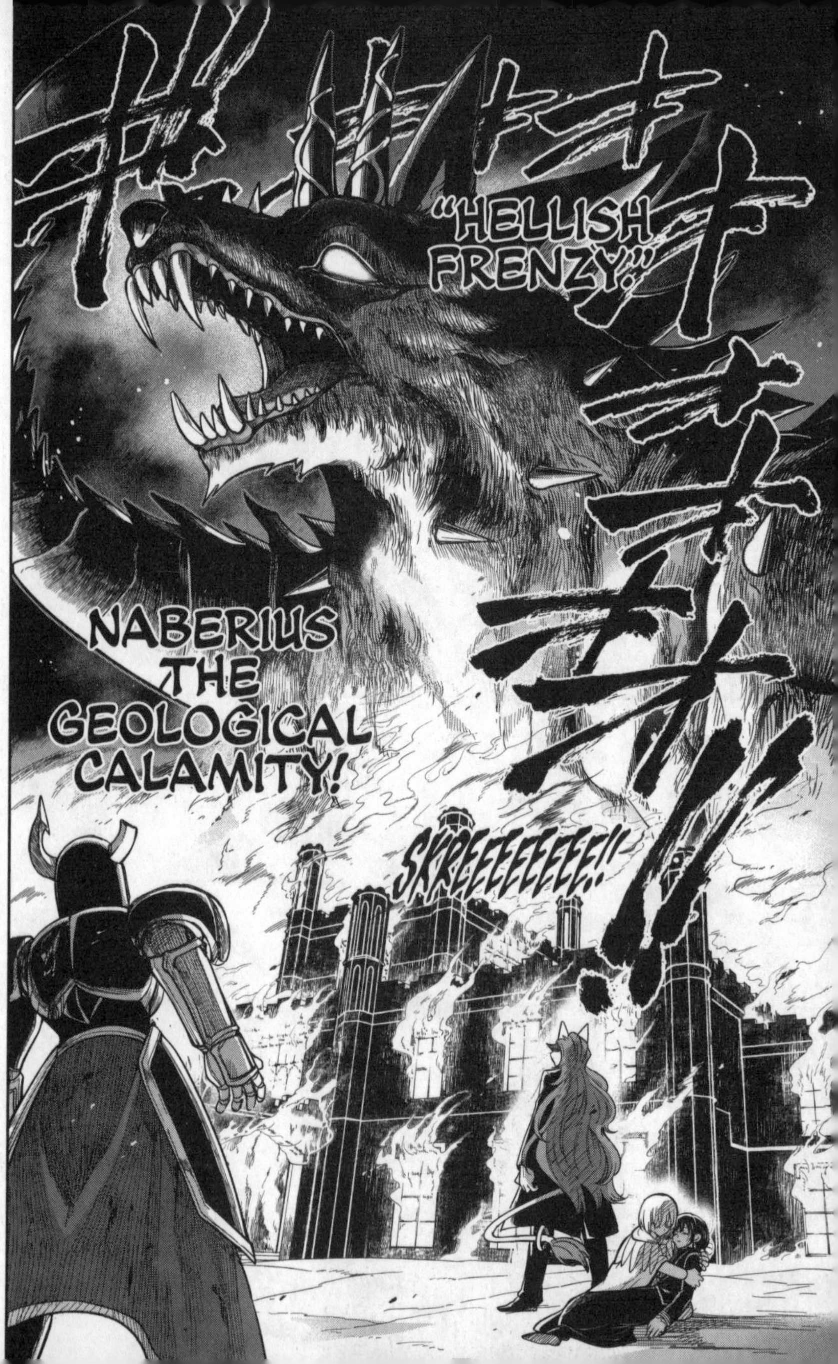
"HELLISH FRENZY!"
NABERIUS THE GEOLOGICAL CALAMITY!
SKREEEEEEEE!!

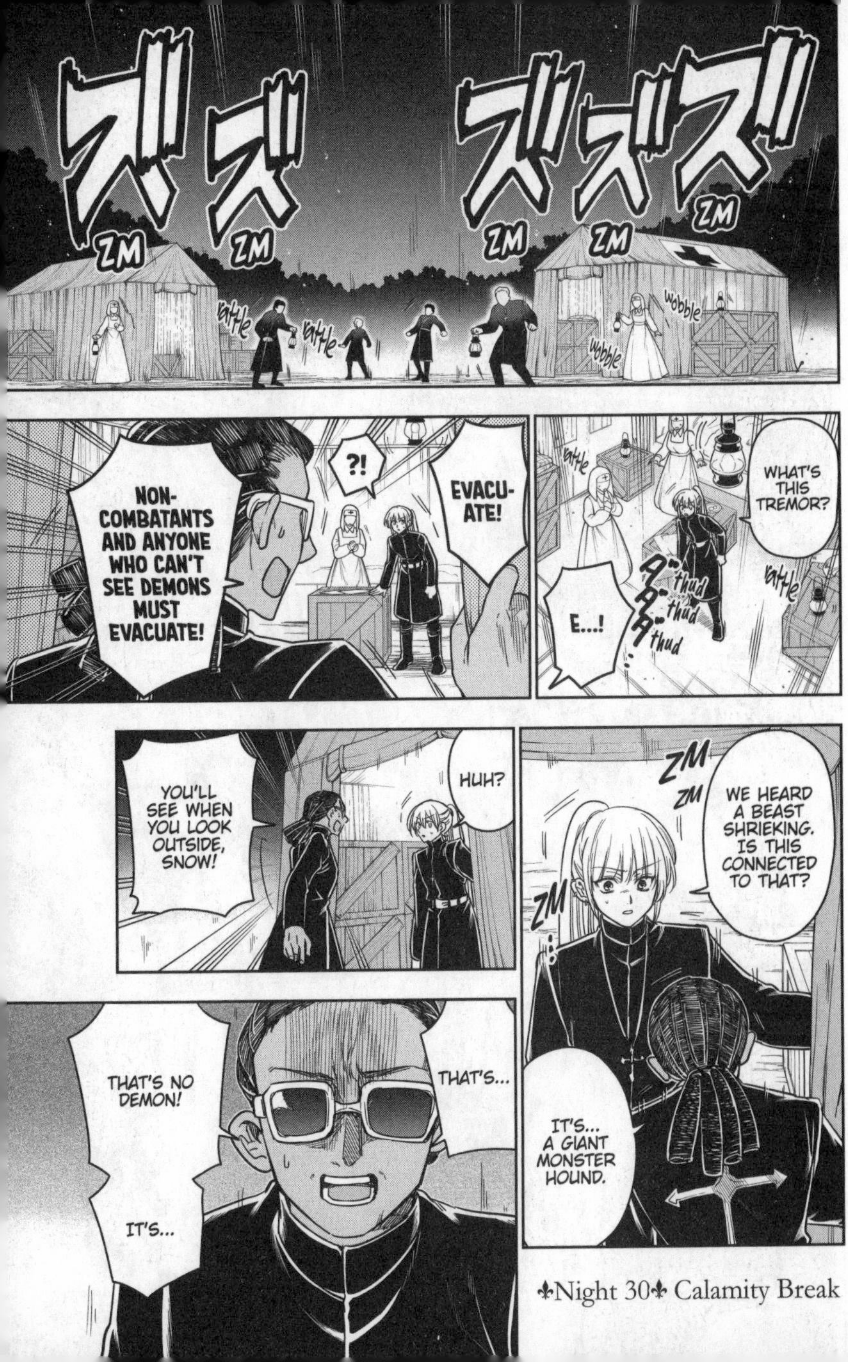
ズ
ズ
ズズズ
ZM
ZM
ZM
ZM
ZM
rattle
rattle
wobble
wobble
WHAT'S THIS TREMOR?
rattle
thud
thud
thud
E...!
EVACU-ATE!
?!
NON-COMBATANTS AND ANYONE WHO CAN'T SEE DEMONS MUST EVACUATE!
ZM
ZM
WE HEARD A BEAST SHRIEKING. IS THIS CONNECTED TO THAT?
ZM
IT'S... A GIANT MONSTER HOUND.
HUH?
YOU'LL SEE WHEN YOU LOOK OUTSIDE, SNOW!
THAT'S...
THAT'S NO DEMON!
IT'S...

⚜Night 30⚜ Calamity Break

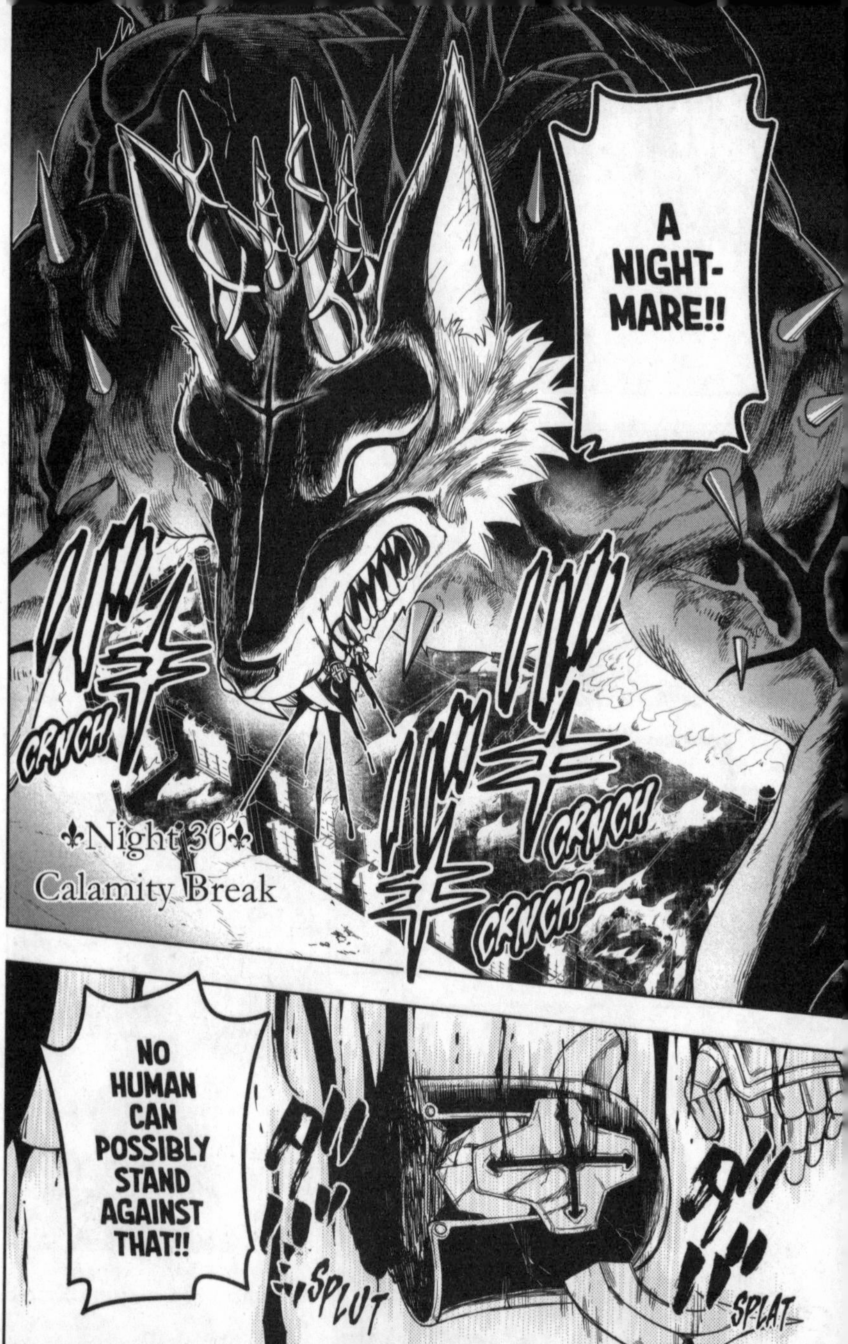
A NIGHT-MARE!!
CRNCH
CRNCH
CRNCH
Night 30
Calamity Break
NO HUMAN CAN POSSIBLY STAND AGAINST THAT!!
SPLAT
SPLUT

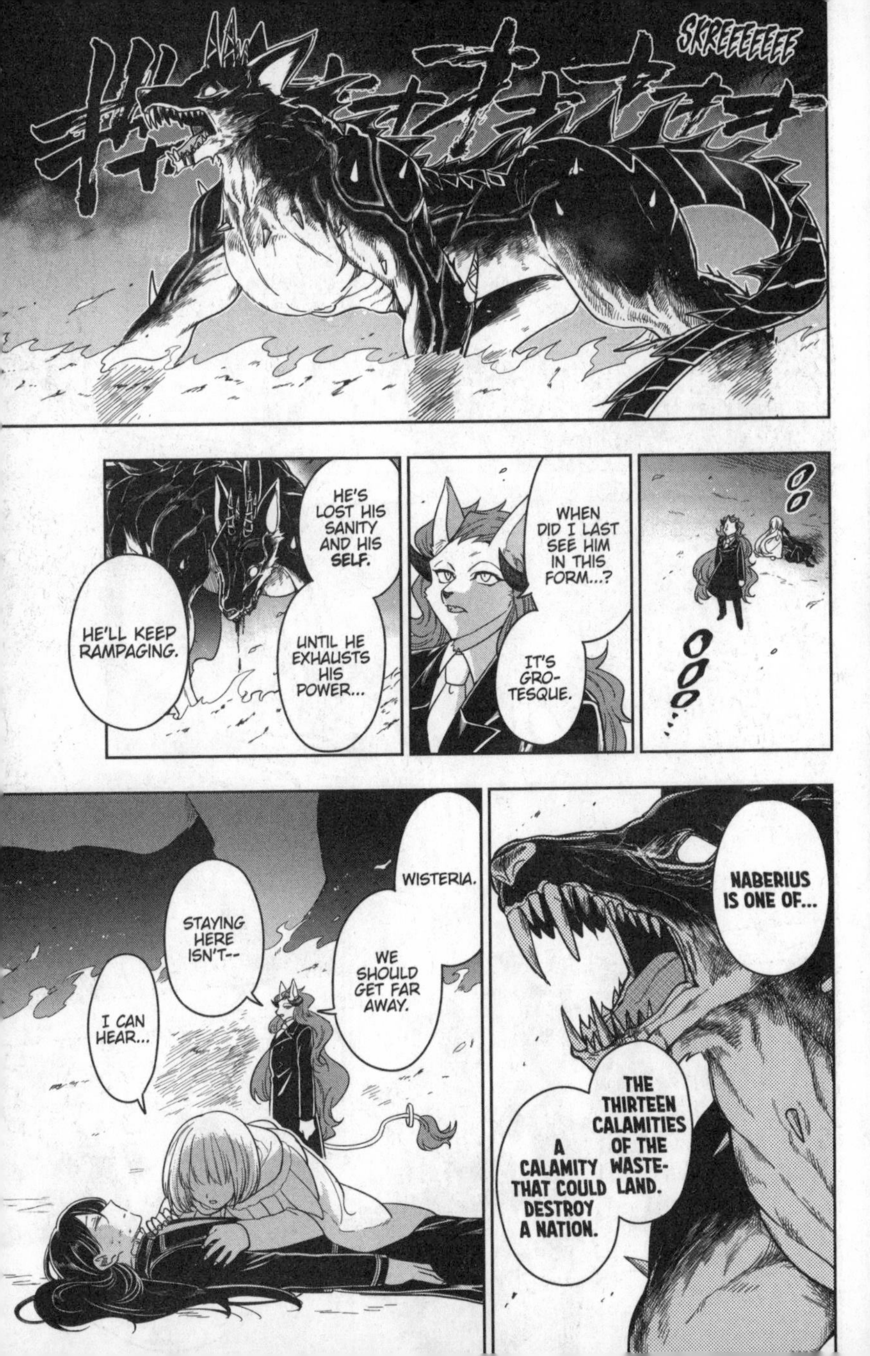
SKREEEEEEE
WHEN DID I LAST SEE HIM IN THIS FORM...?
IT'S GRO-TESQUE.
HE'S LOST HIS SANITY AND HIS SELF.
UNTIL HE EXHAUSTS HIS POWER...
HE'LL KEEP RAMPAGING.
NABERIUS IS ONE OF...
THE THIRTEEN CALAMITIES OF THE WASTE-LAND.
A CALAMITY THAT COULD DESTROY A NATION.
WISTERIA.
WE SHOULD GET FAR AWAY.
STAYING HERE ISN'T--
I CAN HEAR...

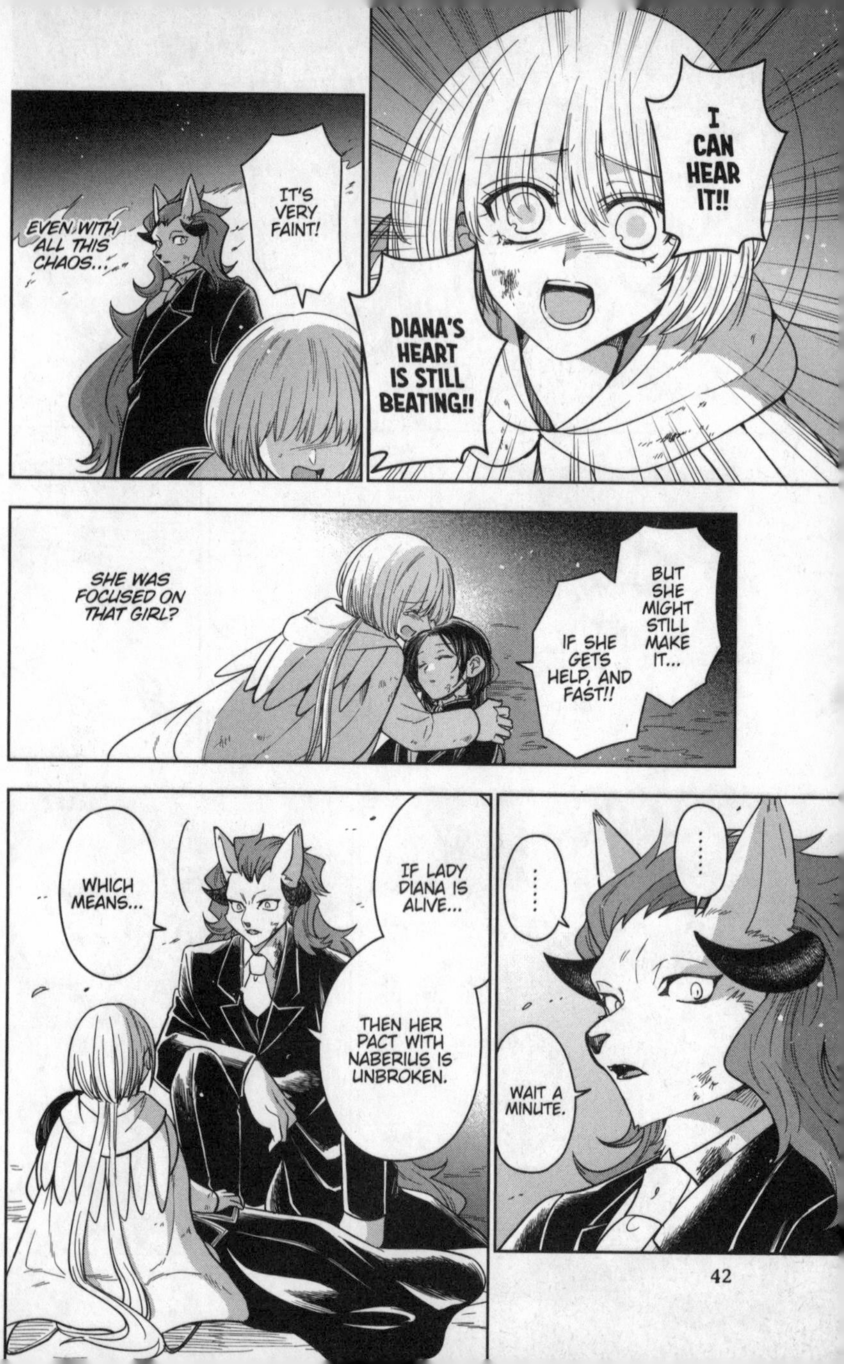
I CAN HEAR IT!!
IT'S VERY FAINT!
DIANA'S HEART IS STILL BEATING!!
EVEN WITH ALL THIS CHAOS...
BUT SHE MIGHT STILL MAKE IT...
IF SHE GETS HELP, AND FAST!!
SHE WAS FOCUSED ON THAT GIRL?
......
......
WAIT A MINUTE.
IF LADY DIANA IS ALIVE...
THEN HER PACT WITH NABERIUS IS UNBROKEN.
WHICH MEANS...

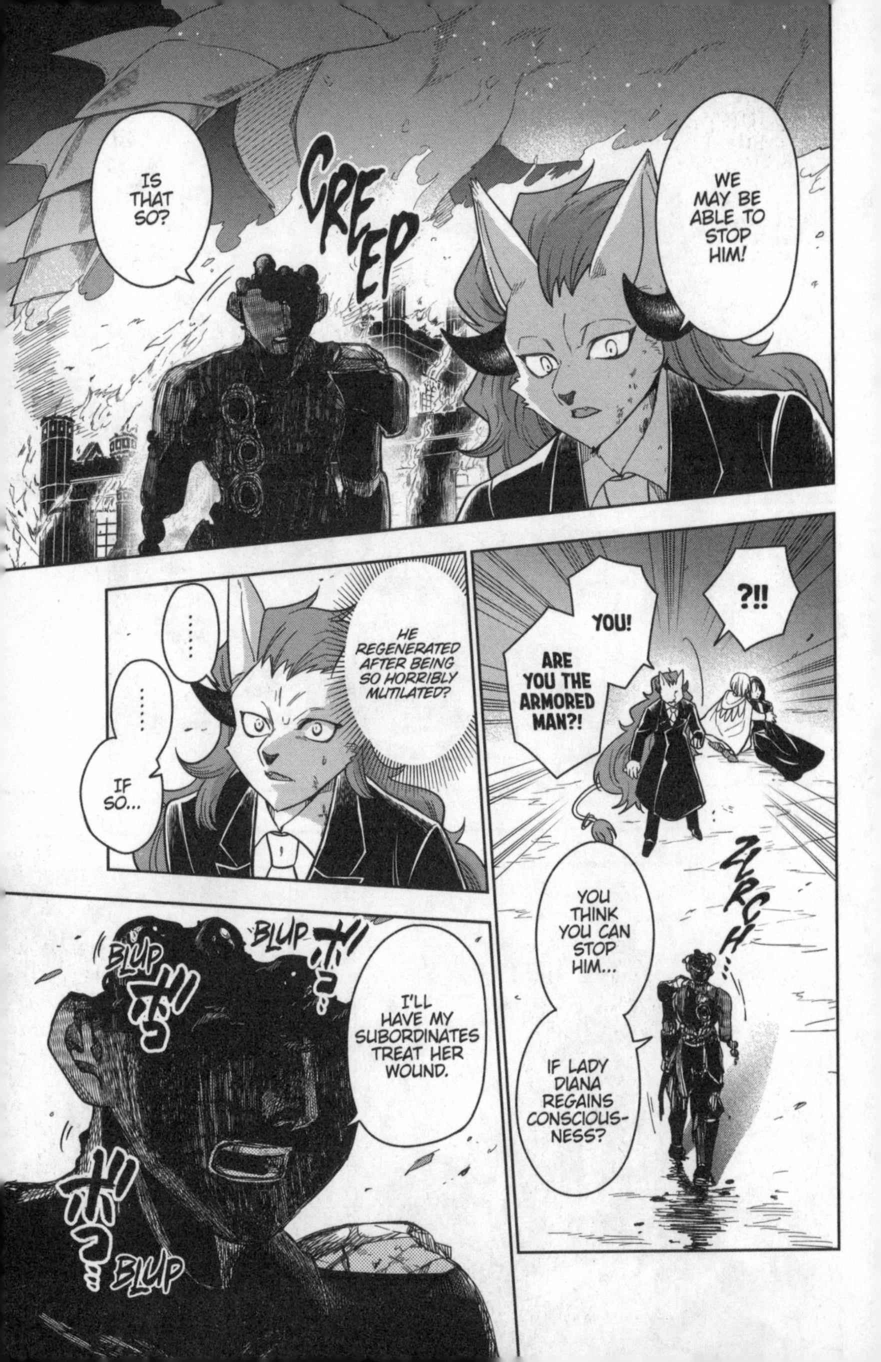
WE MAY BE ABLE TO STOP HIM!
CREEP
IS THAT SO?
?!!
YOU!
ARE YOU THE ARMORED MAN?!
HE REGENERATED AFTER BEING SO HORRIBLY MUTILATED?
......
......
IF SO...
ZLRCH...
YOU THINK YOU CAN STOP HIM...
IF LADY DIANA REGAINS CONSCIOUS-NESS?
I'LL HAVE MY SUBORDINATES TREAT HER WOUND.
BLUP
BLUP
BLUP

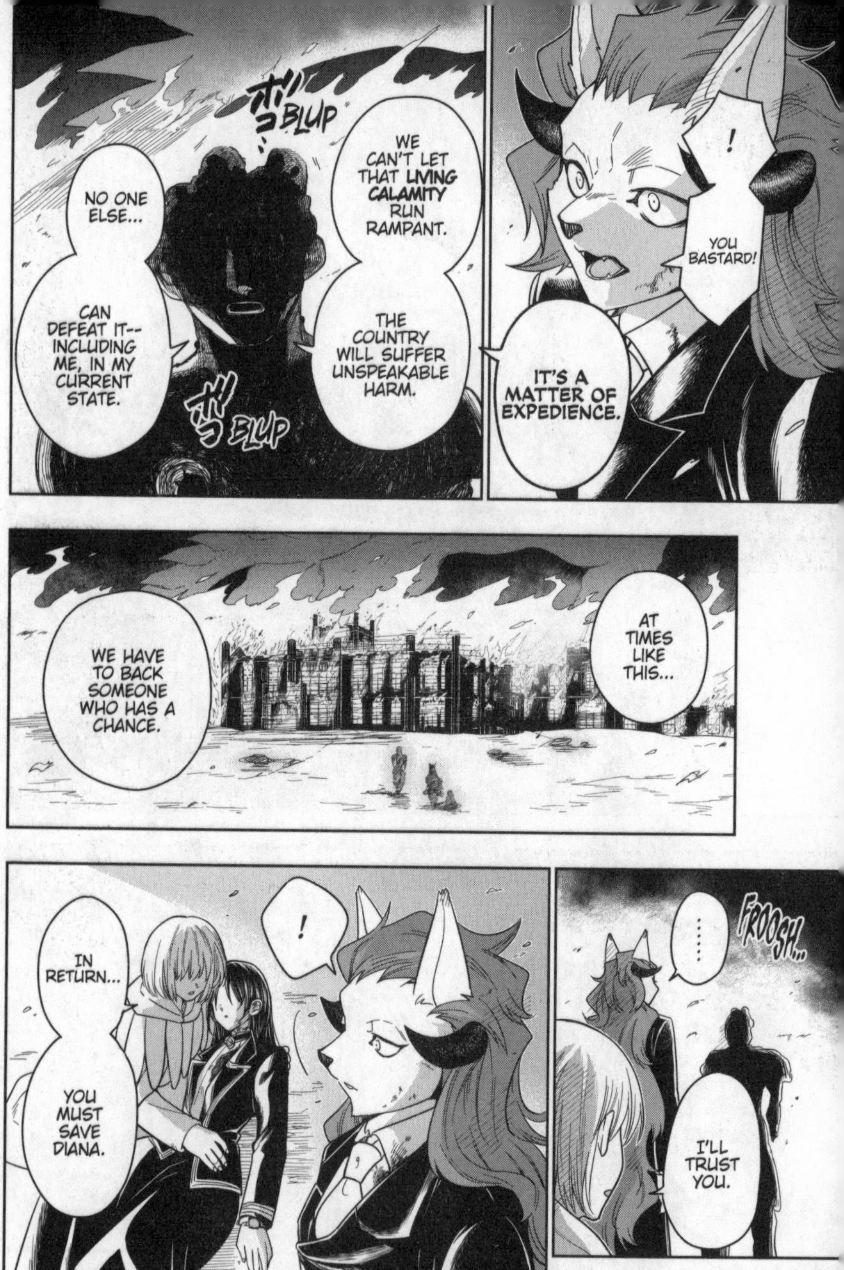
!
YOU BASTARD!
IT'S A MATTER OF EXPEDIENCE.
BLUP
WE CAN'T LET THAT LIVING CALAMITY RUN RAMPANT.
THE COUNTRY WILL SUFFER UNSPEAKABLE HARM.
NO ONE ELSE...
CAN DEFEAT IT-- INCLUDING ME, IN MY CURRENT STATE.
BLUP
AT TIMES LIKE THIS...
WE HAVE TO BACK SOMEONE WHO HAS A CHANCE.
......
FROOSH...
I'LL TRUST YOU.
!
IN RETURN...
YOU MUST SAVE DIANA.

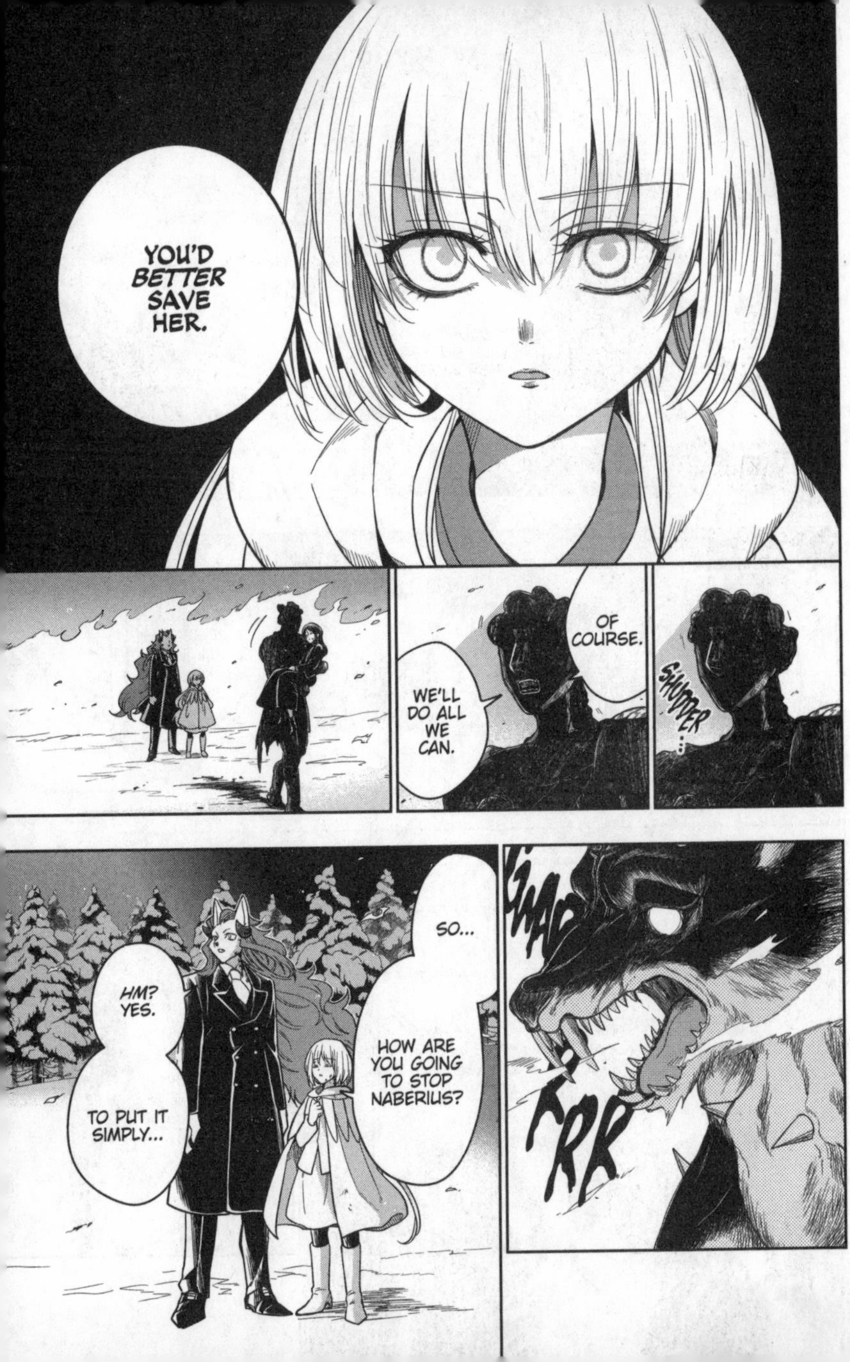
YOU'D BETTER SAVE HER.
SHUDDER...
OF COURSE.
WE'LL DO ALL WE CAN.
KRR
SO...
HOW ARE YOU GOING TO STOP NABERIUS?
HM? YES.
TO PUT IT SIMPLY...

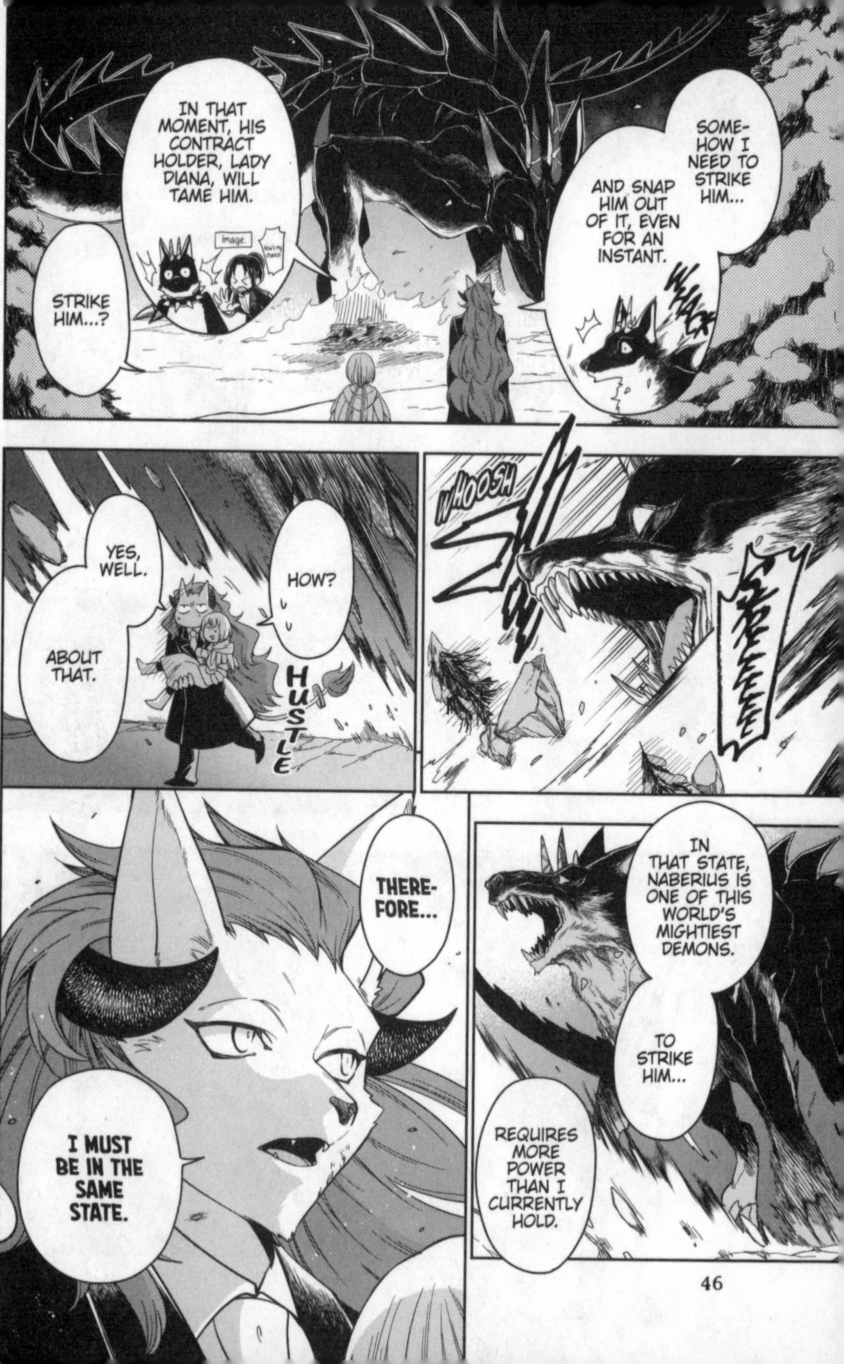
SOME-HOW I NEED TO STRIKE HIM...
AND SNAP HIM OUT OF IT, EVEN FOR AN INSTANT.
WHACK
IN THAT MOMENT, HIS CONTRACT HOLDER, LADY DIANA, WILL TAME HIM.
Now's my chance!
Image.
STRIKE HIM...?
WHOOSH
HOW?
YES, WELL.
ABOUT THAT.
HUSTLE
IN THAT STATE, NABERIUS IS ONE OF THIS WORLD'S MIGHTIEST DEMONS.
TO STRIKE HIM...
REQUIRES MORE POWER THAN I CURRENTLY HOLD.
THERE-FORE...
I MUST BE IN THE SAME STATE.

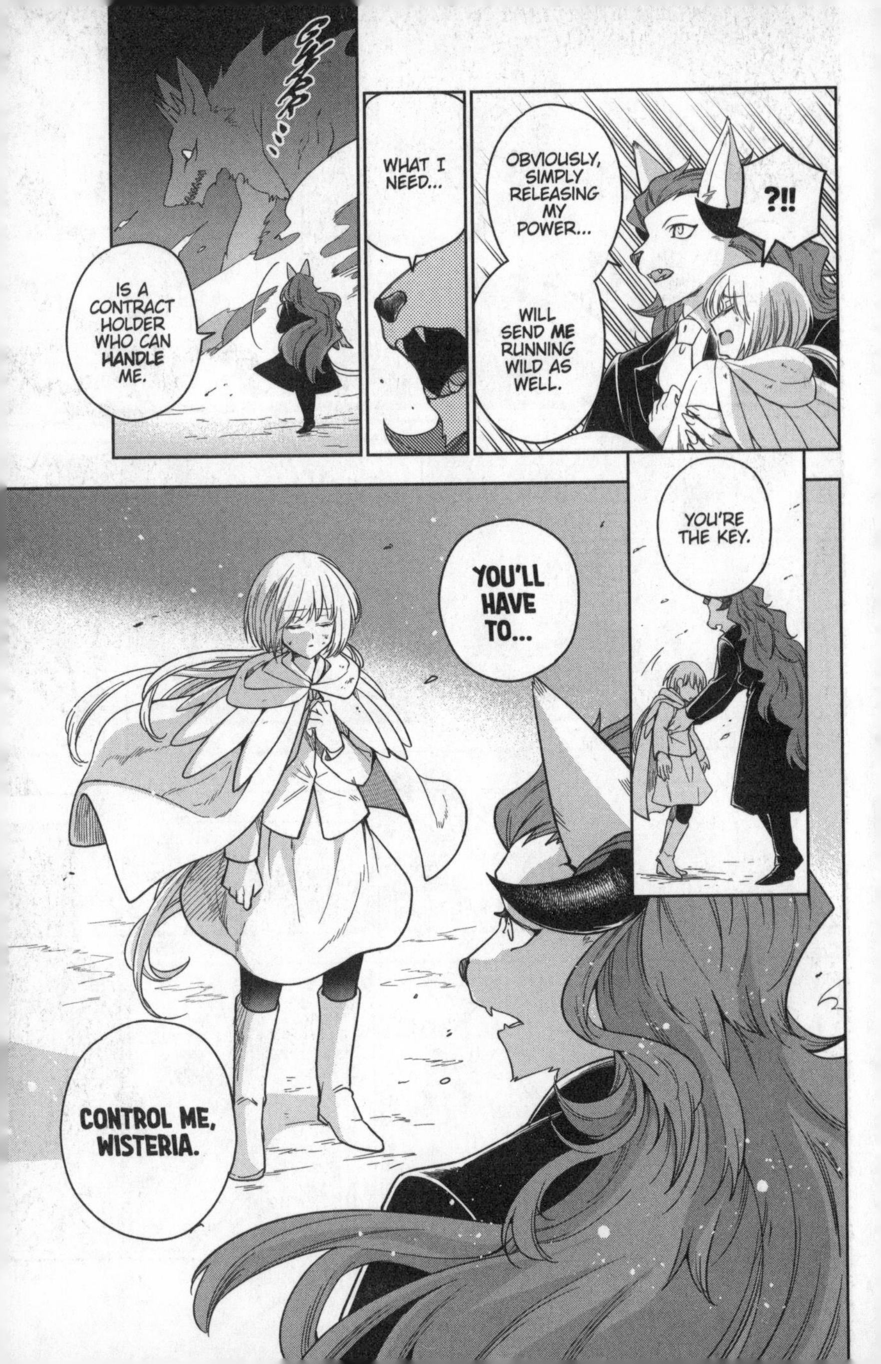
?!!
OBVIOUSLY, SIMPLY RELEASING MY POWER...
WILL SEND ME RUNNING WILD AS WELL.
WHAT I NEED...
IS A CONTRACT HOLDER WHO CAN HANDLE ME.
YOU'RE THE KEY.
YOU'LL HAVE TO...
CONTROL ME, WISTERIA.

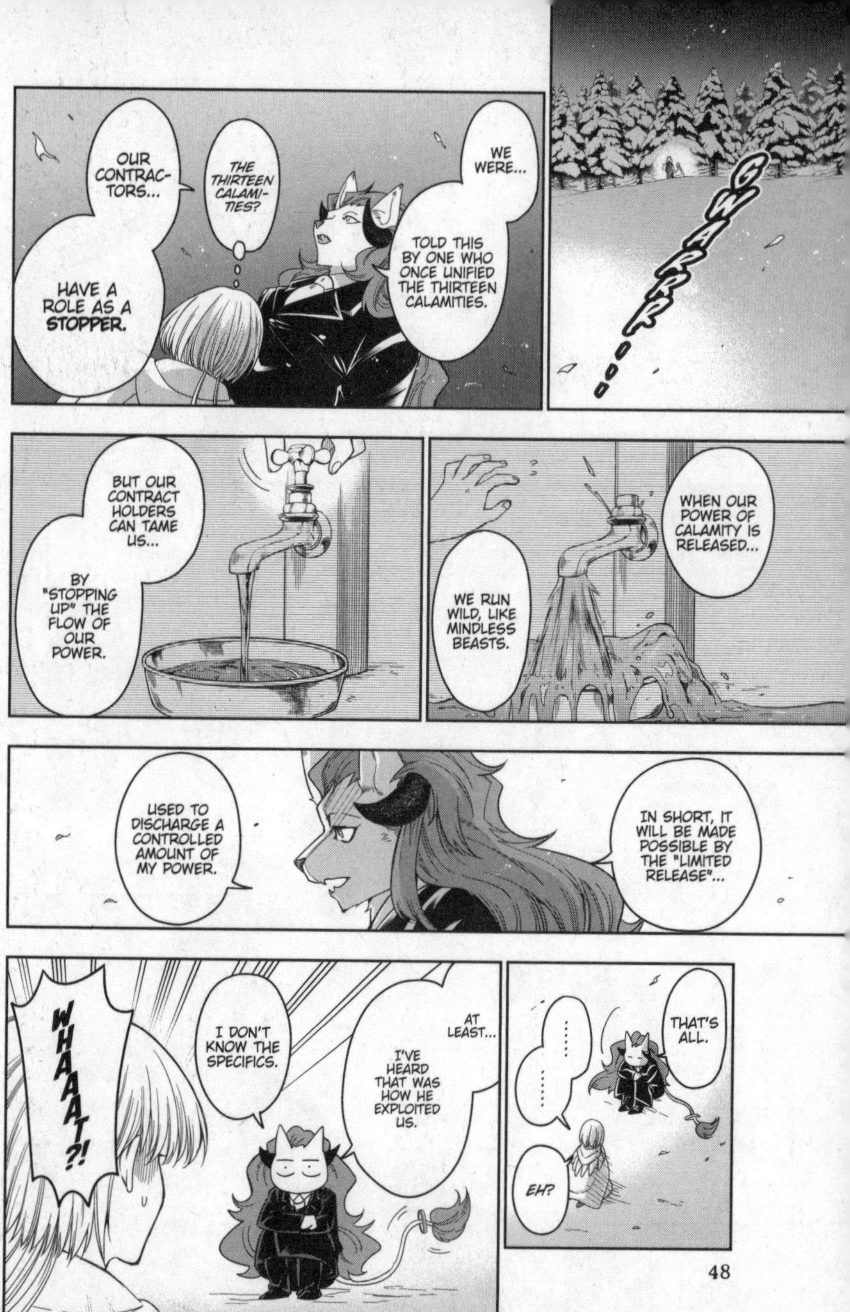
GWARRR...
WE WERE...
TOLD THIS BY ONE WHO ONCE UNIFIED THE THIRTEEN CALAMITIES.
THE THIRTEEN CALAMITIES?
OUR CONTRACTORS...
HAVE A ROLE AS A STOPPER.
WHEN OUR POWER OF CALAMITY IS RELEASED...
WE RUN WILD, LIKE MINDLESS BEASTS.
BUT OUR CONTRACT HOLDERS CAN TAME US...
BY "STOPPING UP" THE FLOW OF OUR POWER.
IN SHORT, IT WILL BE MADE POSSIBLE BY THE "LIMITED RELEASE"...
USED TO DISCHARGE A CONTROLLED AMOUNT OF MY POWER.
THAT'S ALL.
......
EH?
AT LEAST...
I'VE HEARD THAT WAS HOW HE EXPLOITED US.
I DON'T KNOW THE SPECIFICS.
WHAAAAT?!

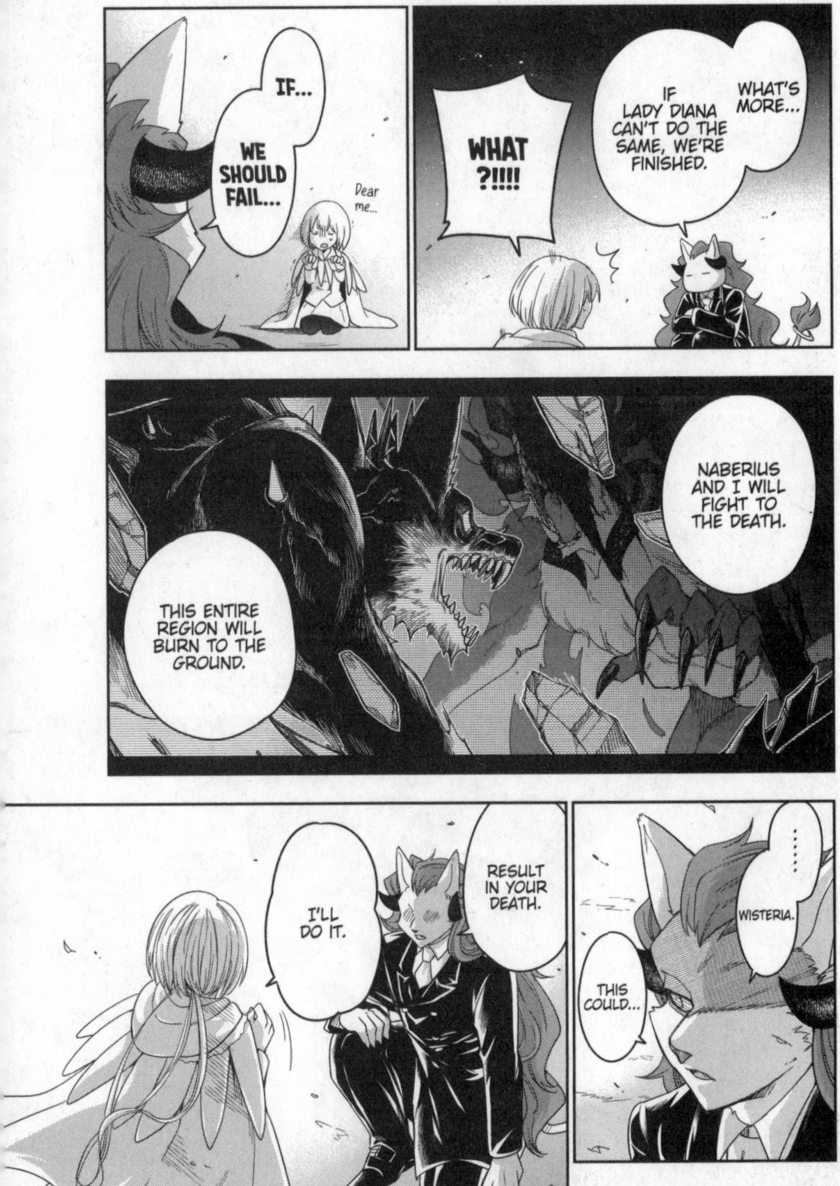
WHAT'S MORE...
IF LADY DIANA CAN'T DO THE SAME, WE'RE FINISHED.
WHAT ?!!!!
IF...
WE SHOULD FAIL...
Dear me...
NABERIUS AND I WILL FIGHT TO THE DEATH.
THIS ENTIRE REGION WILL BURN TO THE GROUND.
......
WISTERIA.
THIS COULD...
RESULT IN YOUR DEATH.
I'LL DO IT.

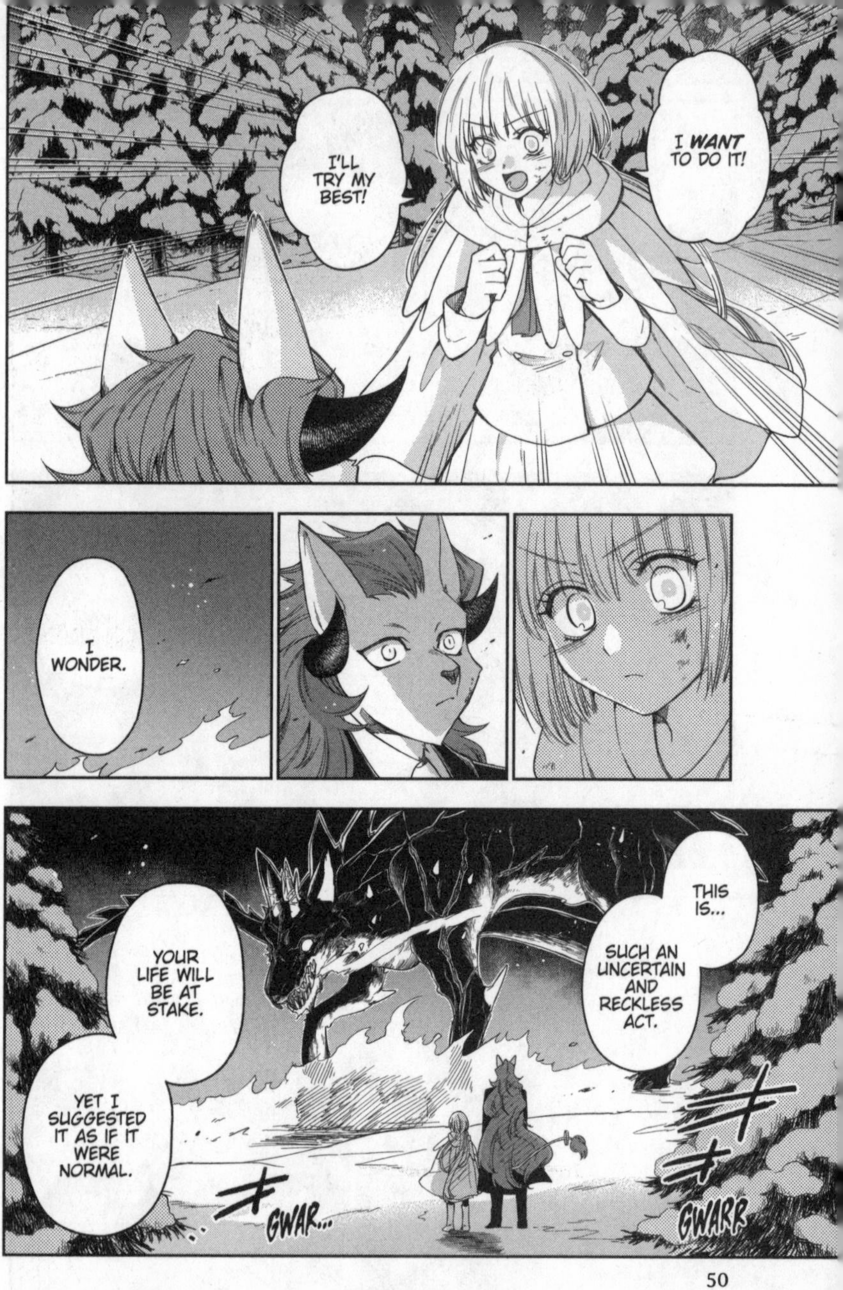
I WANT TO DO IT!
I'LL TRY MY BEST!
I WONDER.
THIS IS...
SUCH AN UNCERTAIN AND RECKLESS ACT.
YOUR LIFE WILL BE AT STAKE.
YET I SUGGESTED IT AS IF IT WERE NORMAL.
GWARR
GWAR...

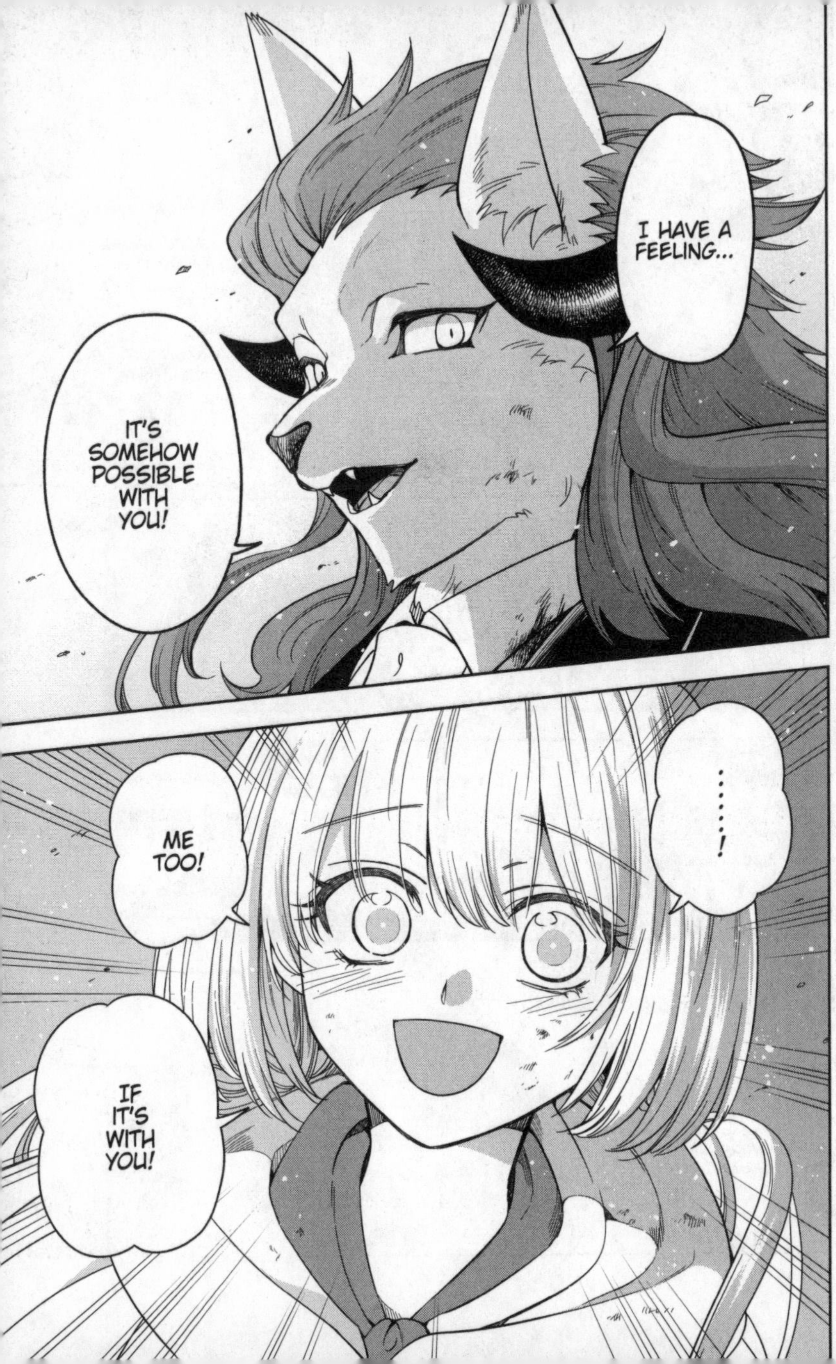
I HAVE A FEELING...
IT'S SOMEHOW POSSIBLE WITH YOU!
......!
ME TOO!
IF IT'S WITH YOU!

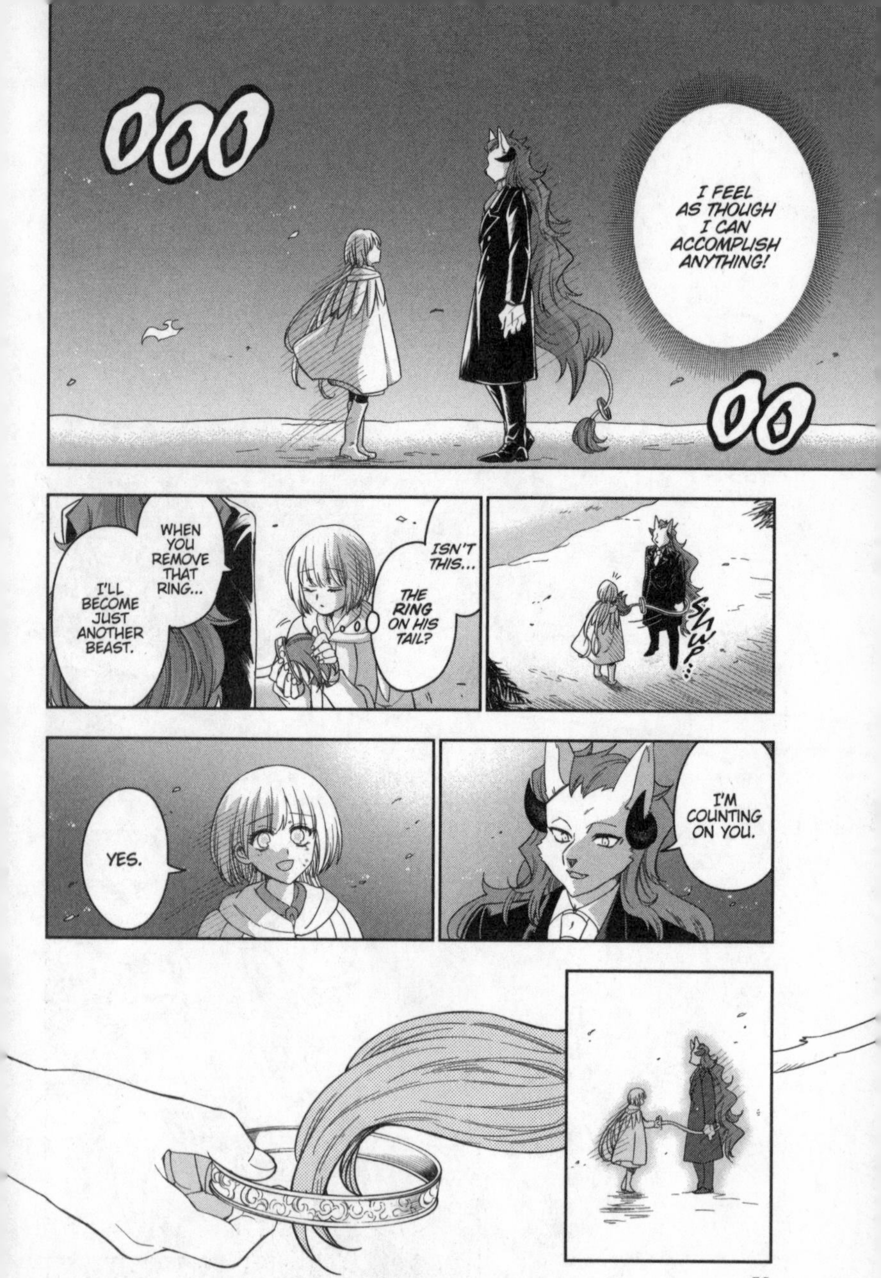
I FEEL AS THOUGH I CAN ACCOMPLISH ANYTHING!
OOO
OO
SHWUP...
ISN'T THIS...
THE RING ON HIS TAIL?
WHEN YOU REMOVE THAT RING...
I'LL BECOME JUST ANOTHER BEAST.
I'M COUNTING ON YOU.
YES.

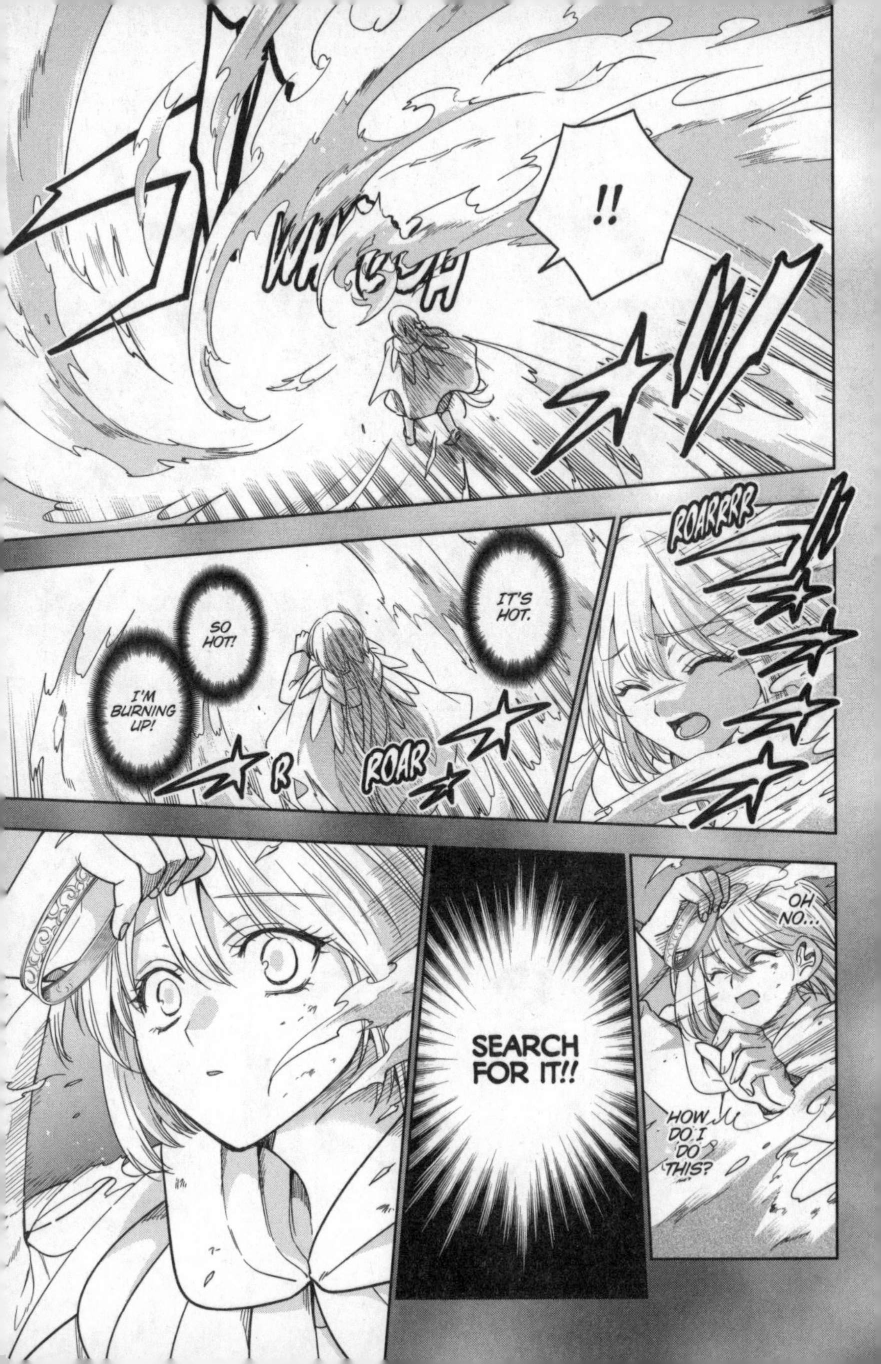
!!
WHOOSH
ROARRRR
IT'S HOT.
SO HOT!
I'M BURNING UP!
ROAR
R
OH NO...
HOW DO I DO THIS?
SEARCH FOR IT!!

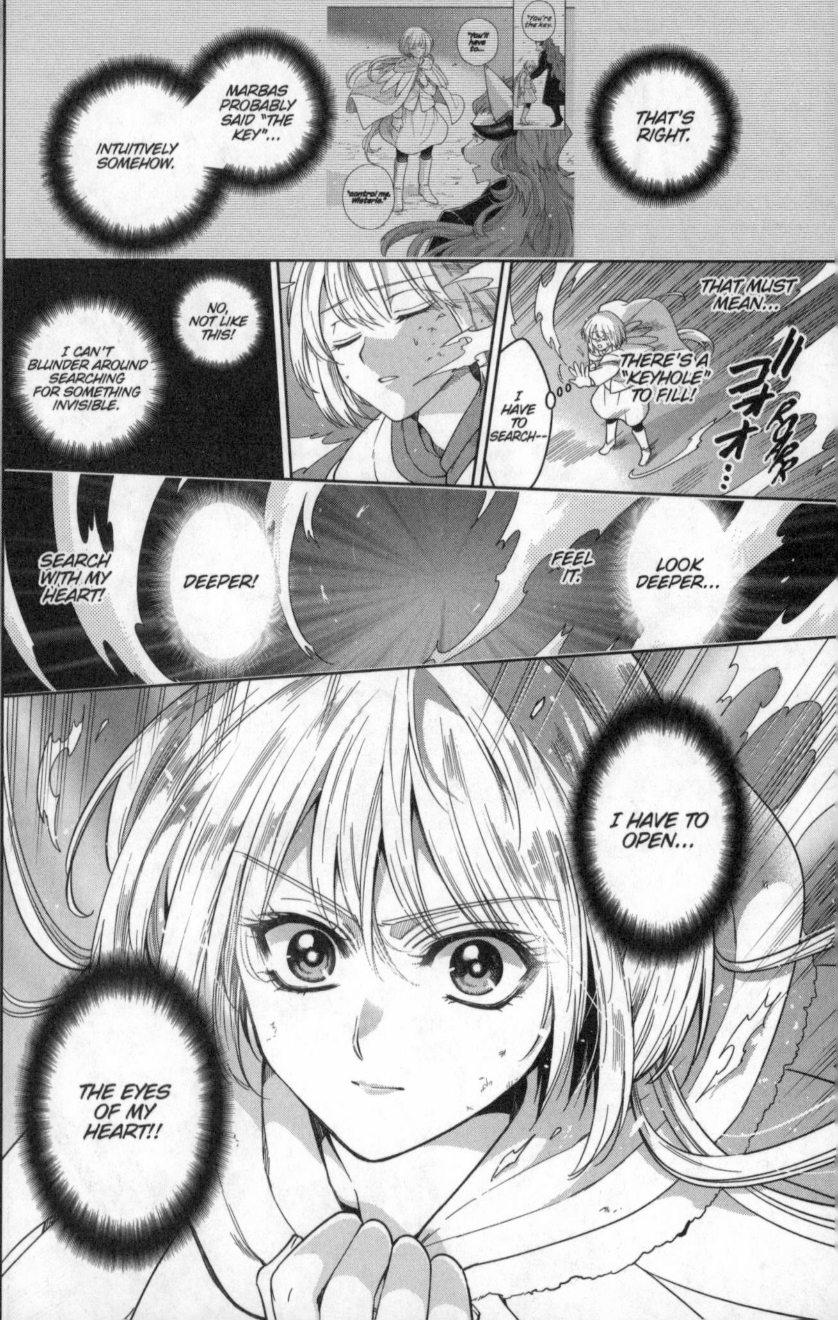
THAT'S RIGHT.
"You're the key.
"You'll have to...
"control me, Wisteria."
MARBAS PROBABLY SAID "THE KEY"...
INTUITIVELY SOMEHOW.
THAT MUST MEAN...
THERE'S A "KEYHOLE" TO FILL!
I HAVE TO SEARCH--
NO, NOT LIKE THIS!
I CAN'T BLUNDER AROUND SEARCHING FOR SOMETHING INVISIBLE.
LOOK DEEPER...
FEEL IT.
DEEPER!
SEARCH WITH MY HEART!
I HAVE TO OPEN...
THE EYES OF MY HEART!!

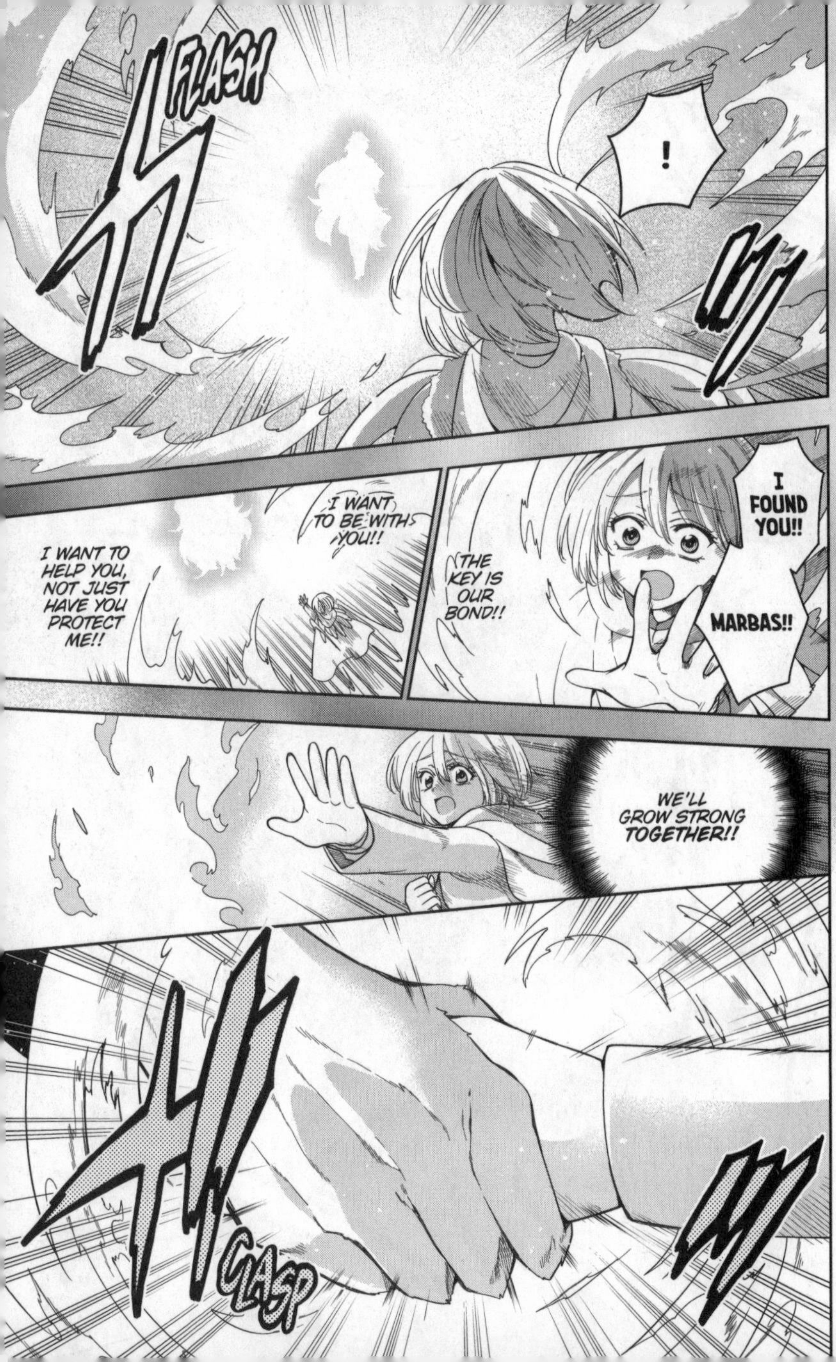
!
FLASH
I FOUND YOU!!
MARBAS!!
THE KEY IS OUR BOND!!
I WANT TO BE WITH YOU!!
I WANT TO HELP YOU, NOT JUST HAVE YOU PROTECT ME!!
WE'LL GROW STRONG TOGETHER!!
CLASP

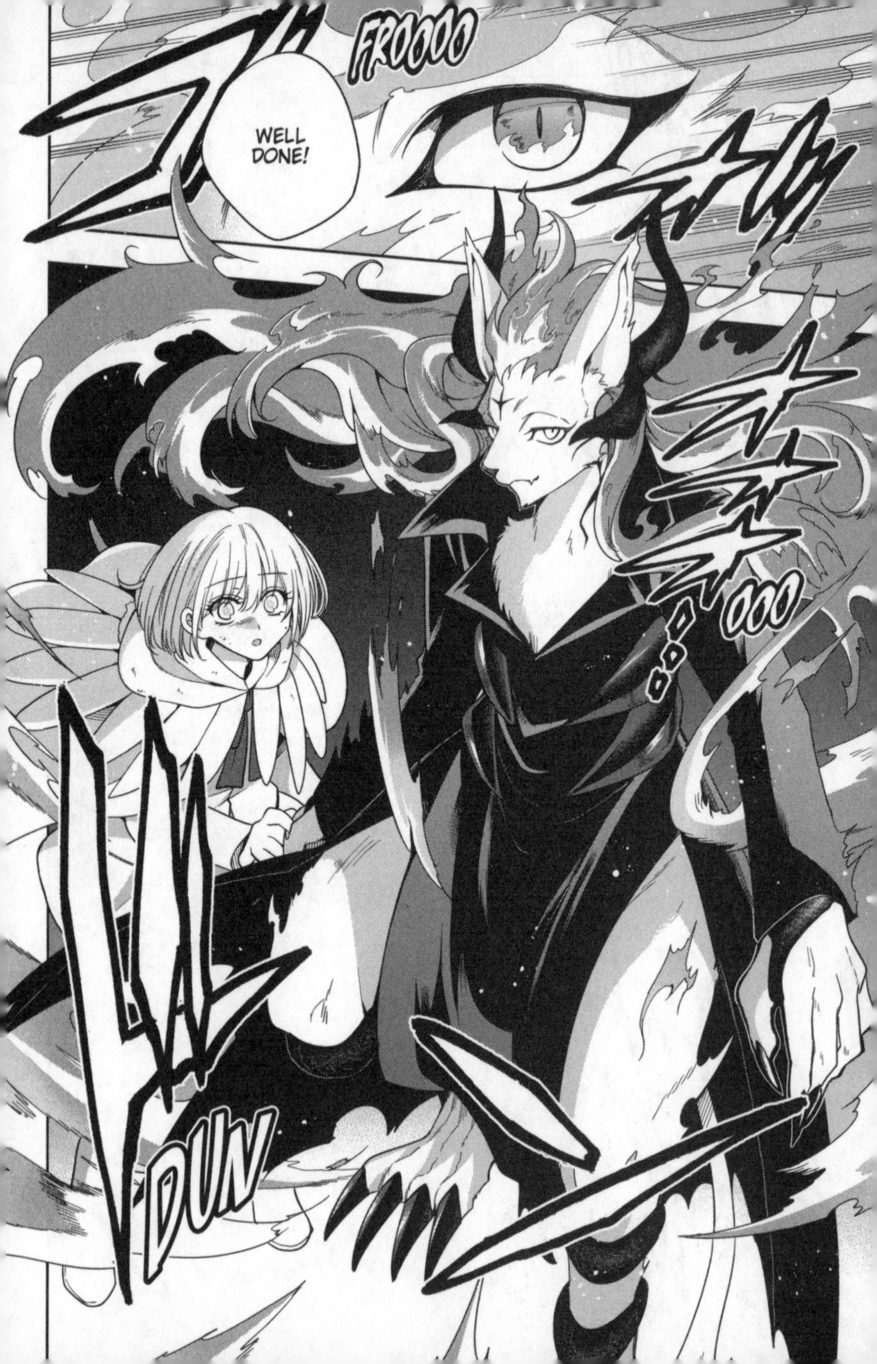
FROOOO
WELL DONE!
DUN

The Tale of the Outcasts

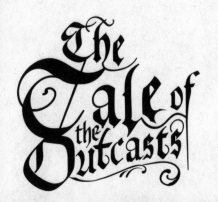

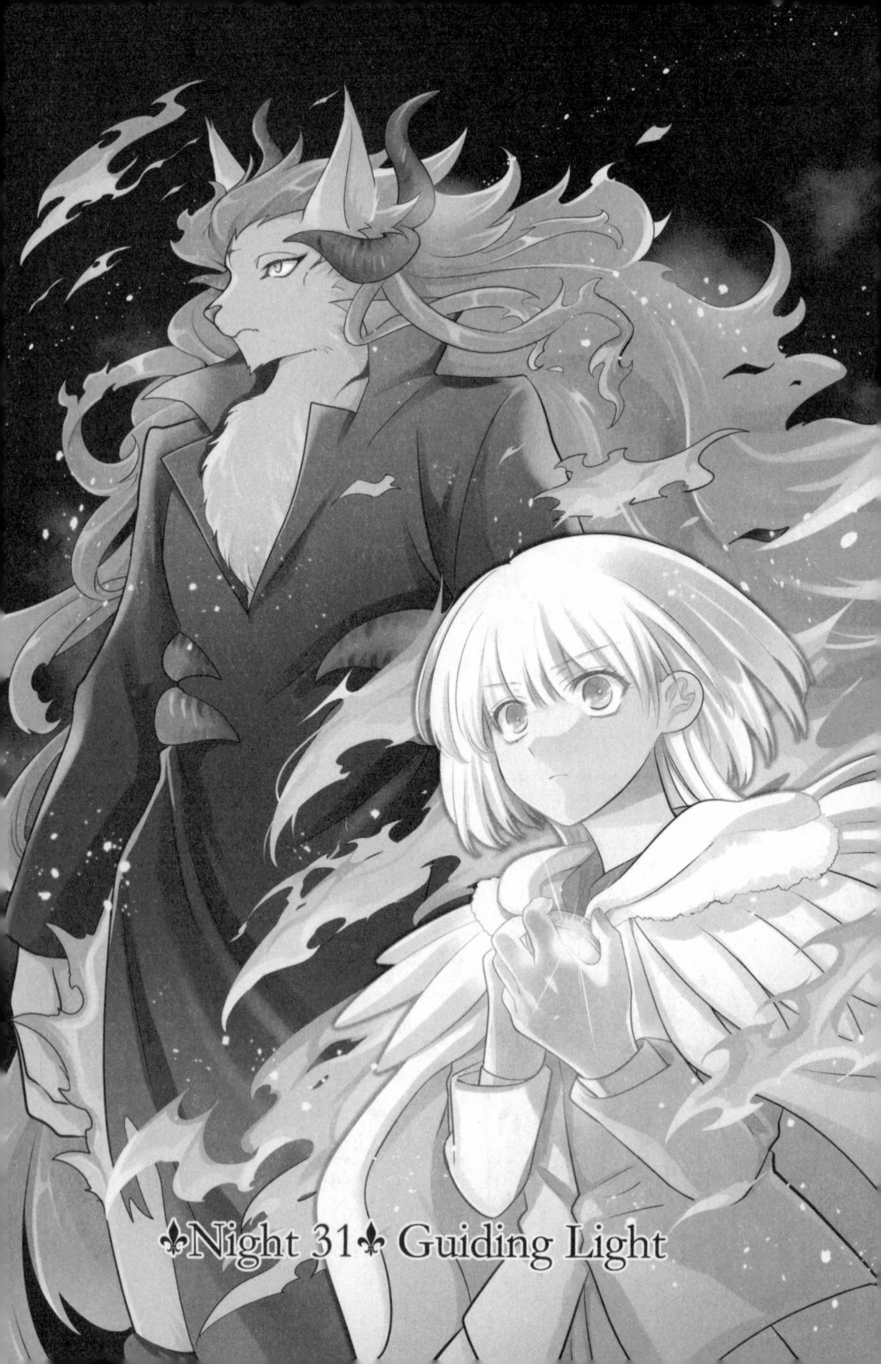
Night 31 Guiding Light

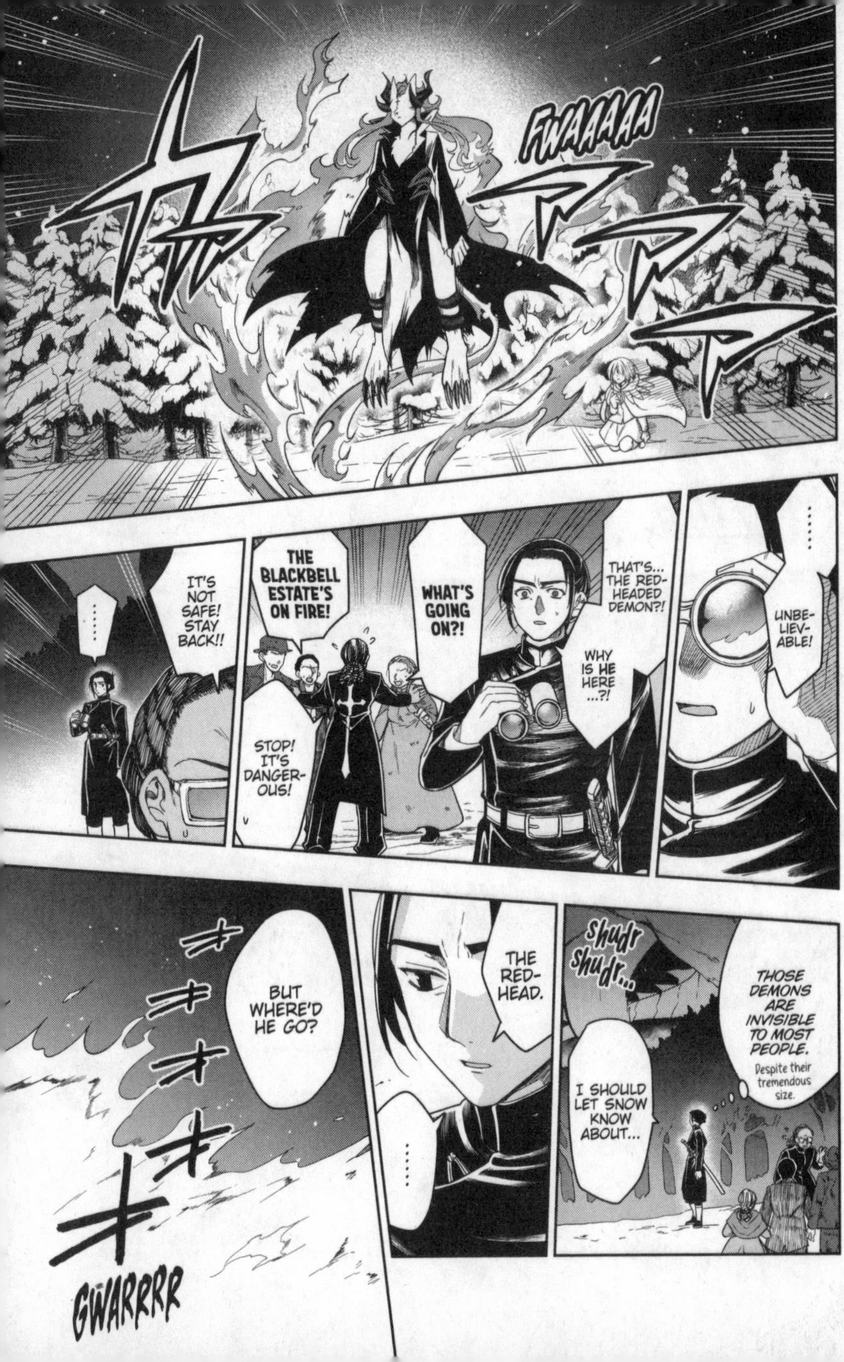
FWAAAAAA
......
UNBE-LIEV-ABLE!
THAT'S... THE RED-HEADED DEMON?!
WHY IS HE HERE ...?!
WHAT'S GOING ON?!
THE BLACKBELL ESTATE'S ON FIRE!
STOP! IT'S DANGER-OUS!
IT'S NOT SAFE! STAY BACK!!
......
Shudr shudr...
THOSE DEMONS ARE INVISIBLE TO MOST PEOPLE.
Despite their tremendous size.
I SHOULD LET SNOW KNOW ABOUT...
THE RED-HEAD.
......
BUT WHERE'D HE GO?
GWARRRR

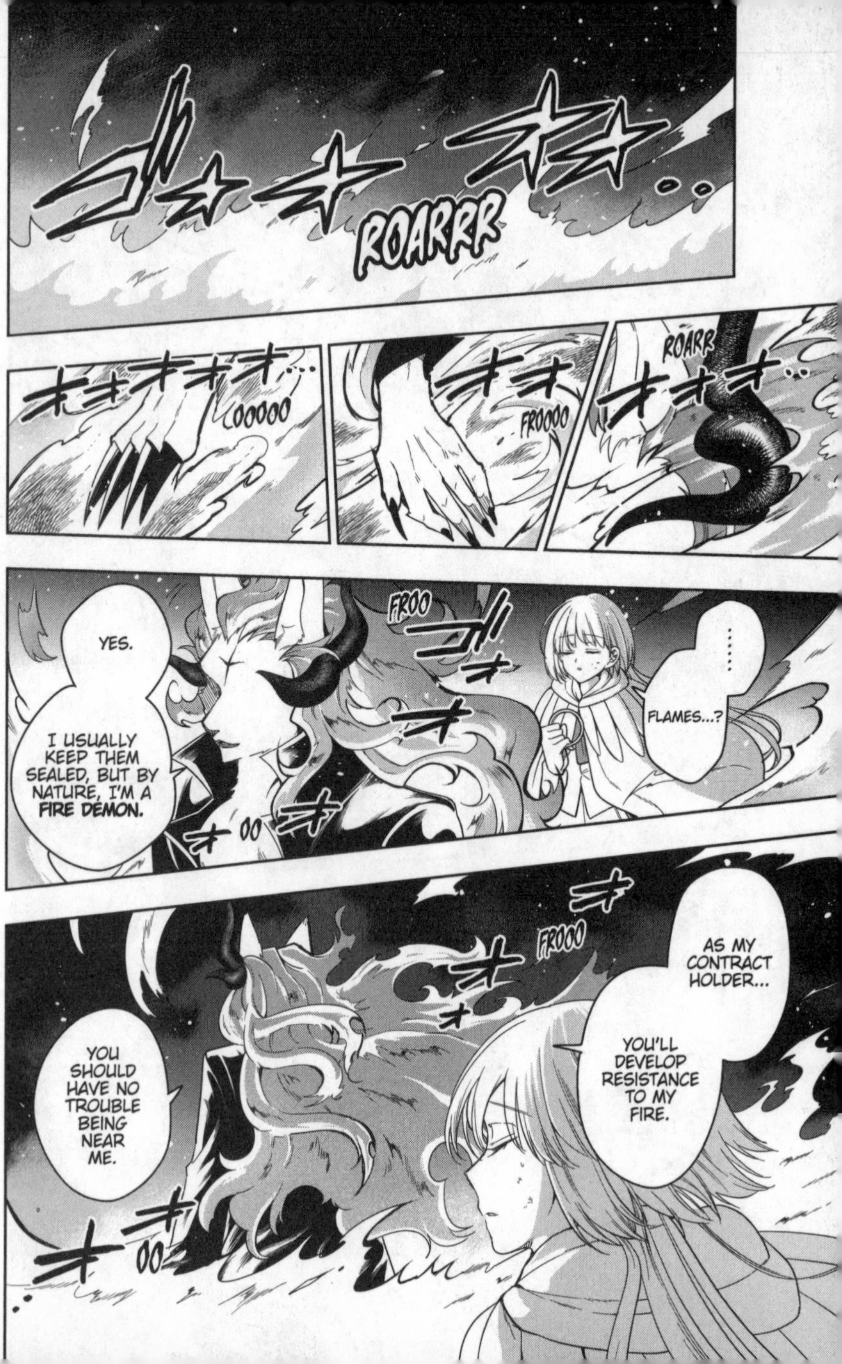
ROARRR
ROARR
FROOOO
OOOOO
......
FLAMES...?
FROO
YES.
I USUALLY KEEP THEM SEALED, BUT BY NATURE, I'M A **FIRE DEMON.**
OO
FROOO
AS MY CONTRACT HOLDER...
YOU'LL DEVELOP RESISTANCE TO MY FIRE.
YOU SHOULD HAVE NO TROUBLE BEING NEAR ME.
OO

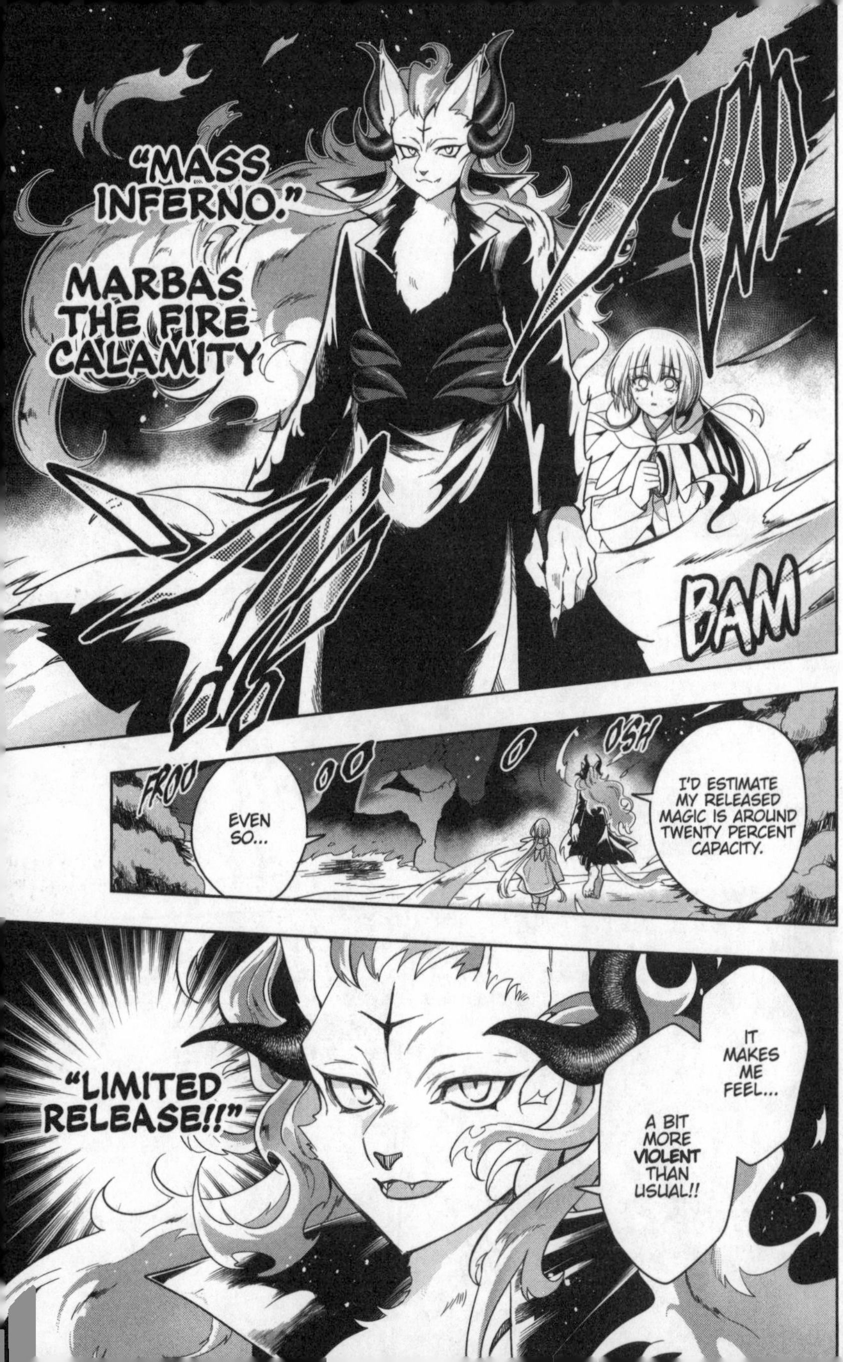
"MASS INFERNO."
MARBAS THE FIRE CALAMITY
BAM
OSH
I'D ESTIMATE MY RELEASED MAGIC IS AROUND TWENTY PERCENT CAPACITY.
FROO
EVEN SO...
IT MAKES ME FEEL...
A BIT MORE **VIOLENT** THAN USUAL!!
"LIMITED RELEASE!!"

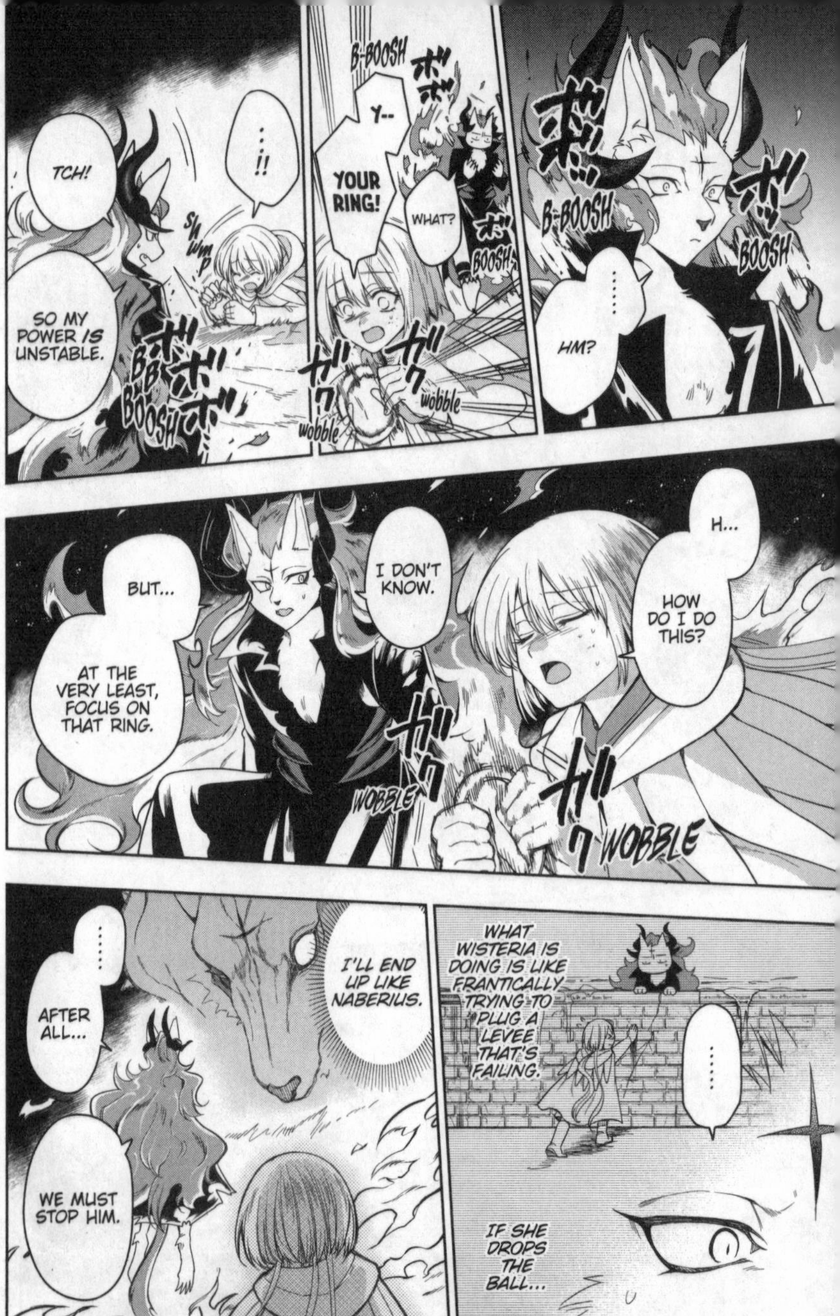
B-BOOSH
......
HM?
BOOSH
B-BOOSH
Y--
YOUR RING!
WHAT?
BOOSH
wobble
wobble
TCH!
...!!
SHWMP
SO MY POWER IS UNSTABLE.
B-B-BOOSH
H...
HOW DO I DO THIS?
WOBBLE
I DON'T KNOW.
BUT...
AT THE VERY LEAST, FOCUS ON THAT RING.
WOBBLE
WHAT WISTERIA IS DOING IS LIKE FRANTICALLY TRYING TO PLUG A LEVEE THAT'S FAILING.
......
IF SHE DROPS THE BALL...
I'LL END UP LIKE NABERIUS.
......
AFTER ALL...
WE MUST STOP HIM.

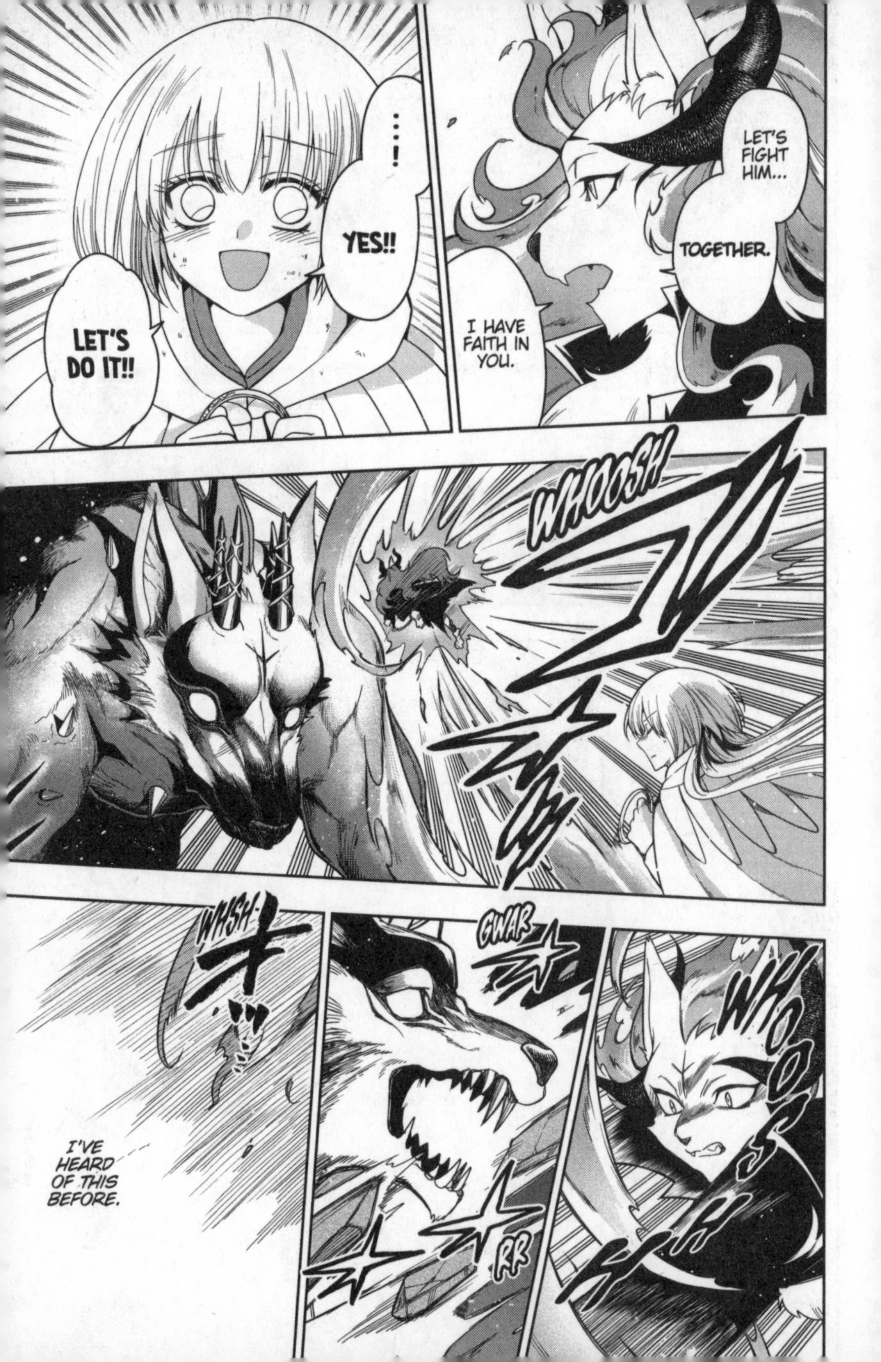
LET'S FIGHT HIM...
TOGETHER.
I HAVE FAITH IN YOU.
...!
YES!!
LET'S DO IT!!
WHOOOSH
WHOOOSSH
GWAR
RR
WHSH
I'VE HEARD OF THIS BEFORE.

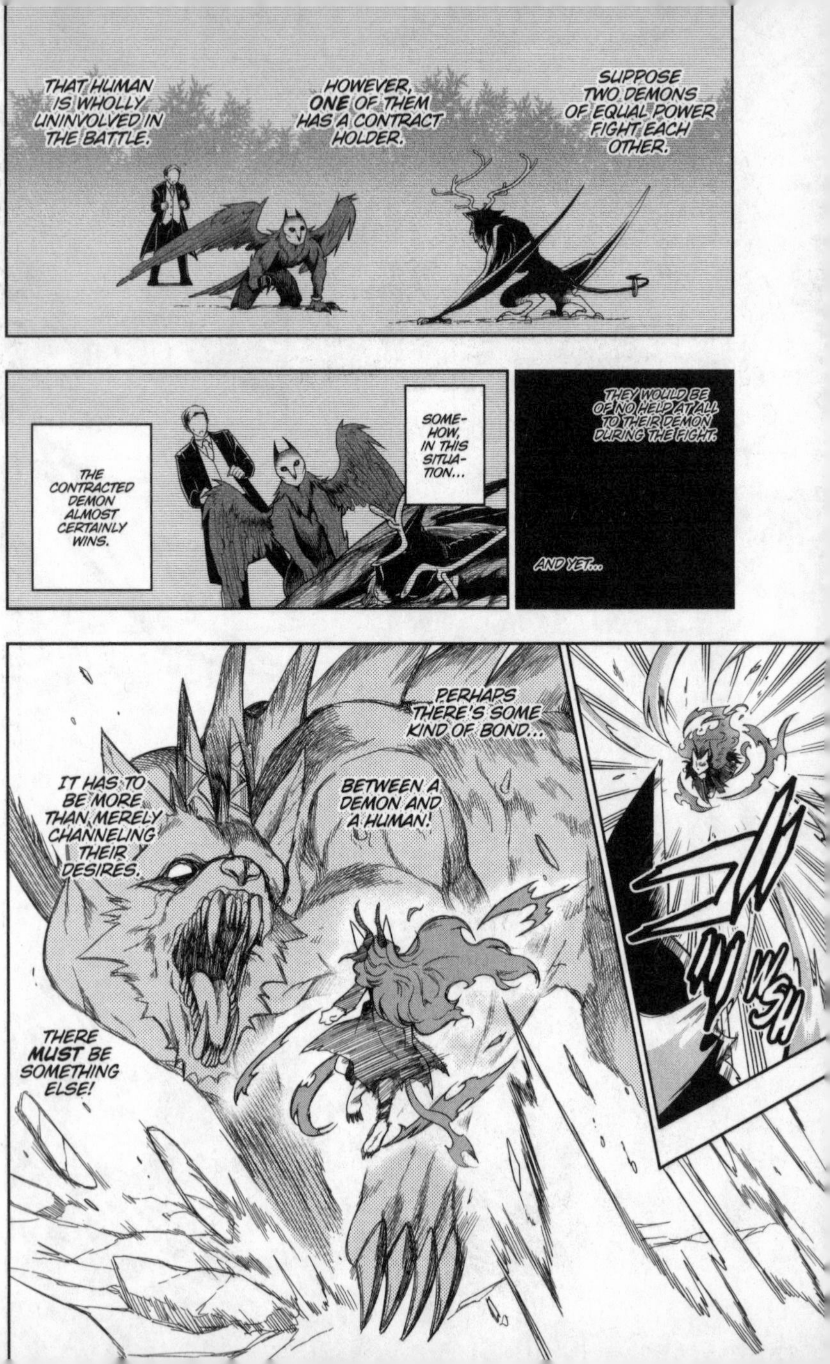
SUPPOSE TWO DEMONS OF EQUAL POWER FIGHT EACH OTHER.
HOWEVER, **ONE** OF THEM HAS A CONTRACT HOLDER.
THAT HUMAN IS WHOLLY UNINVOLVED IN THE BATTLE.
THEY WOULD BE OF NO HELP AT ALL TO THEIR DEMON DURING THE FIGHT.
AND YET...
SOME-HOW, IN THIS SITUA-TION...
THE CONTRACTED DEMON ALMOST CERTAINLY WINS.
WHSH
PERHAPS THERE'S SOME KIND OF BOND...
BETWEEN A DEMON AND A HUMAN!
IT HAS TO BE MORE THAN MERELY CHANNELING THEIR DESIRES.
THERE **MUST** BE SOMETHING ELSE!

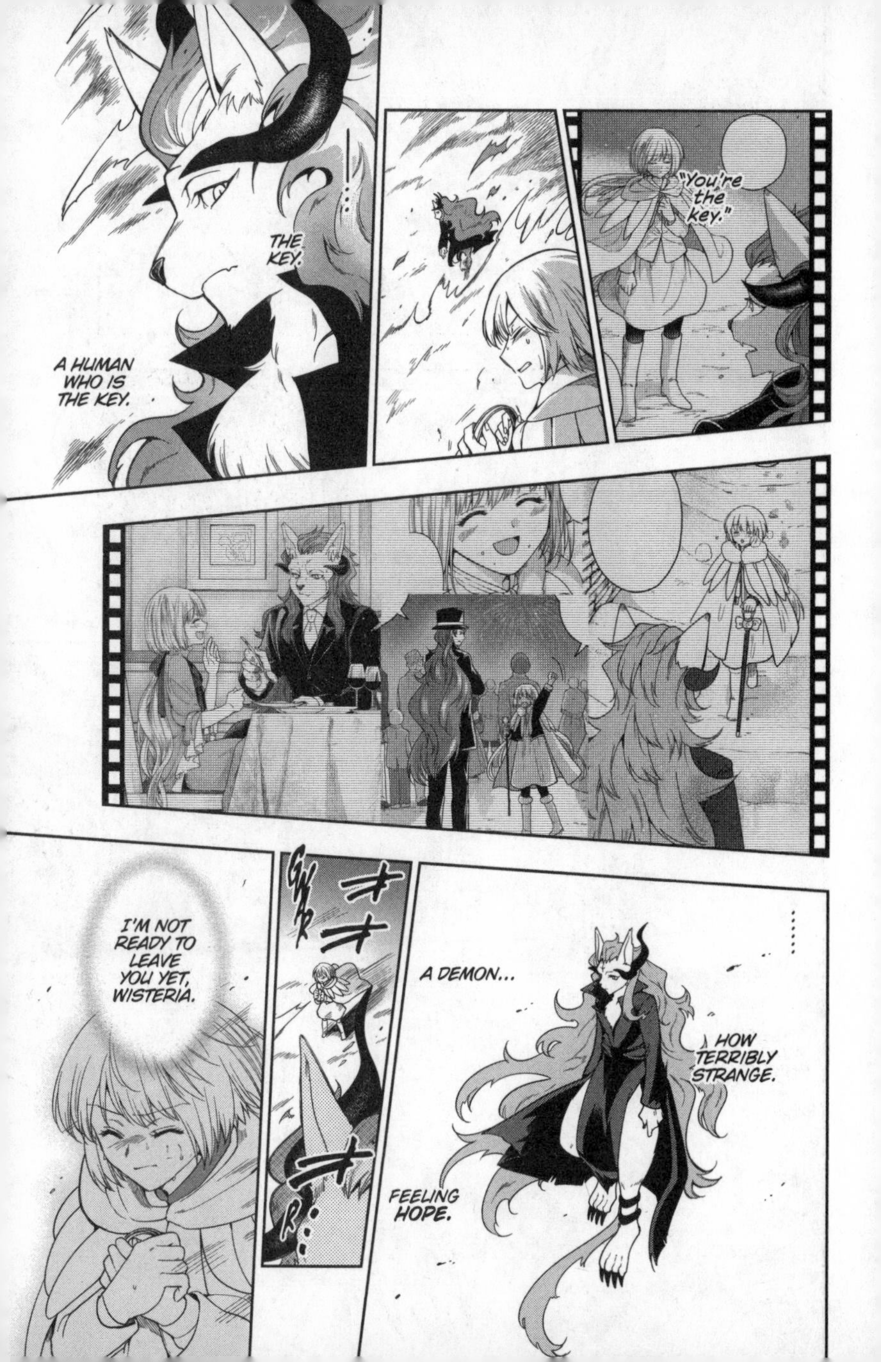
"You're the key."
THE KEY.
A HUMAN WHO IS THE KEY.
......
A DEMON...
HOW TERRIBLY STRANGE.
FEELING HOPE.
GWAR
I'M NOT READY TO LEAVE YOU YET, WISTERIA.

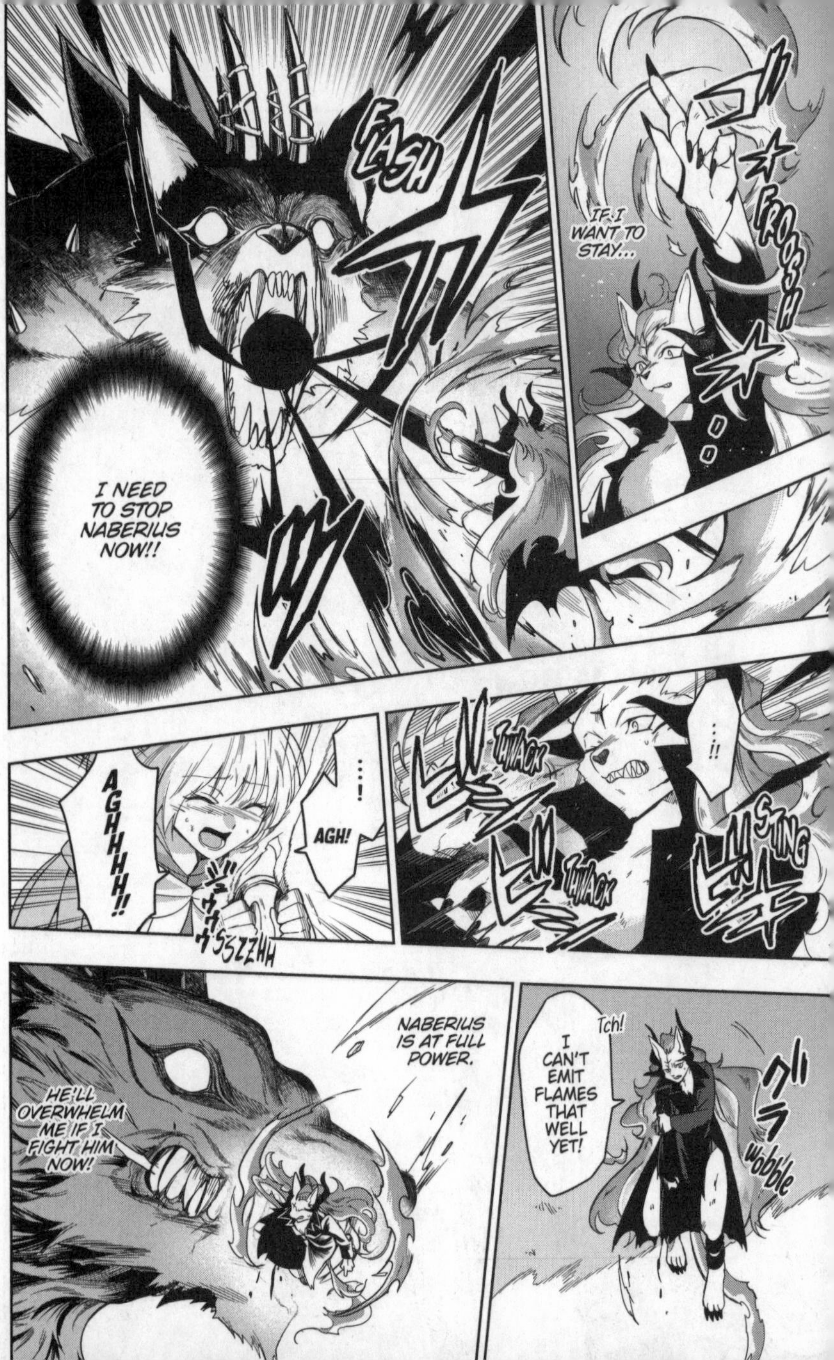
IF I WANT TO STAY...
FROOSH
FLASH
I NEED TO STOP NABERIUS NOW!!
...!!
THWACK
THWACK
STING
...!
AGH!
AGHHHHH!!
SSZZZHH
Tch!
I CAN'T EMIT FLAMES THAT WELL YET!
wobble
NABERIUS IS AT FULL POWER.
HE'LL OVERWHELM ME IF I FIGHT HIM NOW!

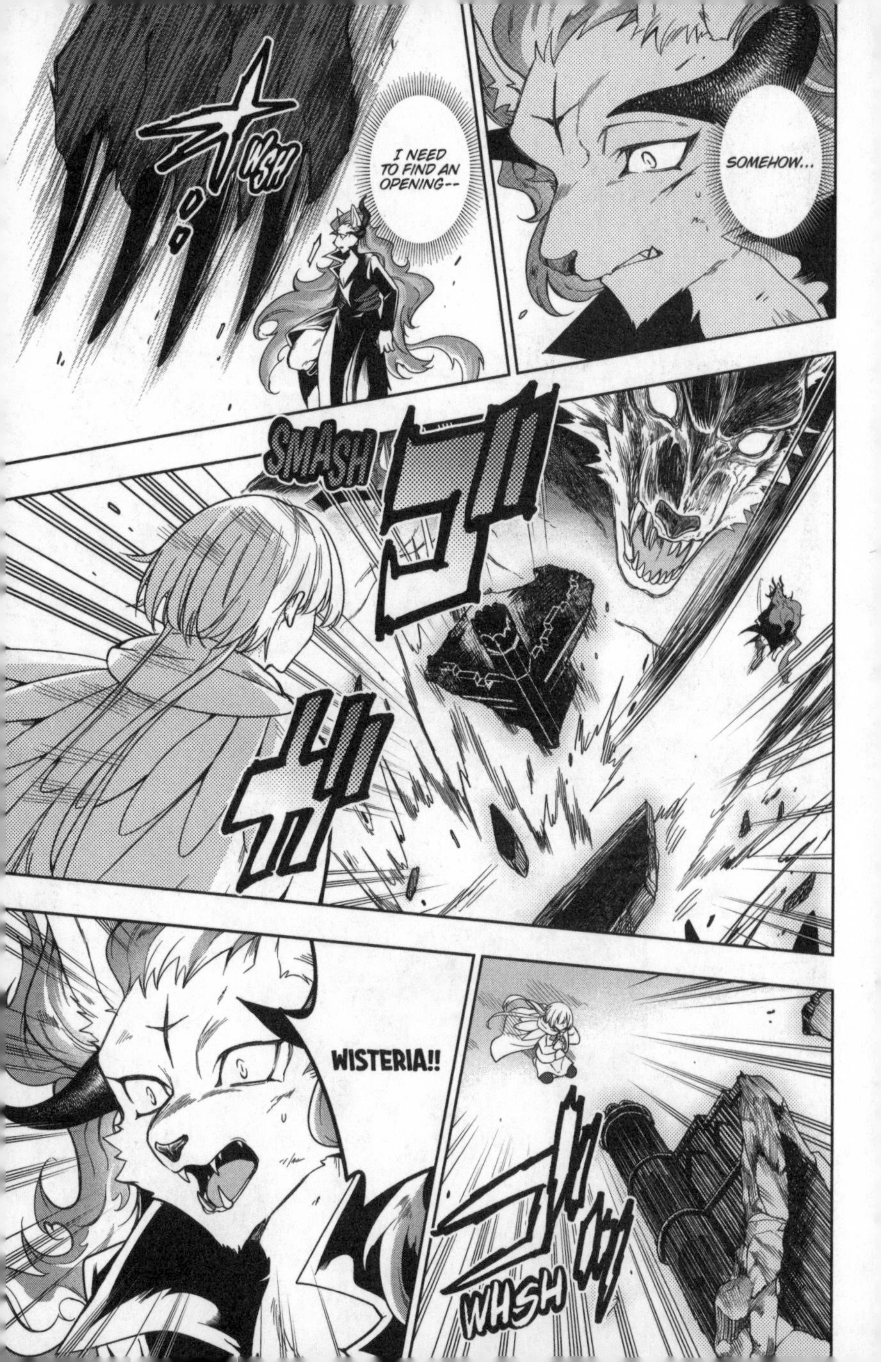
SOMEHOW...
I NEED TO FIND AN OPENING--
WSH
SMASH
WHSH
WISTERIA!!

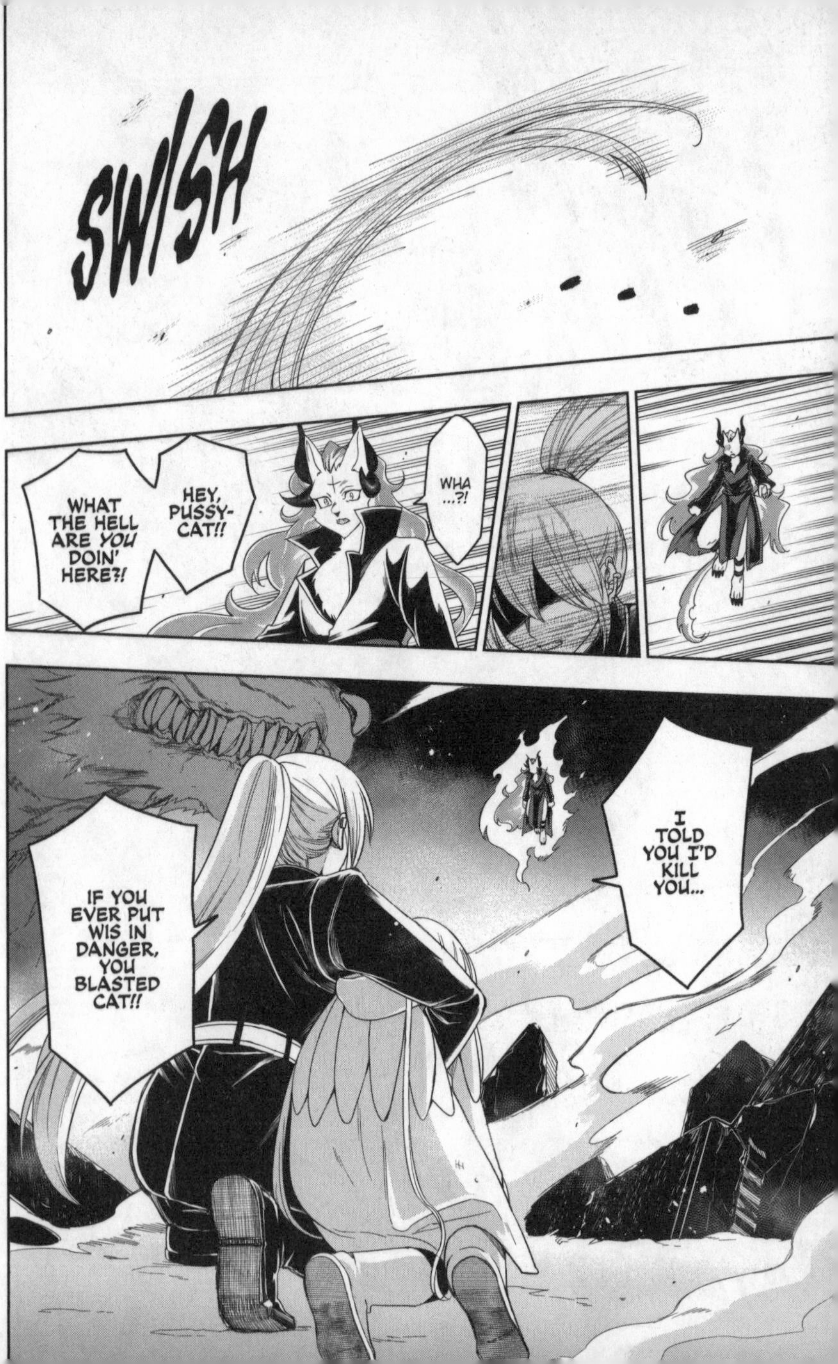
SWISH
...
WHA ...?!
HEY, PUSSY-CAT!!
WHAT THE HELL ARE YOU DOIN' HERE?!
I TOLD YOU I'D KILL YOU...
IF YOU EVER PUT WIS IN DANGER, YOU BLASTED CAT!!

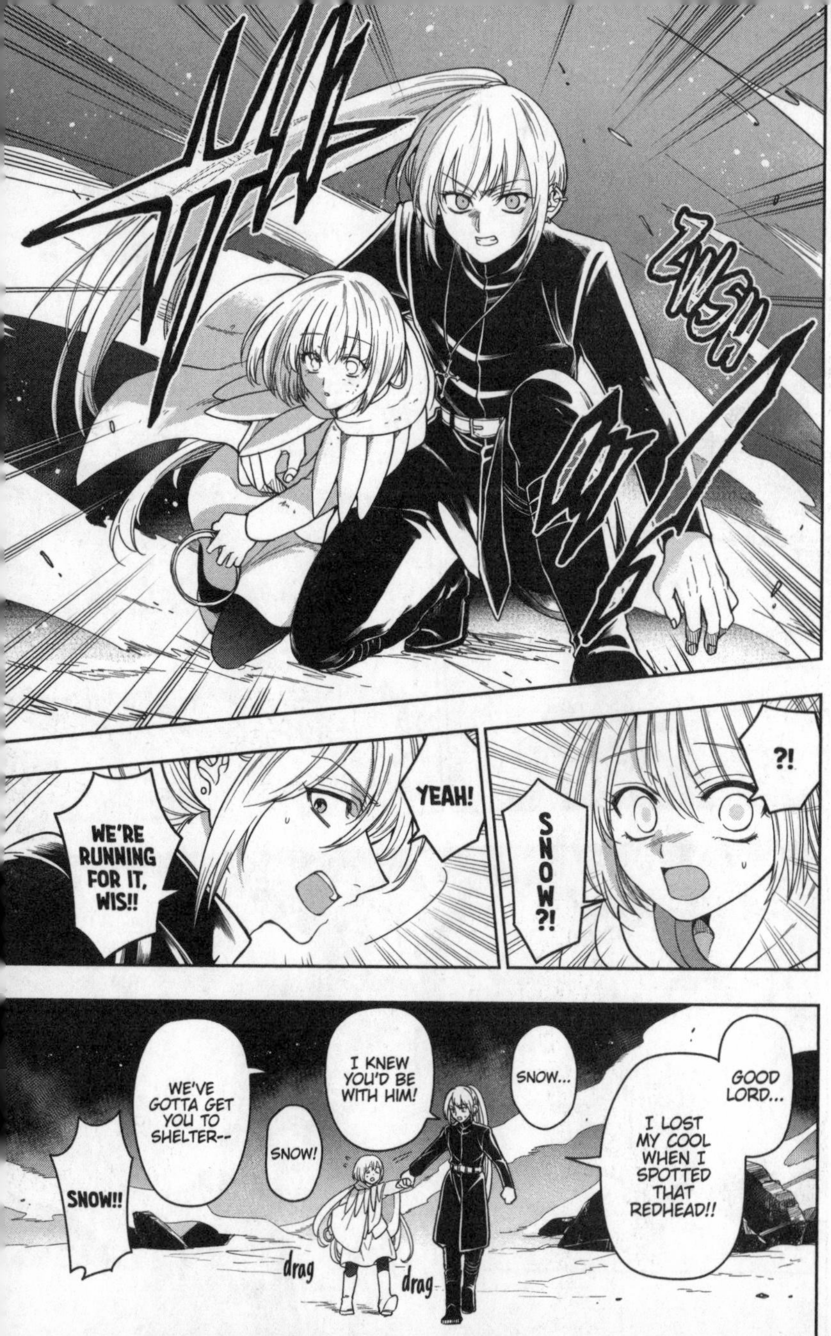
ZWISH
?!
SNOW?!
WE'RE RUNNING FOR IT, WIS!!
YEAH!
GOOD LORD...
I LOST MY COOL WHEN I SPOTTED THAT REDHEAD!!
SNOW...
I KNEW YOU'D BE WITH HIM!
SNOW!
WE'VE GOTTA GET YOU TO SHELTER--
SNOW!!
drag
drag

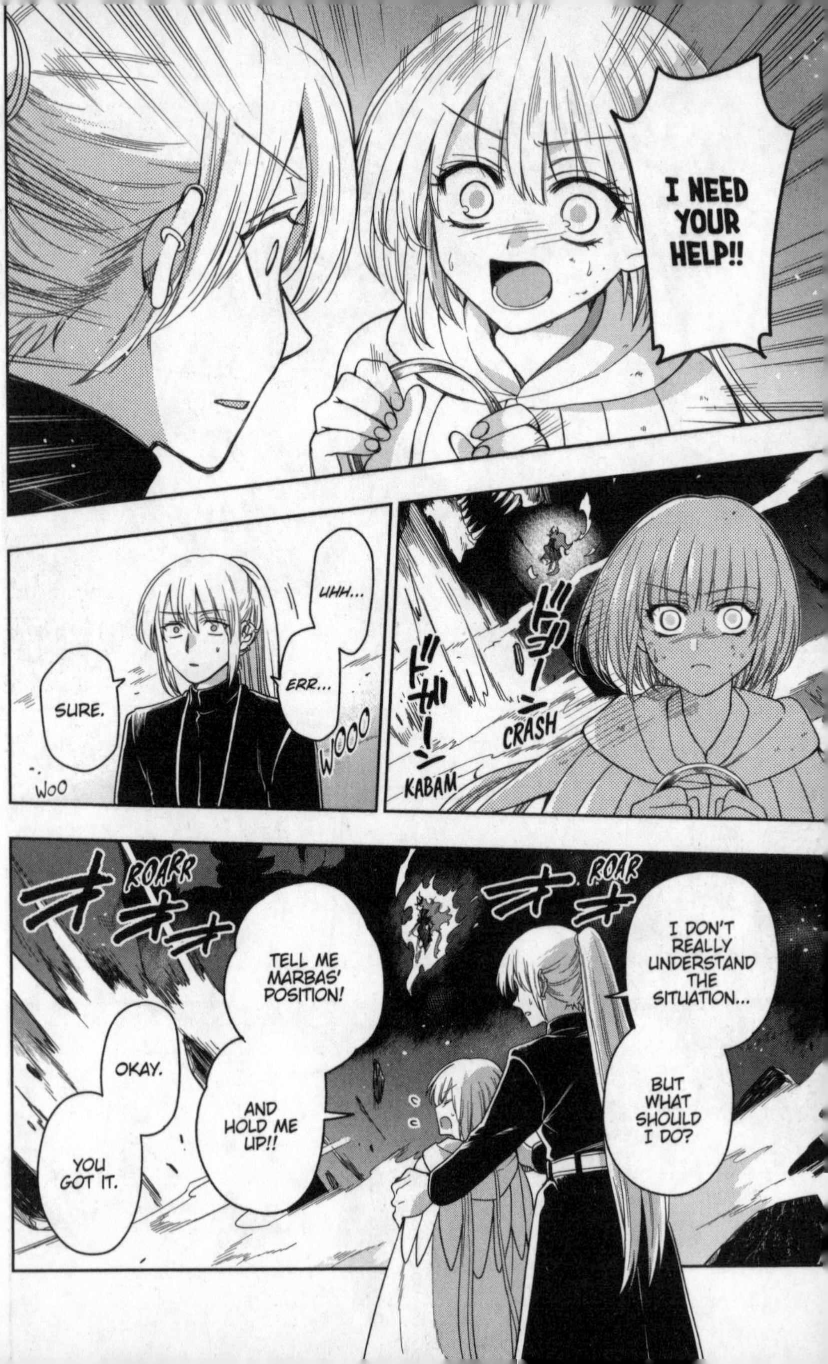
I NEED YOUR HELP!!
CRASH
KABAM
UHH...
ERR...
WOOO
SURE.
WOO
ROAR
I DON'T REALLY UNDERSTAND THE SITUATION...
BUT WHAT SHOULD I DO?
ROARR
TELL ME MARBAS' POSITION!
AND HOLD ME UP!!
OKAY.
YOU GOT IT.

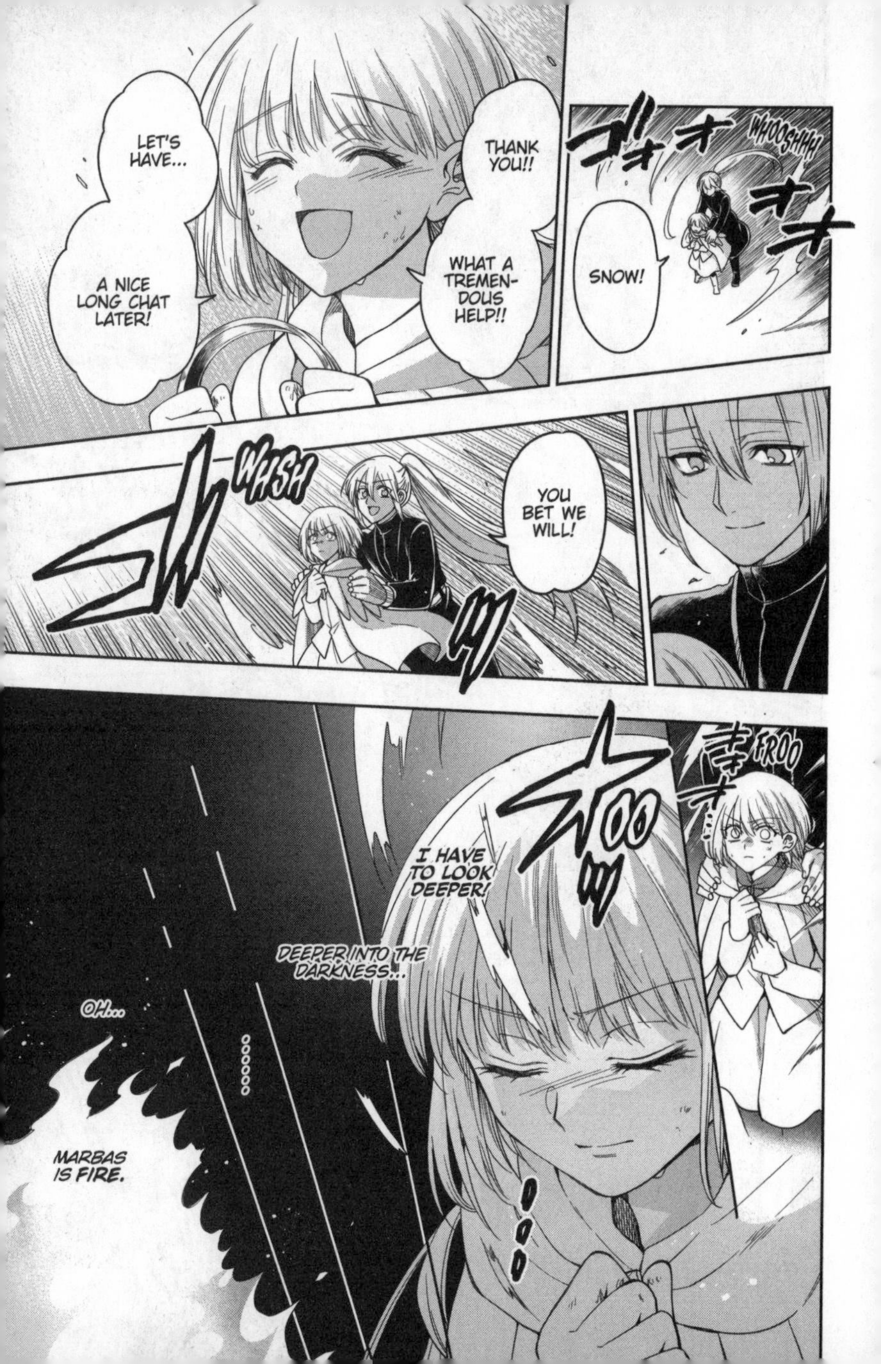
WHOOSHHH
SNOW!
THANK YOU!!
WHAT A TREMENDOUS HELP!!
LET'S HAVE...
A NICE LONG CHAT LATER!
YOU BET WE WILL!
WHISH
FROO
I HAVE TO LOOK DEEPER!
DEEPER INTO THE DARKNESS...
OH...
OOOOOO
MARBAS IS FIRE.

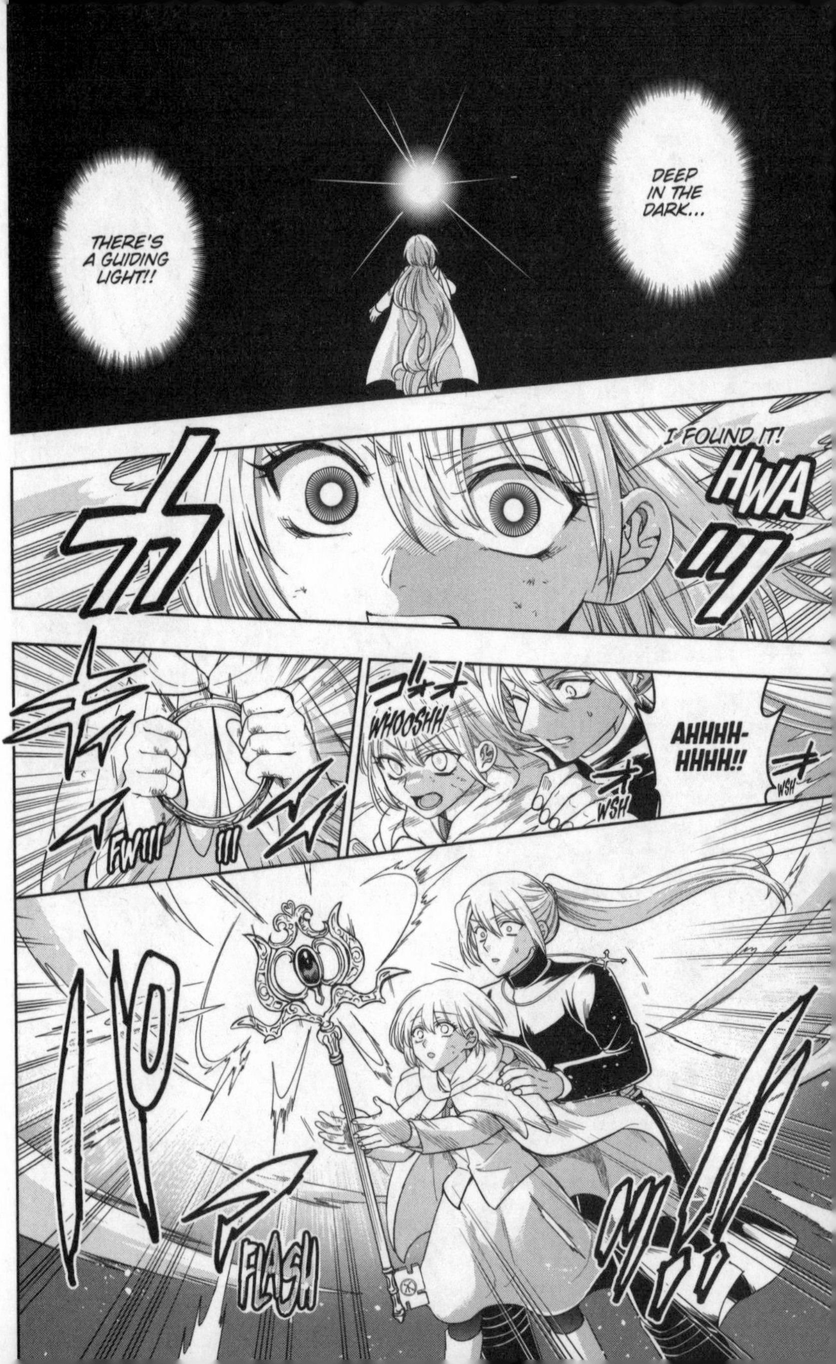
DEEP IN THE DARK...
THERE'S A GUIDING LIGHT!!
I FOUND IT!
HWA
WSH
AHHHH-HHHH!!
WSH
WHOOSHH
FWIII III
FLASH

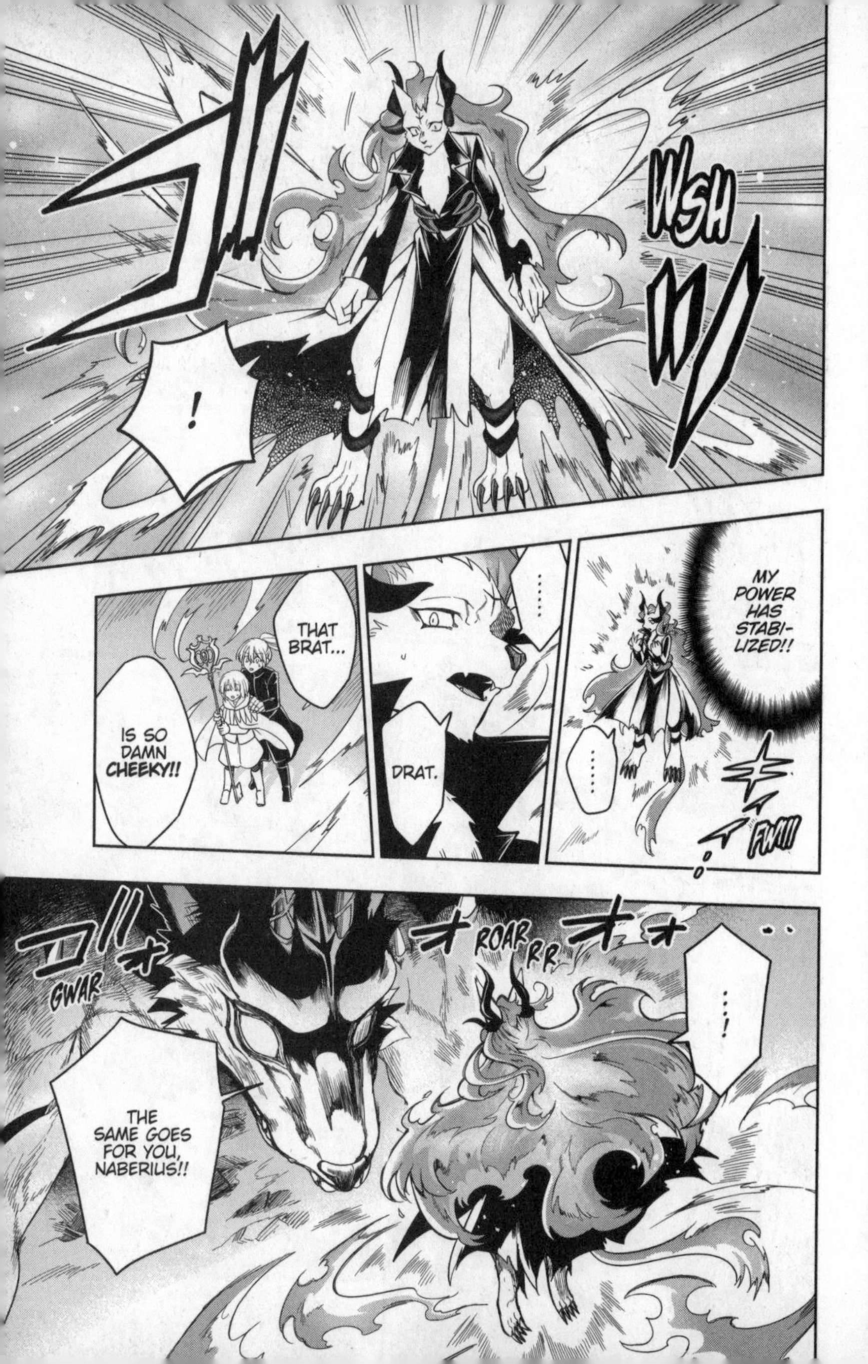
WSH
!
MY POWER HAS STABILIZED!!
......
FWIII
......
DRAT.
THAT BRAT...
IS SO DAMN CHEEKY!!
ROAR RR
GWAR
...!
THE SAME GOES FOR YOU, NABERIUS!!

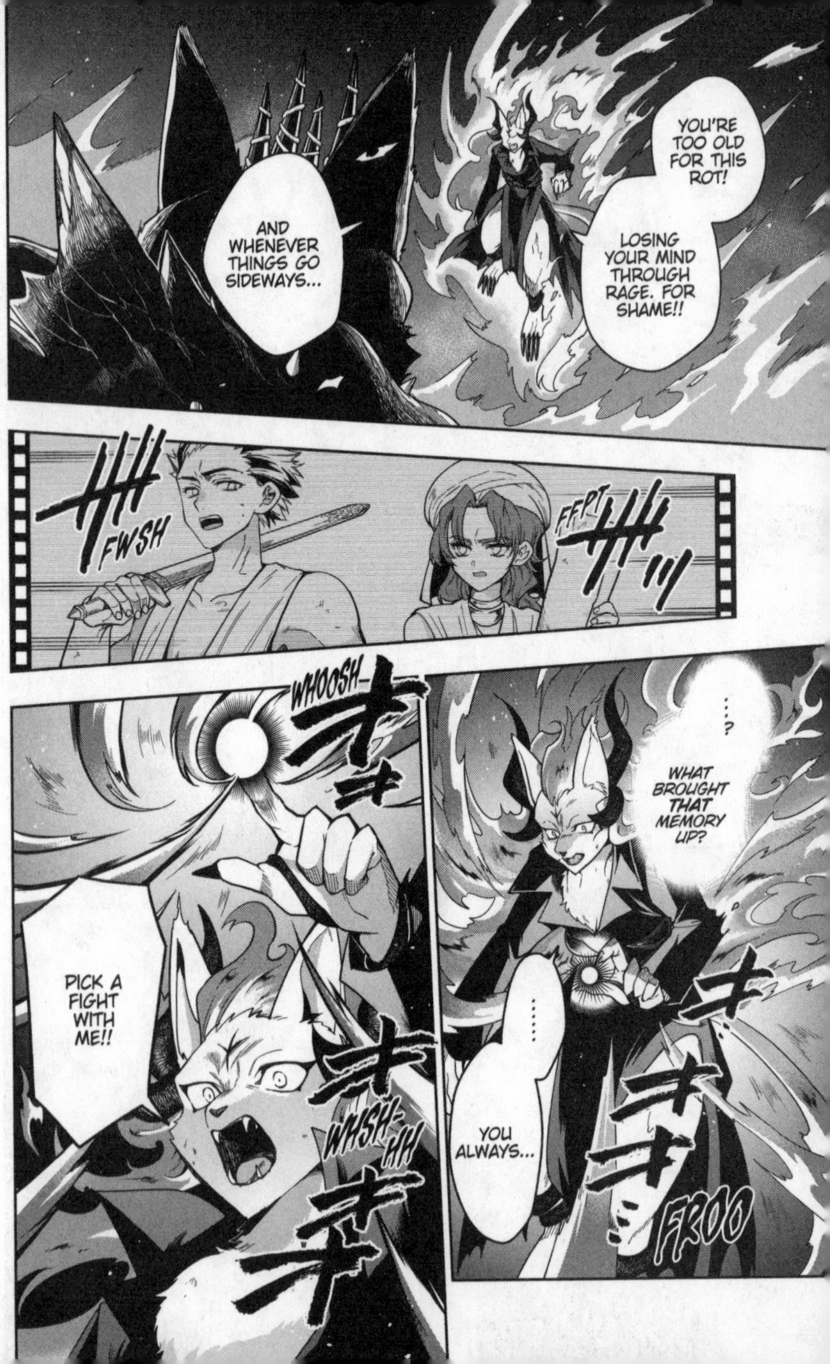
YOU'RE TOO OLD FOR THIS ROT!
LOSING YOUR MIND THROUGH RAGE. FOR SHAME!!
AND WHENEVER THINGS GO SIDEWAYS...
FFPT
FWSH
...?
WHAT BROUGHT THAT MEMORY UP?
......
YOU ALWAYS...
FROO
WHOOSH-
PICK A FIGHT WITH ME!!
WHSH-HH

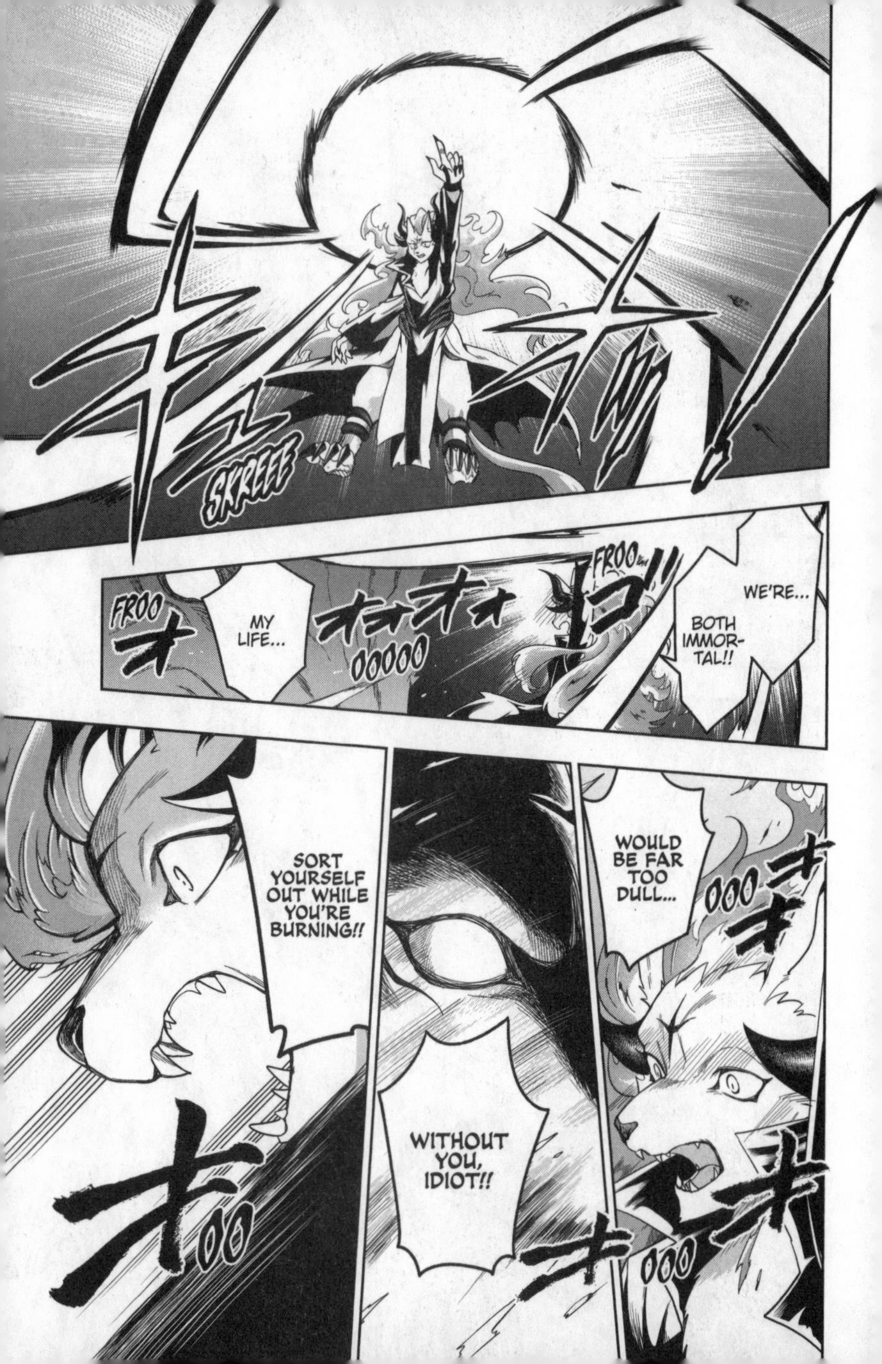
SKREEE
WE'RE...
BOTH IMMORTAL!!
FROOM
OOOOO
MY LIFE...
FROO
WOULD BE FAR TOO DULL...
OOO
WITHOUT YOU, IDIOT!!
OOO
SORT YOURSELF OUT WHILE YOU'RE BURNING!!
OO

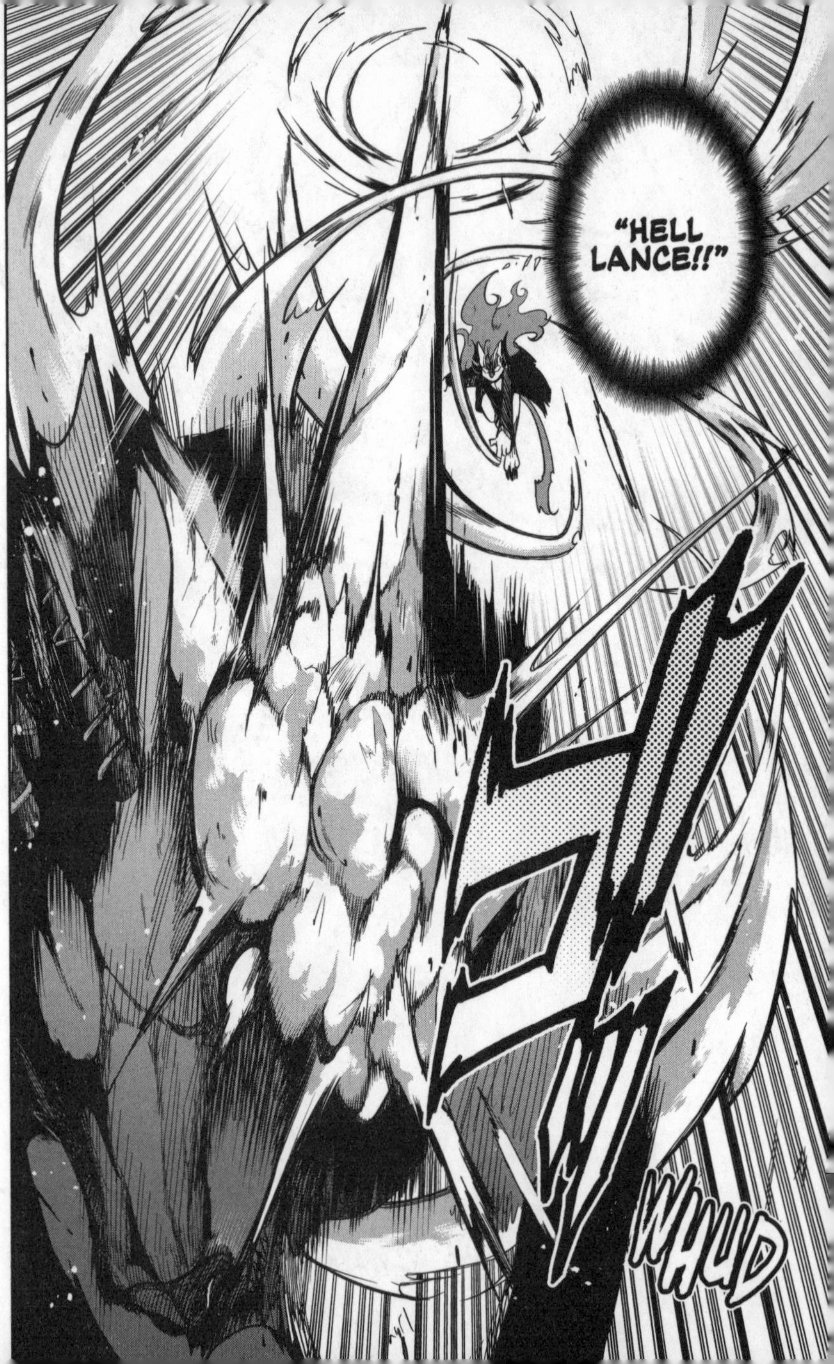
"HELL LANCE!!"
WHUD

Night 32
A New Way

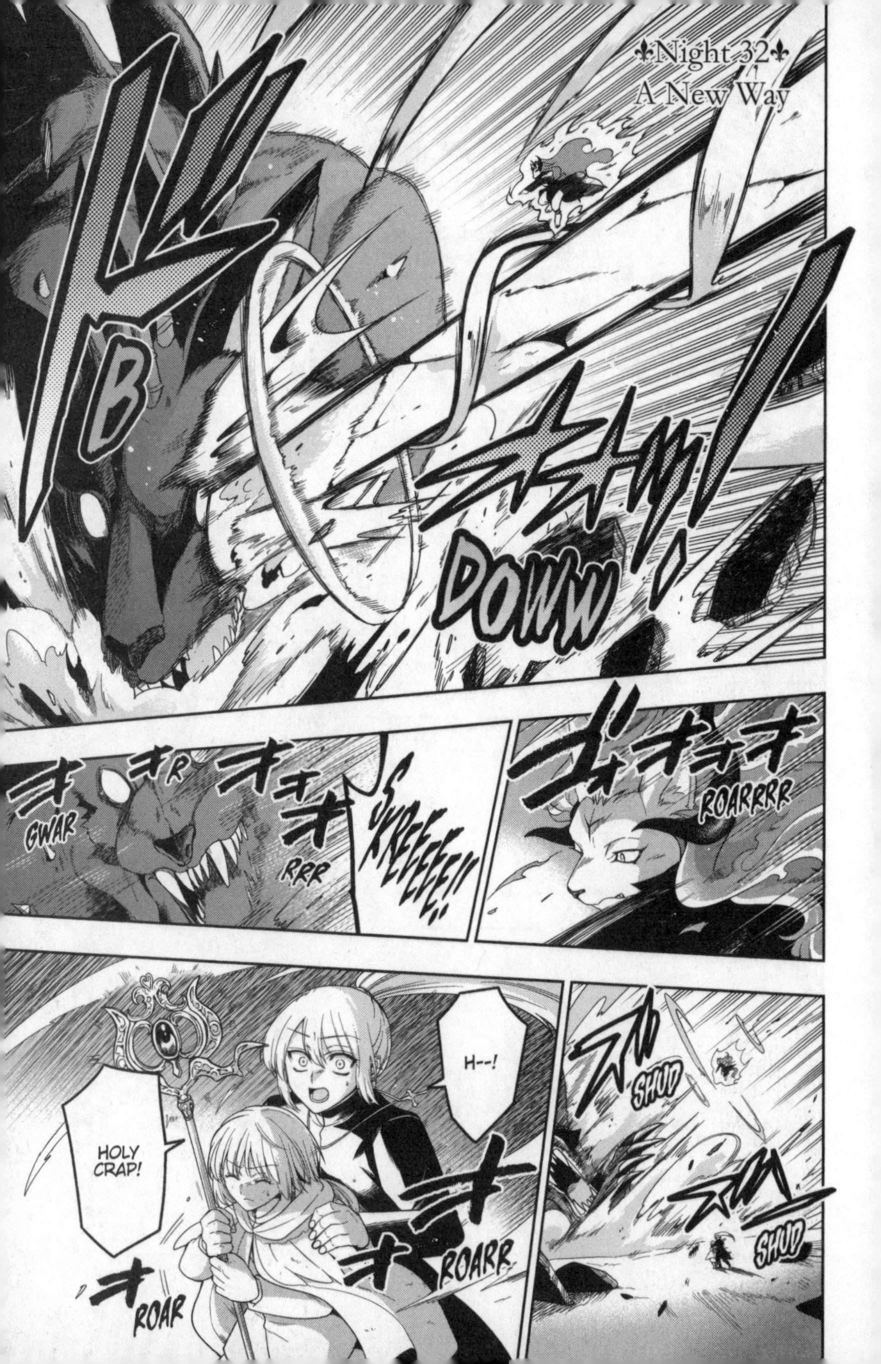

B
DOWW
ROARRRR
SKREEEEE!!
RRR
GWAR
SHUD
SHUD
H--!
HOLY CRAP!
ROARR
ROAR

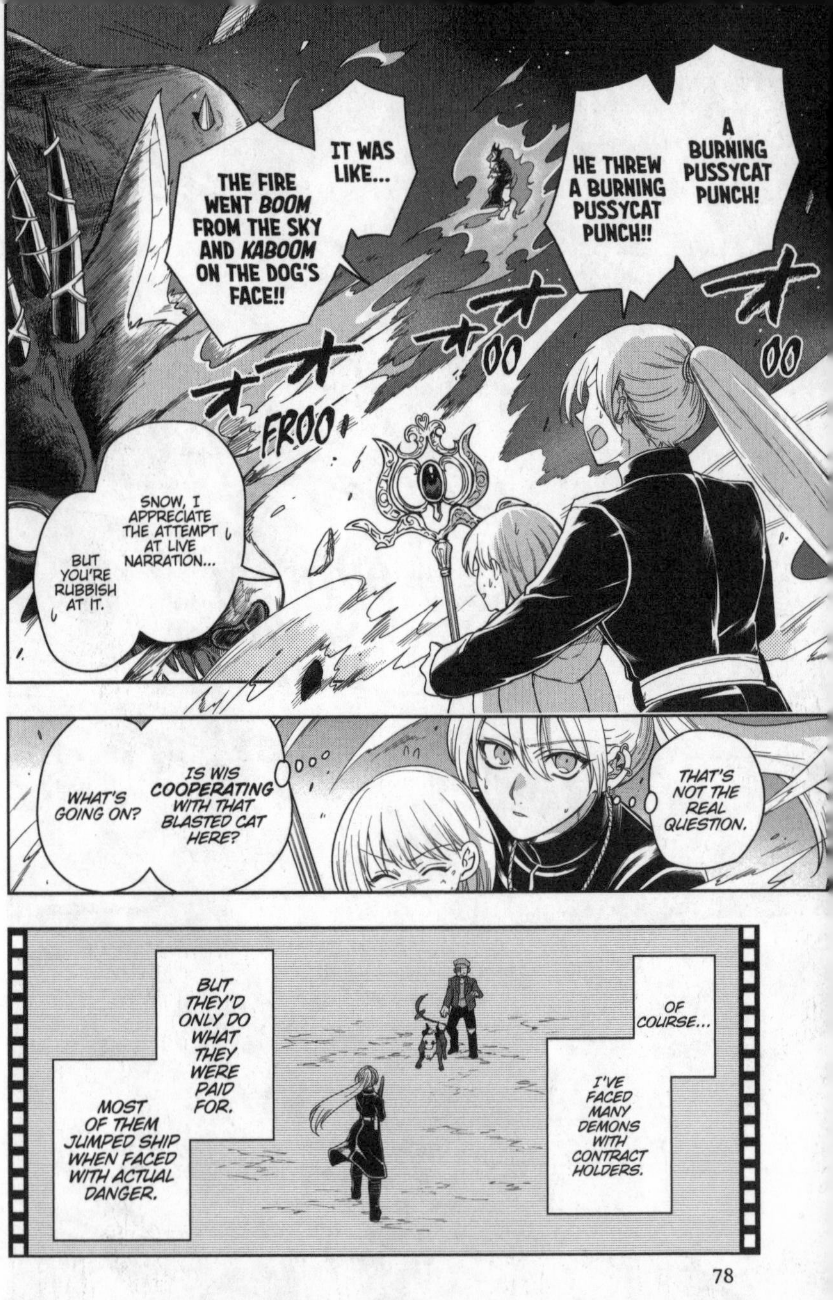
A BURNING PUSSYCAT PUNCH!
HE THREW A BURNING PUSSYCAT PUNCH!!
IT WAS LIKE...
THE FIRE WENT *BOOM* FROM THE SKY AND *KABOOM* ON THE DOG'S FACE!!
OO
OO
FROO
SNOW, I APPRECIATE THE ATTEMPT AT LIVE NARRATION...
BUT YOU'RE RUBBISH AT IT.
THAT'S NOT THE REAL QUESTION.
IS WIS COOPERATING WITH THAT BLASTED CAT HERE?
WHAT'S GOING ON?
OF COURSE...
I'VE FACED MANY DEMONS WITH CONTRACT HOLDERS.
BUT THEY'D ONLY DO WHAT THEY WERE PAID FOR.
MOST OF THEM JUMPED SHIP WHEN FACED WITH ACTUAL DANGER.

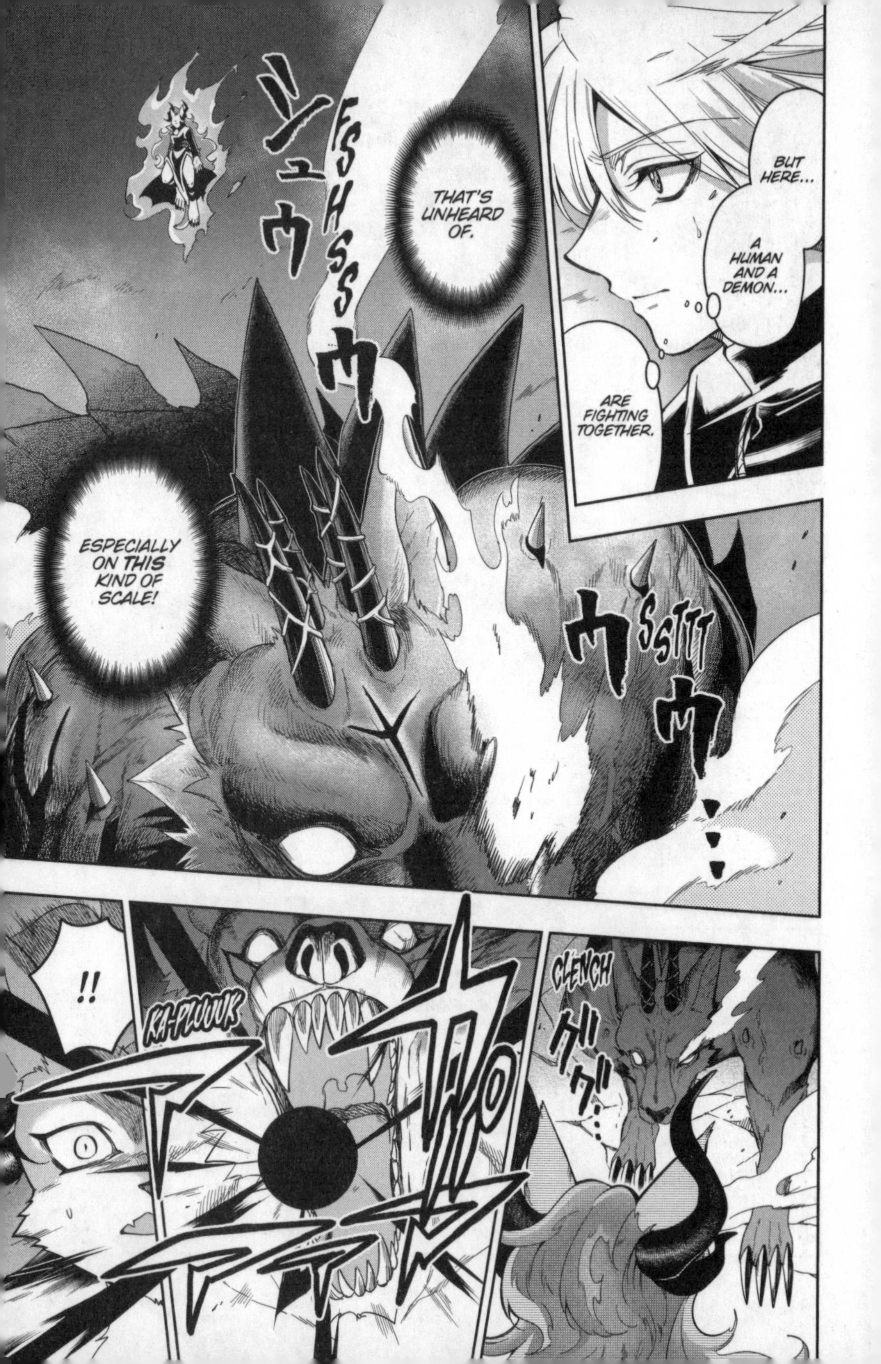

BUT HERE...
A HUMAN AND A DEMON...
ARE FIGHTING TOGETHER.
THAT'S UNHEARD OF.
FSHSSS
ESPECIALLY ON THIS KIND OF SCALE!
SSTTT
CLENCH
KA-PLOOOK
!!

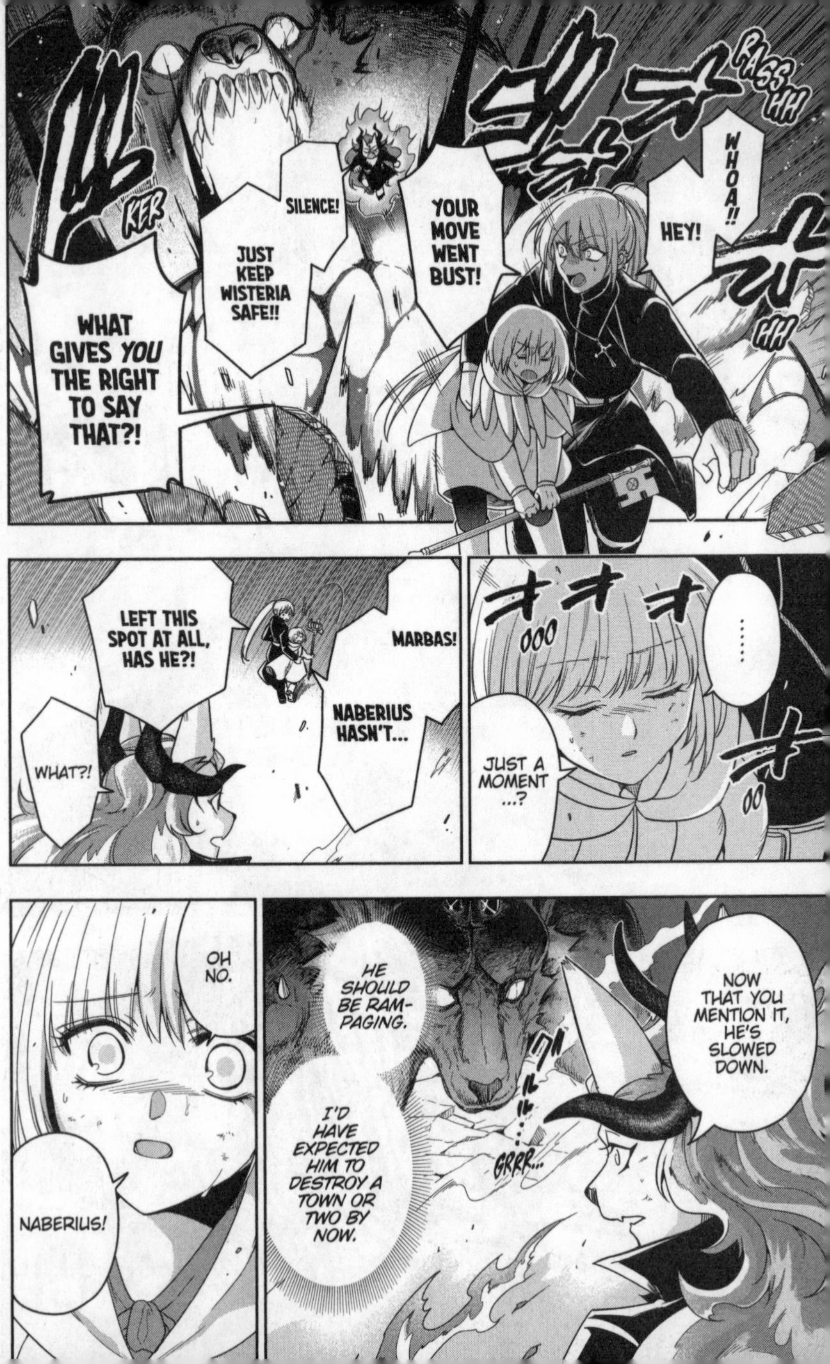
RASSHH
WHOA!!
HEY!
PHH
YOUR MOVE WENT BUST!
SILENCE!
JUST KEEP WISTERIA SAFE!!
KER
WHAT GIVES YOU THE RIGHT TO SAY THAT?!
......
OOO
OO
JUST A MOMENT ...?
MARBAS!
NABERIUS HASN'T...
LEFT THIS SPOT AT ALL, HAS HE?!
WHAT?!
NOW THAT YOU MENTION IT, HE'S SLOWED DOWN.
HE SHOULD BE RAM-PAGING.
GRRR...
I'D HAVE EXPECTED HIM TO DESTROY A TOWN OR TWO BY NOW.
OH NO.
NABERIUS!

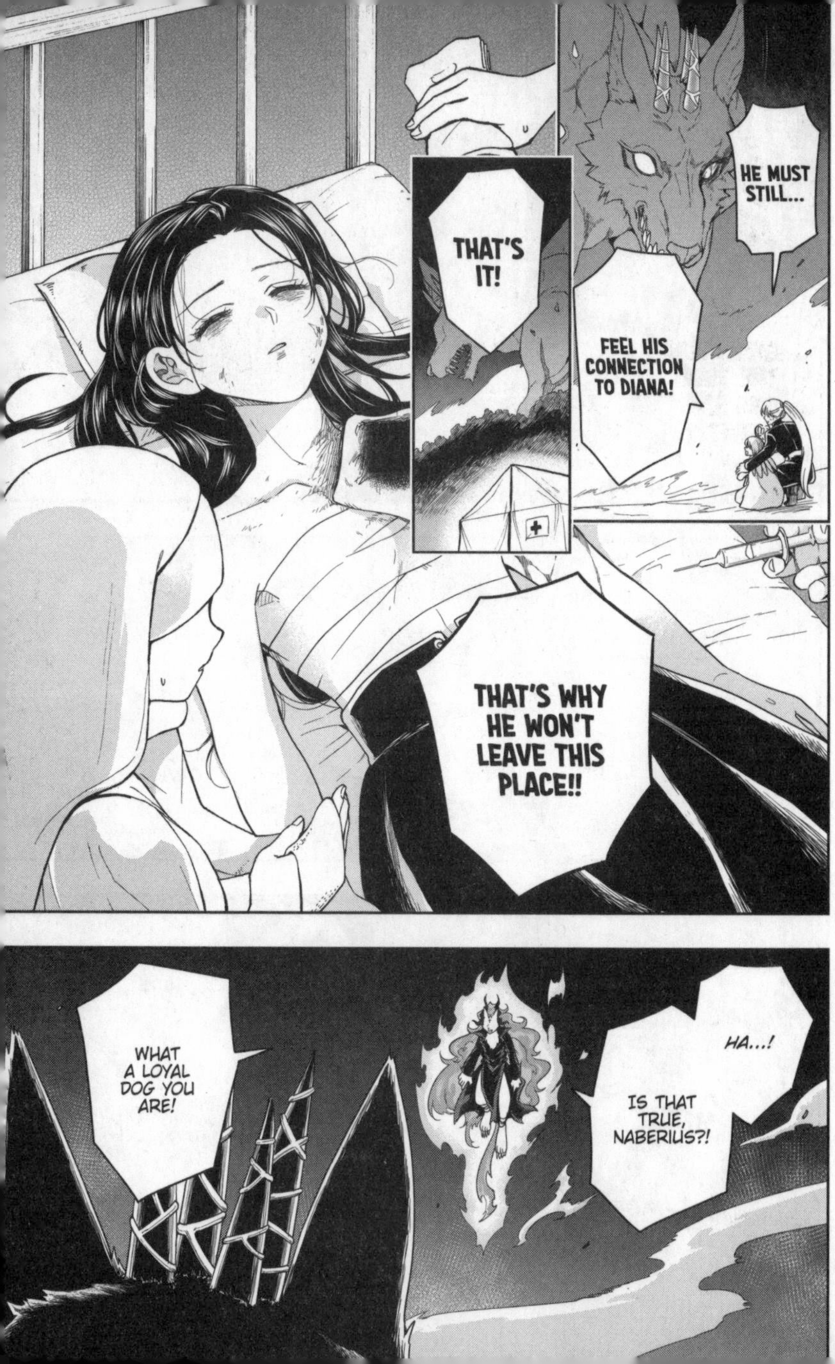
HE MUST STILL...
FEEL HIS CONNECTION TO DIANA!
THAT'S IT!
THAT'S WHY HE WON'T LEAVE THIS PLACE!!
HA...!
IS THAT TRUE, NABERIUS?!
WHAT A LOYAL DOG YOU ARE!

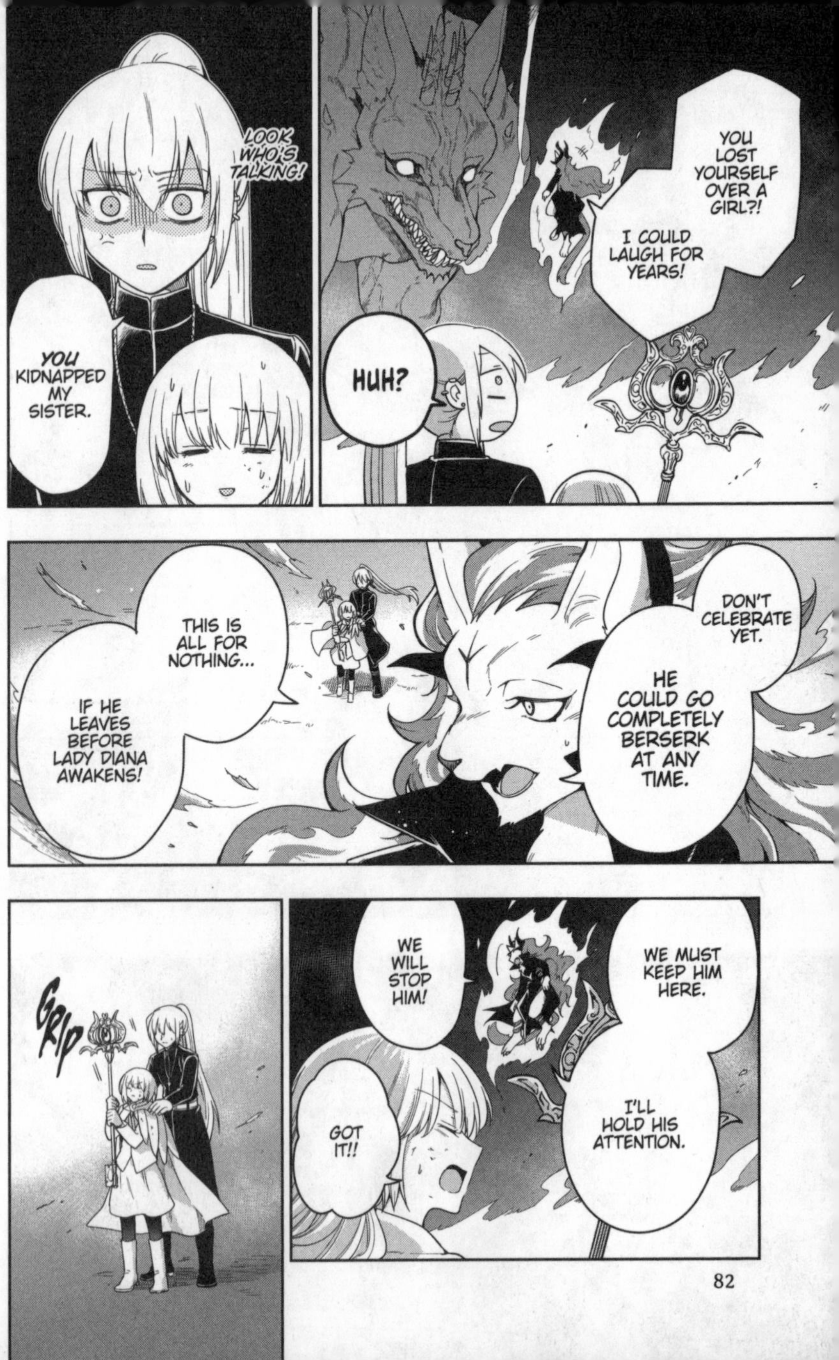
YOU LOST YOURSELF OVER A GIRL?!
I COULD LAUGH FOR YEARS!
HUH?
LOOK WHO'S TALKING!
YOU KIDNAPPED MY SISTER.
DON'T CELEBRATE YET.
HE COULD GO COMPLETELY BERSERK AT ANY TIME.
THIS IS ALL FOR NOTHING...
IF HE LEAVES BEFORE LADY DIANA AWAKENS!
WE MUST KEEP HIM HERE.
WE WILL STOP HIM!
I'LL HOLD HIS ATTENTION.
GOT IT!!
GRIP

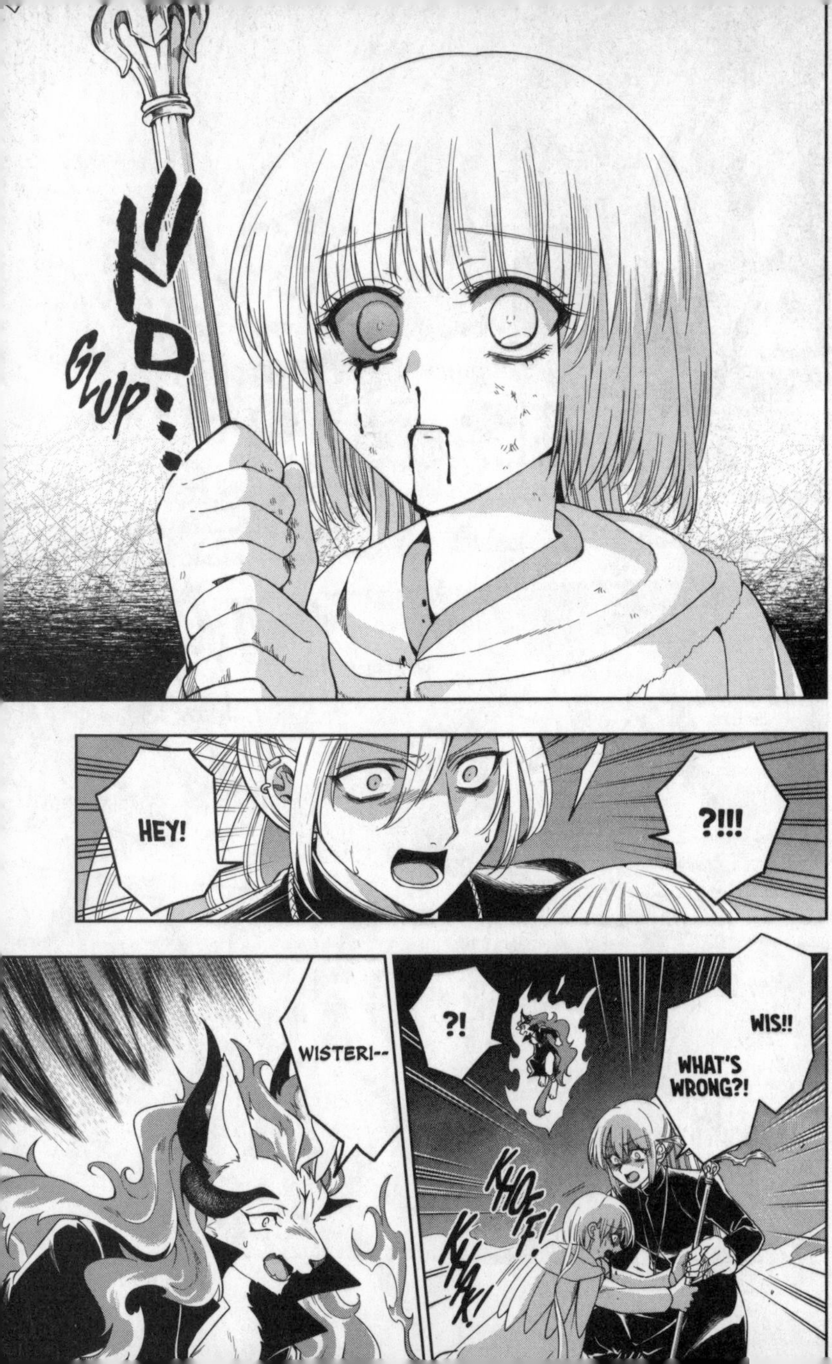
ド
GLUP
?!!!
HEY!
WIS!! WHAT'S WRONG?!
?!
KHOFF!
KHAK!
WISTERI--

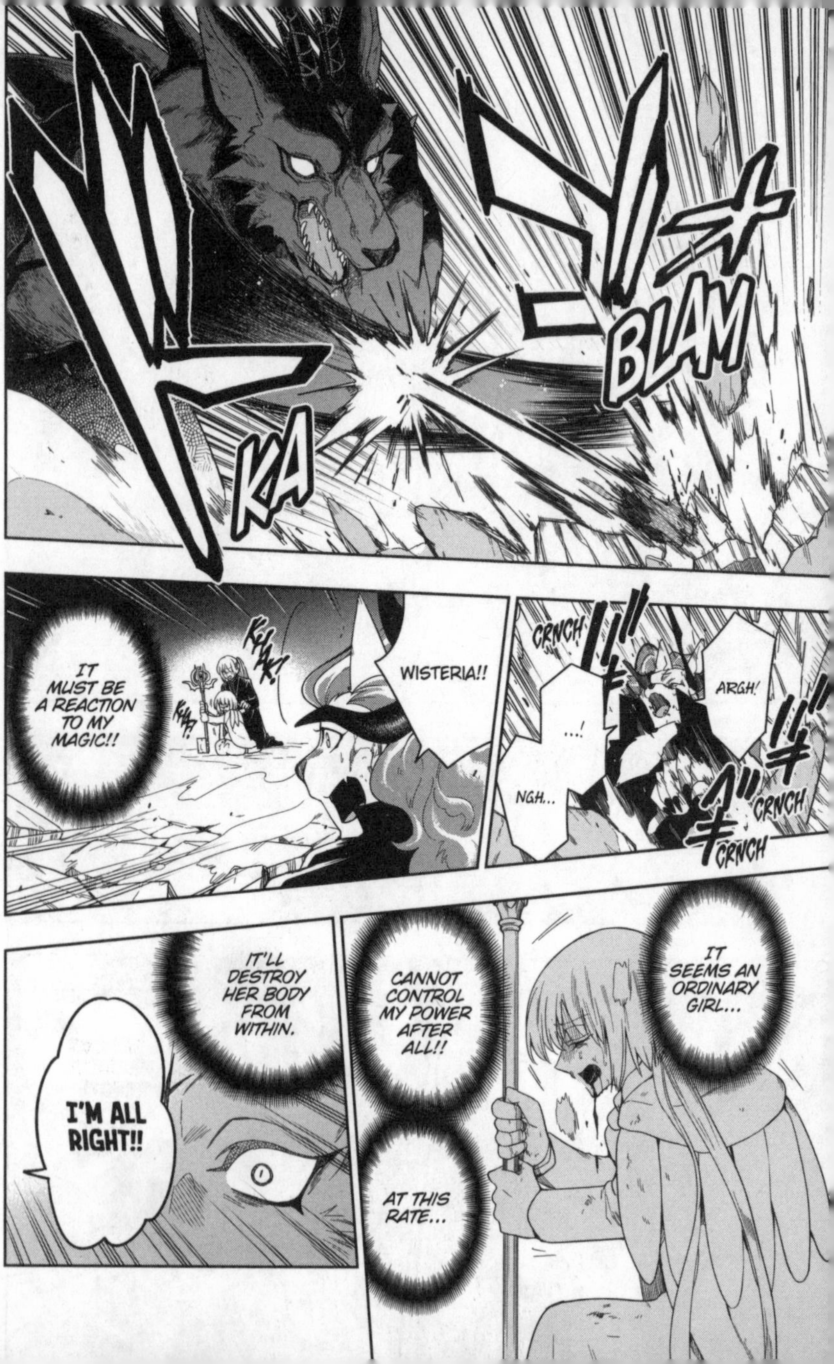
BLAM
KA
CRNCH
ARGH!
...!
NGH...
CRNCH
CRNCH
WISTERIA!!
IT MUST BE A REACTION TO MY MAGIC!!
IT SEEMS AN ORDINARY GIRL...
CANNOT CONTROL MY POWER AFTER ALL!!
AT THIS RATE...
IT'LL DESTROY HER BODY FROM WITHIN.
I'M ALL RIGHT!!

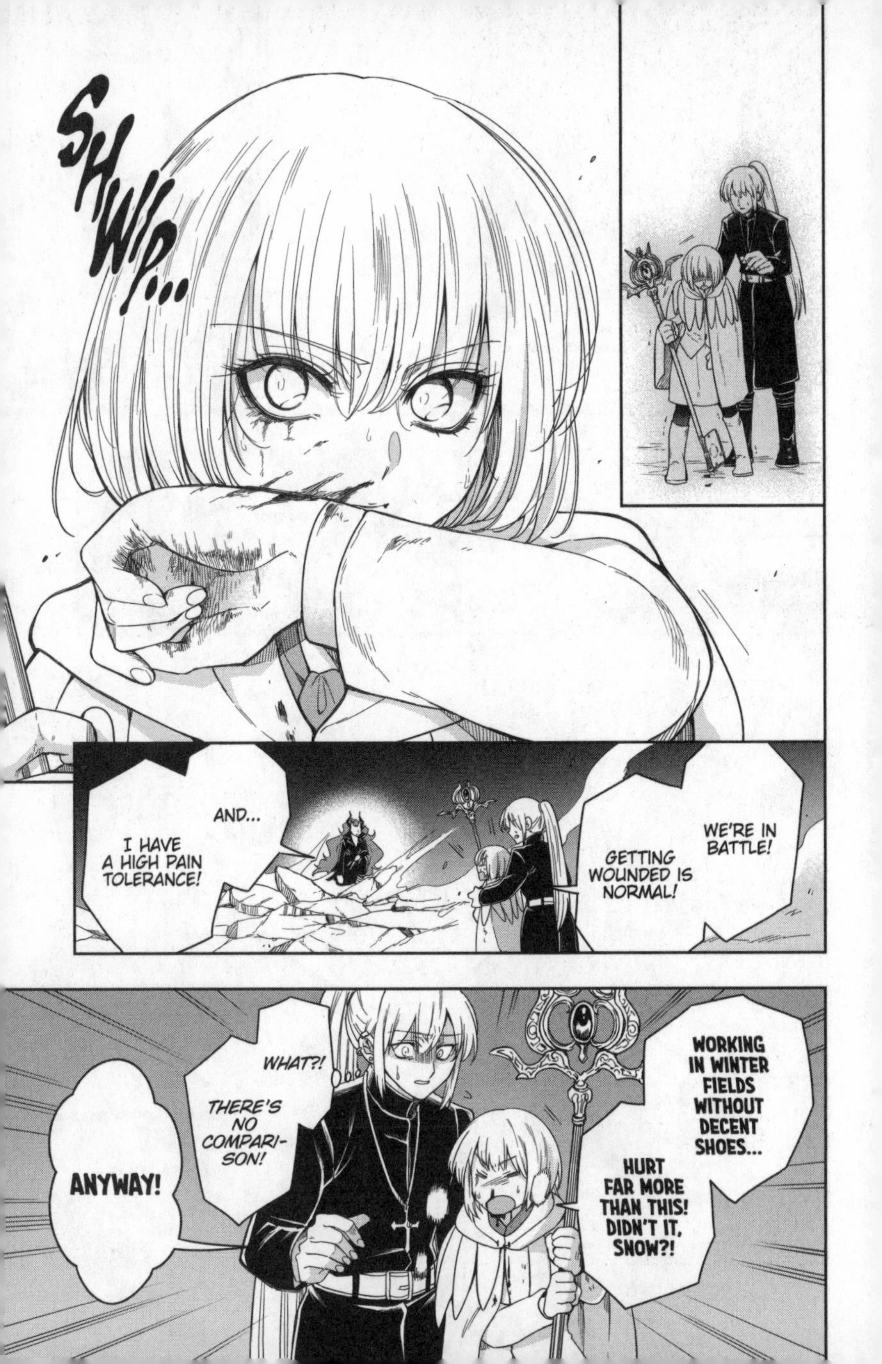
SHWIP...
WE'RE IN BATTLE!
GETTING WOUNDED IS NORMAL!
AND...
I HAVE A HIGH PAIN TOLERANCE!
WORKING IN WINTER FIELDS WITHOUT DECENT SHOES...
HURT FAR MORE THAN THIS! DIDN'T IT, SNOW?!
WHAT?!
THERE'S NO COMPARISON!
ANYWAY!

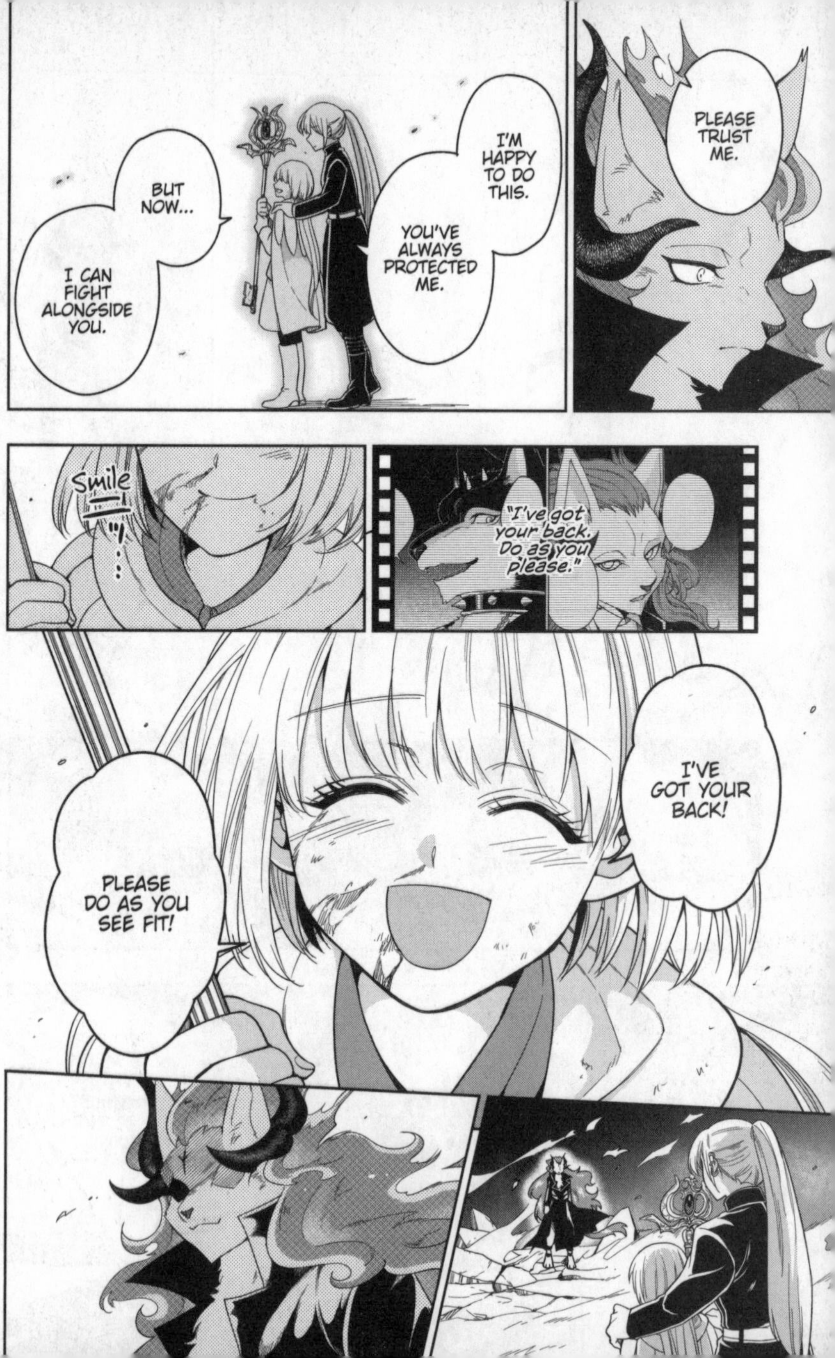
PLEASE TRUST ME.
I'M HAPPY TO DO THIS.
YOU'VE ALWAYS PROTECTED ME.
BUT NOW...
I CAN FIGHT ALONGSIDE YOU.
"I've got your back. Do as you please."
Smile
I'VE GOT YOUR BACK!
PLEASE DO AS YOU SEE FIT!

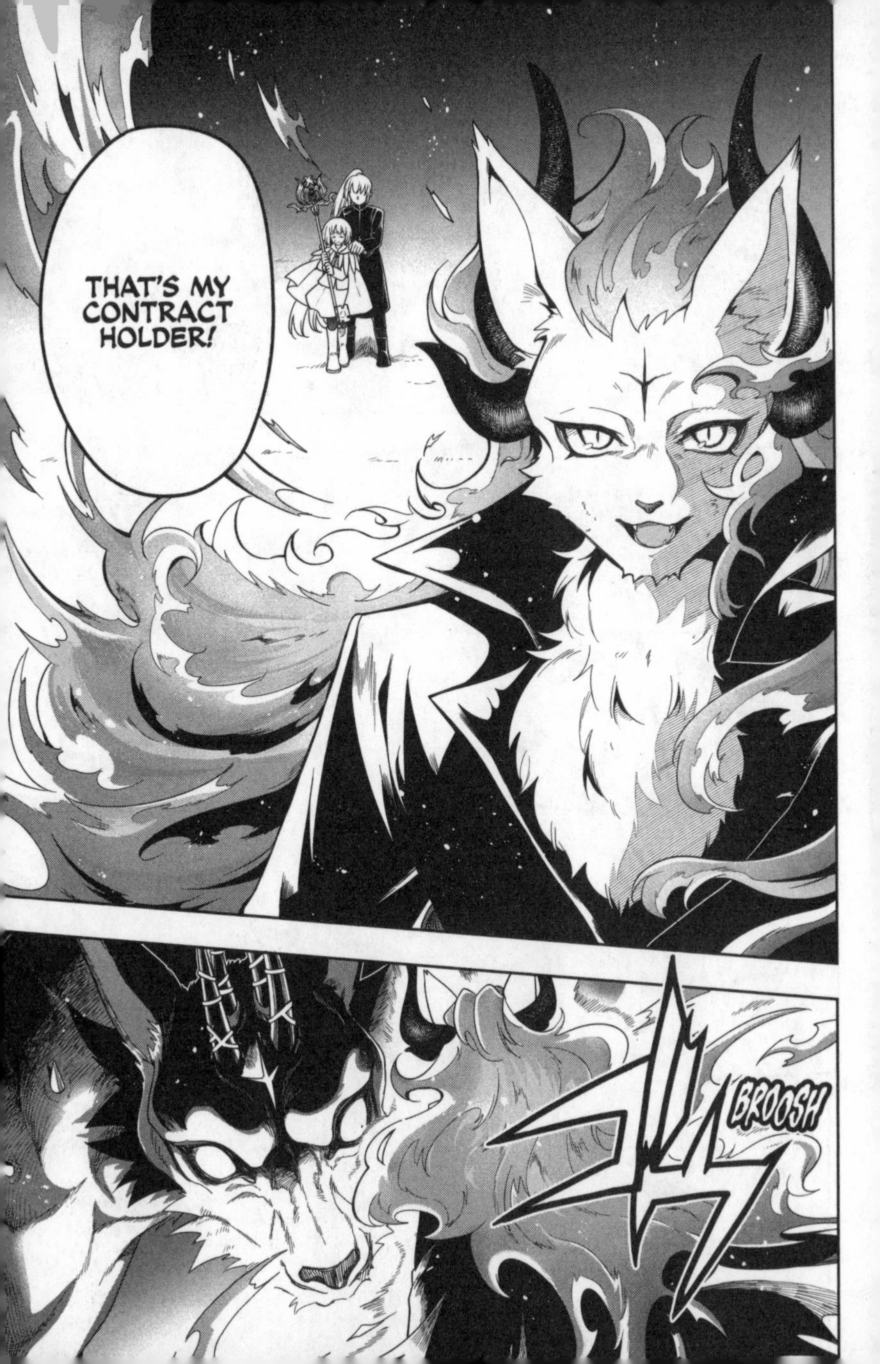
THAT'S MY CONTRACT HOLDER!
BROOSH

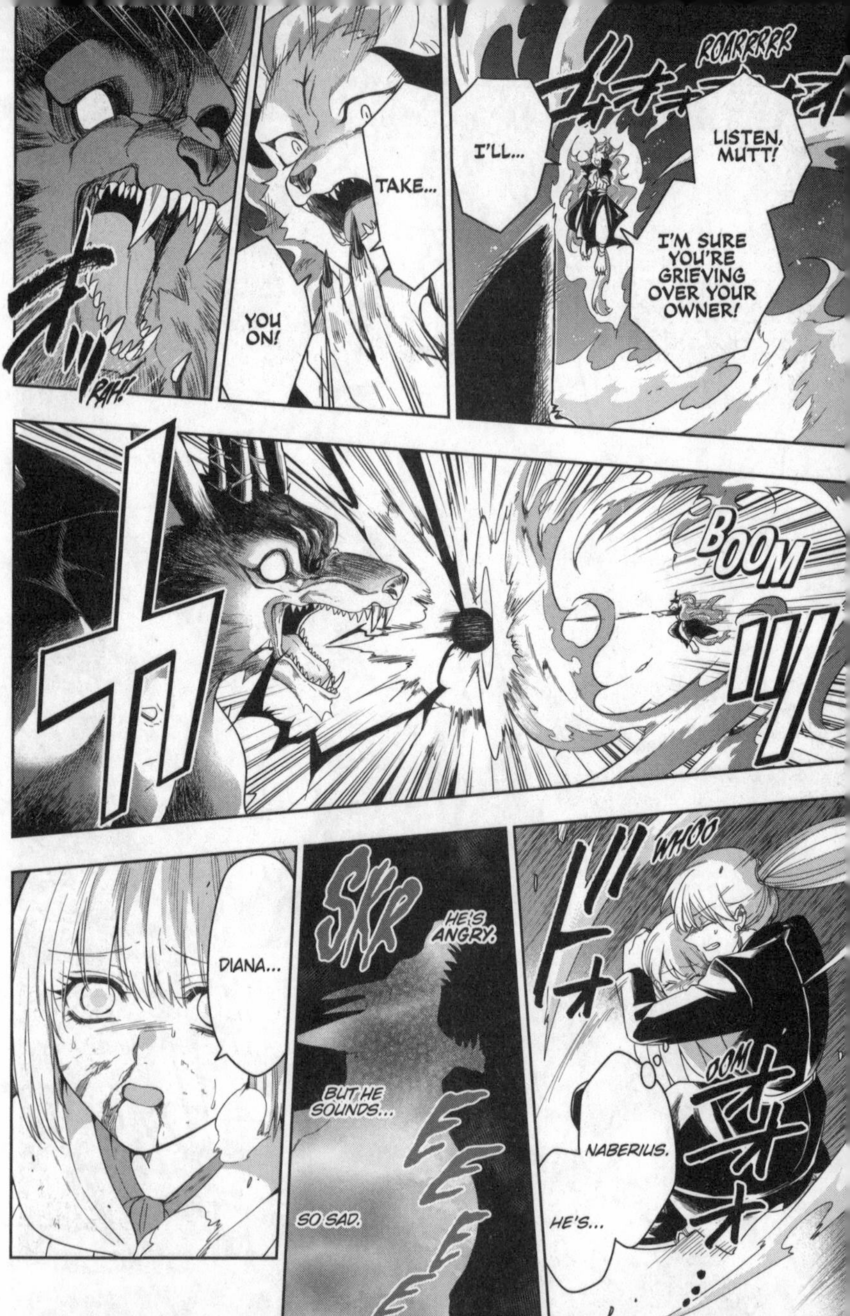
ROARRRRR
LISTEN, MUTT!
I'M SURE YOU'RE GRIEVING OVER YOUR OWNER!
I'LL...
TAKE...
YOU ON!
RAH!
BOOM
WHOO
OOM
NABERIUS.
HE'S...
HE'S ANGRY.
BUT HE SOUNDS...
SO SAD.
DIANA...

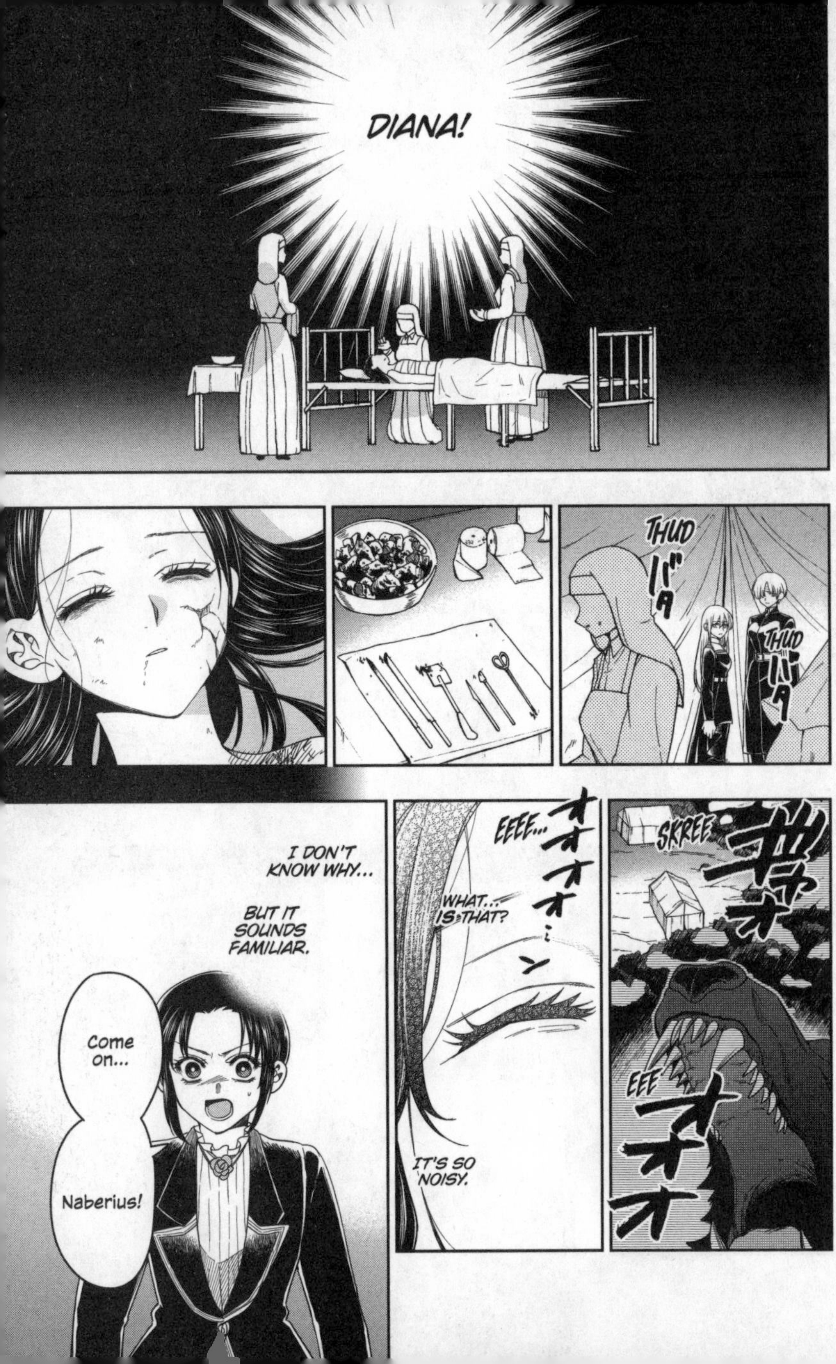
DIANA!
THUD
バタ
THUD
バタ
SKREE
EEE
EEEE...
WHAT... IS THAT?
IT'S SO NOISY.
I DON'T KNOW WHY...
BUT IT SOUNDS FAMILIAR.
Come on...
Naberius!

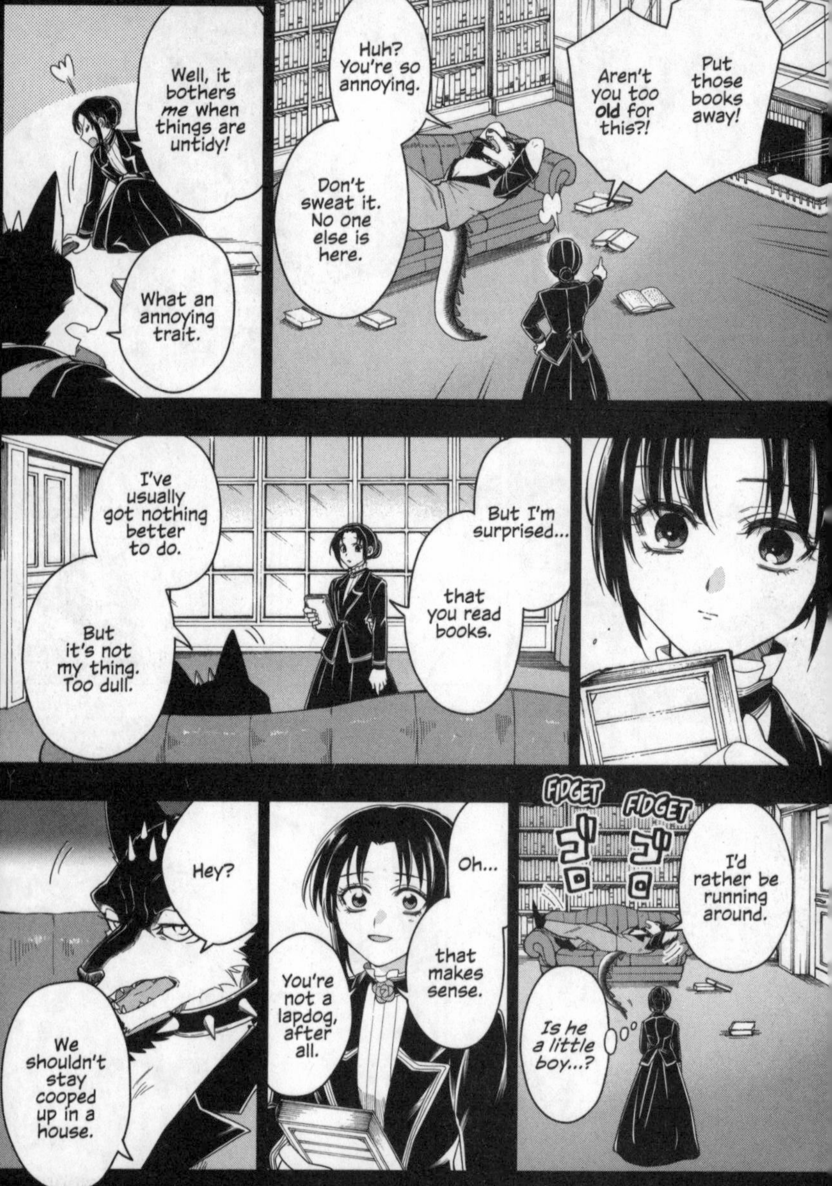
Put those books away!
Aren't you too **old** for this?!
Huh? You're so annoying.
Don't sweat it. No one else is here.
Well, it bothers *me* when things are untidy!
What an annoying trait.
But I'm surprised...
that you read books.
I've usually got nothing better to do.
But it's not my thing. Too dull.
FIDGET
FIDGET
ゴロ
ゴロ
I'd rather be running around.
Is he a little boy...?
Oh...
that makes sense.
You're not a lapdog, after all.
Hey?
We shouldn't stay cooped up in a house.

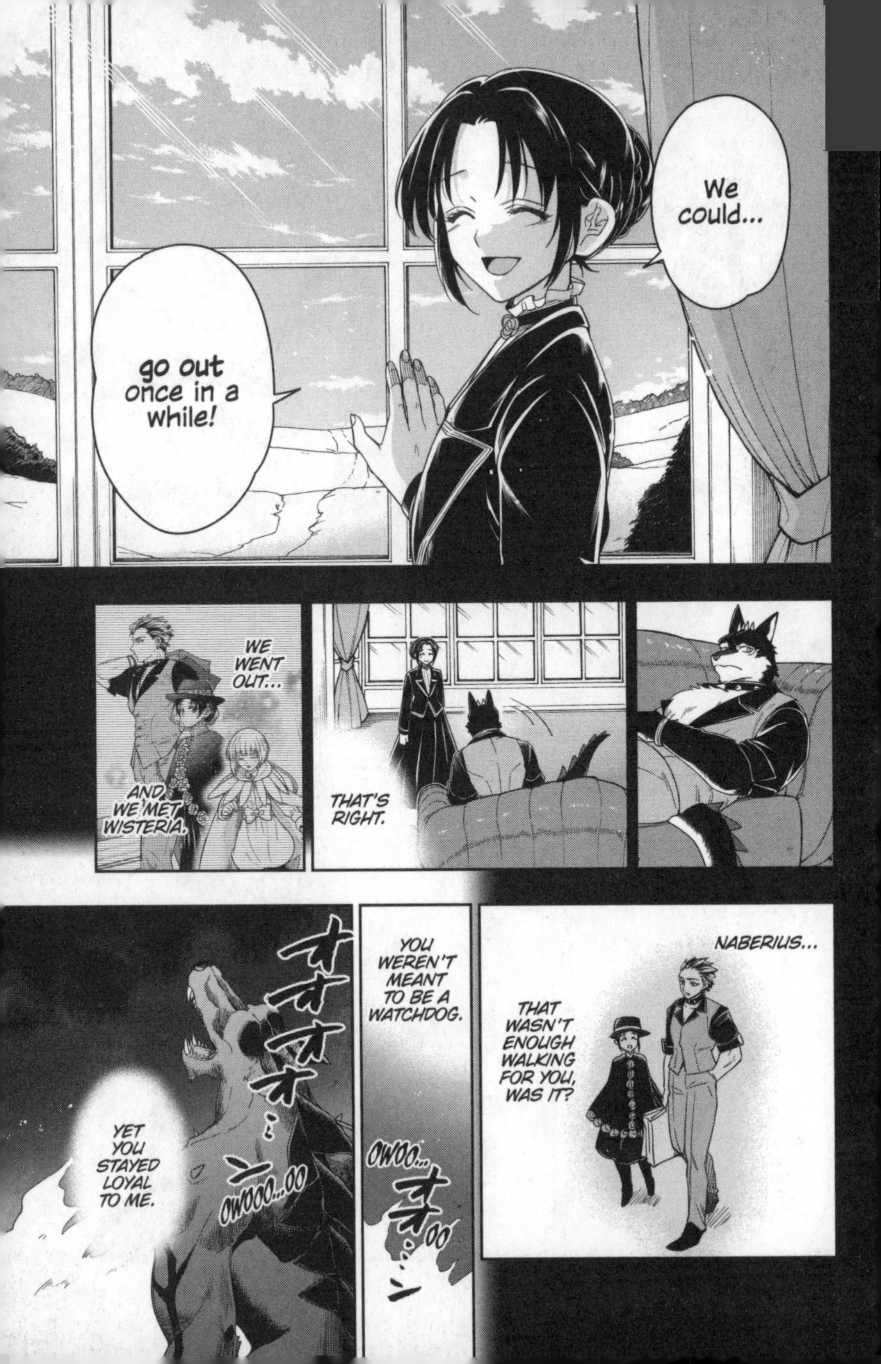
We could...
go out once in a while!
THAT'S RIGHT.
WE WENT OUT...
AND WE MET WISTERIA.
NABERIUS...
THAT WASN'T ENOUGH WALKING FOR YOU, WAS IT?
YOU WEREN'T MEANT TO BE A WATCHDOG.
OWOO...
OO
YET YOU STAYED LOYAL TO ME.
OWOOO...OO

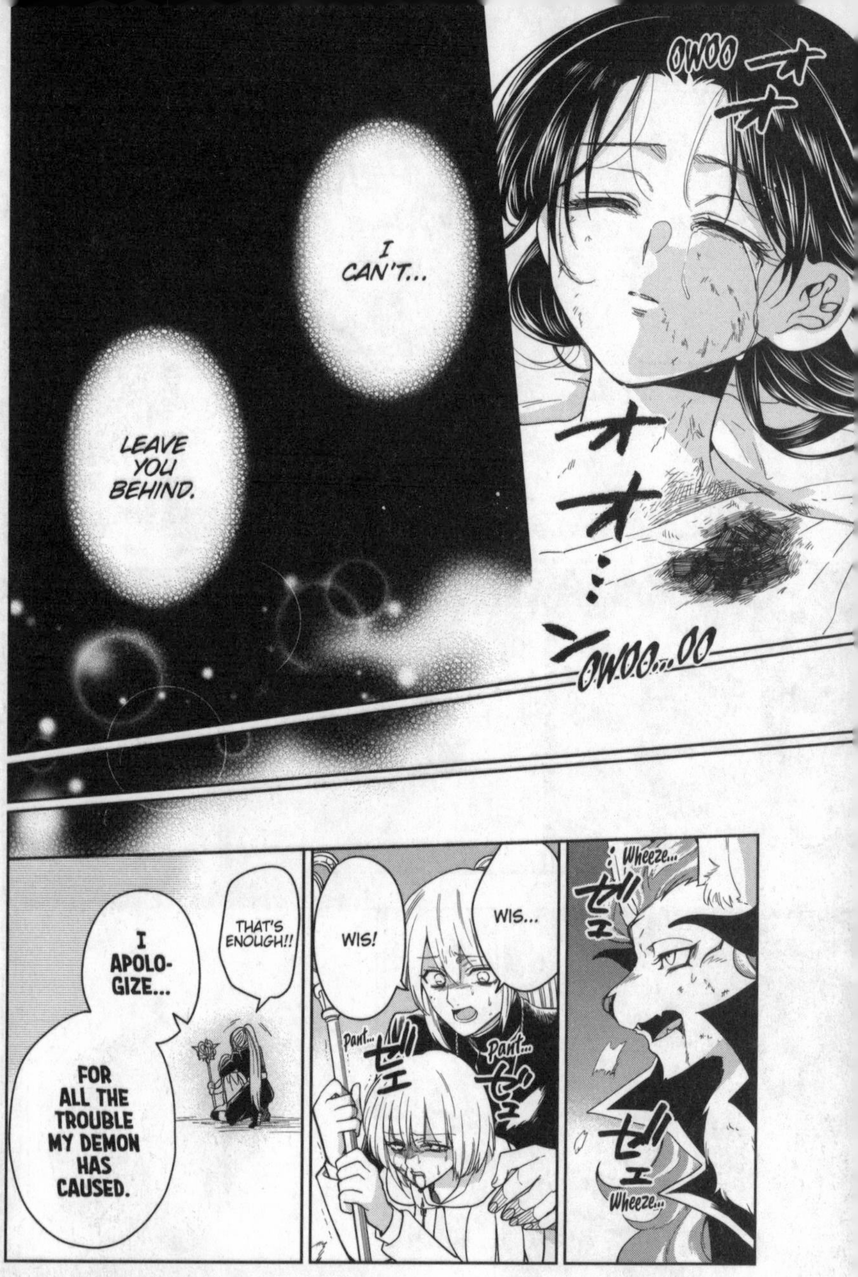
OWOO
オオ
I CAN'T...
LEAVE YOU BEHIND.
オオ…ン
OWOO...OO
Wheeze...
ゼェ
ゼェ
Wheeze...
WIS...
WIS!
Pant...
ゼェ
Pant...
ゼェ
THAT'S ENOUGH!!
I APOLOGIZE...
FOR ALL THE TROUBLE MY DEMON HAS CAUSED.

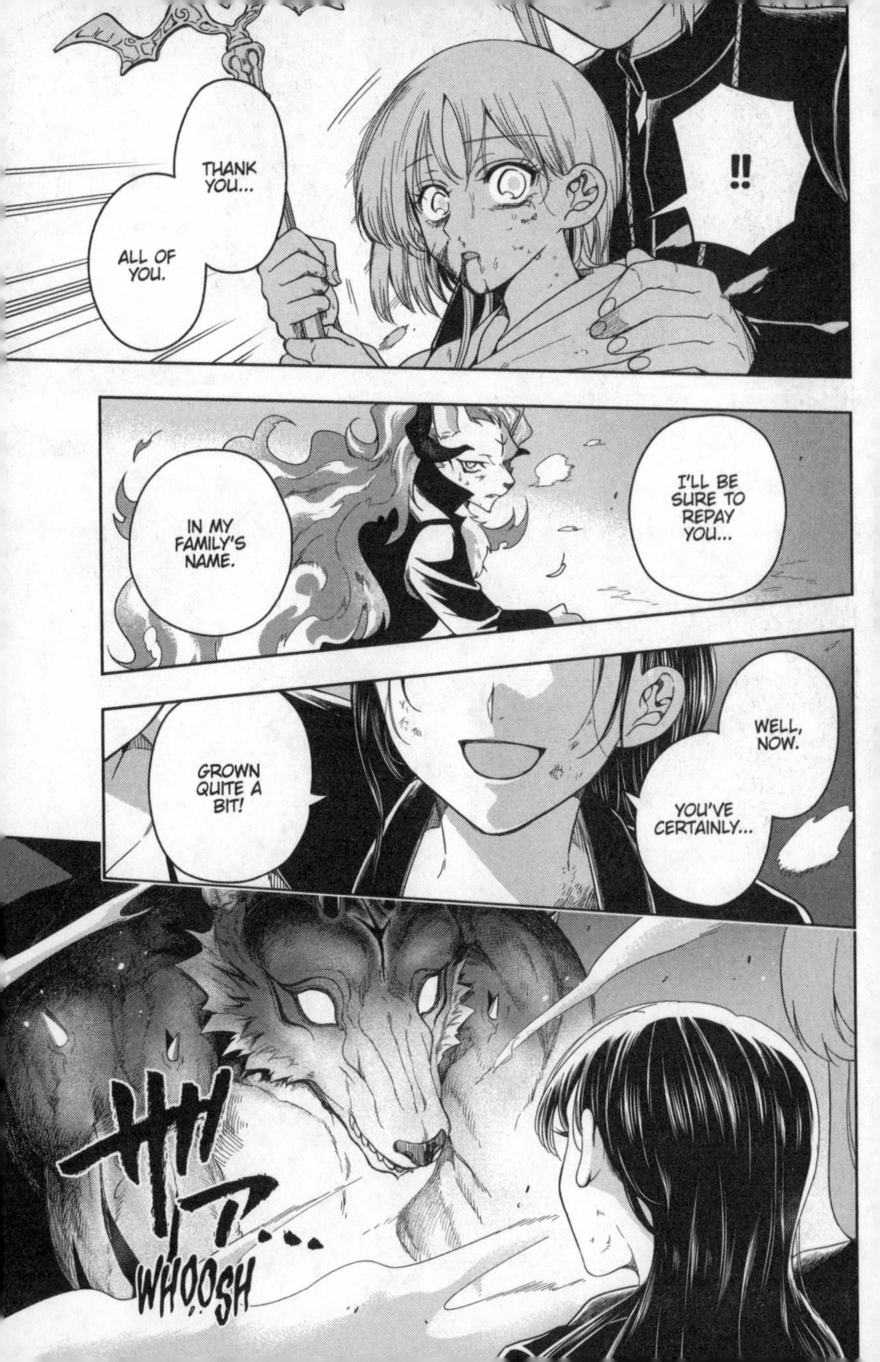
!!
THANK YOU...
ALL OF YOU.
I'LL BE SURE TO REPAY YOU...
IN MY FAMILY'S NAME.
WELL, NOW.
YOU'VE CERTAINLY...
GROWN QUITE A BIT!
WHOOSH

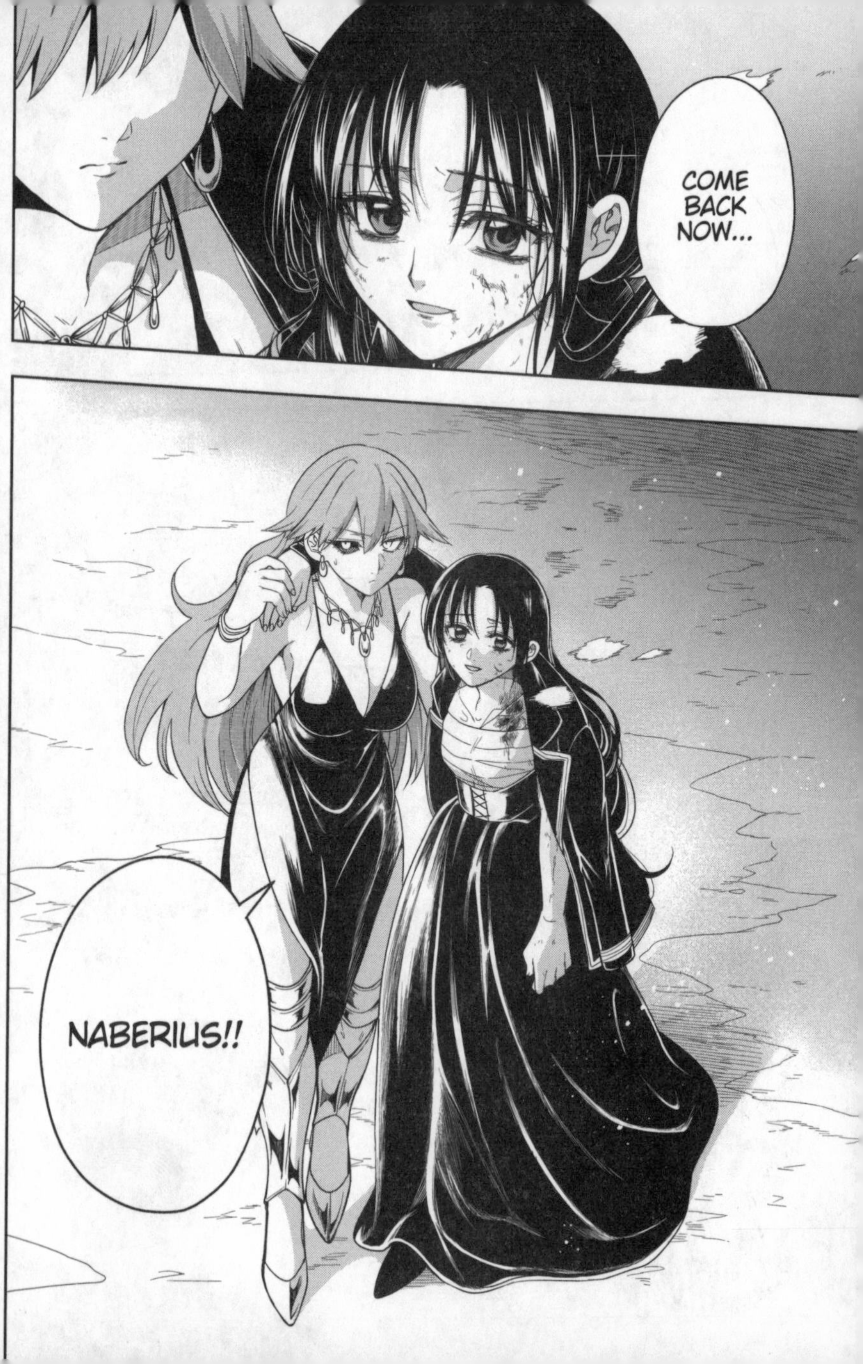
COME BACK NOW...
NABERIUS!!

The Tale of the Outcasts

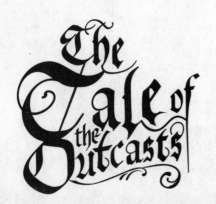

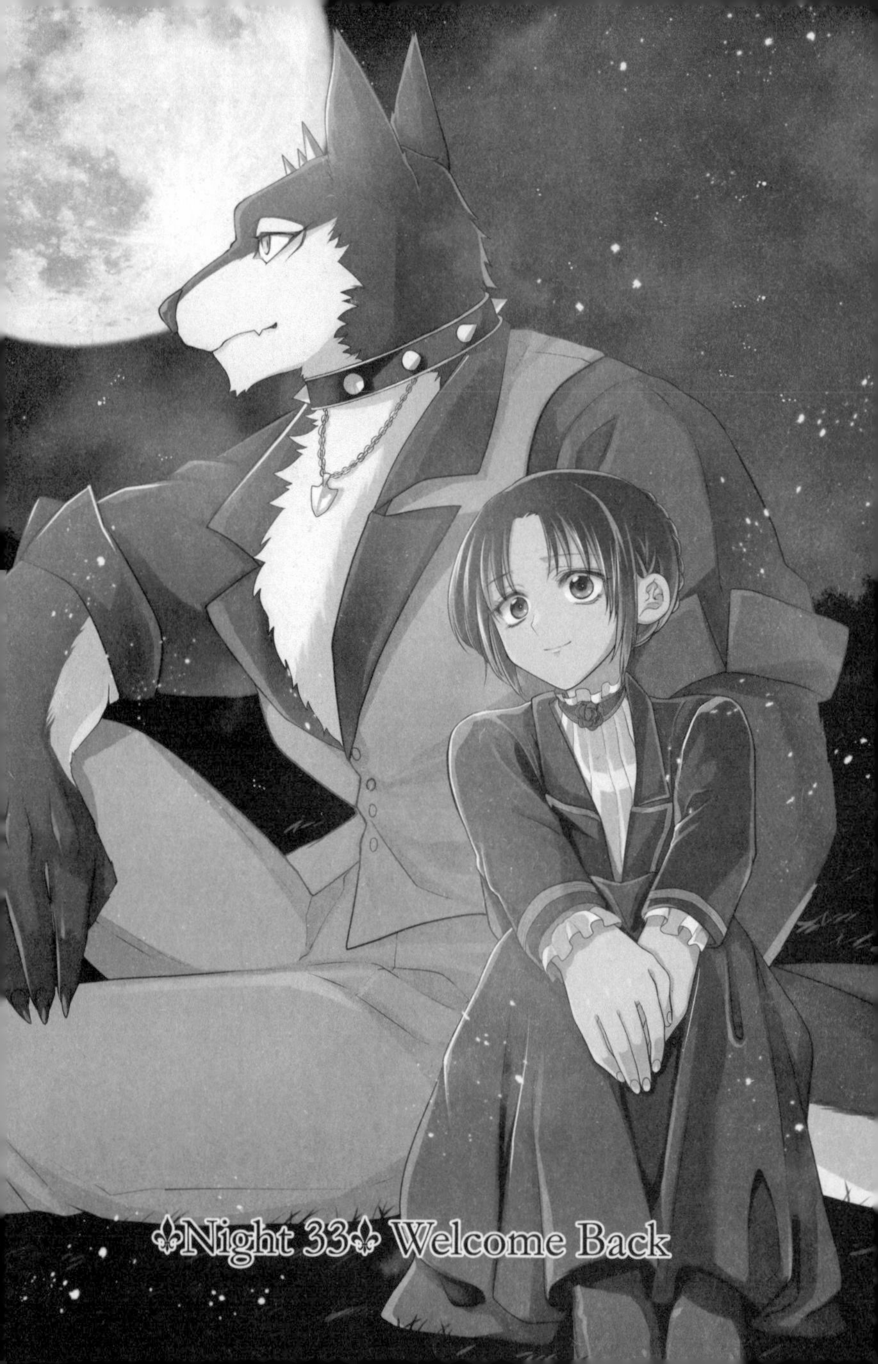
Night 33 Welcome Back

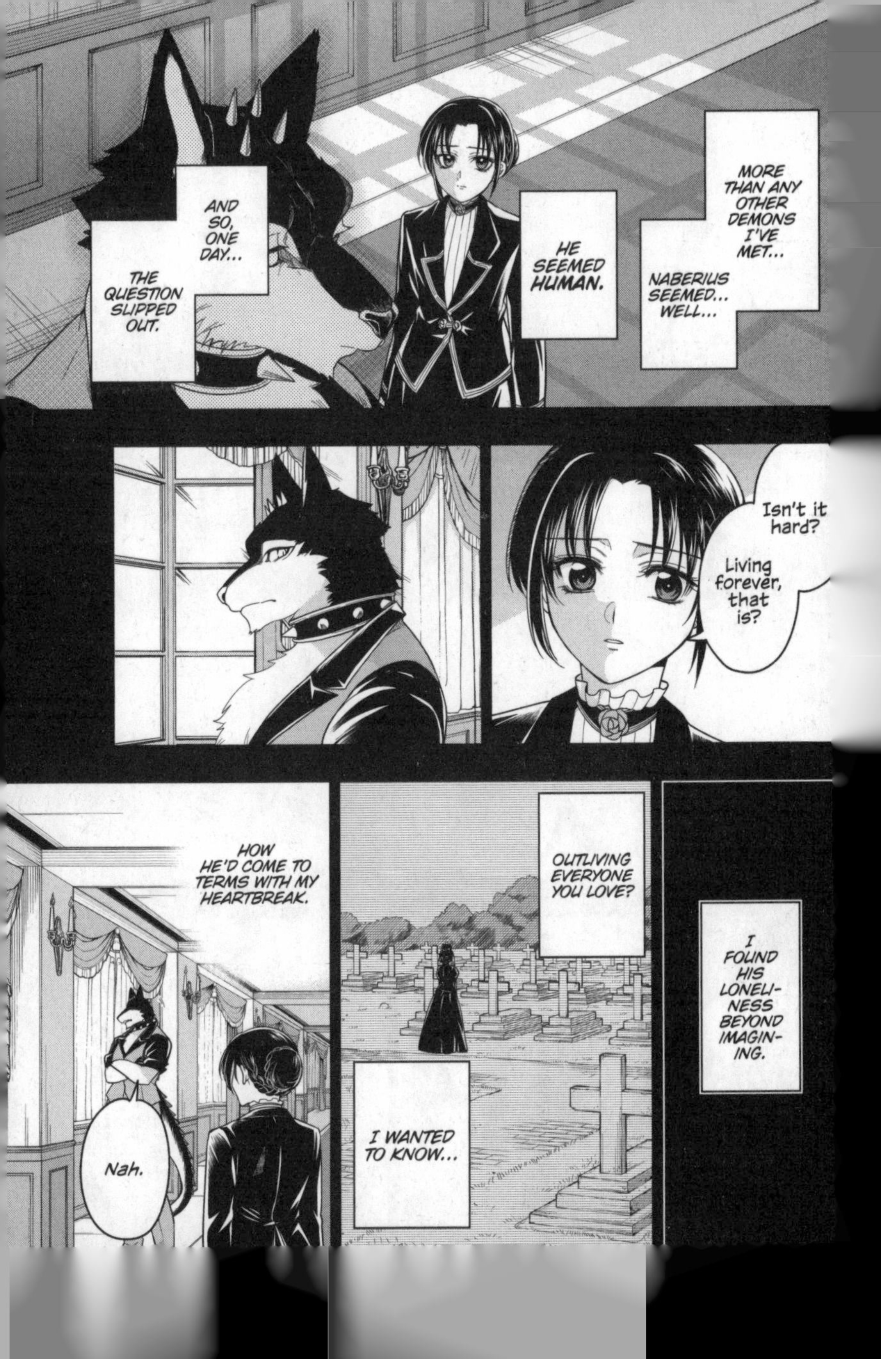
MORE THAN ANY OTHER DEMONS I'VE MET...
NABERIUS SEEMED... WELL...
HE SEEMED **HUMAN.**
AND SO, ONE DAY...
THE QUESTION SLIPPED OUT.
Isn't it hard?
Living forever, that is?
I FOUND HIS LONELI-NESS BEYOND IMAGIN-ING.
OUTLIVING EVERYONE YOU LOVE?
I WANTED TO KNOW...
HOW HE'D COME TO TERMS WITH MY HEARTBREAK.
Nah.

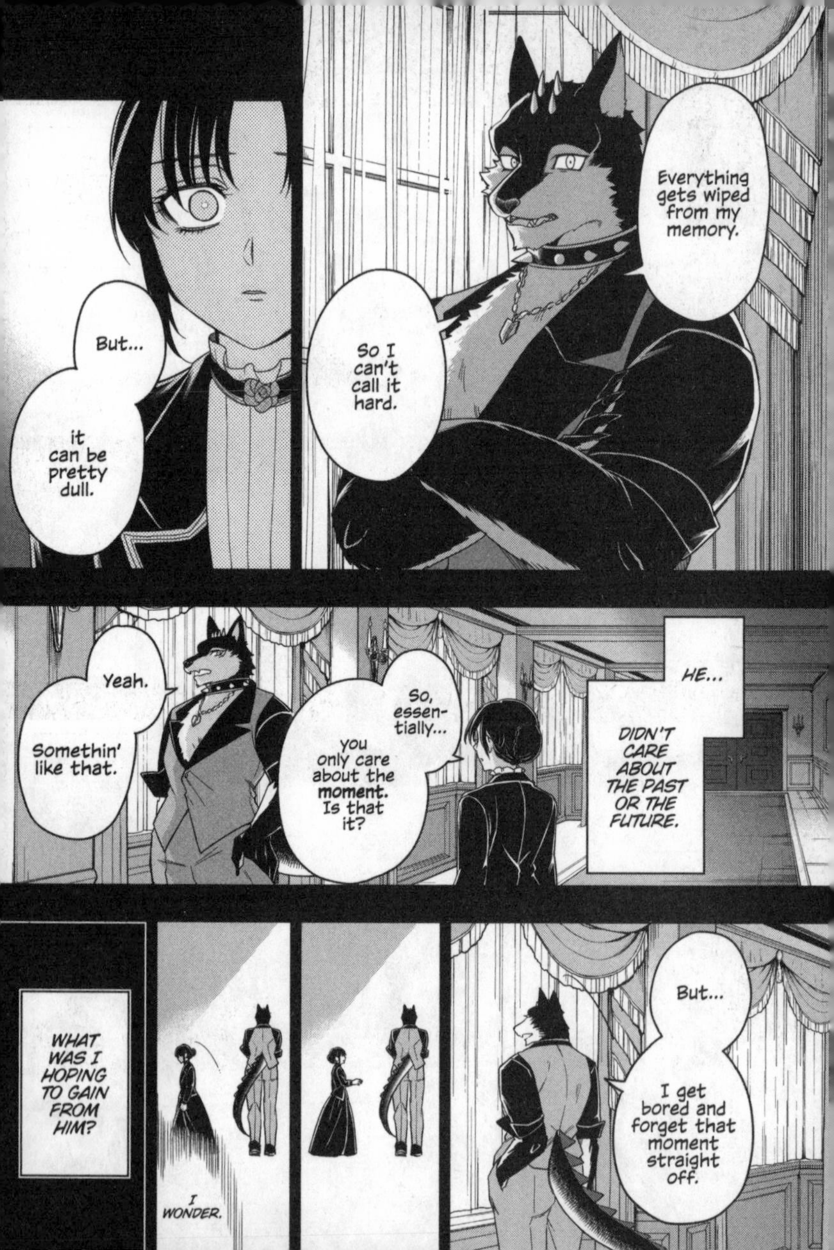
Everything gets wiped from my memory.
So I can't call it hard.
But...
it can be pretty dull.
HE...
DIDN'T CARE ABOUT THE PAST OR THE FUTURE.
So, essentially...
you only care about the **moment.** Is that it?
Yeah.
Somethin' like that.
But...
I get bored and forget that moment straight off.
I WONDER.
WHAT WAS I HOPING TO GAIN FROM HIM?

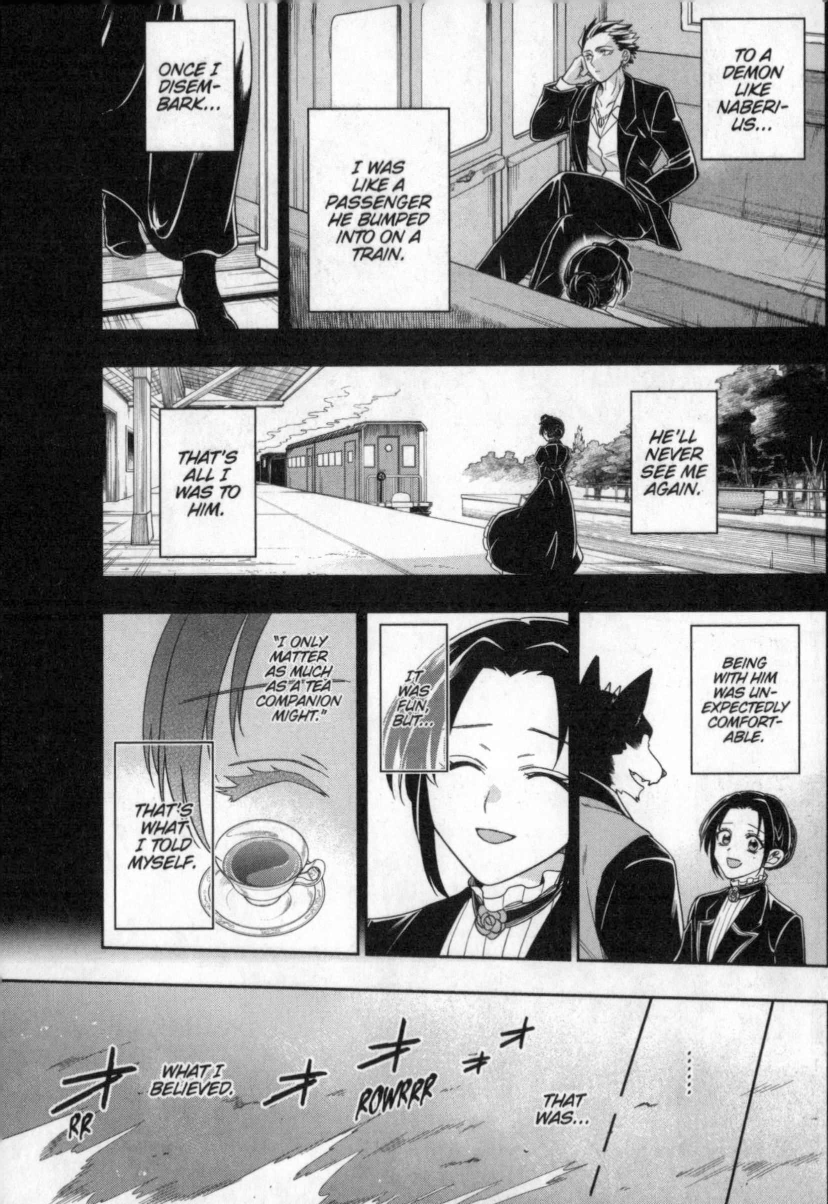

TO A DEMON LIKE NABERIUS...
I WAS LIKE A PASSENGER HE BUMPED INTO ON A TRAIN.
ONCE I DISEMBARK...
HE'LL NEVER SEE ME AGAIN.
THAT'S ALL I WAS TO HIM.
BEING WITH HIM WAS UNEXPECTEDLY COMFORTABLE.
IT WAS FUN, BUT...
"I ONLY MATTER AS MUCH AS A TEA COMPANION MIGHT."
THAT'S WHAT I TOLD MYSELF.
......
THAT WAS...
ROWRRR
WHAT I BELIEVED.
RR

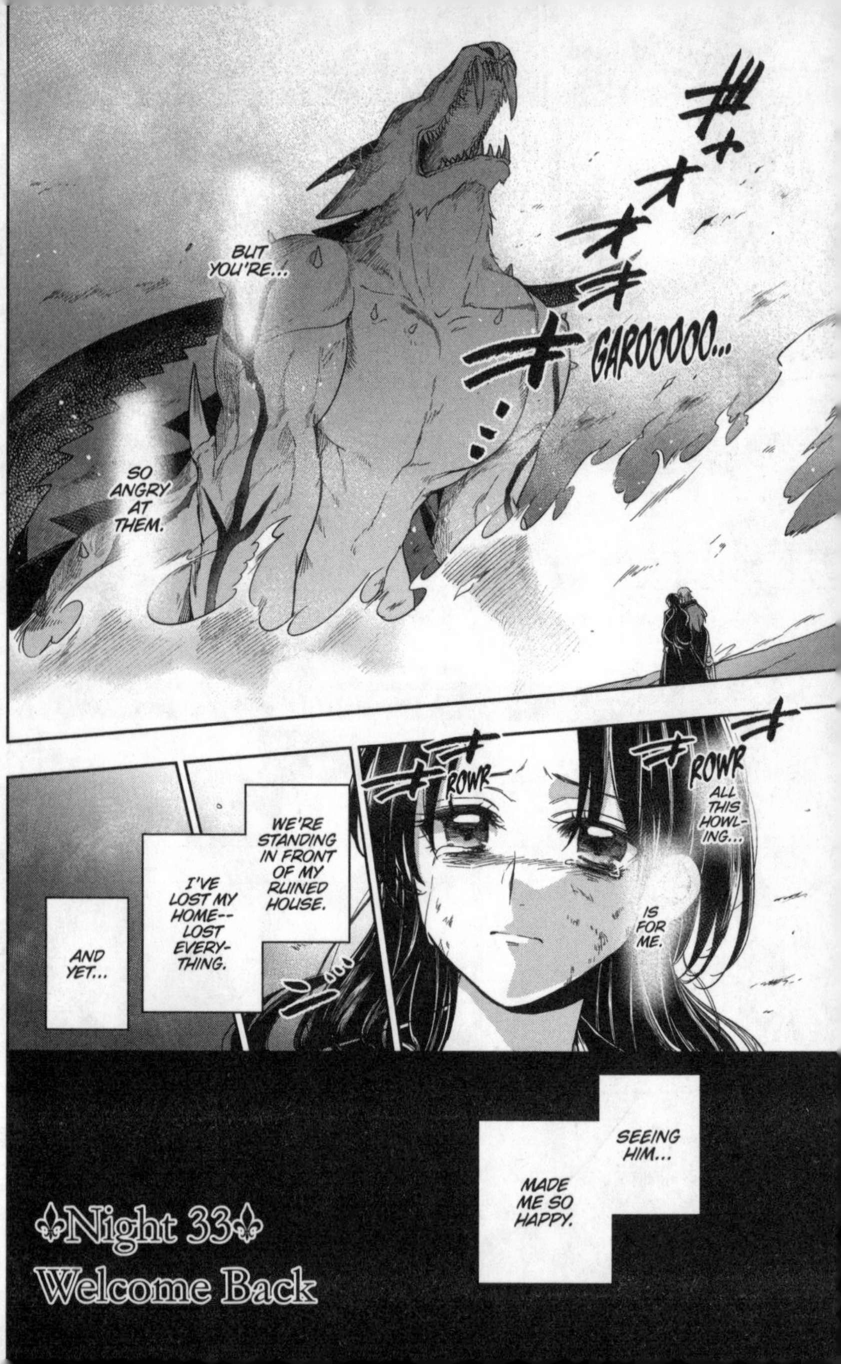
GAROOOOO...
BUT YOU'RE...
SO ANGRY AT THEM.
ROWR
ALL THIS HOWLING...
ROWR
IS FOR ME.
WE'RE STANDING IN FRONT OF MY RUINED HOUSE.
I'VE LOST MY HOME--LOST EVERYTHING.
AND YET...
SEEING HIM...
MADE ME SO HAPPY.
Night 33
Welcome Back

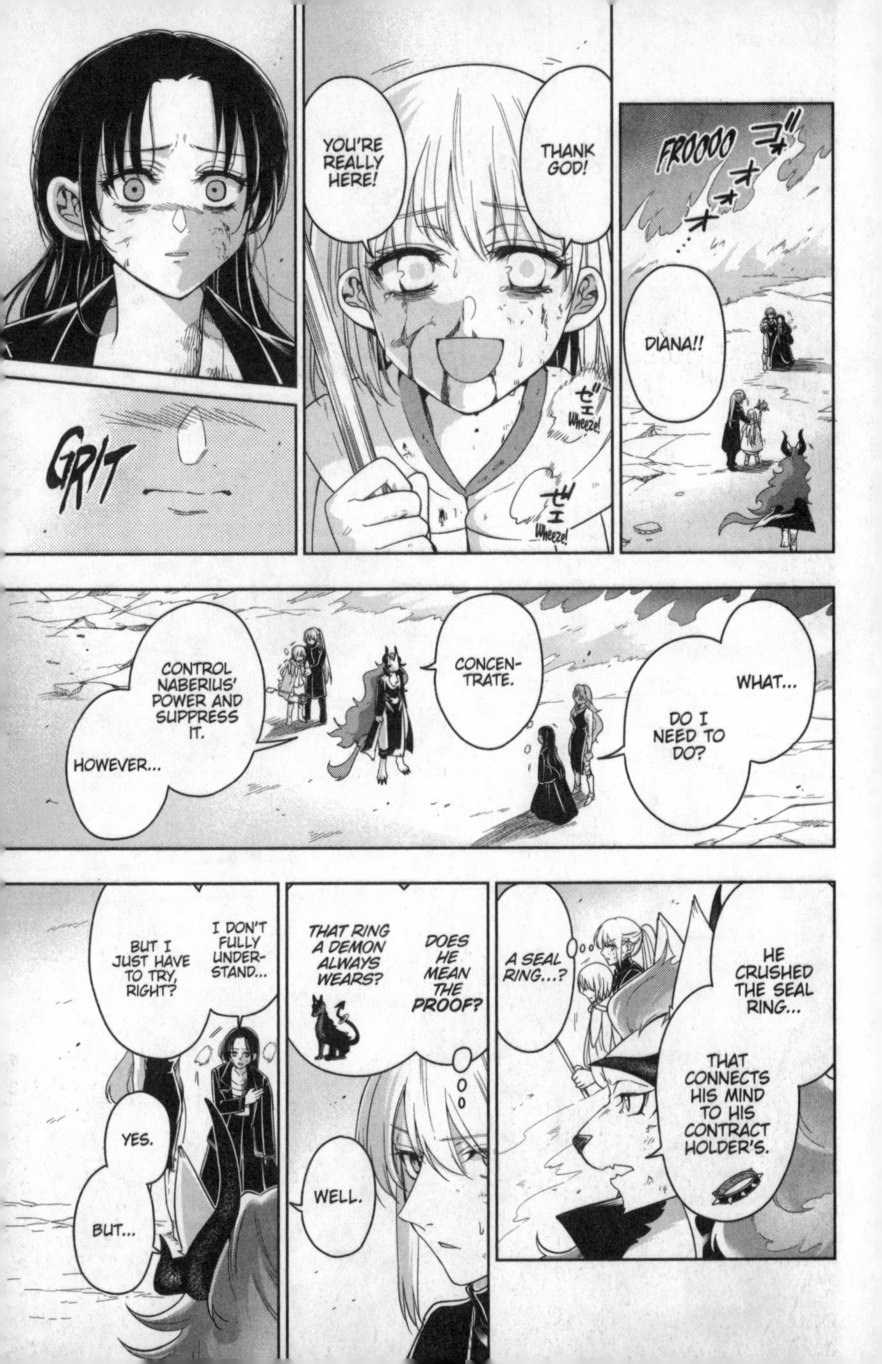
FROOOO
DIANA!!
THANK GOD!
YOU'RE REALLY HERE!
ゼェ
Wheeze!
ゼェ
Wheeze!
GRIT
WHAT... DO I NEED TO DO?
CONCENTRATE.
CONTROL NABERIUS' POWER AND SUPPRESS IT.
HOWEVER...
HE CRUSHED THE SEAL RING...
THAT CONNECTS HIS MIND TO HIS CONTRACT HOLDER'S.
A SEAL RING...?
DOES HE MEAN THE PROOF?
THAT RING A DEMON ALWAYS WEARS?
WELL.
I DON'T FULLY UNDERSTAND...
BUT I JUST HAVE TO TRY, RIGHT?
YES.
BUT...

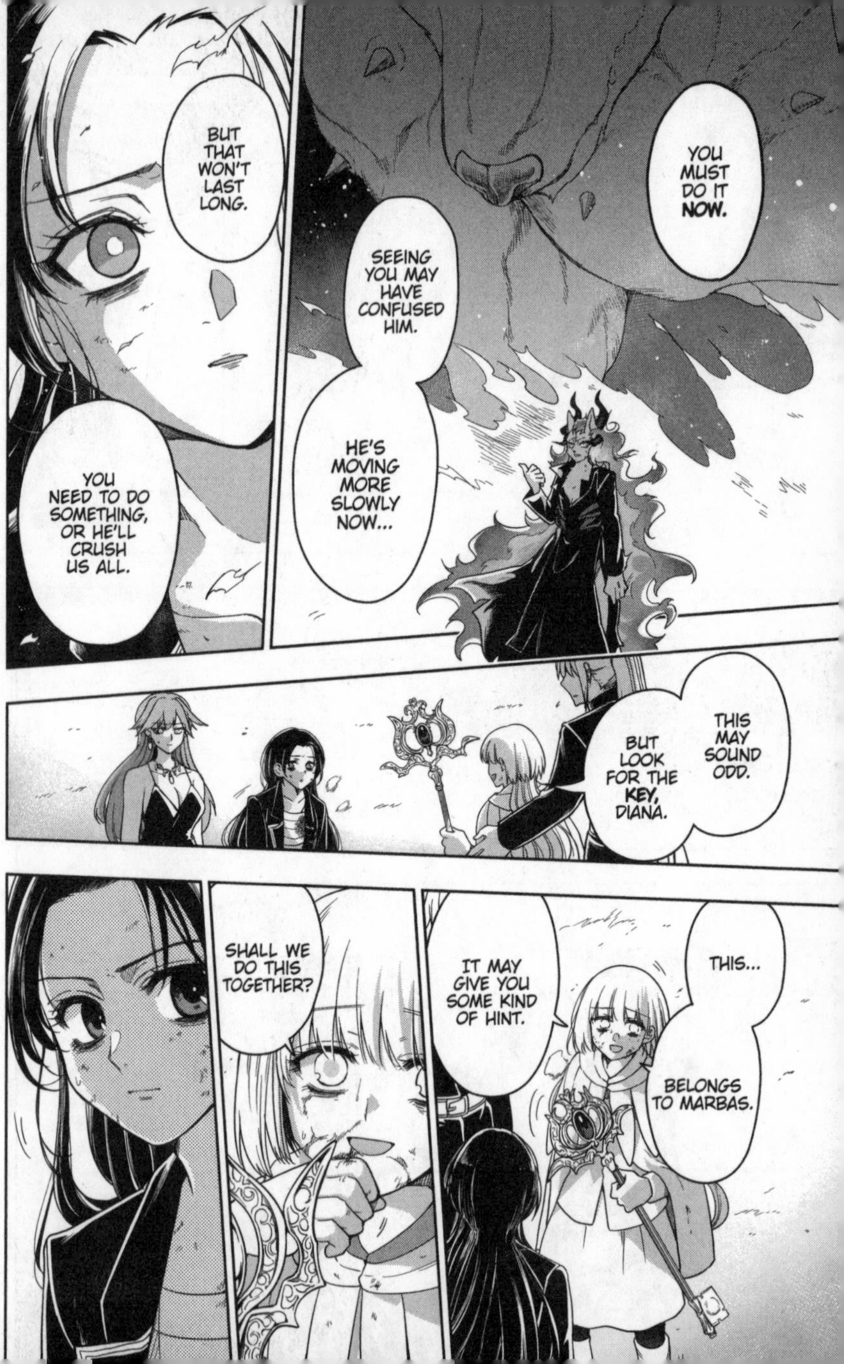
YOU MUST DO IT NOW.
SEEING YOU MAY HAVE CONFUSED HIM.
HE'S MOVING MORE SLOWLY NOW...
BUT THAT WON'T LAST LONG.
YOU NEED TO DO SOMETHING, OR HE'LL CRUSH US ALL.
THIS MAY SOUND ODD.
BUT LOOK FOR THE KEY, DIANA.
THIS...
BELONGS TO MARBAS.
IT MAY GIVE YOU SOME KIND OF HINT.
SHALL WE DO THIS TOGETHER?

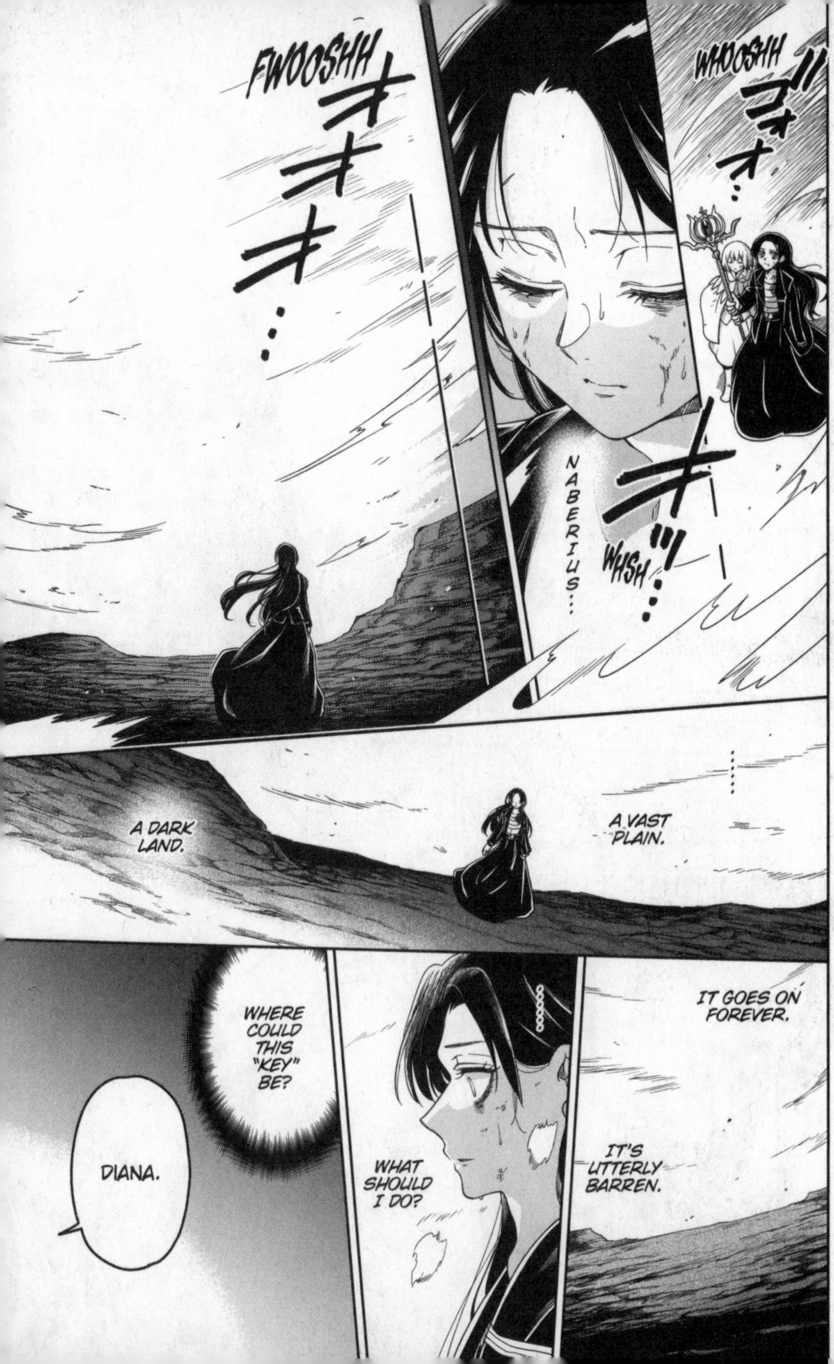
WHOOSHH
ゴォォ…
WHSH
キッ…
NABERIUS…
FWOOSHH
オォォォ…
……
A VAST PLAIN.
A DARK LAND.
IT GOES ON FOREVER.
IT'S UTTERLY BARREN.
WHERE COULD THIS "KEY" BE?
WHAT SHOULD I DO?
DIANA.

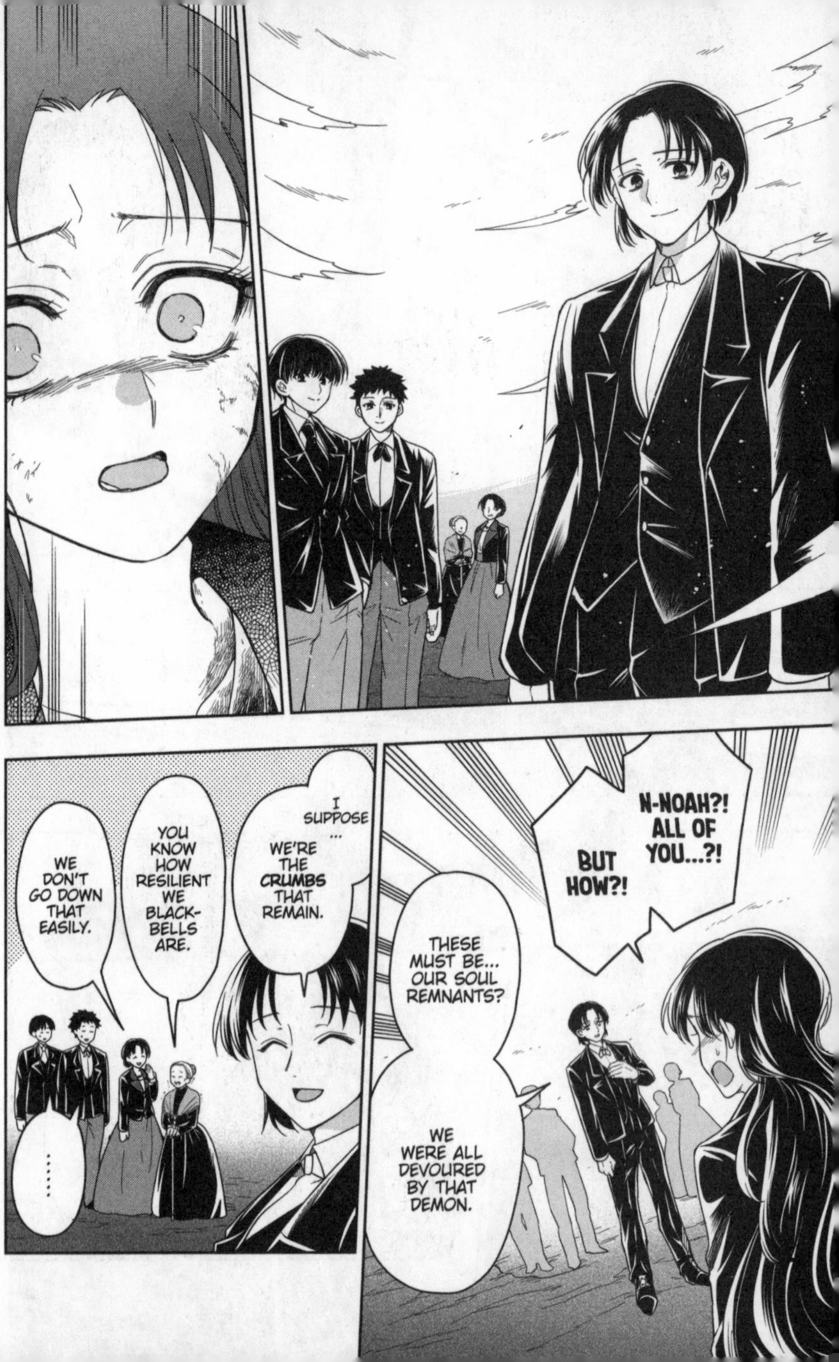
N-NOAH?! ALL OF YOU...?!
BUT HOW?!
THESE MUST BE... OUR SOUL REMNANTS?
WE WERE ALL DEVOURED BY THAT DEMON.
I SUPPOSE... WE'RE THE CRUMBS THAT REMAIN.
YOU KNOW HOW RESILIENT WE BLACK-BELLS ARE.
WE DON'T GO DOWN THAT EASILY.
......

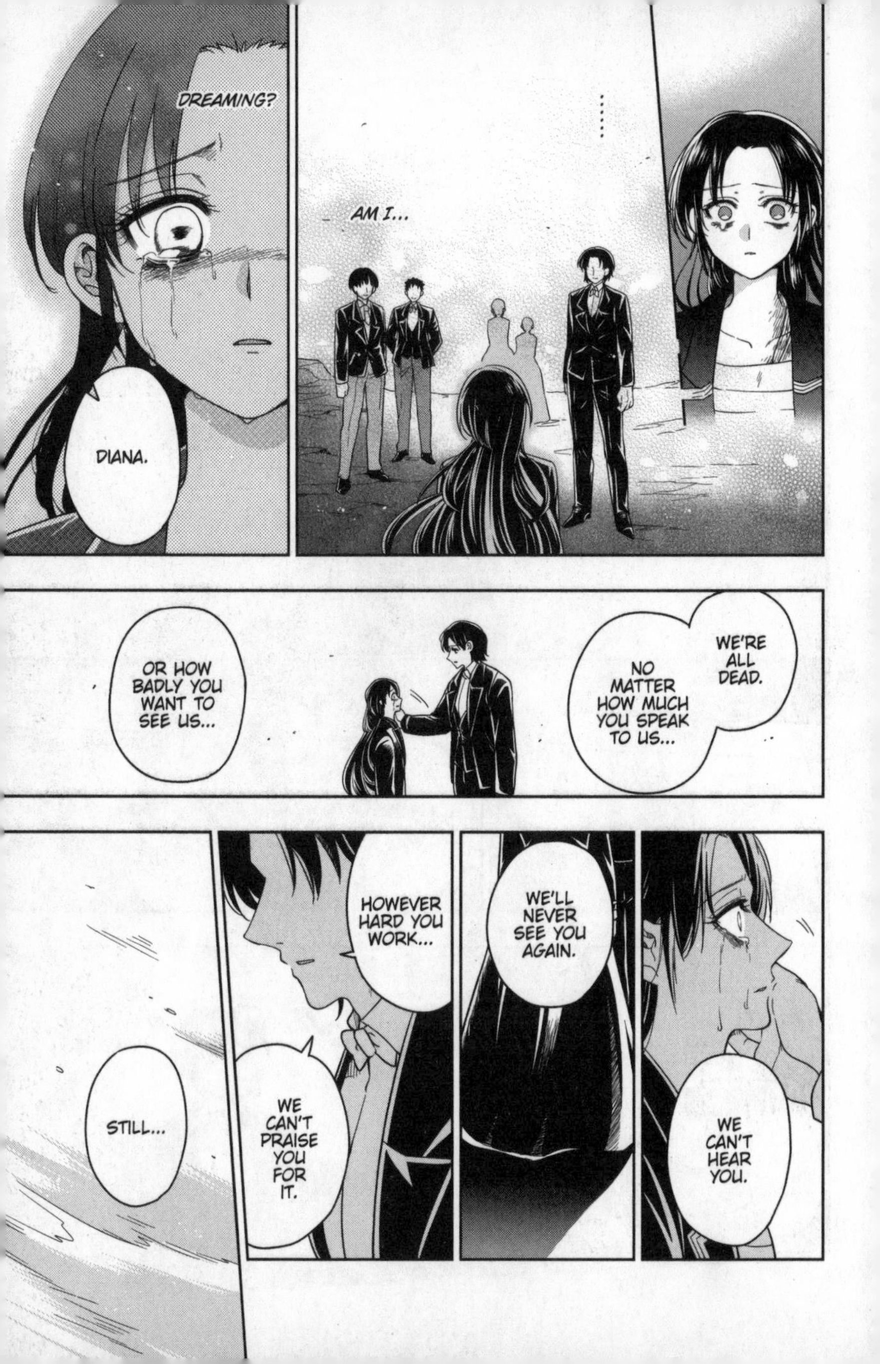
......
AM I...
DREAMING?
DIANA.
WE'RE ALL DEAD.
NO MATTER HOW MUCH YOU SPEAK TO US...
OR HOW BADLY YOU WANT TO SEE US...
WE CAN'T HEAR YOU.
WE'LL NEVER SEE YOU AGAIN.
HOWEVER HARD YOU WORK...
WE CAN'T PRAISE YOU FOR IT.
STILL...

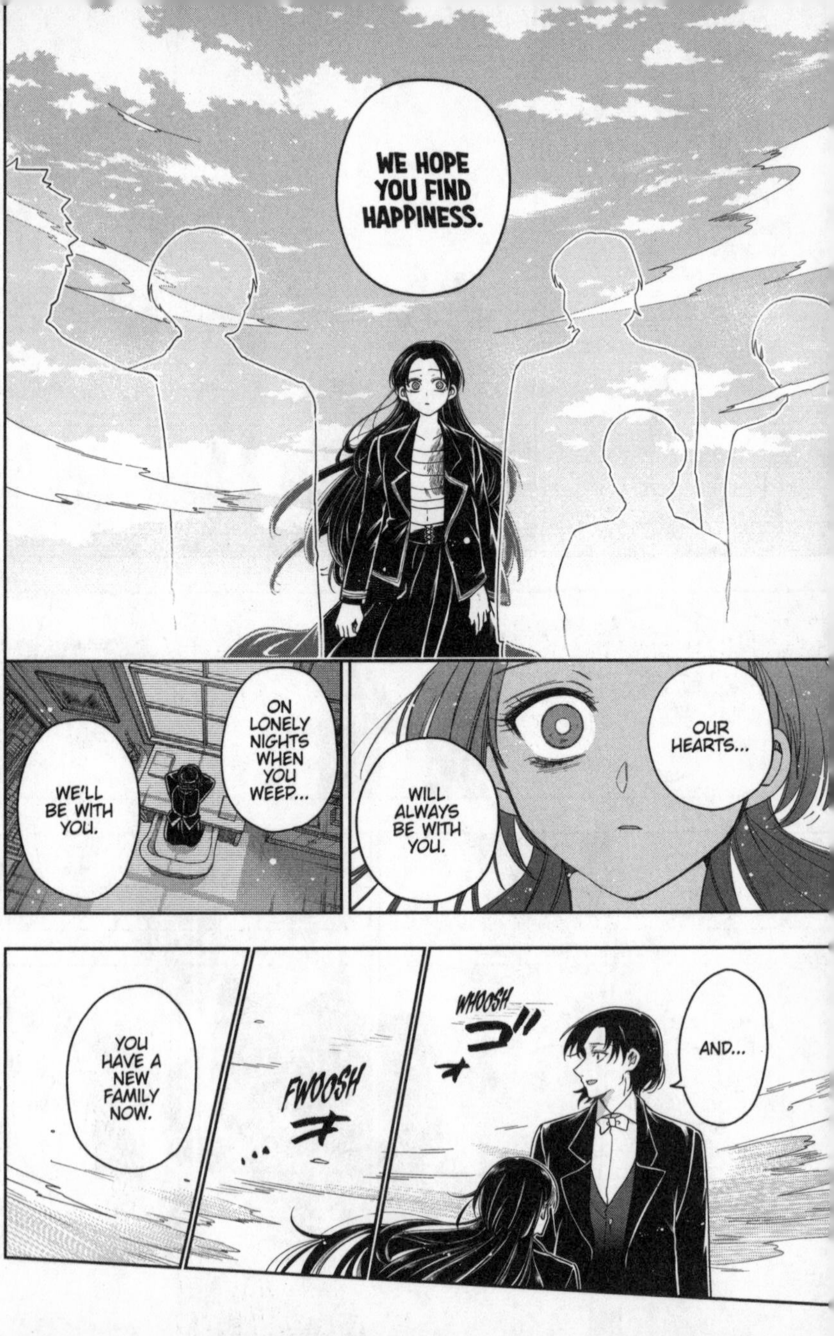
WE HOPE YOU FIND HAPPINESS.
OUR HEARTS...
WILL ALWAYS BE WITH YOU.
ON LONELY NIGHTS WHEN YOU WEEP...
WE'LL BE WITH YOU.
AND...
WHOOSH
ゴオ
FWOOSH
オ
...
YOU HAVE A NEW FAMILY NOW.

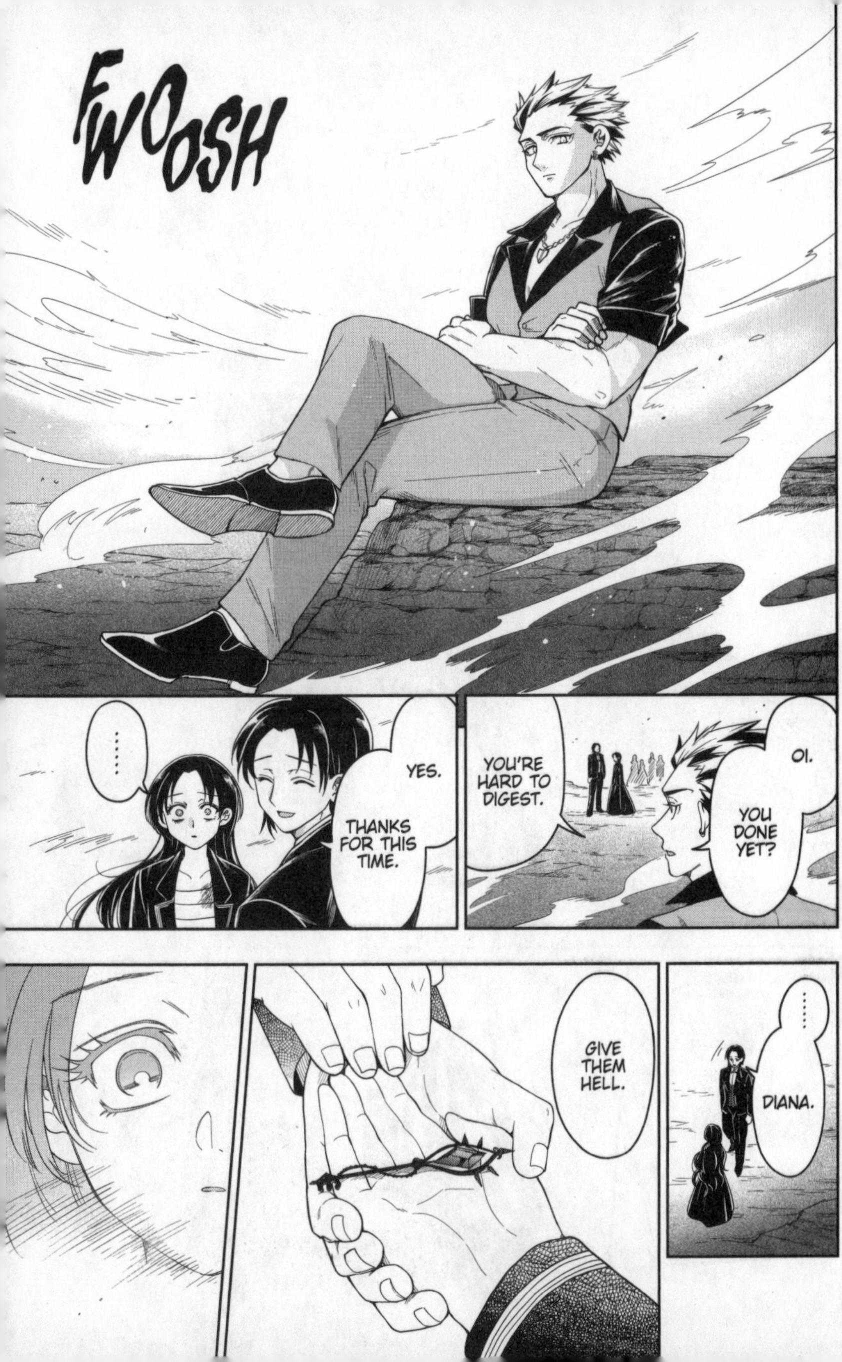
FWOOSH
OI.
YOU DONE YET?
YOU'RE HARD TO DIGEST.
YES.
THANKS FOR THIS TIME.
......
......
DIANA.
GIVE THEM HELL.

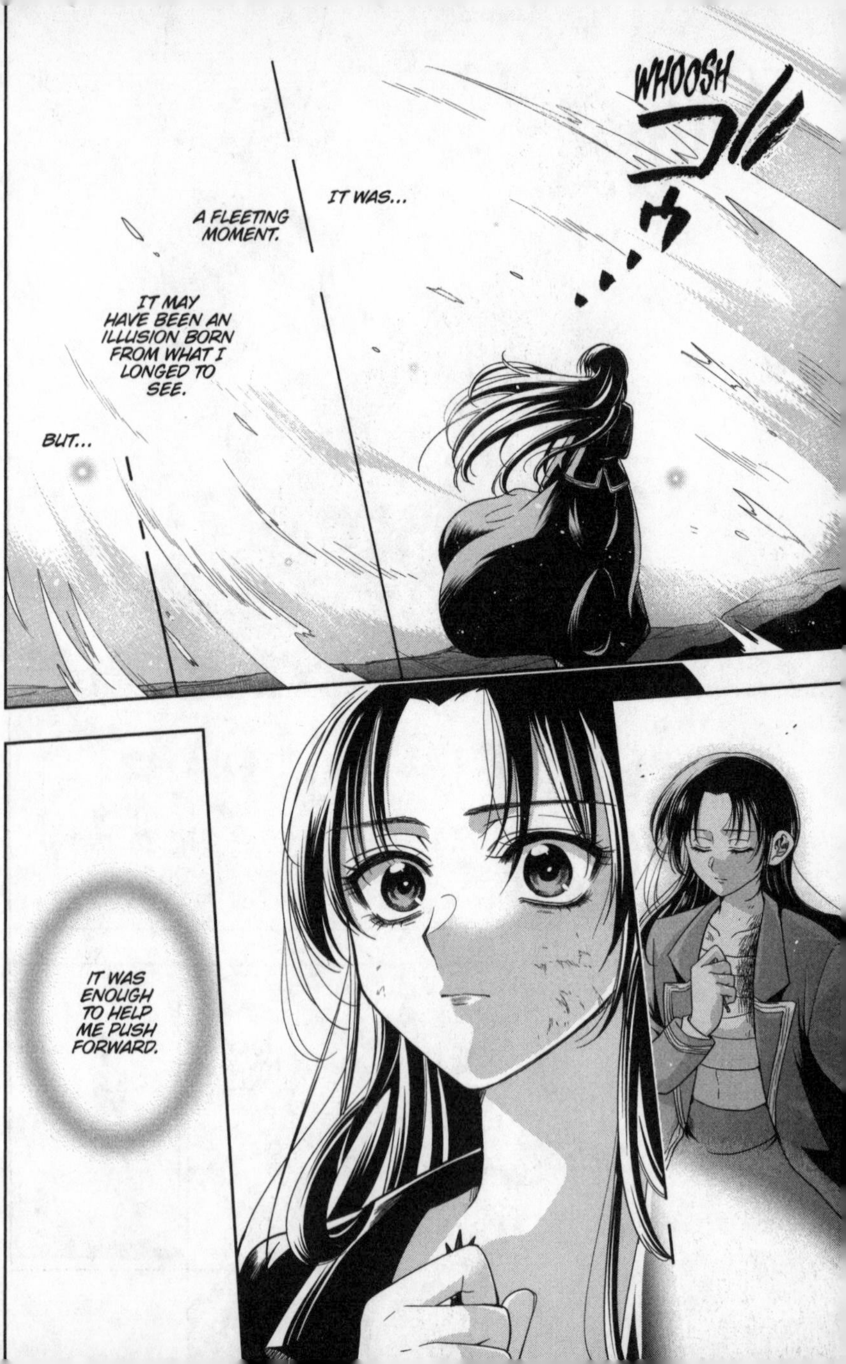
WHOOSH
ゴウ…
IT WAS…
A FLEETING MOMENT.
IT MAY HAVE BEEN AN ILLUSION BORN FROM WHAT I LONGED TO SEE.
BUT…
IT WAS ENOUGH TO HELP ME PUSH FORWARD.

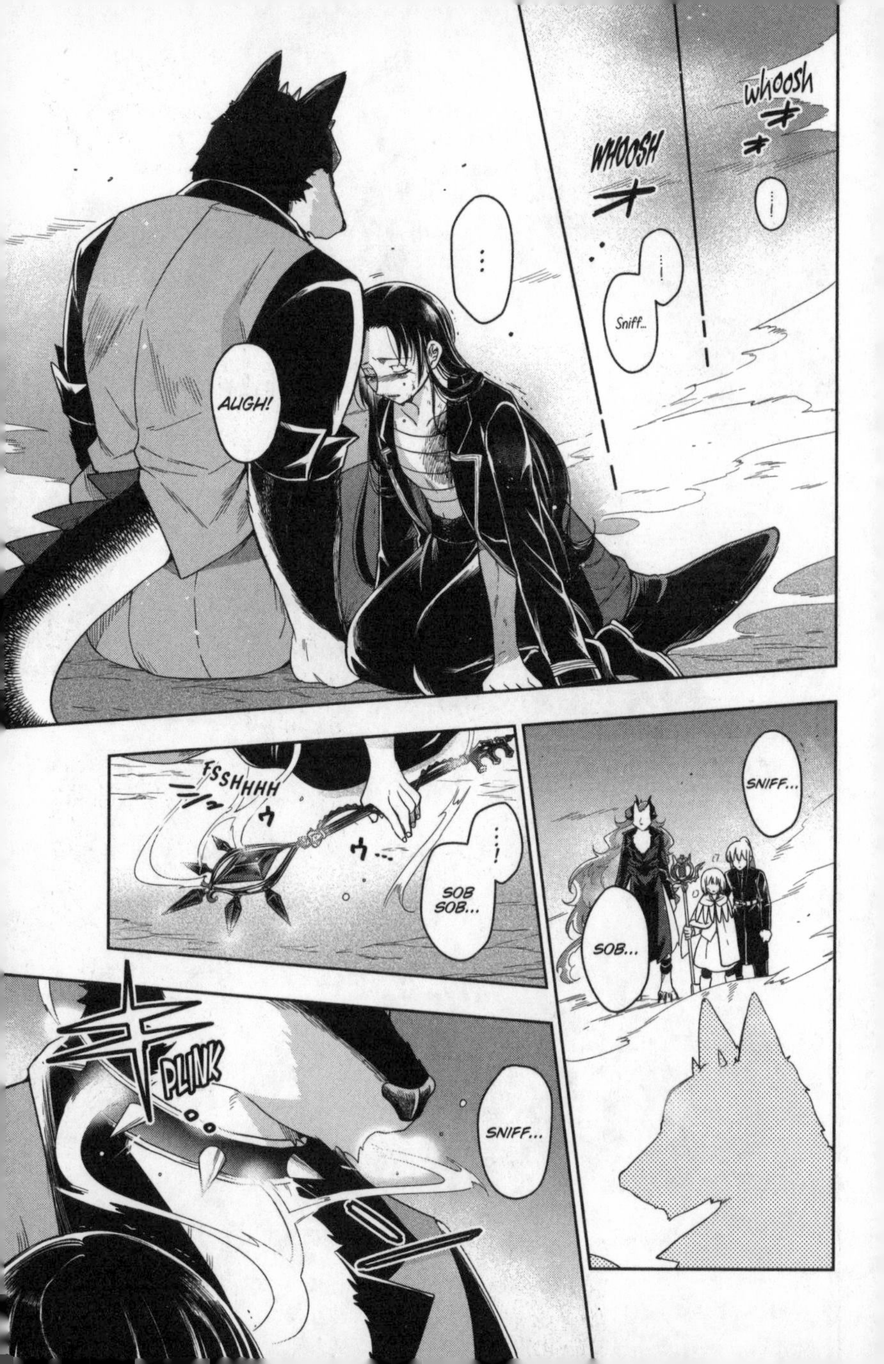
whoosh
WHOOSH
!
!
Sniff...
...
AUGH!
SNIFF...
SOB...
FSSHHHH
...!
SOB SOB...
SNIFF...
PLINK

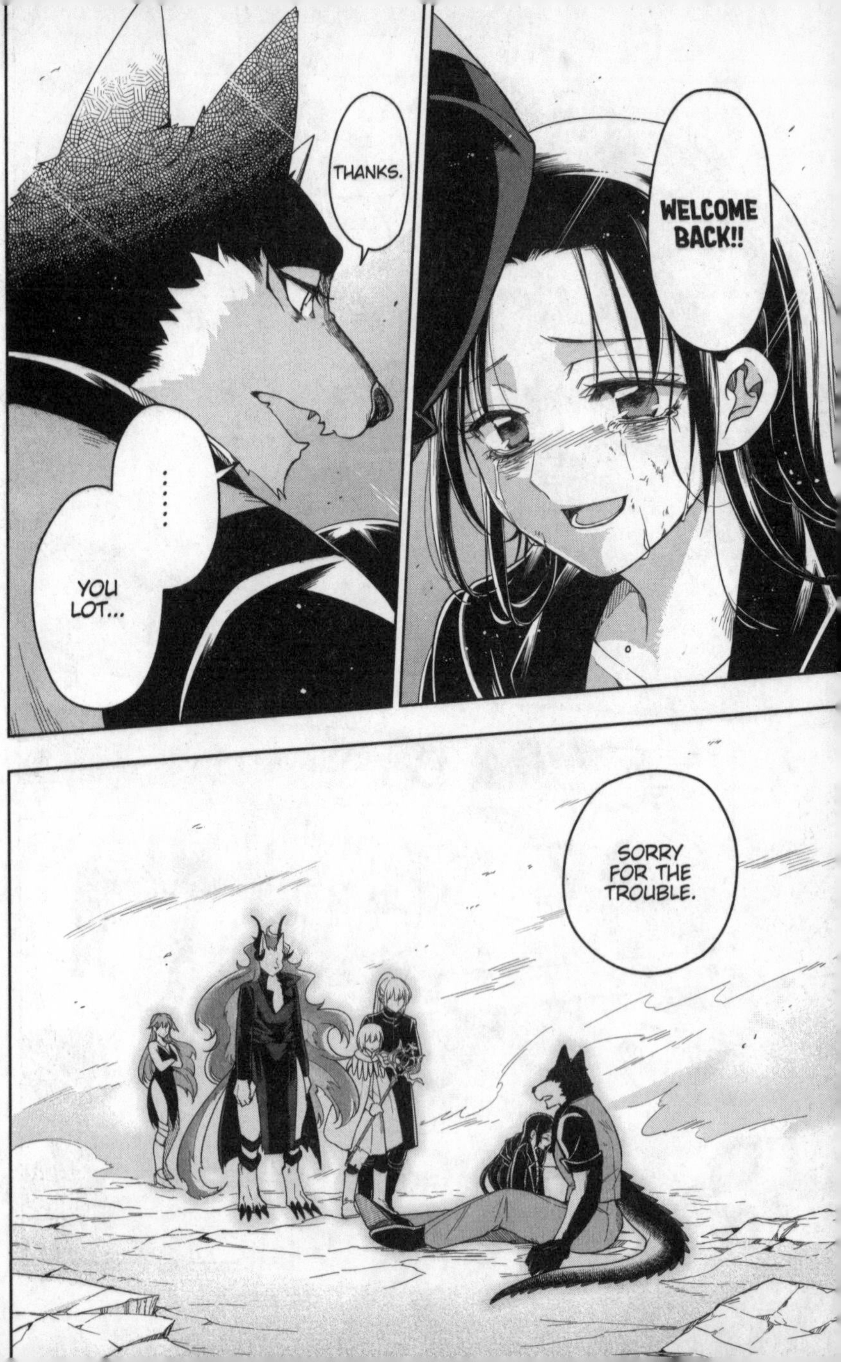
WELCOME BACK!!
THANKS.
..... YOU LOT...
SORRY FOR THE TROUBLE.

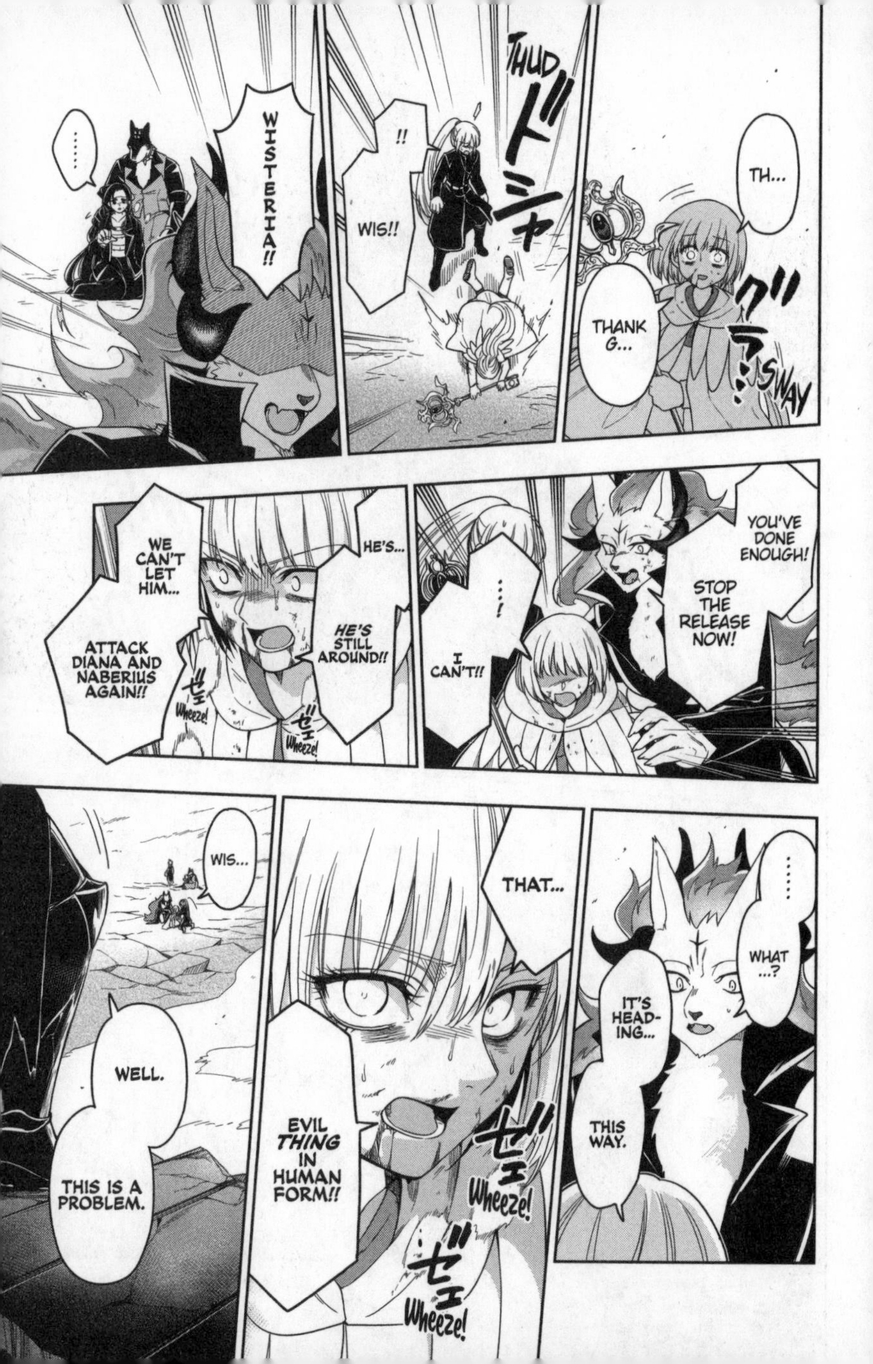
TH...
THANK G...
SWAY
THUD
!!
WIS!!
WISTERIA!!
......
YOU'VE DONE ENOUGH!
STOP THE RELEASE NOW!
...!
I CAN'T!!
HE'S...
HE'S STILL AROUND!!
WE CAN'T LET HIM...
ATTACK DIANA AND NABERIUS AGAIN!!
Wheeze!
Wheeze!
......
WHAT ...?
IT'S HEAD-ING...
THIS WAY.
THAT...
EVIL *THING* IN HUMAN FORM!!
Wheeze!
Wheeze!
WIS...
WELL.
THIS IS A PROBLEM.

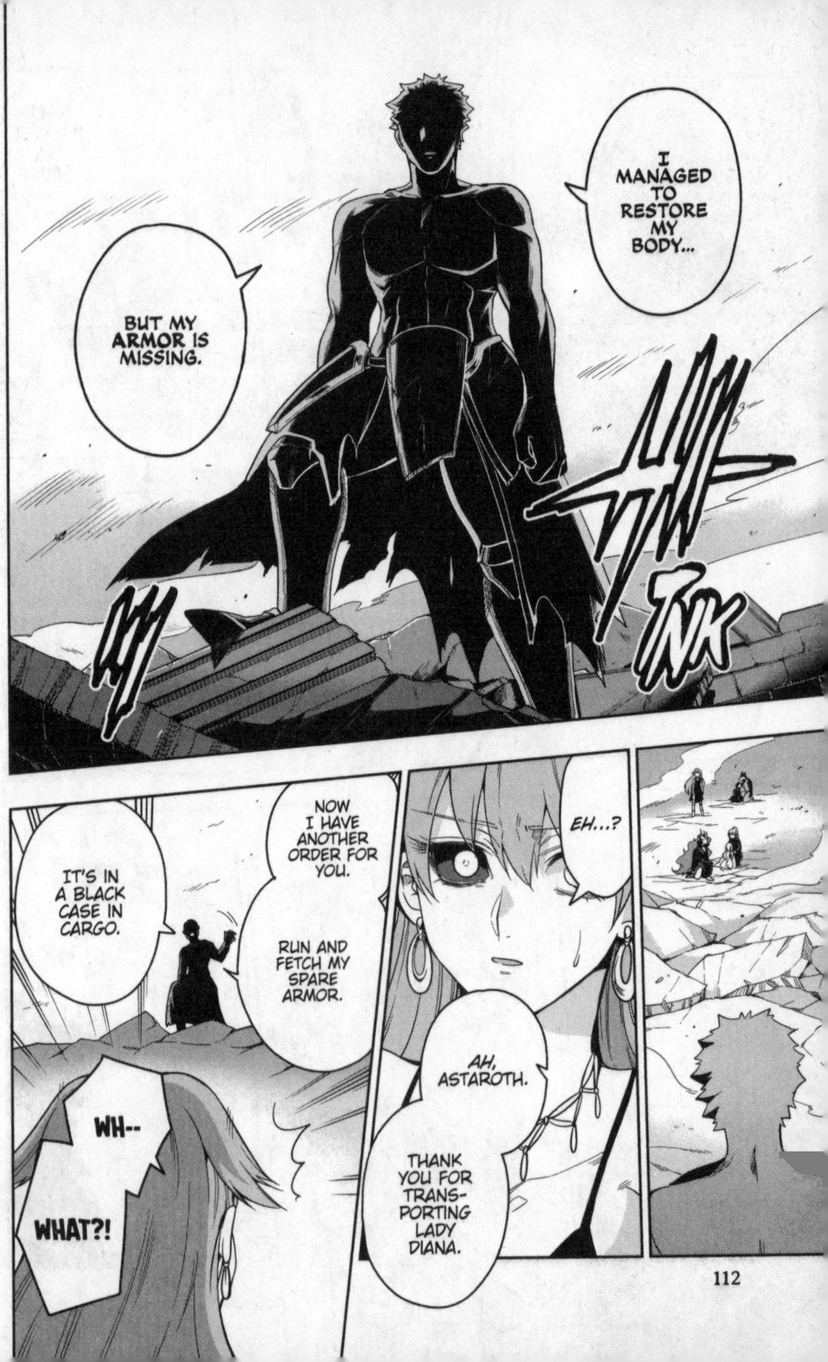

I MANAGED TO RESTORE MY BODY...
BUT MY ARMOR IS MISSING.
EH...?
AH, ASTAROTH.
THANK YOU FOR TRANS-PORTING LADY DIANA.
NOW I HAVE ANOTHER ORDER FOR YOU.
RUN AND FETCH MY SPARE ARMOR.
IT'S IN A BLACK CASE IN CARGO.
WH--
WHAT?!

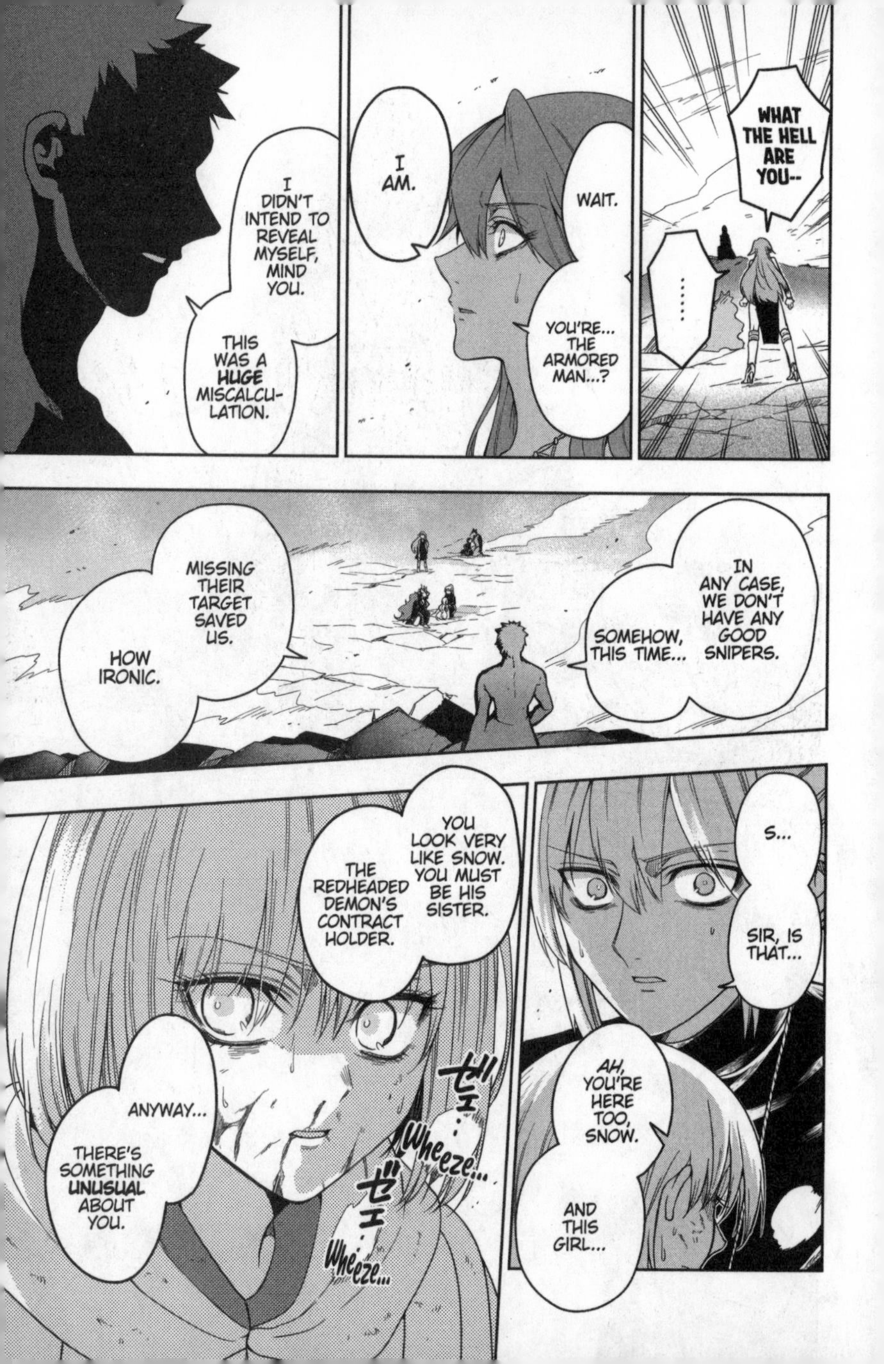
WHAT THE HELL ARE YOU--
......
WAIT.
YOU'RE... THE ARMORED MAN...?
I AM.
I DIDN'T INTEND TO REVEAL MYSELF, MIND YOU.
THIS WAS A HUGE MISCALCULATION.
IN ANY CASE, WE DON'T HAVE ANY GOOD SNIPERS.
SOMEHOW, THIS TIME...
MISSING THEIR TARGET SAVED US.
HOW IRONIC.
S...
SIR, IS THAT...
AH, YOU'RE HERE TOO, SNOW.
AND THIS GIRL...
YOU LOOK VERY LIKE SNOW. YOU MUST BE HIS SISTER.
THE REDHEADED DEMON'S CONTRACT HOLDER.
ゼェ… Wheeze...
ゼェ… Wheeze...
ANYWAY...
THERE'S SOMETHING UNUSUAL ABOUT YOU.

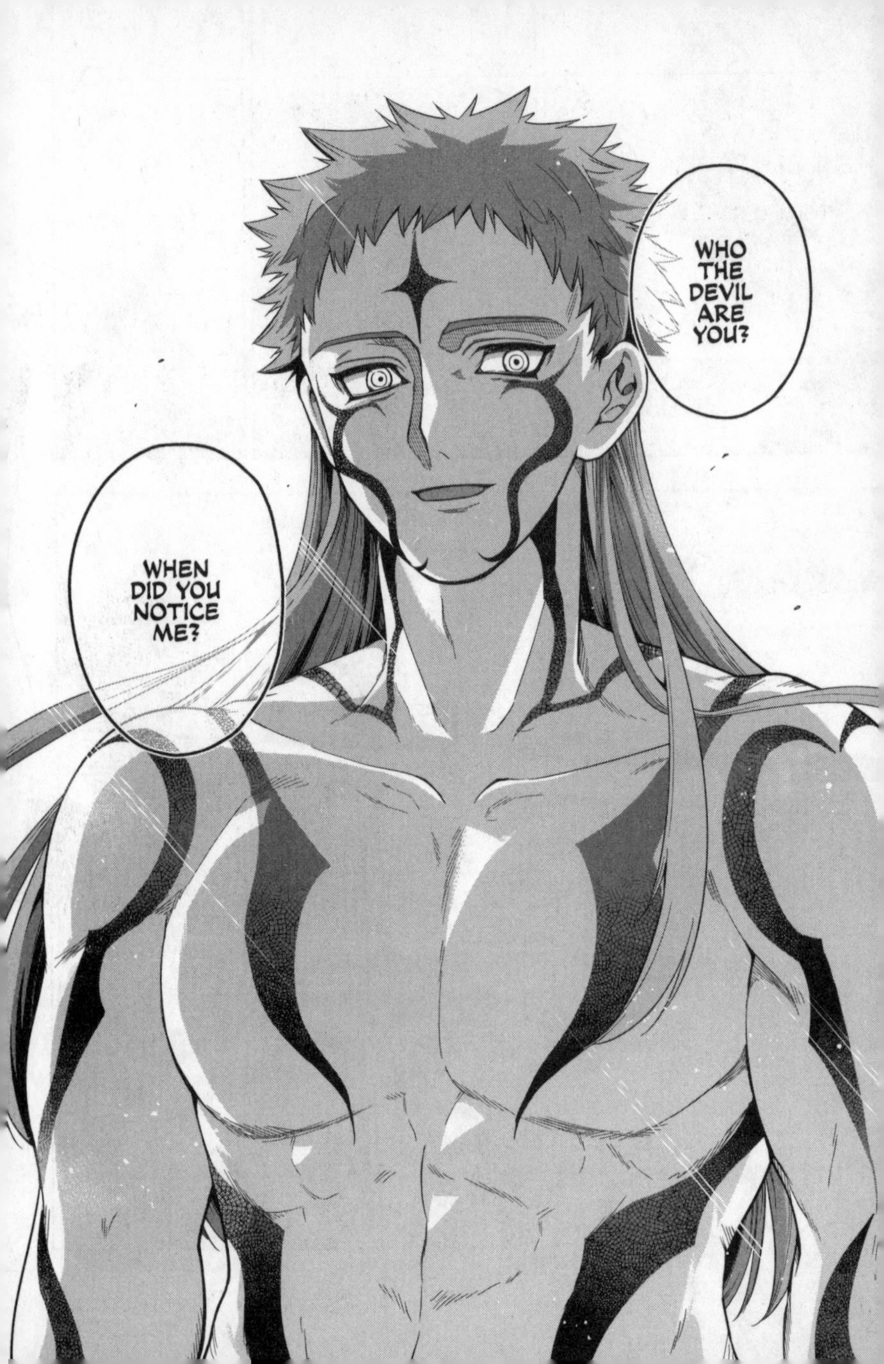
WHO THE DEVIL ARE YOU?
WHEN DID YOU NOTICE ME?

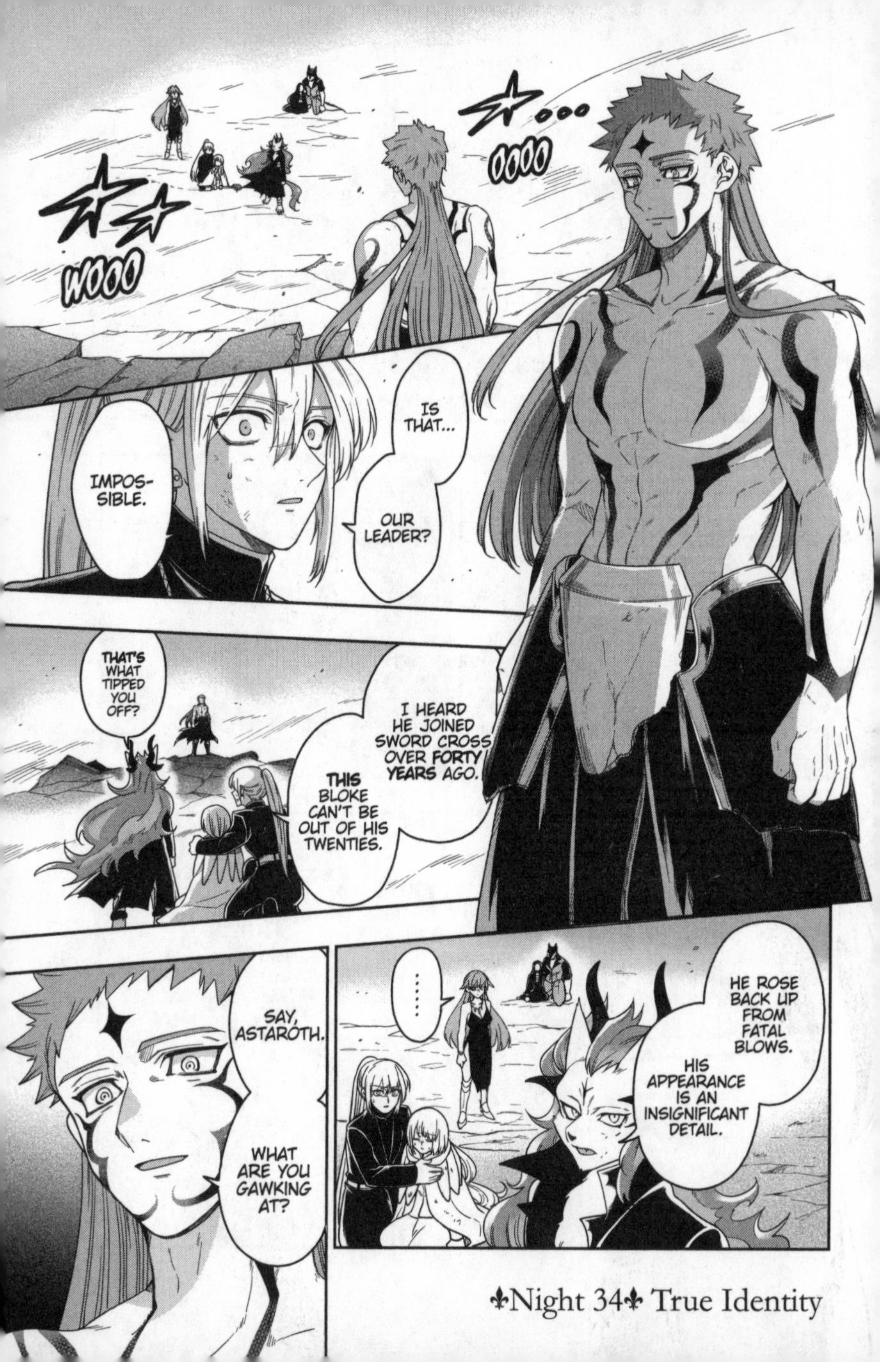

OOO
OOOO
WOOO
IS THAT...
OUR LEADER?
IMPOSSIBLE.
I HEARD HE JOINED SWORD CROSS OVER FORTY YEARS AGO.
THIS BLOKE CAN'T BE OUT OF HIS TWENTIES.
THAT'S WHAT TIPPED YOU OFF?
HE ROSE BACK UP FROM FATAL BLOWS.
HIS APPEARANCE IS AN INSIGNIFICANT DETAIL.
......
SAY, ASTAROTH.
WHAT ARE YOU GAWKING AT?

⚜Night 34⚜ True Identity

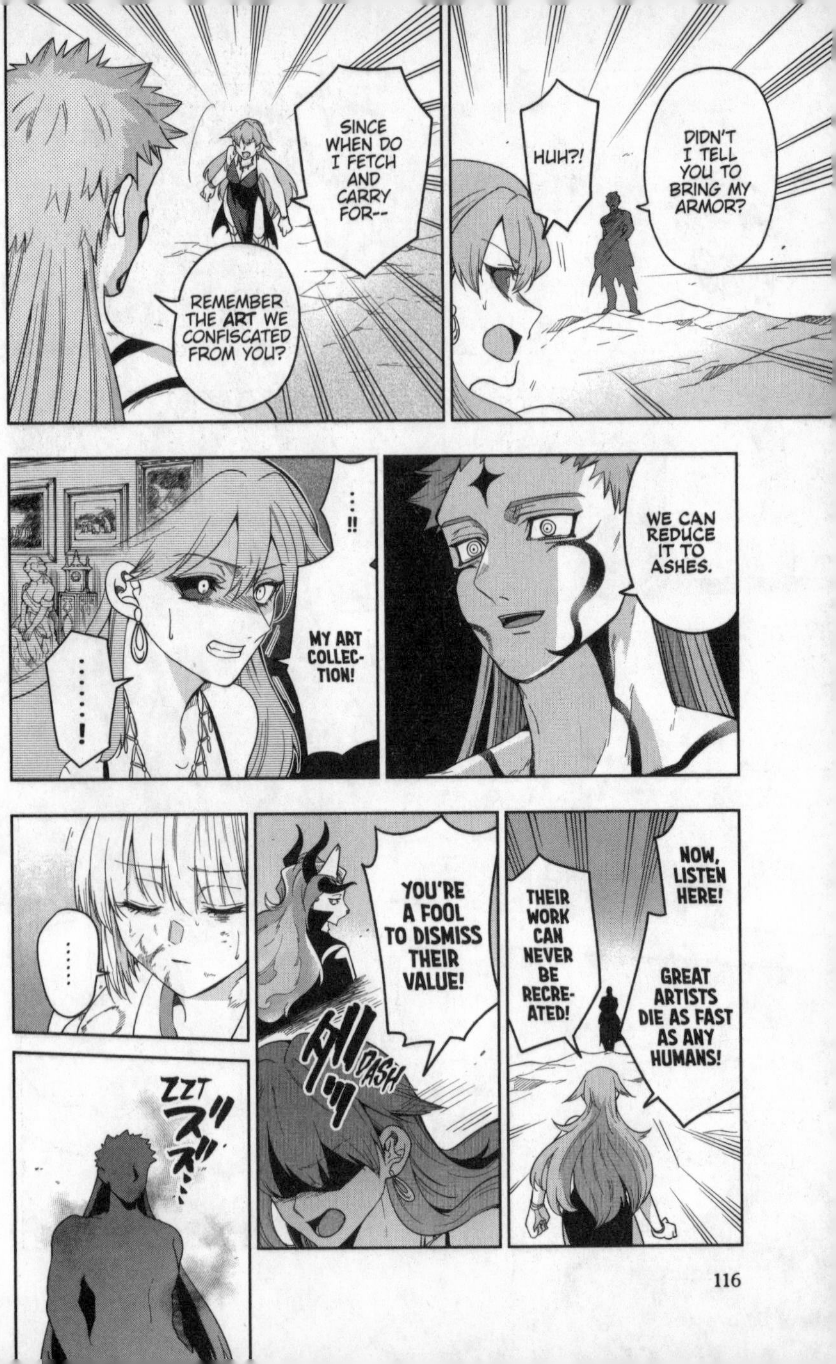
DIDN'T I TELL YOU TO BRING MY ARMOR?
HUH?!
SINCE WHEN DO I FETCH AND CARRY FOR--
REMEMBER THE ART WE CONFISCATED FROM YOU?
WE CAN REDUCE IT TO ASHES.
...!!
MY ART COLLECTION!
......!
NOW, LISTEN HERE!
THEIR WORK CAN NEVER BE RECREATED!
GREAT ARTISTS DIE AS FAST AS ANY HUMANS!
YOU'RE A FOOL TO DISMISS THEIR VALUE!
DASH
......
ZZT

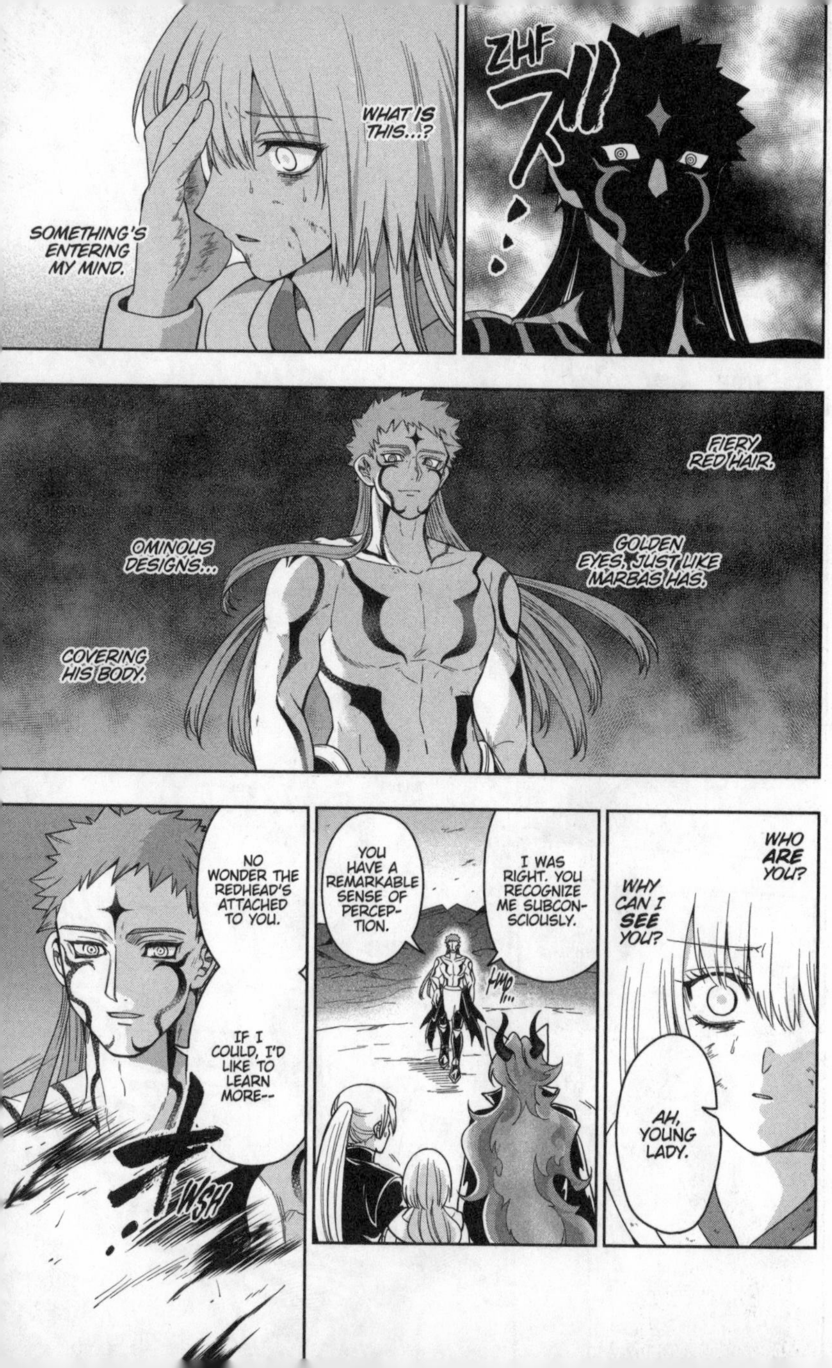
ZHF
WHAT IS THIS...?
SOMETHING'S ENTERING MY MIND.
FIERY RED HAIR.
GOLDEN EYES, JUST LIKE MARBAS HAS.
OMINOUS DESIGNS...
COVERING HIS BODY.
WHO ARE YOU?
WHY CAN I SEE YOU?
AH, YOUNG LADY.
I WAS RIGHT. YOU RECOGNIZE ME SUBCONSCIOUSLY.
YOU HAVE A REMARKABLE SENSE OF PERCEPTION.
NO WONDER THE REDHEAD'S ATTACHED TO YOU.
IF I COULD, I'D LIKE TO LEARN MORE--
WSH

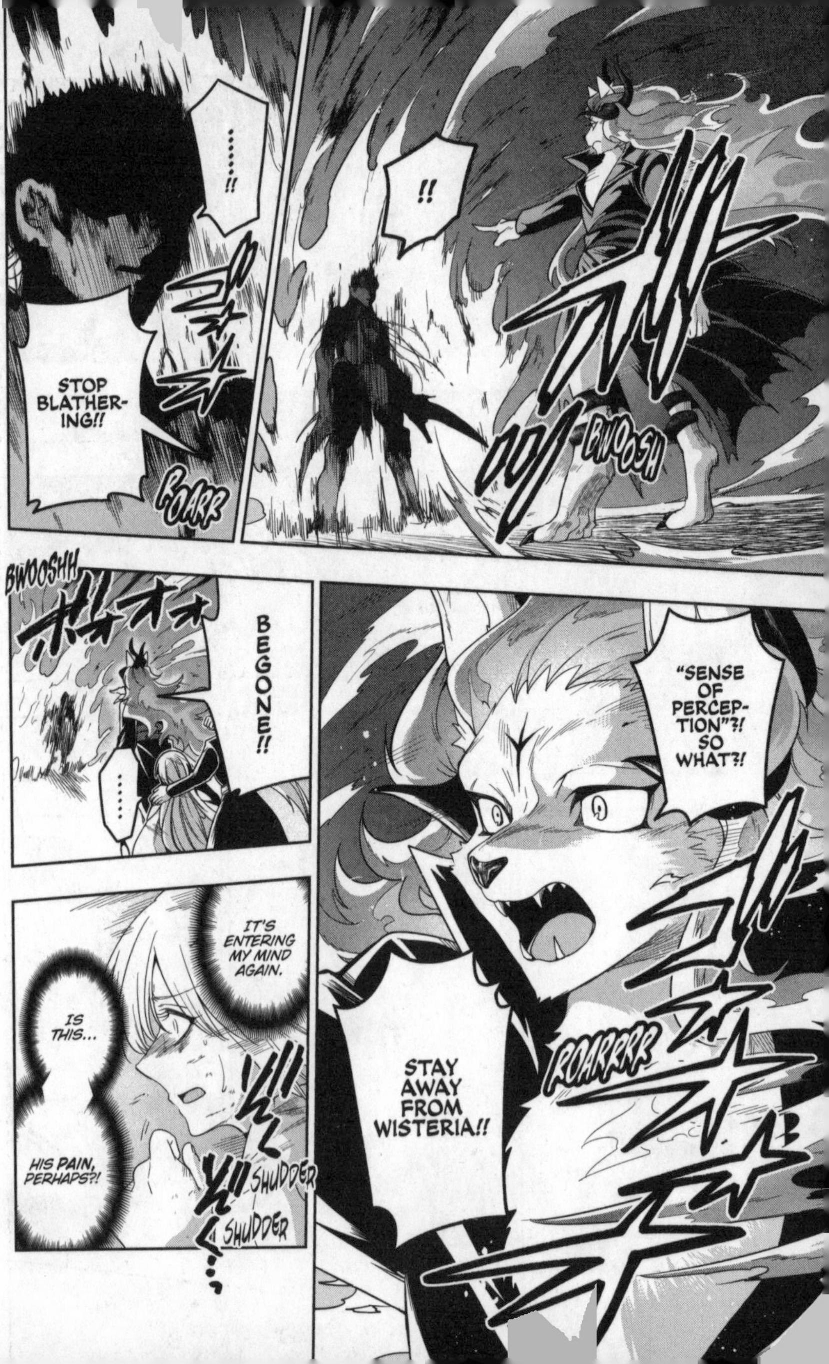
!!
BWOOSH
......!!
STOP BLATHER-ING!!
ROARR
"SENSE OF PERCEP-TION"?! SO WHAT?!
STAY AWAY FROM WISTERIA!!
ROARRRR
BWOOSHH
BEGONE!!
......
IT'S ENTERING MY MIND AGAIN.
IS THIS...
HIS PAIN, PERHAPS?!
SHUDDER
SHUDDER

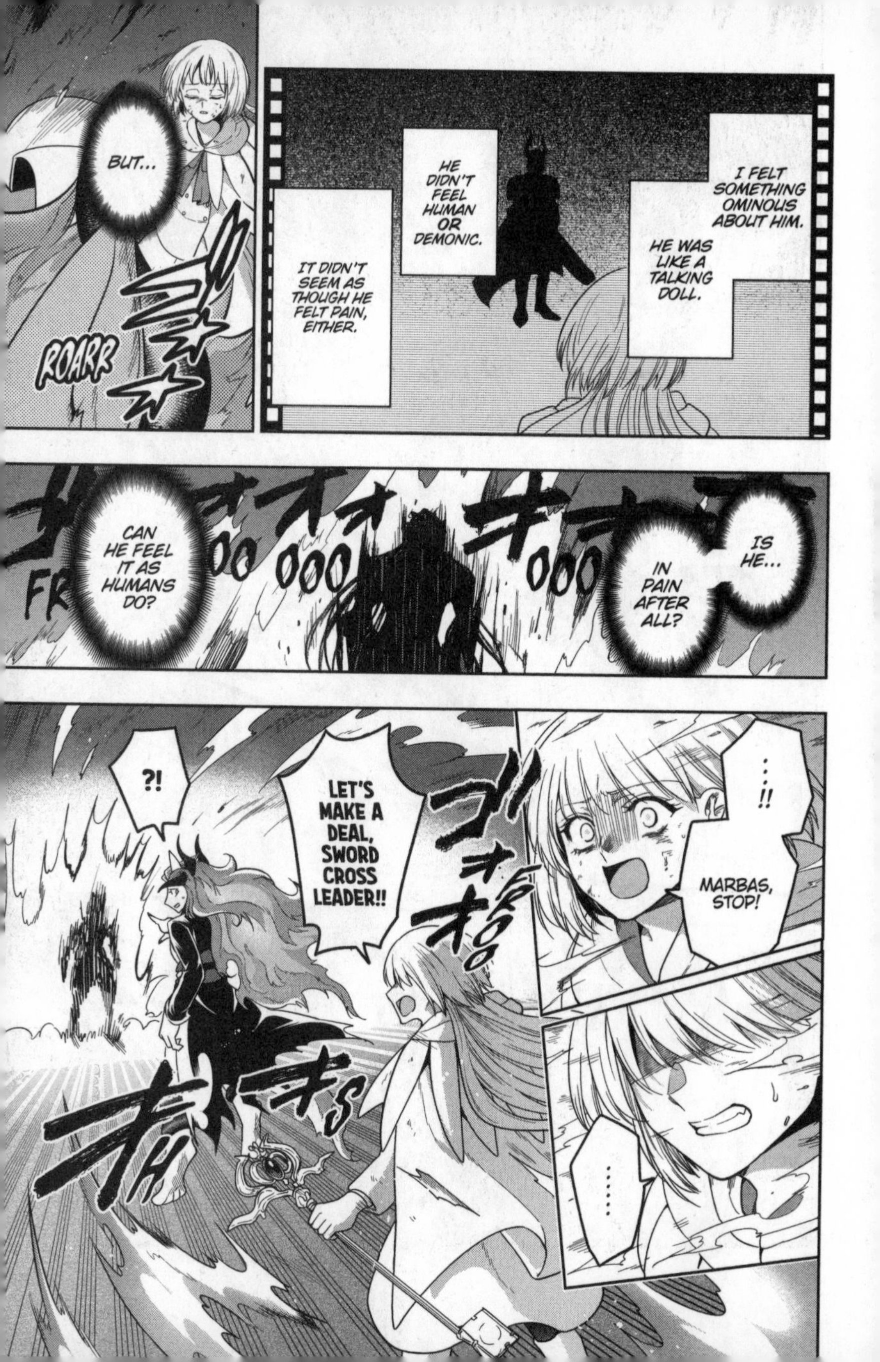
I FELT SOMETHING OMINOUS ABOUT HIM.
HE WAS LIKE A TALKING DOLL.
HE DIDN'T FEEL HUMAN OR DEMONIC.
IT DIDN'T SEEM AS THOUGH HE FELT PAIN, EITHER.
BUT...
ROARR
IS HE...
IN PAIN AFTER ALL?
OOO
OO OOO
FR
CAN HE FEEL IT AS HUMANS DO?
...!!
MARBAS, STOP!
......
LET'S MAKE A DEAL, SWORD CROSS LEADER!!
?!

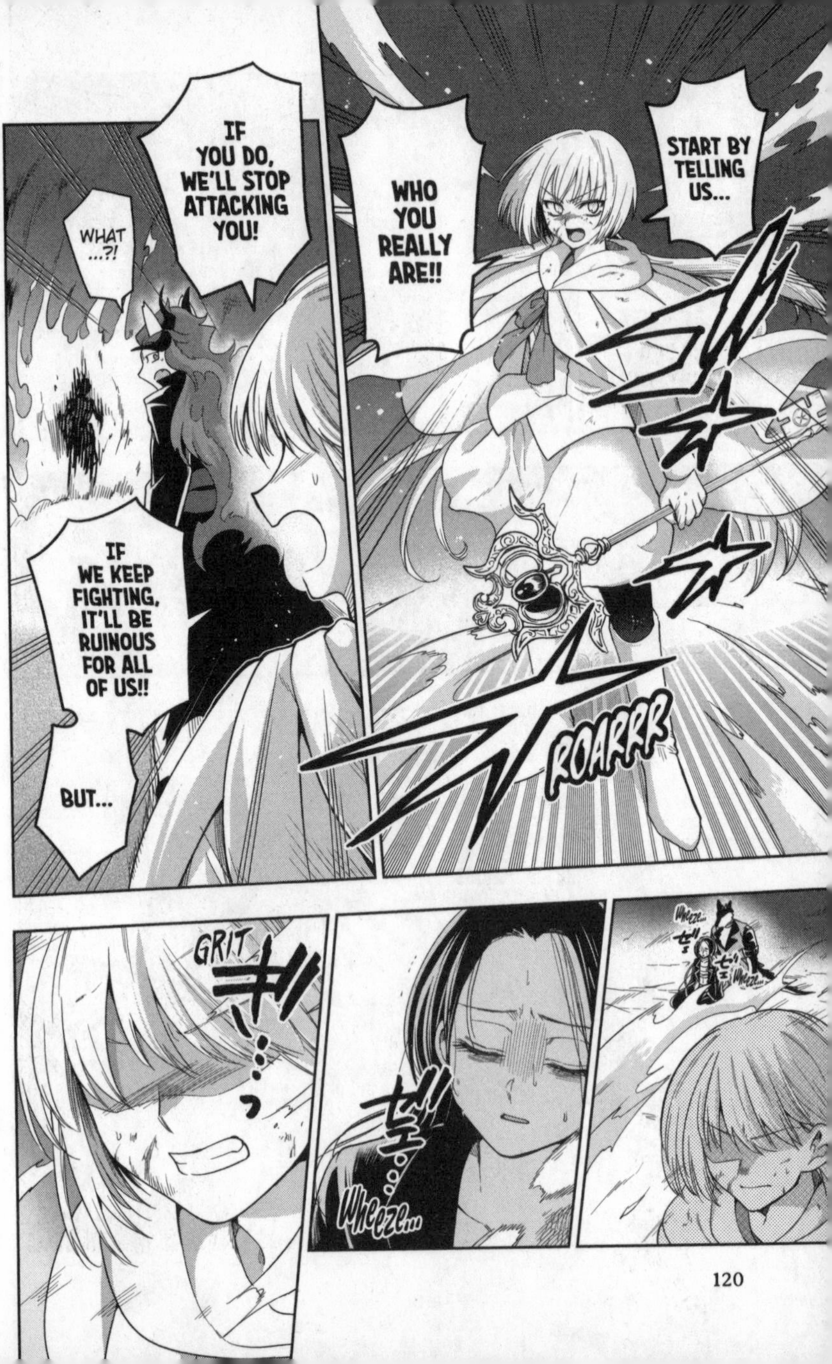
START BY TELLING US...
WHO YOU REALLY ARE!!
ROARRR
IF YOU DO, WE'LL STOP ATTACKING YOU!
WHAT ...?!
IF WE KEEP FIGHTING, IT'LL BE RUINOUS FOR ALL OF US!!
BUT...
Wheeze...
Wheeze...
Wheeze...
GRIT

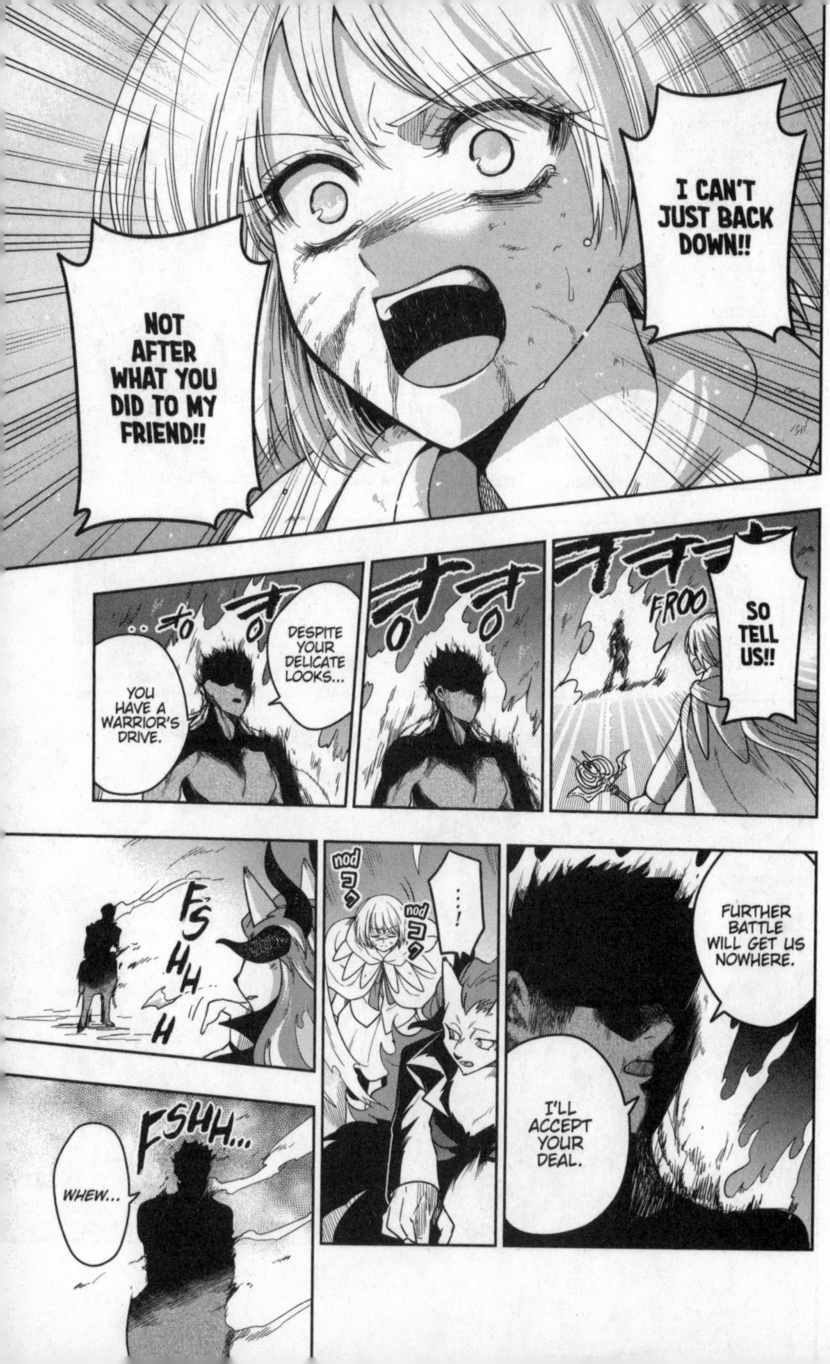
I CAN'T JUST BACK DOWN!!
NOT AFTER WHAT YOU DID TO MY FRIEND!!
FROO
SO TELL US!!
DESPITE YOUR DELICATE LOOKS...
YOU HAVE A WARRIOR'S DRIVE.
FURTHER BATTLE WILL GET US NOWHERE.
I'LL ACCEPT YOUR DEAL.
nod
nod
...!
FSHHH...
FSHH...
WHEW...

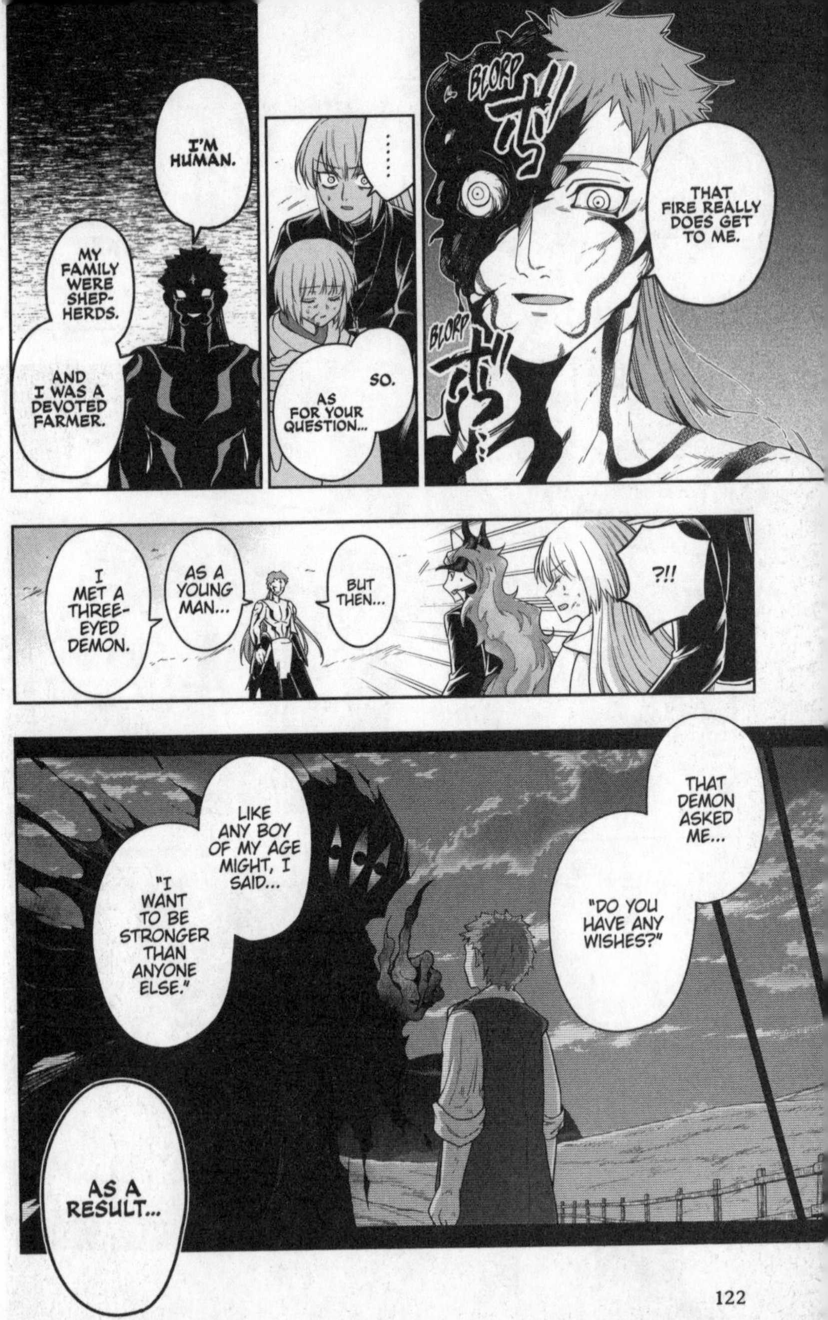
BLORP
THAT FIRE REALLY DOES GET TO ME.
BLORP
......
SO.
AS FOR YOUR QUESTION...
I'M HUMAN.
MY FAMILY WERE SHEPHERDS.
AND I WAS A DEVOTED FARMER.
?!!
BUT THEN...
AS A YOUNG MAN...
I MET A THREE-EYED DEMON.
THAT DEMON ASKED ME...
"DO YOU HAVE ANY WISHES?"
LIKE ANY BOY OF MY AGE MIGHT, I SAID...
"I WANT TO BE STRONGER THAN ANYONE ELSE."
AS A RESULT...

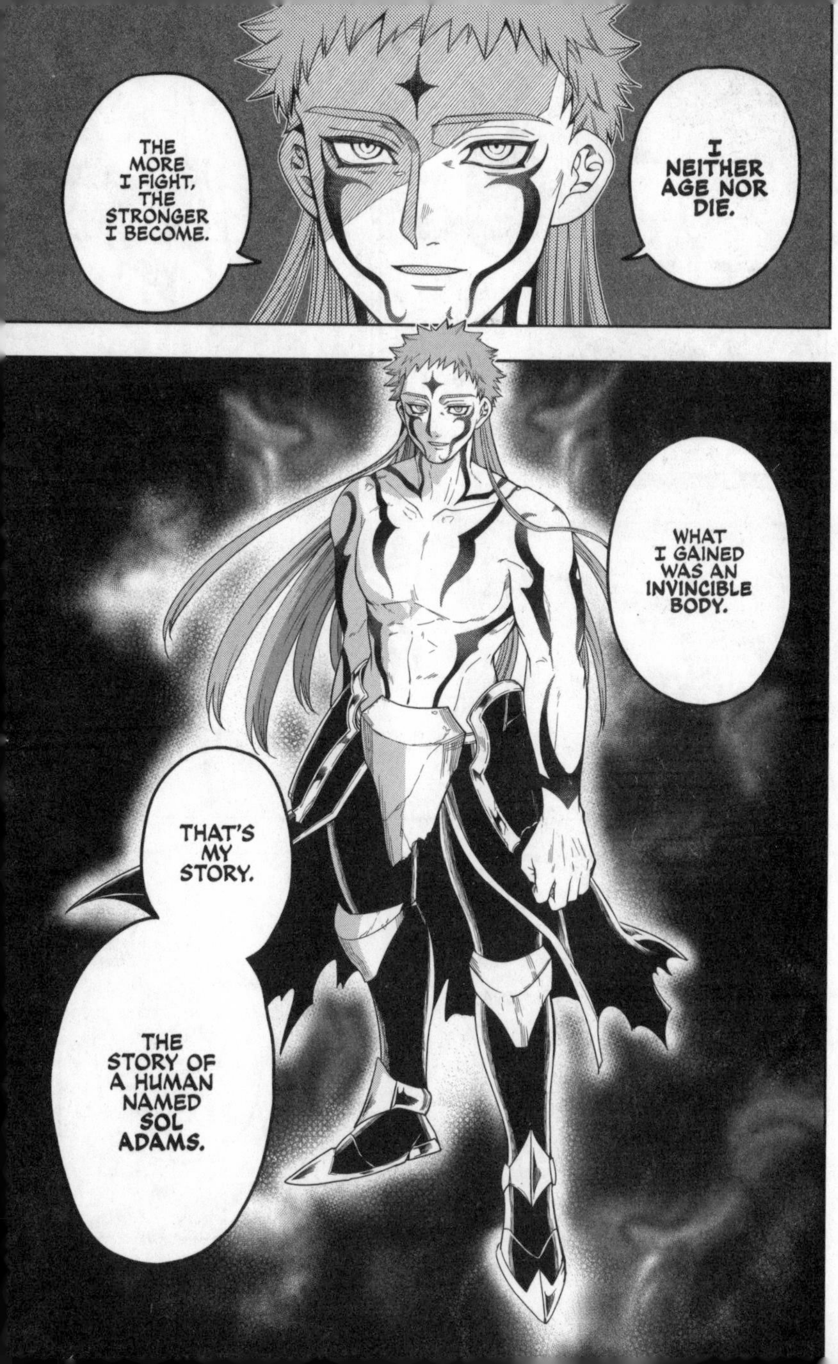
I NEITHER AGE NOR DIE.
THE MORE I FIGHT, THE STRONGER I BECOME.
WHAT I GAINED WAS AN INVINCIBLE BODY.
THAT'S MY STORY.
THE STORY OF A HUMAN NAMED SOL ADAMS.

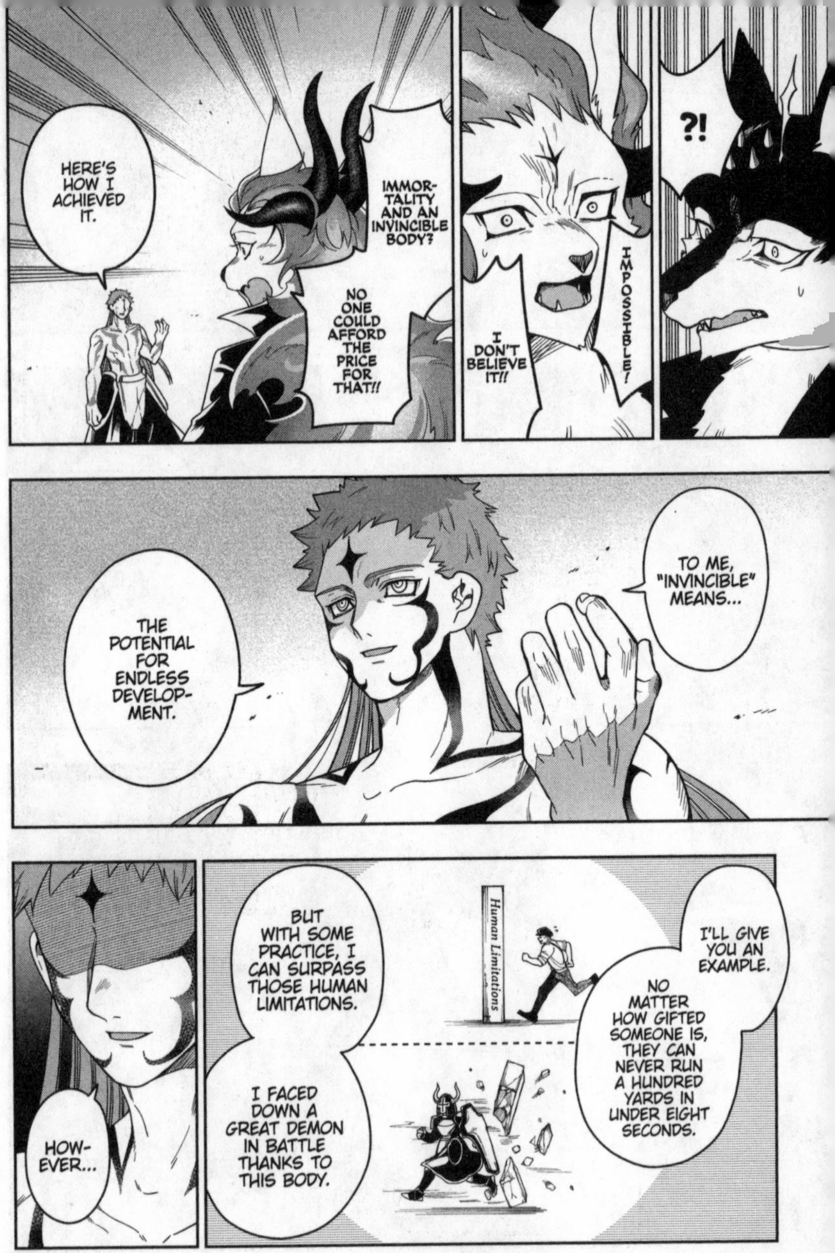
?!
IMPOSSIBLE!
I DON'T BELIEVE IT!!
IMMORTALITY AND AN INVINCIBLE BODY?
NO ONE COULD AFFORD THE PRICE FOR THAT!!
HERE'S HOW I ACHIEVED IT.
TO ME, "INVINCIBLE" MEANS...
THE POTENTIAL FOR ENDLESS DEVELOPMENT.
I'LL GIVE YOU AN EXAMPLE.
NO MATTER HOW GIFTED SOMEONE IS, THEY CAN NEVER RUN A HUNDRED YARDS IN UNDER EIGHT SECONDS.
Human Limitations
BUT WITH SOME PRACTICE, I CAN SURPASS THOSE HUMAN LIMITATIONS.
I FACED DOWN A GREAT DEMON IN BATTLE THANKS TO THIS BODY.
HOWEVER...

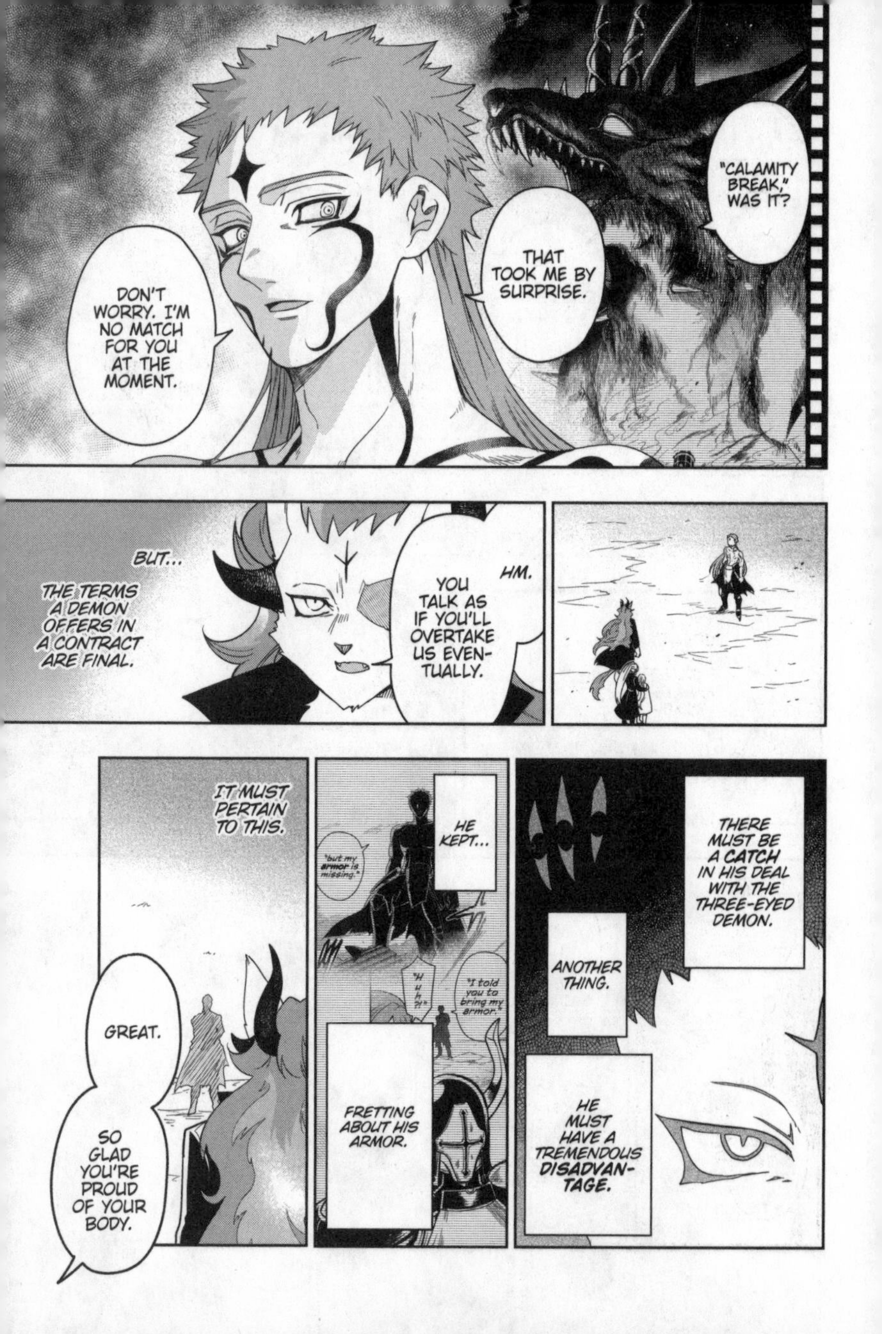
"CALAMITY BREAK," WAS IT?
THAT TOOK ME BY SURPRISE.
DON'T WORRY. I'M NO MATCH FOR YOU AT THE MOMENT.
HM.
YOU TALK AS IF YOU'LL OVERTAKE US EVENTUALLY.
BUT...
THE TERMS A DEMON OFFERS IN A CONTRACT ARE FINAL.
THERE MUST BE A CATCH IN HIS DEAL WITH THE THREE-EYED DEMON.
ANOTHER THING.
HE MUST HAVE A TREMENDOUS DISADVANTAGE.
HE KEPT...
"but my armor is missing."
"I told you to bring my armor."
"Huh?!"
FRETTING ABOUT HIS ARMOR.
IT MUST PERTAIN TO THIS.
GREAT.
SO GLAD YOU'RE PROUD OF YOUR BODY.

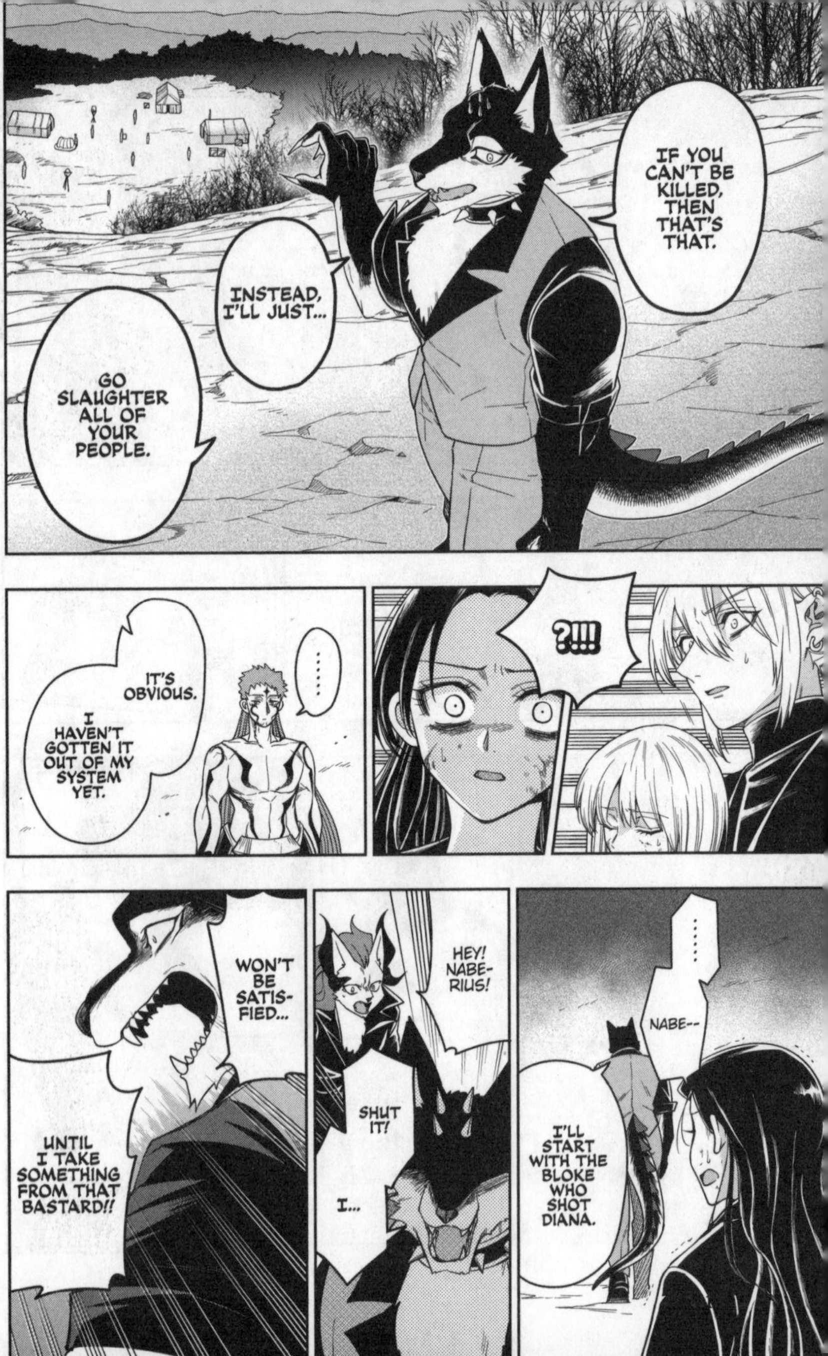
IF YOU CAN'T BE KILLED, THEN THAT'S THAT.
INSTEAD, I'LL JUST...
GO SLAUGHTER ALL OF YOUR PEOPLE.
?!!!
......
IT'S OBVIOUS. I HAVEN'T GOTTEN IT OUT OF MY SYSTEM YET.
......
NABE--
I'LL START WITH THE BLOKE WHO SHOT DIANA.
HEY! NABERIUS!
SHUT IT!
I...
WON'T BE SATISFIED...
UNTIL I TAKE SOMETHING FROM THAT BASTARD!!

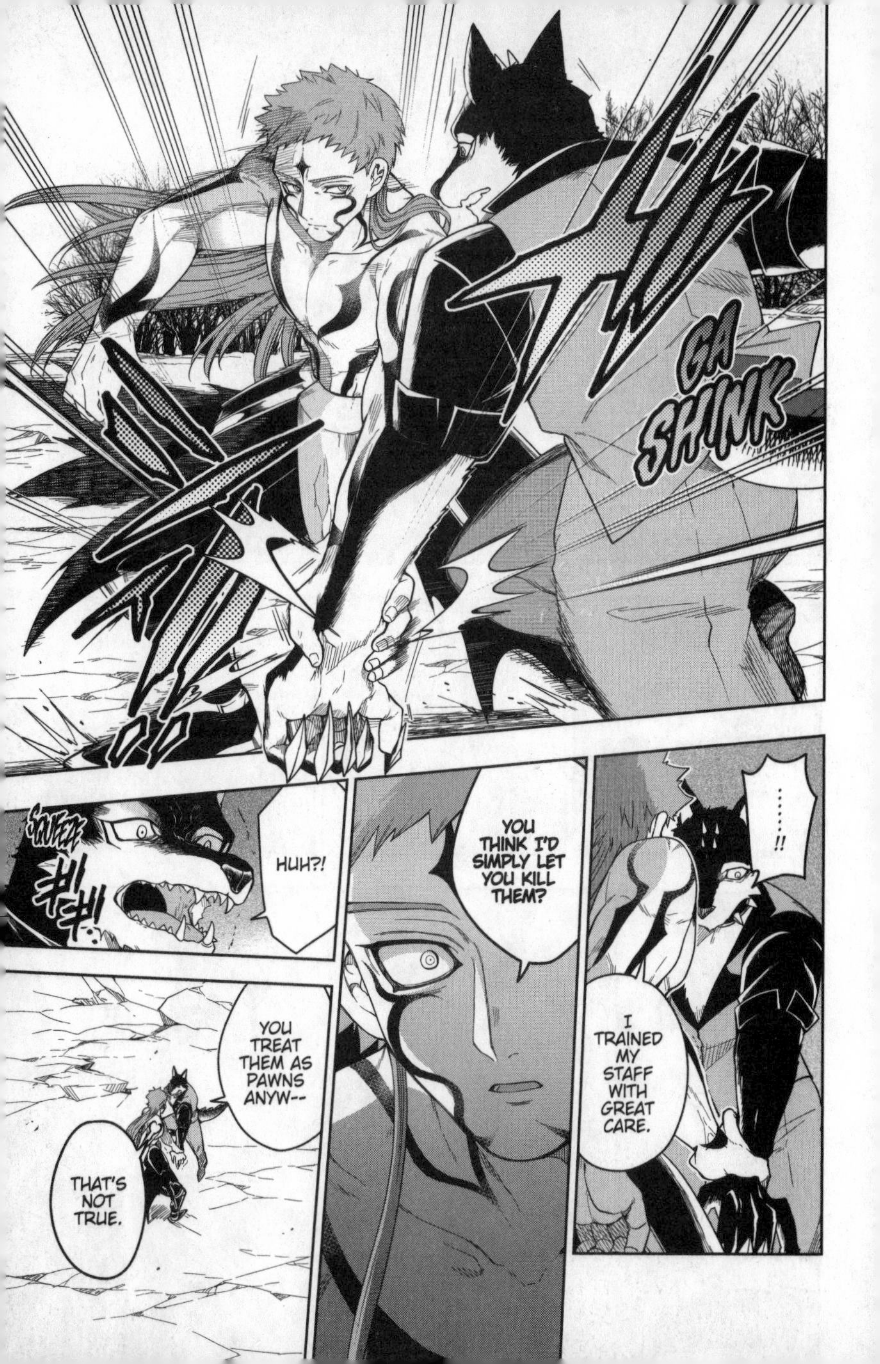
GA SHINK
......!!
I TRAINED MY STAFF WITH GREAT CARE.
YOU THINK I'D SIMPLY LET YOU KILL THEM?
SQUEEZE
HUH?!
YOU TREAT THEM AS PAWNS ANYW--
THAT'S NOT TRUE.

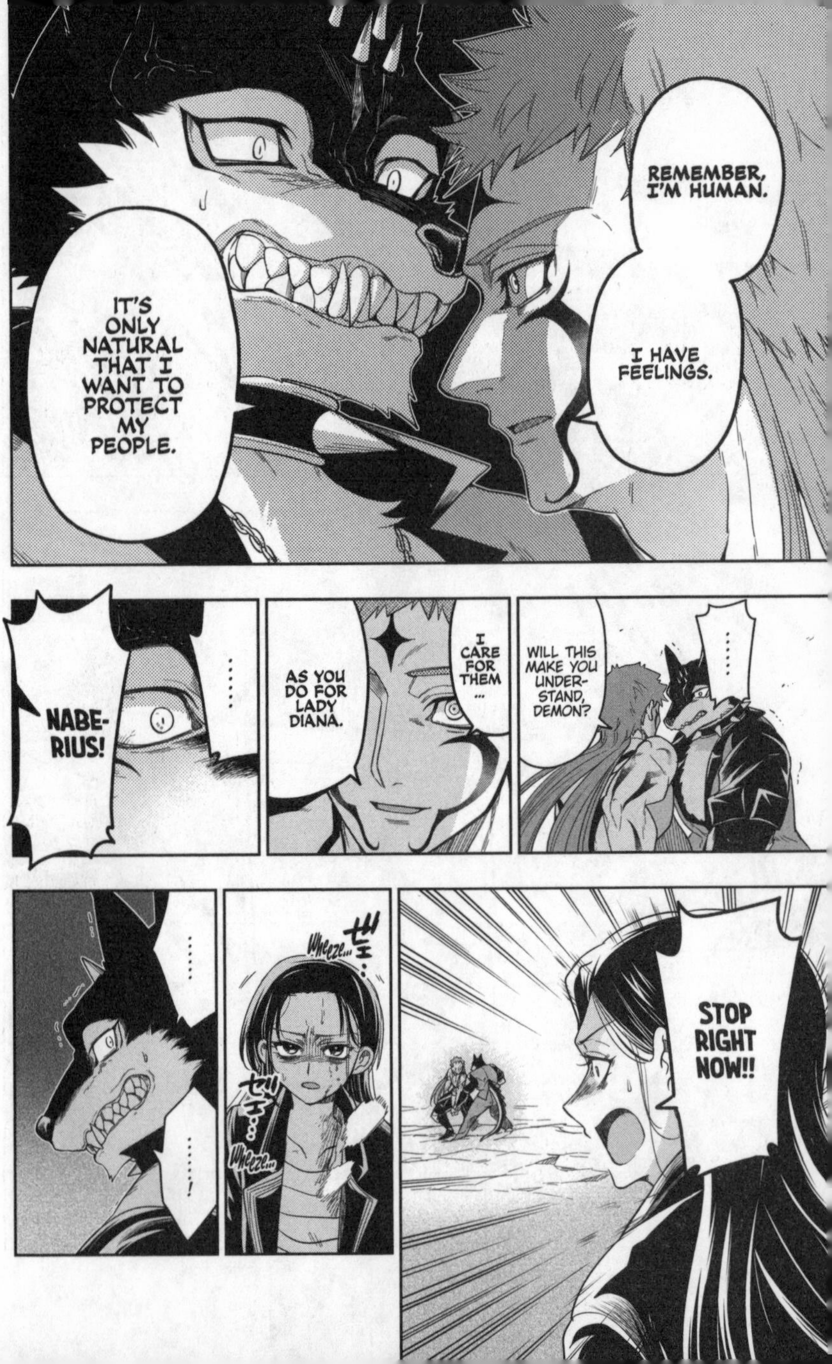

REMEMBER, I'M HUMAN.
I HAVE FEELINGS.
IT'S ONLY NATURAL THAT I WANT TO PROTECT MY PEOPLE.
......
WILL THIS MAKE YOU UNDER-STAND, DEMON?
I CARE FOR THEM...
AS YOU DO FOR LADY DIANA.
......
NABE-RIUS!
STOP RIGHT NOW!!
Wheeze...
Wheeze...
......
......!

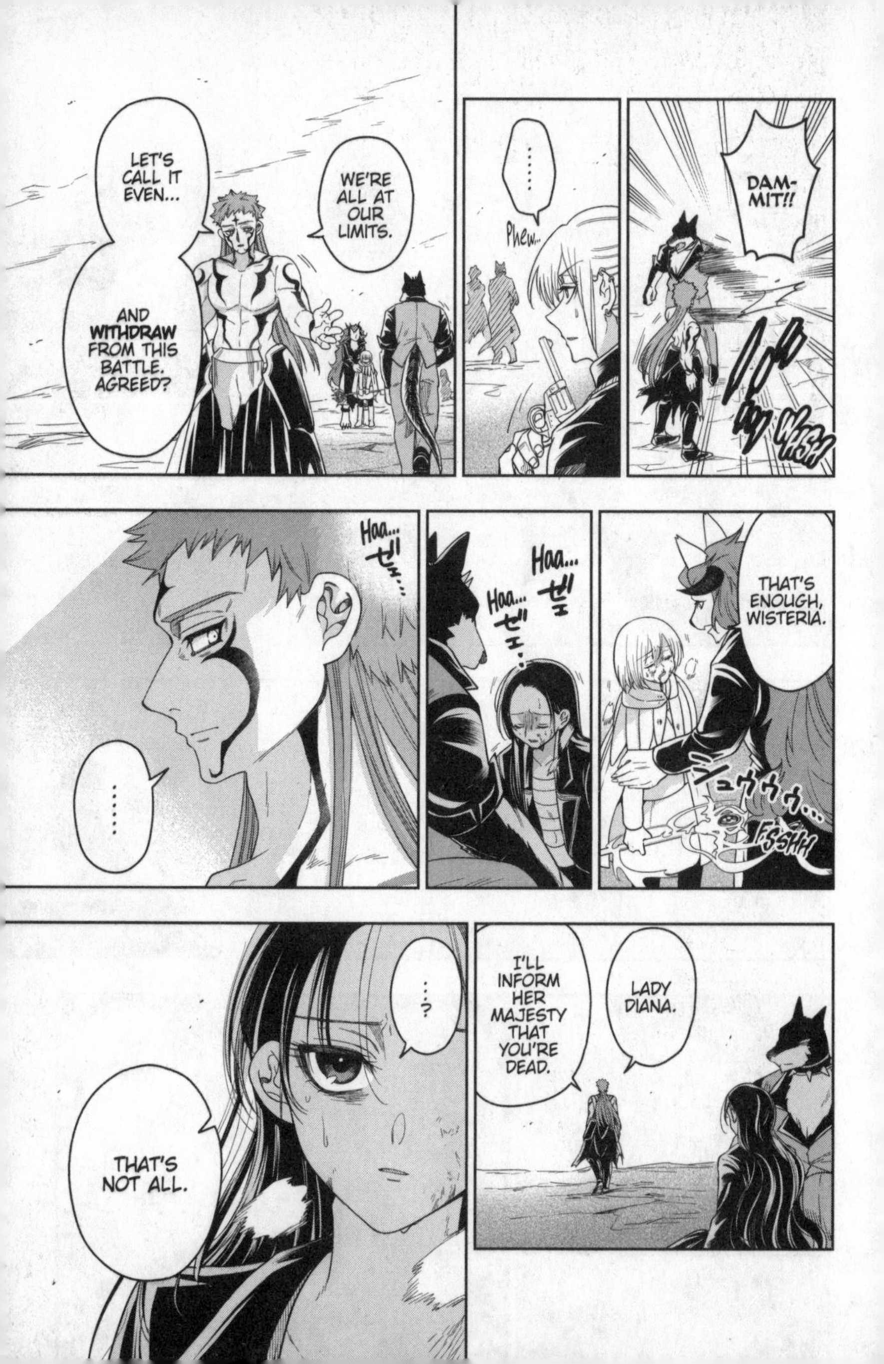
DAM-MIT!!
WHSH
......
Phew...
WE'RE ALL AT OUR LIMITS.
LET'S CALL IT EVEN...
AND WITHDRAW FROM THIS BATTLE. AGREED?
THAT'S ENOUGH, WISTERIA.
シュウウウ...
FSSHH
Haa... ゼェ
Haa... ゼェ...
Haa... ゼェ...
......
LADY DIANA.
I'LL INFORM HER MAJESTY THAT YOU'RE DEAD.
...?
THAT'S NOT ALL.

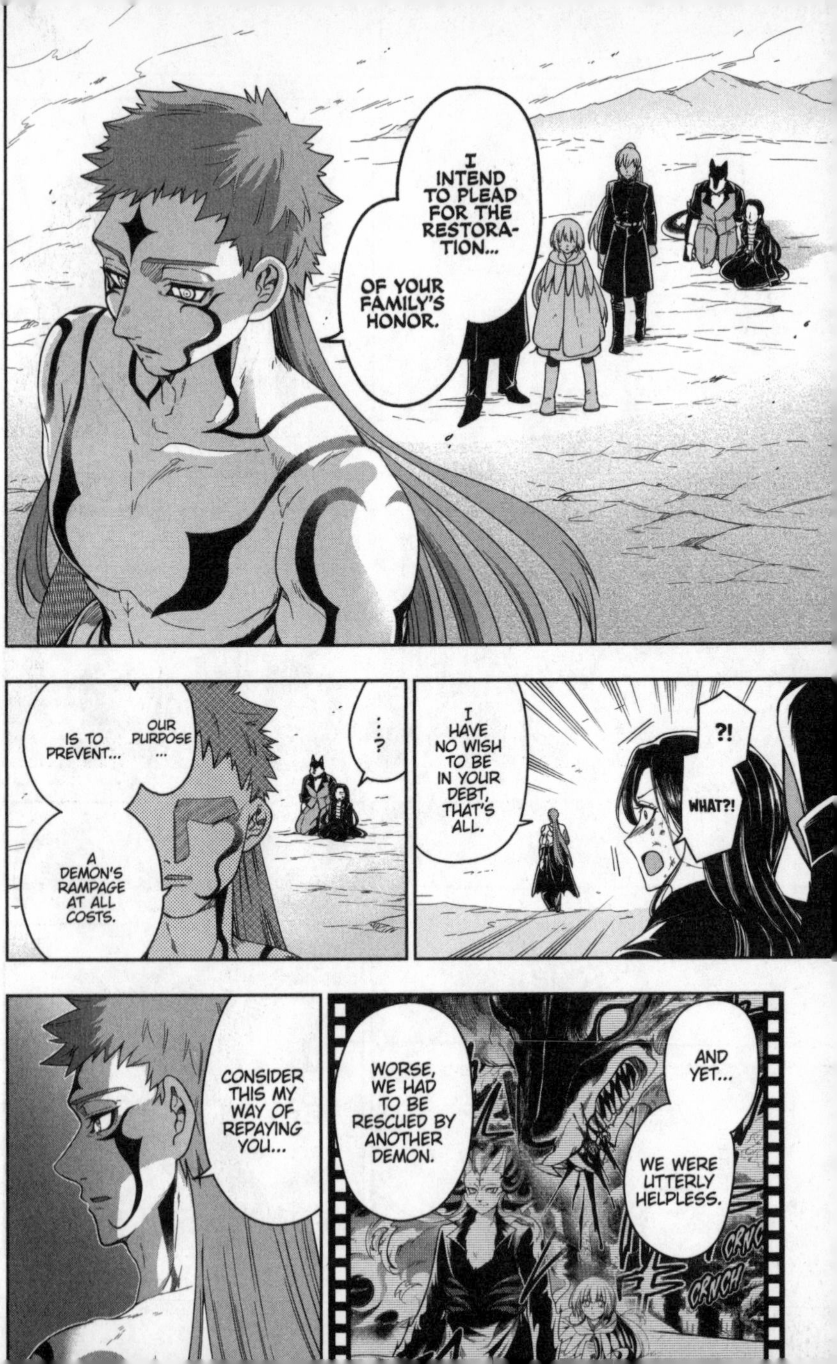

I INTEND TO PLEAD FOR THE RESTORATION...
OF YOUR FAMILY'S HONOR.
?!
WHAT?!
I HAVE NO WISH TO BE IN YOUR DEBT, THAT'S ALL.
...?
OUR PURPOSE ...
IS TO PREVENT...
A DEMON'S RAMPAGE AT ALL COSTS.
AND YET...
WE WERE UTTERLY HELPLESS.
WORSE, WE HAD TO BE RESCUED BY ANOTHER DEMON.
CRNCH
CONSIDER THIS MY WAY OF REPAYING YOU...

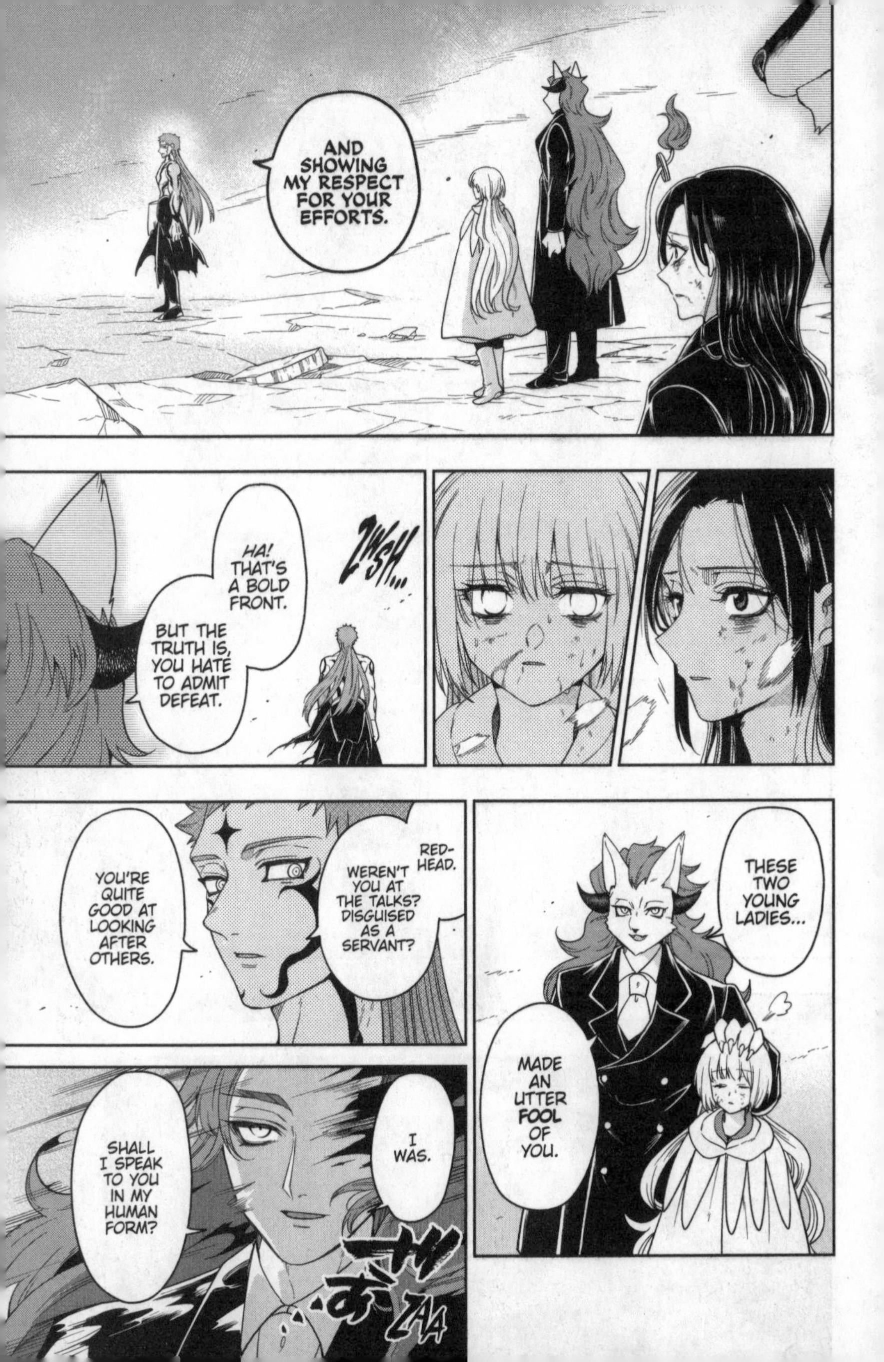
AND SHOWING MY RESPECT FOR YOUR EFFORTS.
ZWSH...
HA! THAT'S A BOLD FRONT.
BUT THE TRUTH IS, YOU HATE TO ADMIT DEFEAT.
THESE TWO YOUNG LADIES...
MADE AN UTTER FOOL OF YOU.
RED-HEAD.
WEREN'T YOU AT THE TALKS? DISGUISED AS A SERVANT?
YOU'RE QUITE GOOD AT LOOKING AFTER OTHERS.
I WAS.
SHALL I SPEAK TO YOU IN MY HUMAN FORM?
ZAA

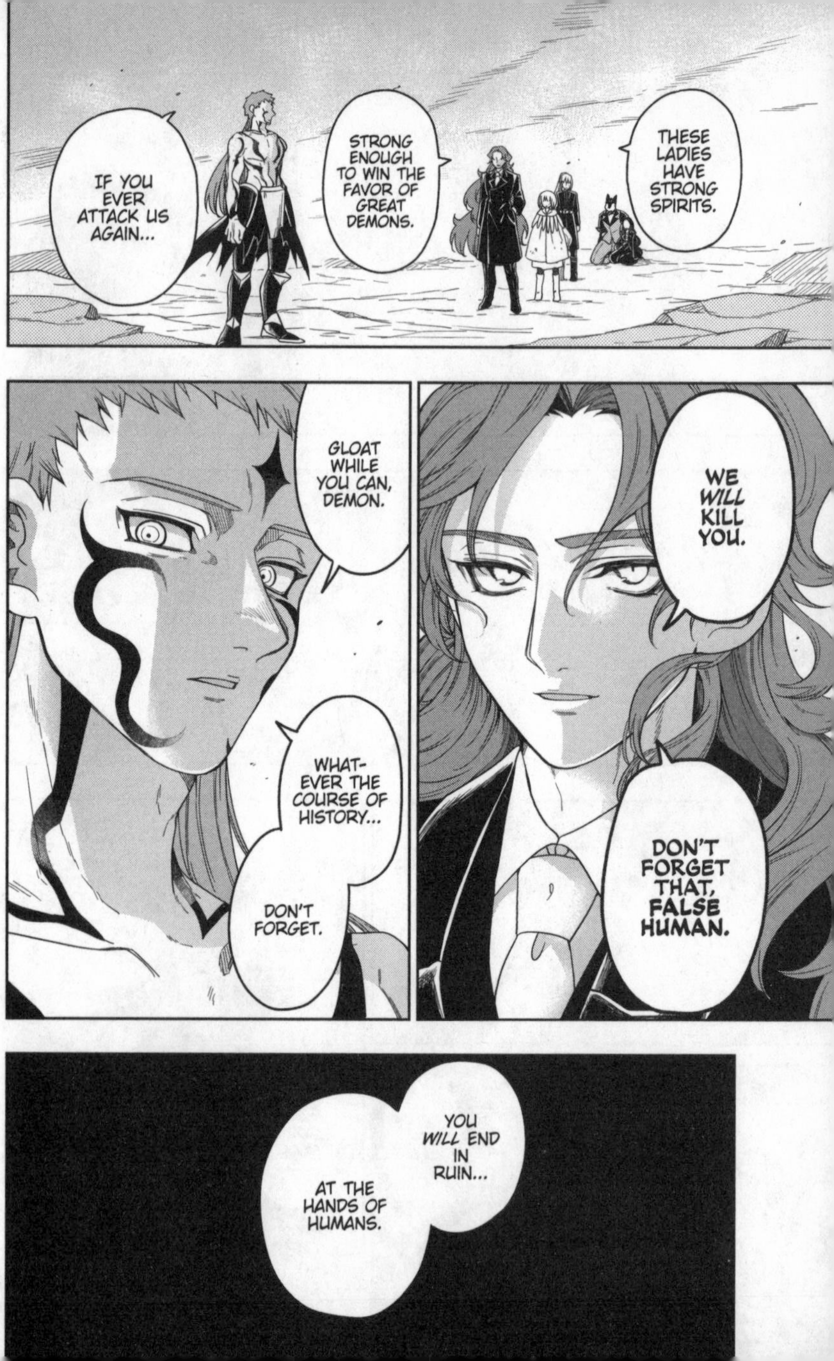
THESE LADIES HAVE STRONG SPIRITS.
STRONG ENOUGH TO WIN THE FAVOR OF GREAT DEMONS.
IF YOU EVER ATTACK US AGAIN...
WE *WILL* KILL YOU.
DON'T FORGET THAT, FALSE HUMAN.
GLOAT WHILE YOU CAN, DEMON.
WHAT-EVER THE COURSE OF HISTORY...
DON'T FORGET.
YOU *WILL* END IN RUIN...
AT THE HANDS OF HUMANS.

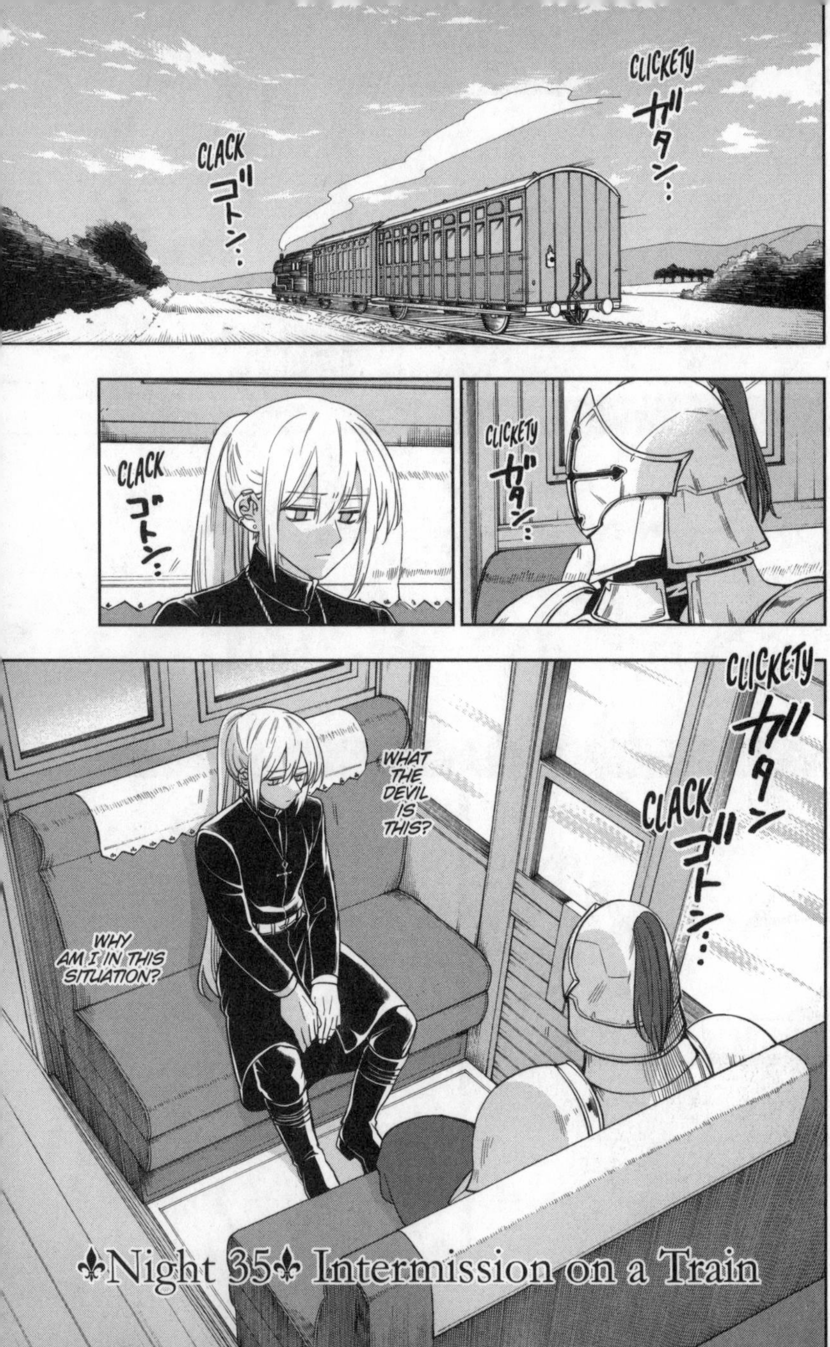
CLICKETY
ガタン…
CLACK
ゴトン…
CLICKETY
ガタン…
CLACK
ゴトン…
CLICKETY
ガタン
CLACK
ゴトン…
WHAT THE DEVIL IS THIS?
WHY AM I IN THIS SITUATION?

⚜Night 35⚜ Intermission on a Train

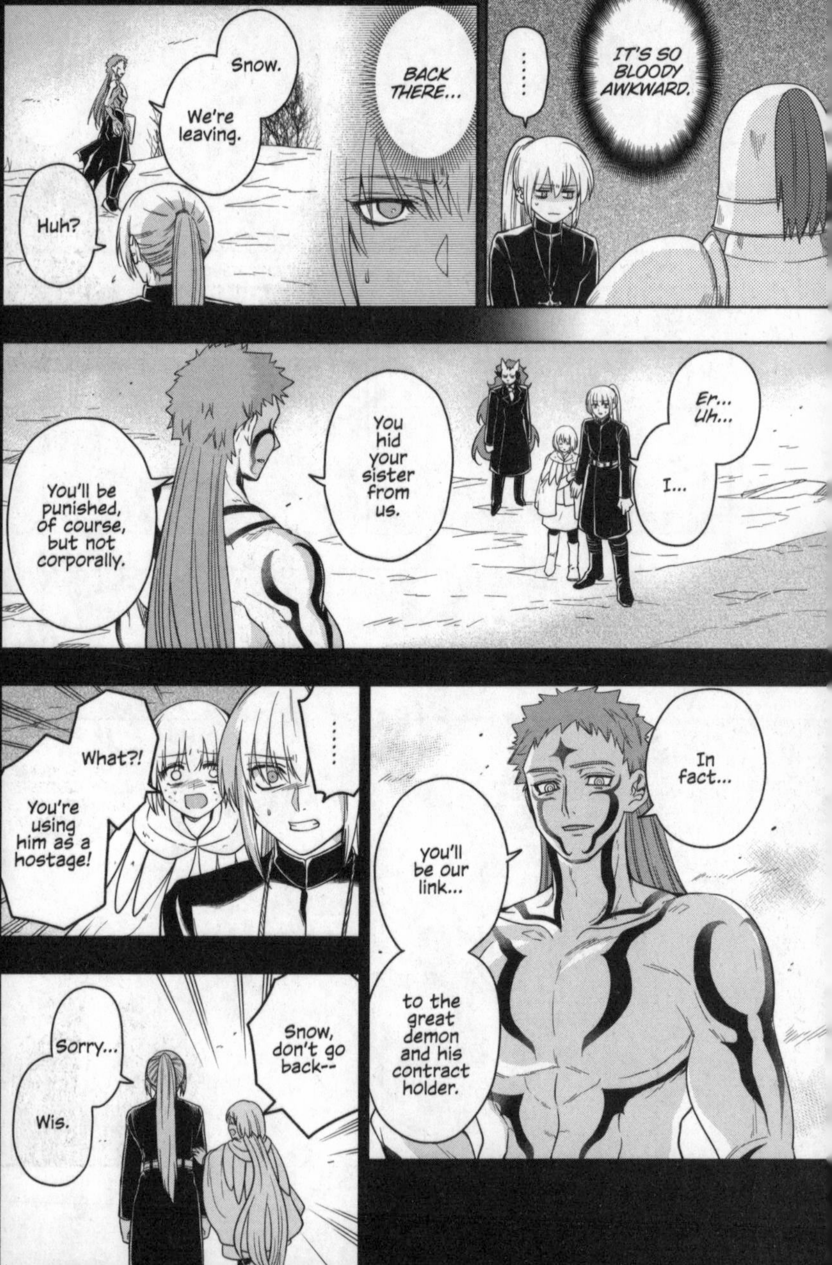
IT'S SO BLOODY AWKWARD.
......
BACK THERE...
Snow.
We're leaving.
Huh?
Er... Uh...
I...
You hid your sister from us.
You'll be punished, of course, but not corporally.
In fact...
you'll be our link...
to the great demon and his contract holder.
......
What?!
You're using him as a hostage!
Snow, don't go back--
Sorry...
Wis.

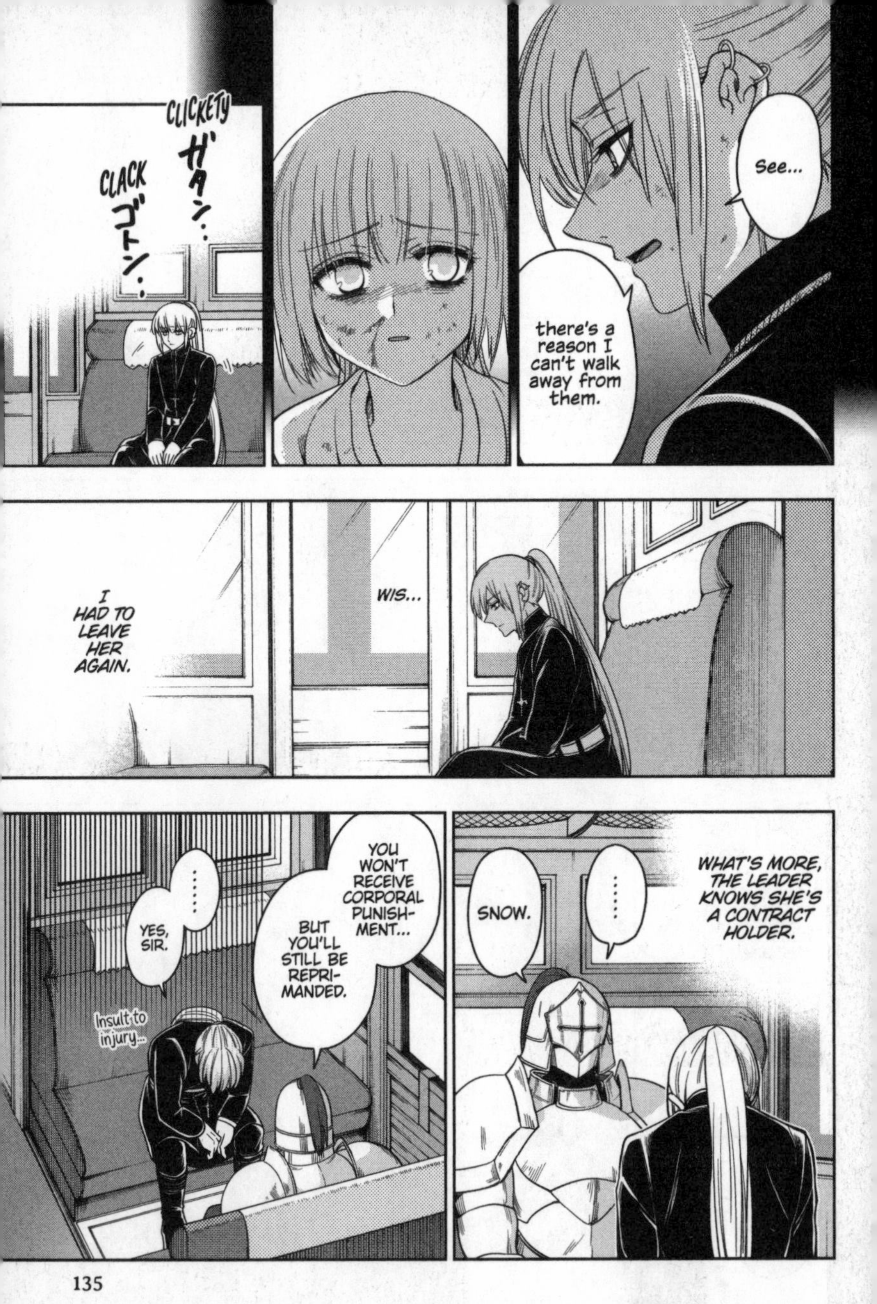
See...
there's a reason I can't walk away from them.
CLICKETY
ガタン..
CLACK
ゴトン..
WIS...
I HAD TO LEAVE HER AGAIN.
WHAT'S MORE, THE LEADER KNOWS SHE'S A CONTRACT HOLDER.
......
SNOW.
YOU WON'T RECEIVE CORPORAL PUNISHMENT...
BUT YOU'LL STILL BE REPRIMANDED.
......
YES, SIR.
Insult to injury...

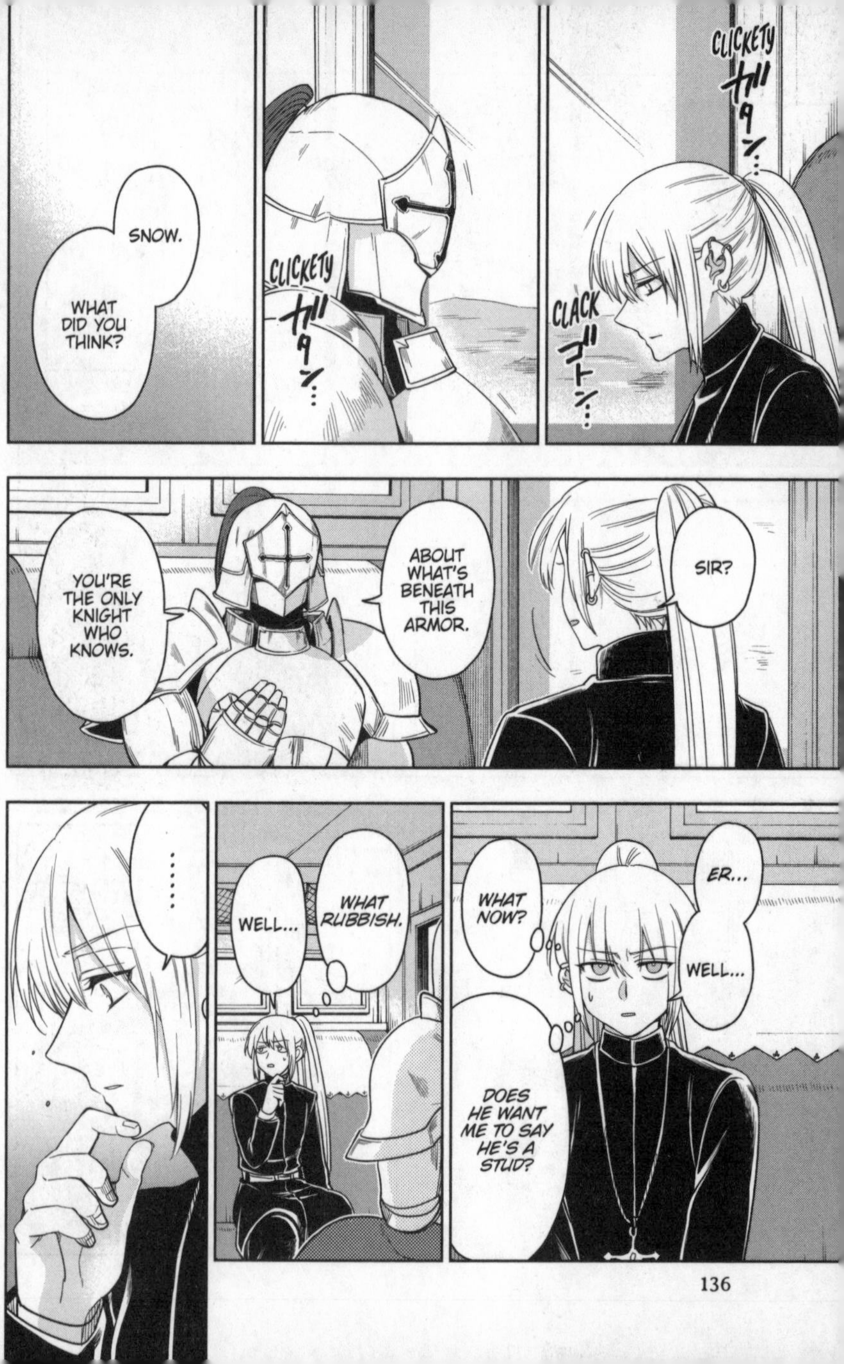
CLICKETY
ガタン…
CLACK
ゴトン…
CLICKETY
ガタン…
SNOW.
WHAT DID YOU THINK?
SIR?
ABOUT WHAT'S BENEATH THIS ARMOR.
YOU'RE THE ONLY KNIGHT WHO KNOWS.
ER...
WELL...
WHAT NOW?
DOES HE WANT ME TO SAY HE'S A STUD?
WHAT RUBBISH.
WELL...
......

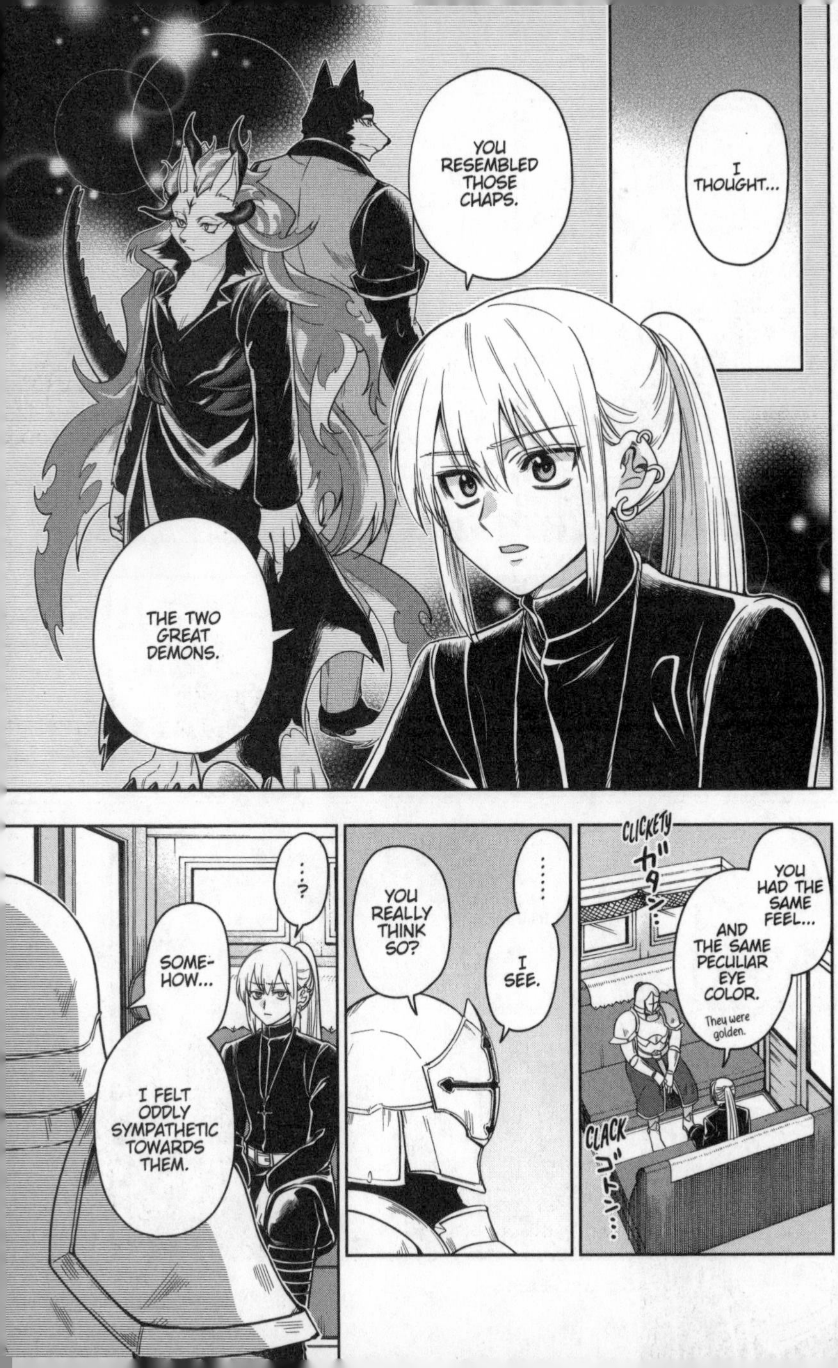
I THOUGHT...
YOU RESEMBLED THOSE CHAPS.
THE TWO GREAT DEMONS.
CLICKETY
ガタン…
YOU HAD THE SAME FEEL...
AND THE SAME PECULIAR EYE COLOR.
They were golden.
CLACK
......
I SEE.
YOU REALLY THINK SO?
...?
SOME-HOW...
I FELT ODDLY SYMPATHETIC TOWARDS THEM.

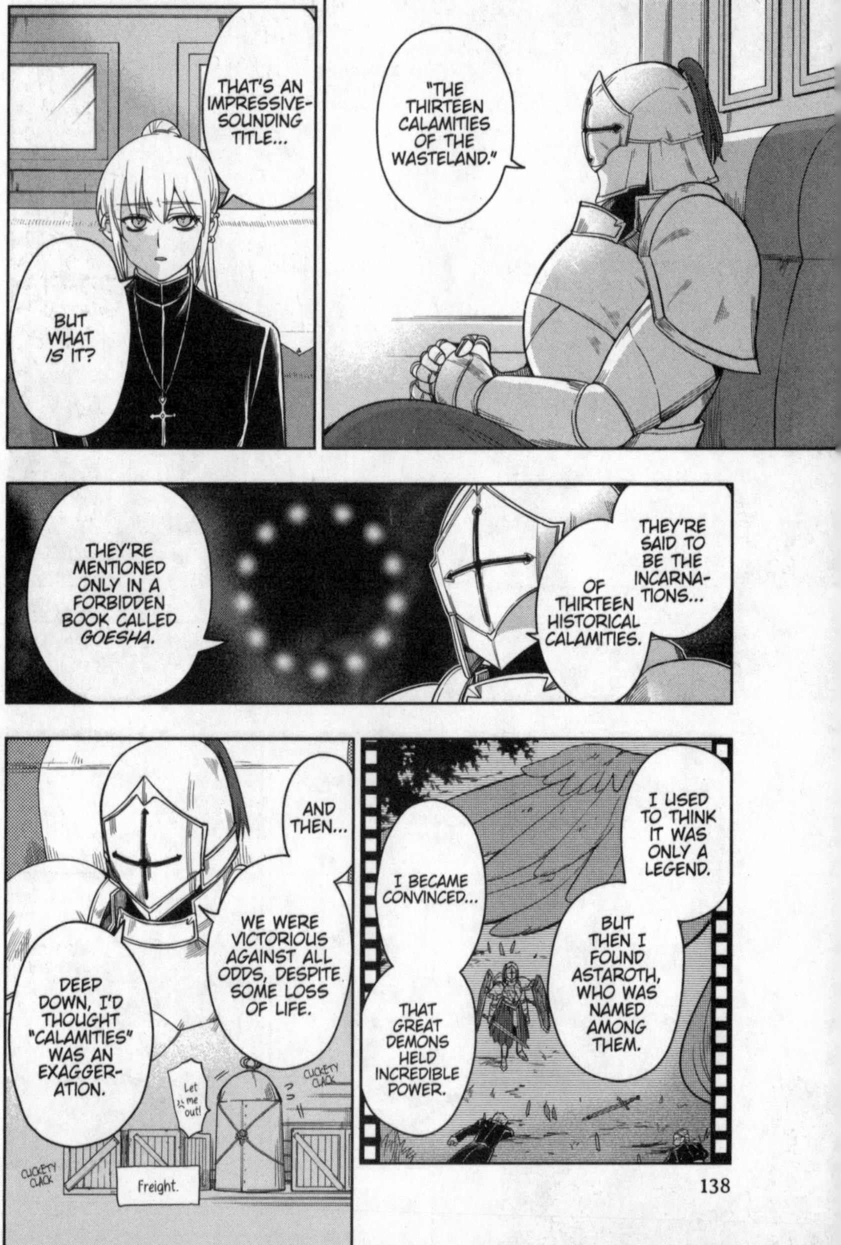
"THE THIRTEEN CALAMITIES OF THE WASTELAND."
THAT'S AN IMPRESSIVE-SOUNDING TITLE...
BUT WHAT *IS* IT?
THEY'RE SAID TO BE THE INCARNA-TIONS...
OF THIRTEEN HISTORICAL CALAMITIES.
THEY'RE MENTIONED ONLY IN A FORBIDDEN BOOK CALLED *GOESHA*.
I USED TO THINK IT WAS ONLY A LEGEND.
BUT THEN I FOUND ASTAROTH, WHO WAS NAMED AMONG THEM.
I BECAME CONVINCED...
THAT GREAT DEMONS HELD INCREDIBLE POWER.
AND THEN...
WE WERE VICTORIOUS AGAINST ALL ODDS, DESPITE SOME LOSS OF LIFE.
DEEP DOWN, I'D THOUGHT "CALAMITIES" WAS AN EXAGGER-ATION.
CLICKETY CLACK
Let me out!
CLICKETY CLACK
Freight.

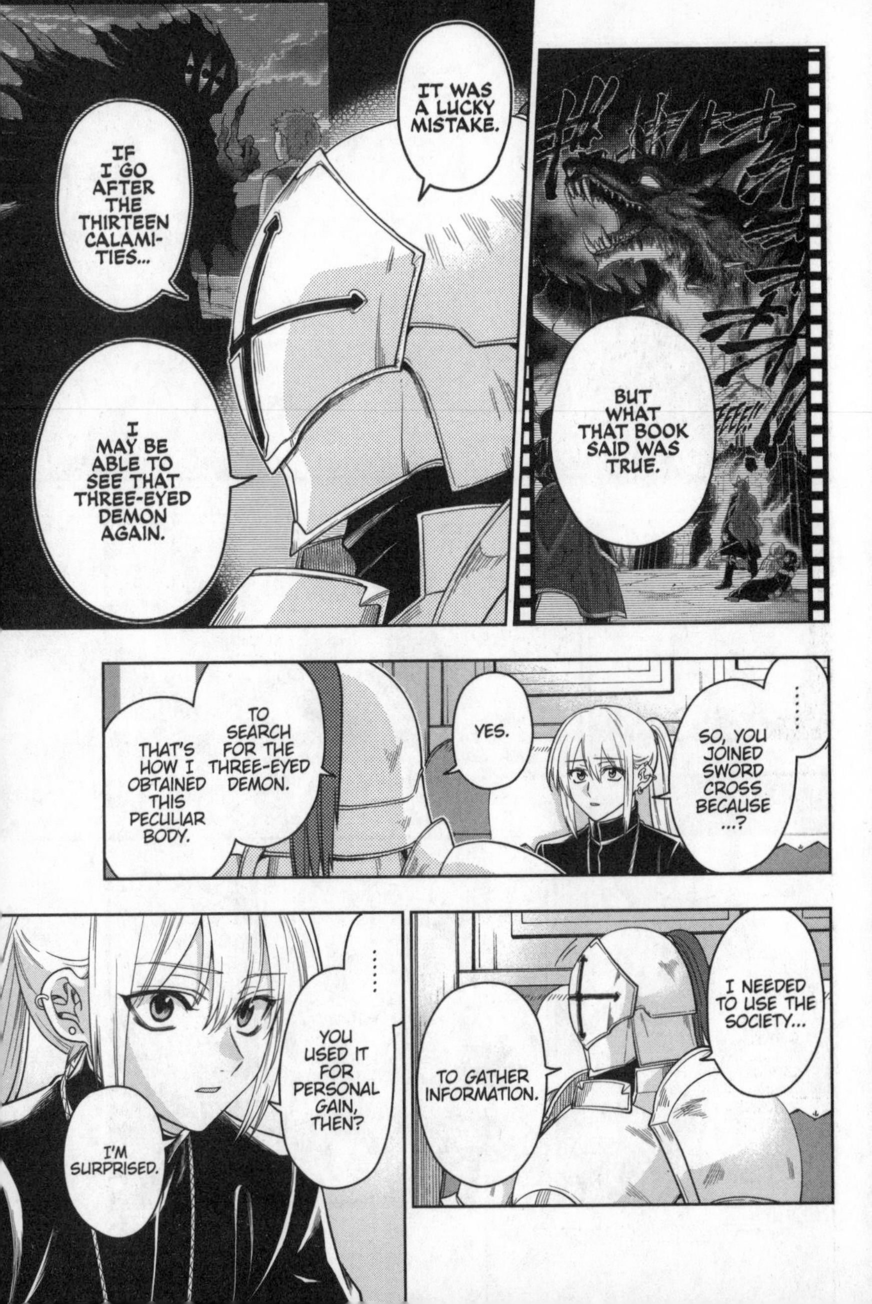

BUT WHAT THAT BOOK SAID WAS TRUE.
IT WAS A LUCKY MISTAKE.
IF I GO AFTER THE THIRTEEN CALAMITIES...
I MAY BE ABLE TO SEE THAT THREE-EYED DEMON AGAIN.
......
SO, YOU JOINED SWORD CROSS BECAUSE ...?
YES.
TO SEARCH FOR THE THREE-EYED DEMON.
THAT'S HOW I OBTAINED THIS PECULIAR BODY.
I NEEDED TO USE THE SOCIETY...
TO GATHER INFORMATION.
......
YOU USED IT FOR PERSONAL GAIN, THEN?
I'M SURPRISED.

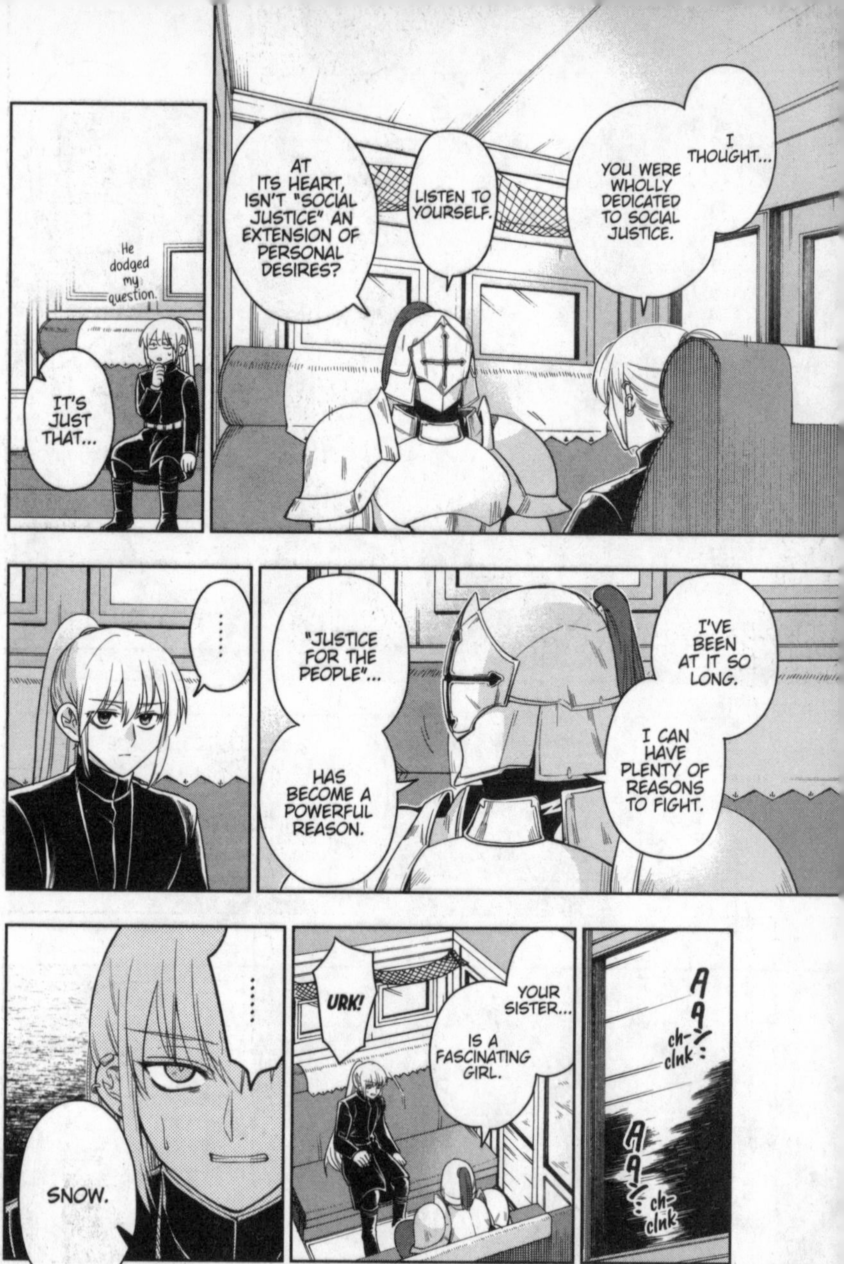
I THOUGHT...
YOU WERE WHOLLY DEDICATED TO SOCIAL JUSTICE.
LISTEN TO YOURSELF.
AT ITS HEART, ISN'T "SOCIAL JUSTICE" AN EXTENSION OF PERSONAL DESIRES?
He dodged my question.
IT'S JUST THAT...
I'VE BEEN AT IT SO LONG.
I CAN HAVE PLENTY OF REASONS TO FIGHT.
"JUSTICE FOR THE PEOPLE"...
HAS BECOME A POWERFUL REASON.
......
ch-clnk
ch-clnk
YOUR SISTER...
IS A FASCINATING GIRL.
URK!
......
SNOW.

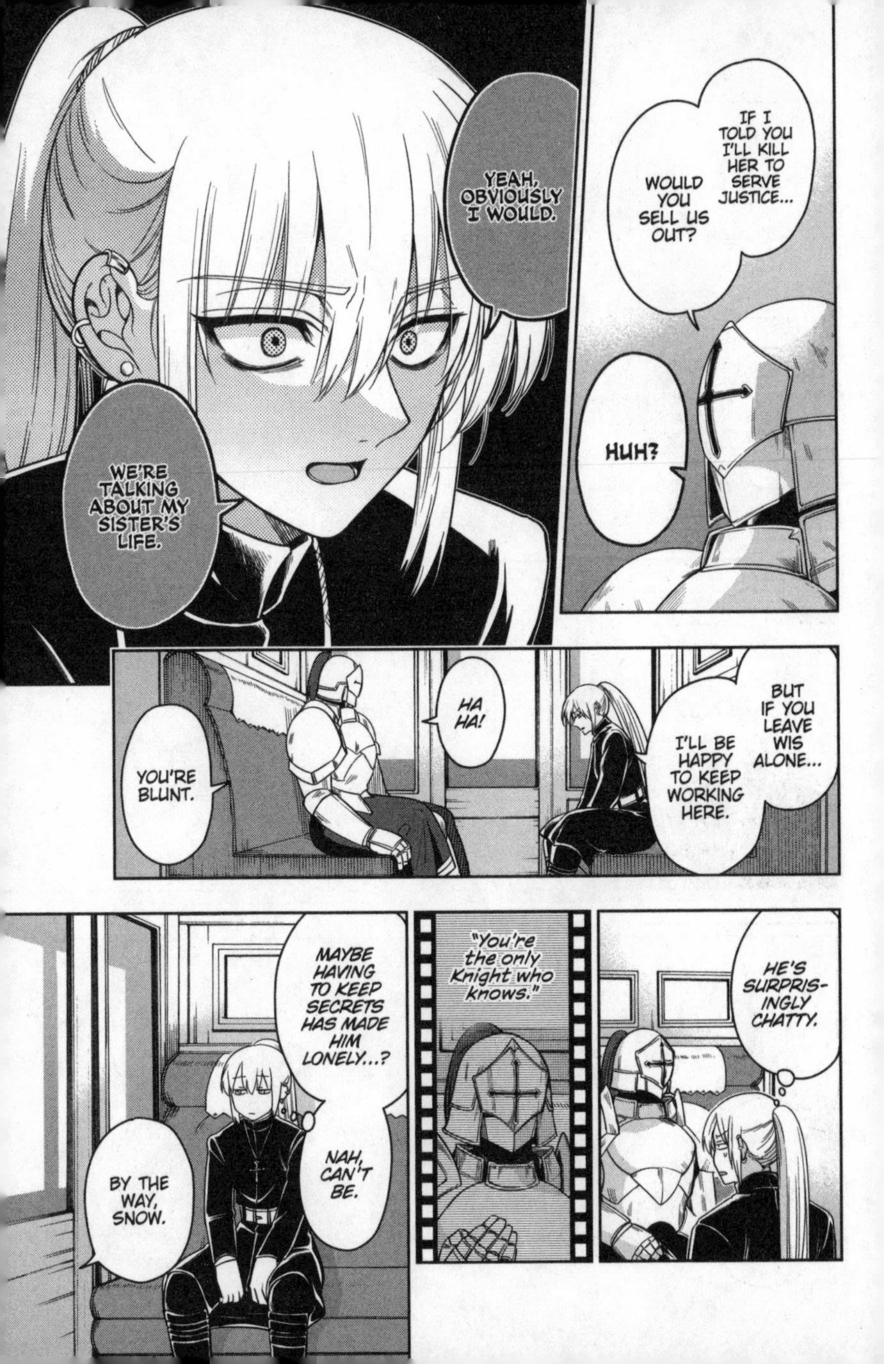
IF I TOLD YOU I'LL KILL HER TO SERVE JUSTICE...
WOULD YOU SELL US OUT?
HUH?
YEAH, OBVIOUSLY I WOULD.
WE'RE TALKING ABOUT MY SISTER'S LIFE.
BUT IF YOU LEAVE WIS ALONE...
I'LL BE HAPPY TO KEEP WORKING HERE.
HA HA!
YOU'RE BLUNT.
HE'S SURPRISINGLY CHATTY.
"You're the only Knight who knows."
MAYBE HAVING TO KEEP SECRETS HAS MADE HIM LONELY...?
NAH, CAN'T BE.
BY THE WAY, SNOW.

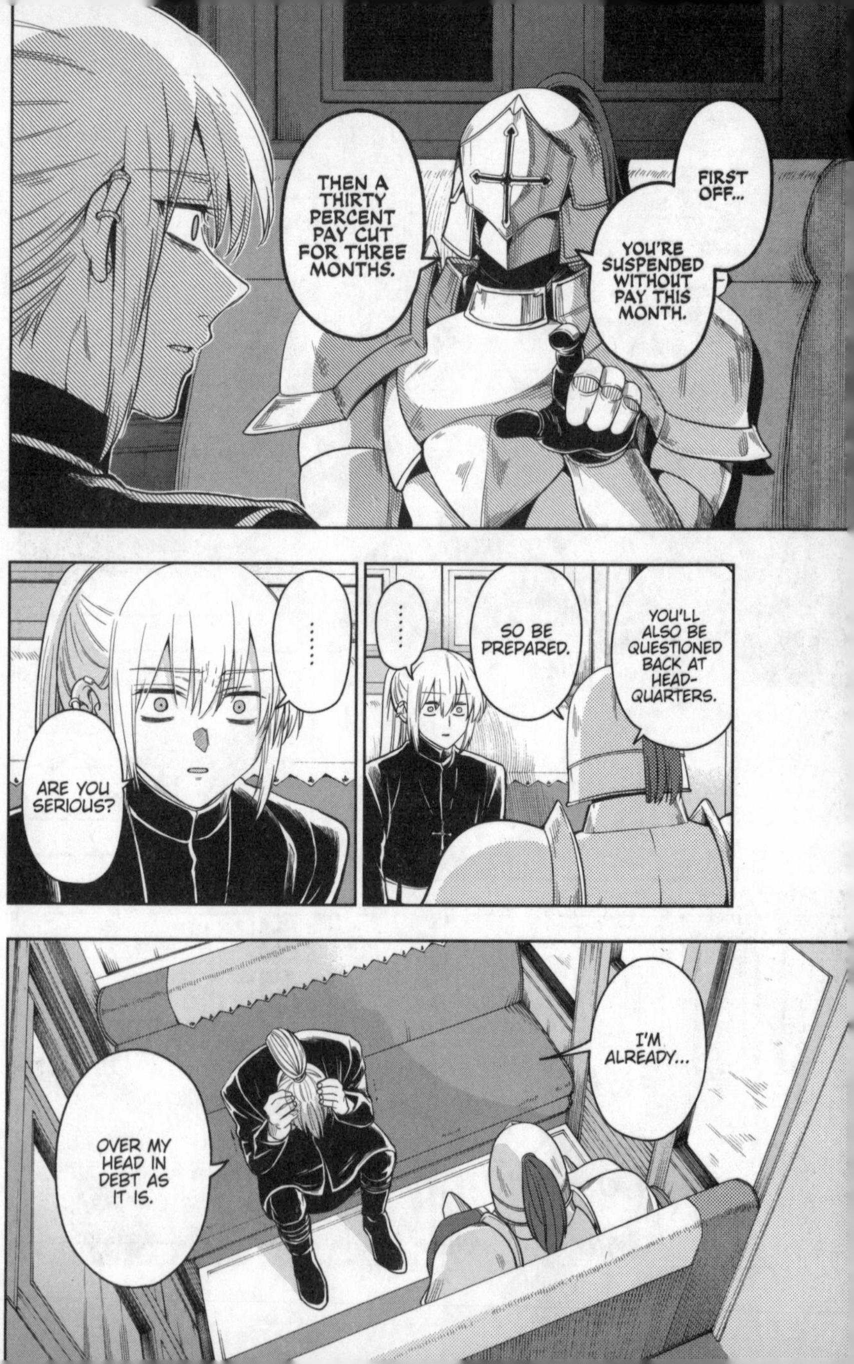
FIRST OFF...
YOU'RE SUSPENDED WITHOUT PAY THIS MONTH.
THEN A THIRTY PERCENT PAY CUT FOR THREE MONTHS.
YOU'LL ALSO BE QUESTIONED BACK AT HEAD-QUARTERS.
SO BE PREPARED.
......
......
ARE YOU SERIOUS?
I'M ALREADY...
OVER MY HEAD IN DEBT AS IT IS.

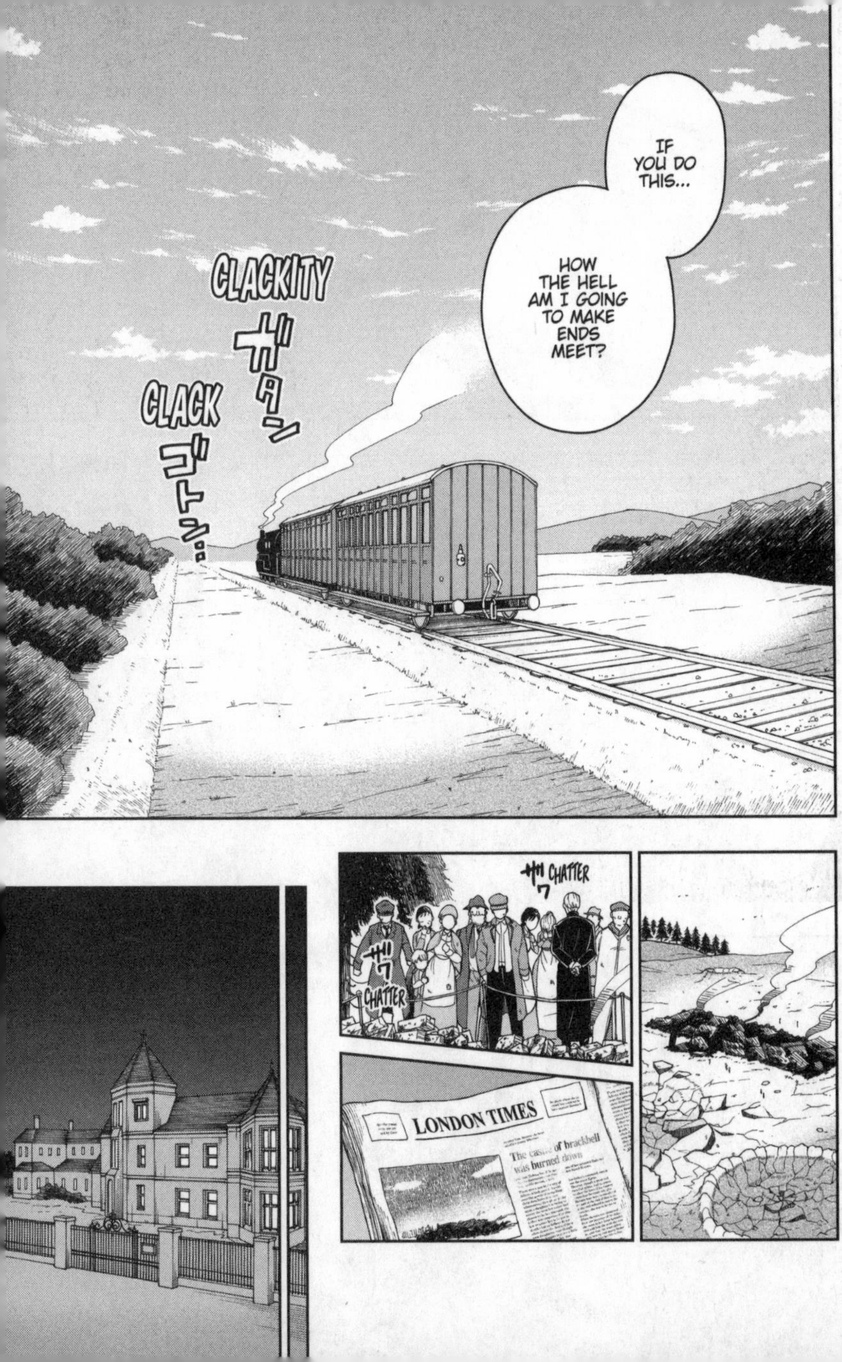
IF YOU DO THIS...
HOW THE HELL AM I GOING TO MAKE ENDS MEET?
CLACKITY
ガタン
CLACK
ゴトン
CHATTER
CHATTER
LONDON TIMES
The castle of brackbell was burned down

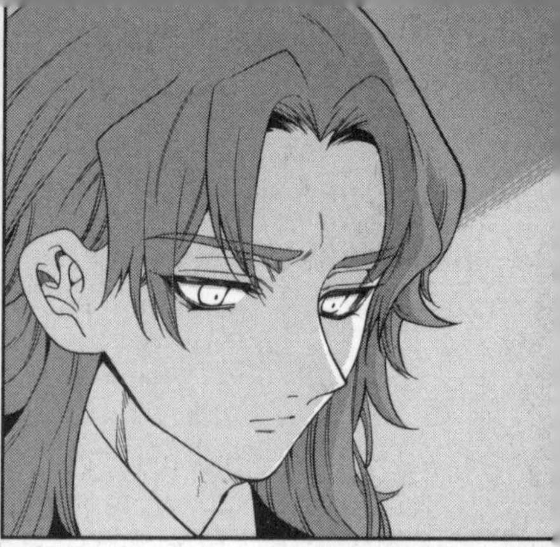
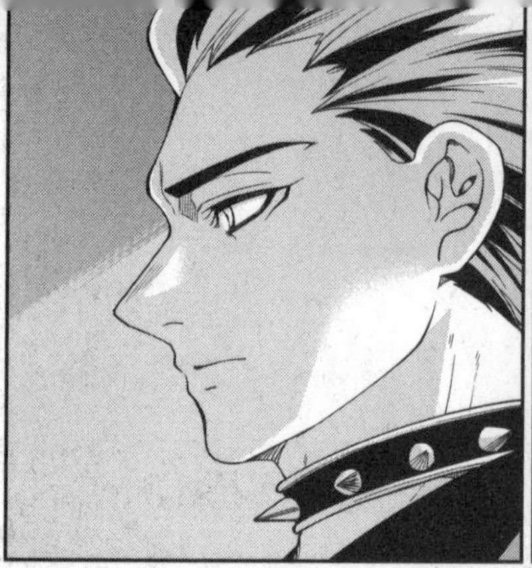
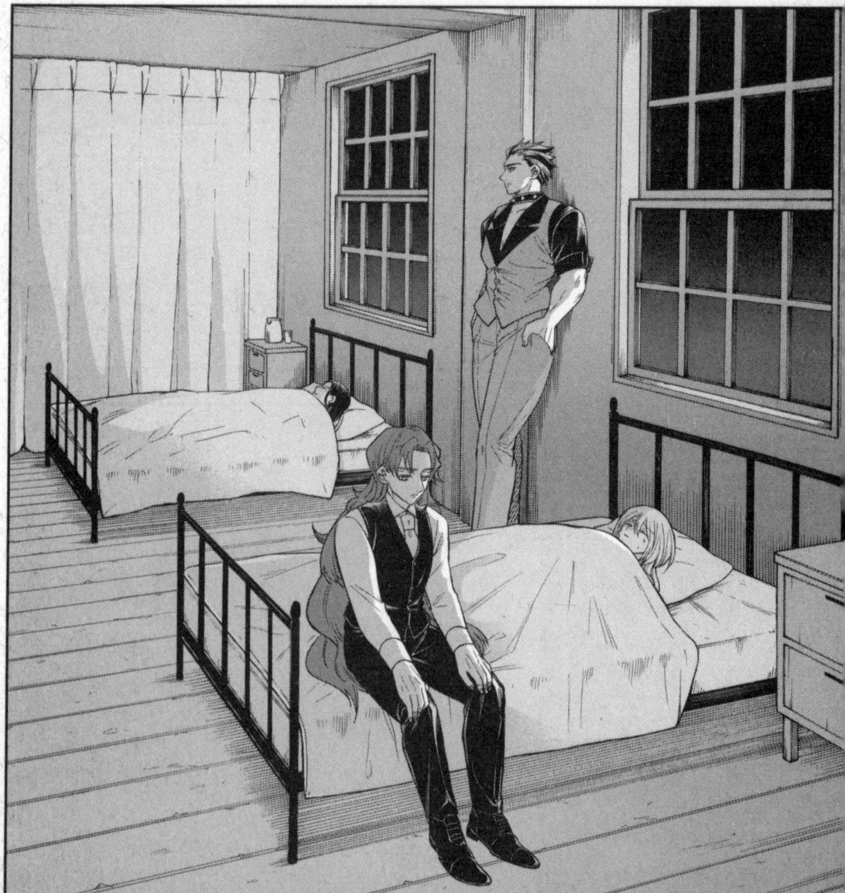

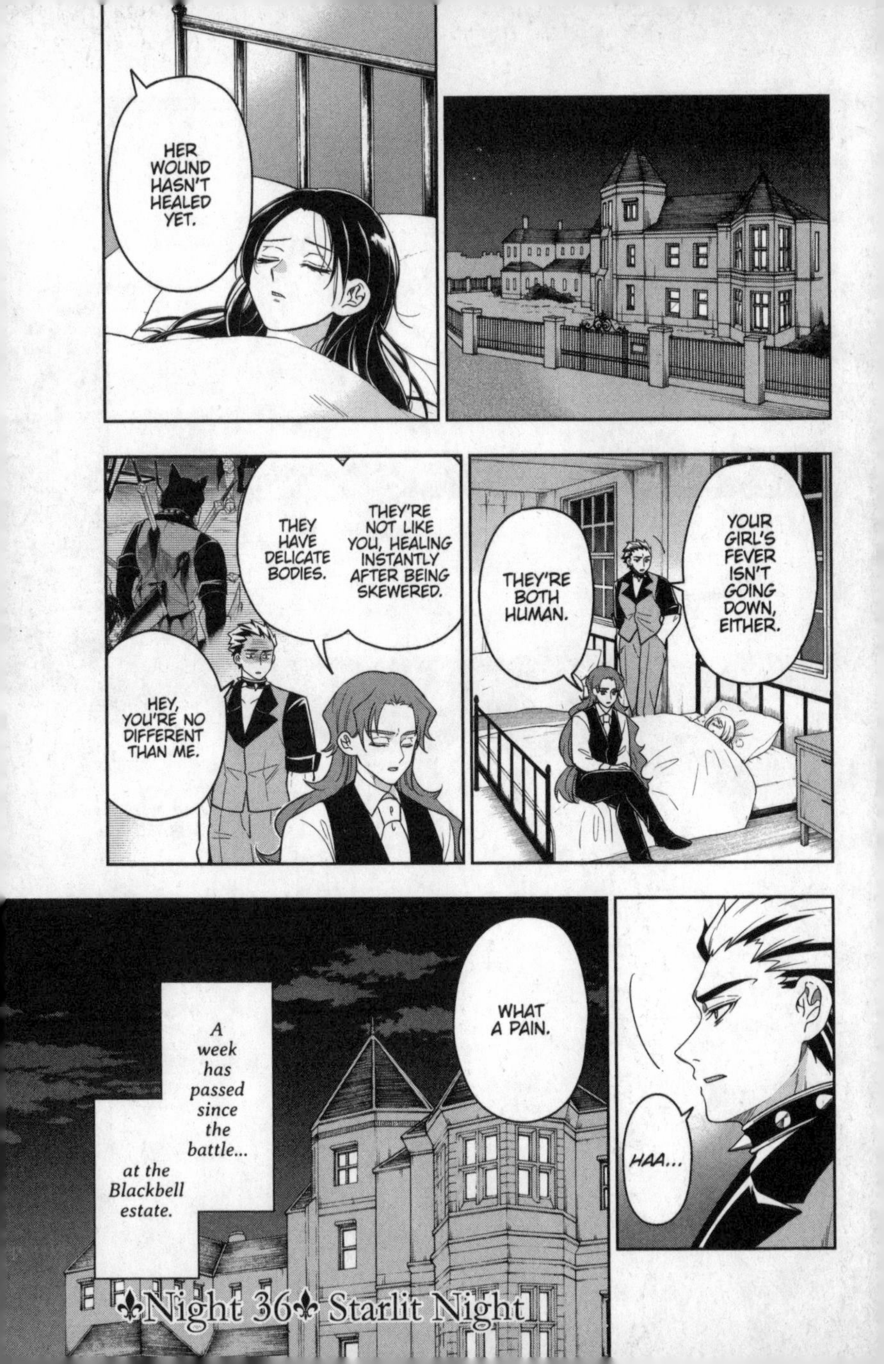
HER WOUND HASN'T HEALED YET.
YOUR GIRL'S FEVER ISN'T GOING DOWN, EITHER.
THEY'RE BOTH HUMAN.
THEY'RE NOT LIKE YOU, HEALING INSTANTLY AFTER BEING SKEWERED.
THEY HAVE DELICATE BODIES.
HEY, YOU'RE NO DIFFERENT THAN ME.
HAA...
WHAT A PAIN.
A week has passed since the battle...
at the Blackbell estate.
Night 36 Starlit Night

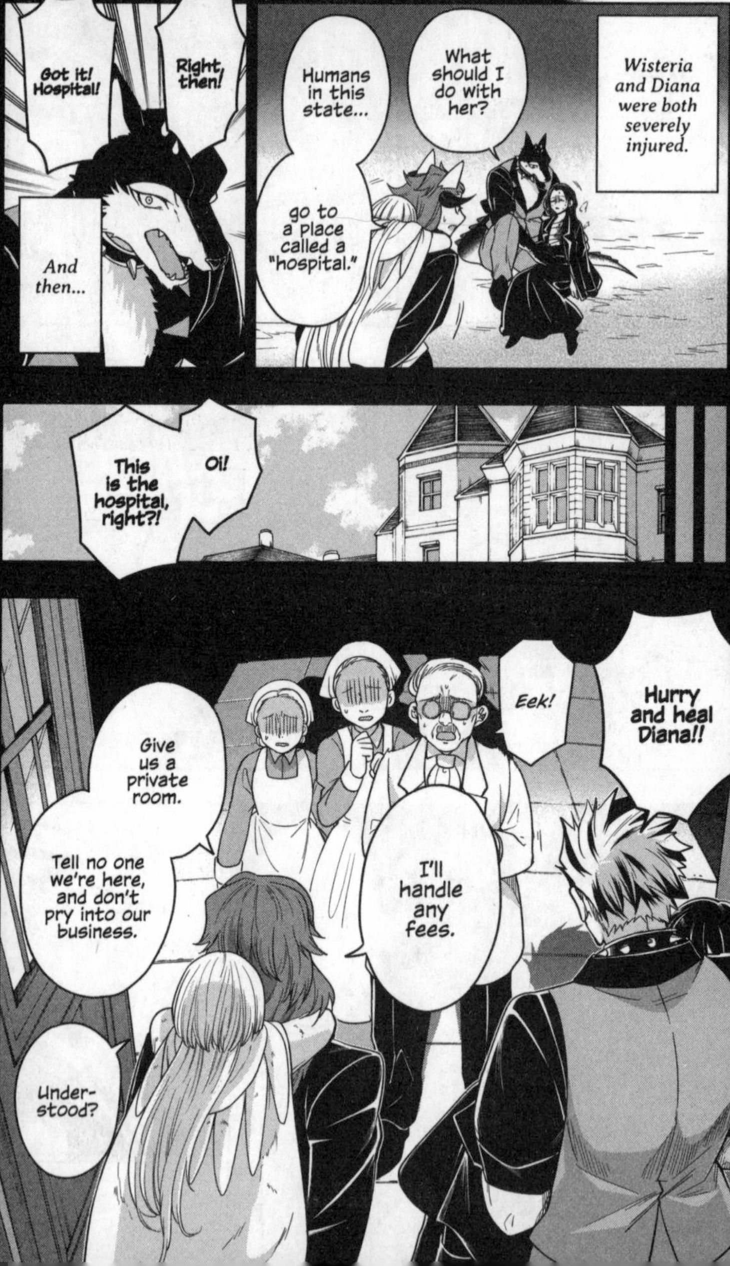
Wisteria and Diana were both severely injured.
What should I do with her?
Humans in this state...
go to a place called a "hospital."
Right, then!
Got it! Hospital!
And then...
Oi!
This is the hospital, right?!
Hurry and heal Diana!!
Eek!
I'll handle any fees.
Give us a private room.
Tell no one we're here, and don't pry into our business.
Understood?

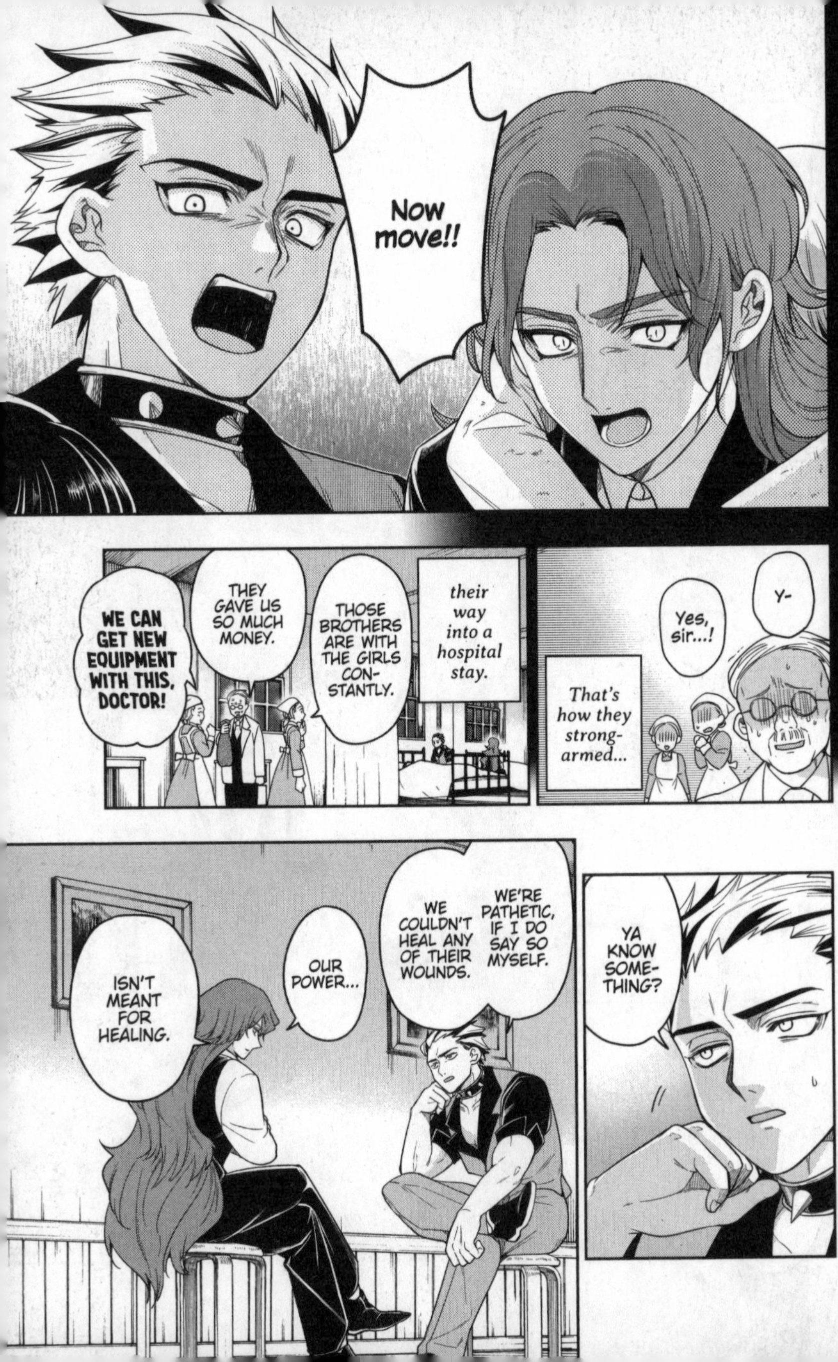
Now move!!
Y-
Yes, sir...!
That's how they strong-armed...
their way into a hospital stay.
THOSE BROTHERS ARE WITH THE GIRLS CONSTANTLY.
THEY GAVE US SO MUCH MONEY.
WE CAN GET NEW EQUIPMENT WITH THIS, DOCTOR!
YA KNOW SOMETHING?
WE'RE PATHETIC, IF I DO SAY SO MYSELF.
WE COULDN'T HEAL ANY OF THEIR WOUNDS.
OUR POWER...
ISN'T MEANT FOR HEALING.

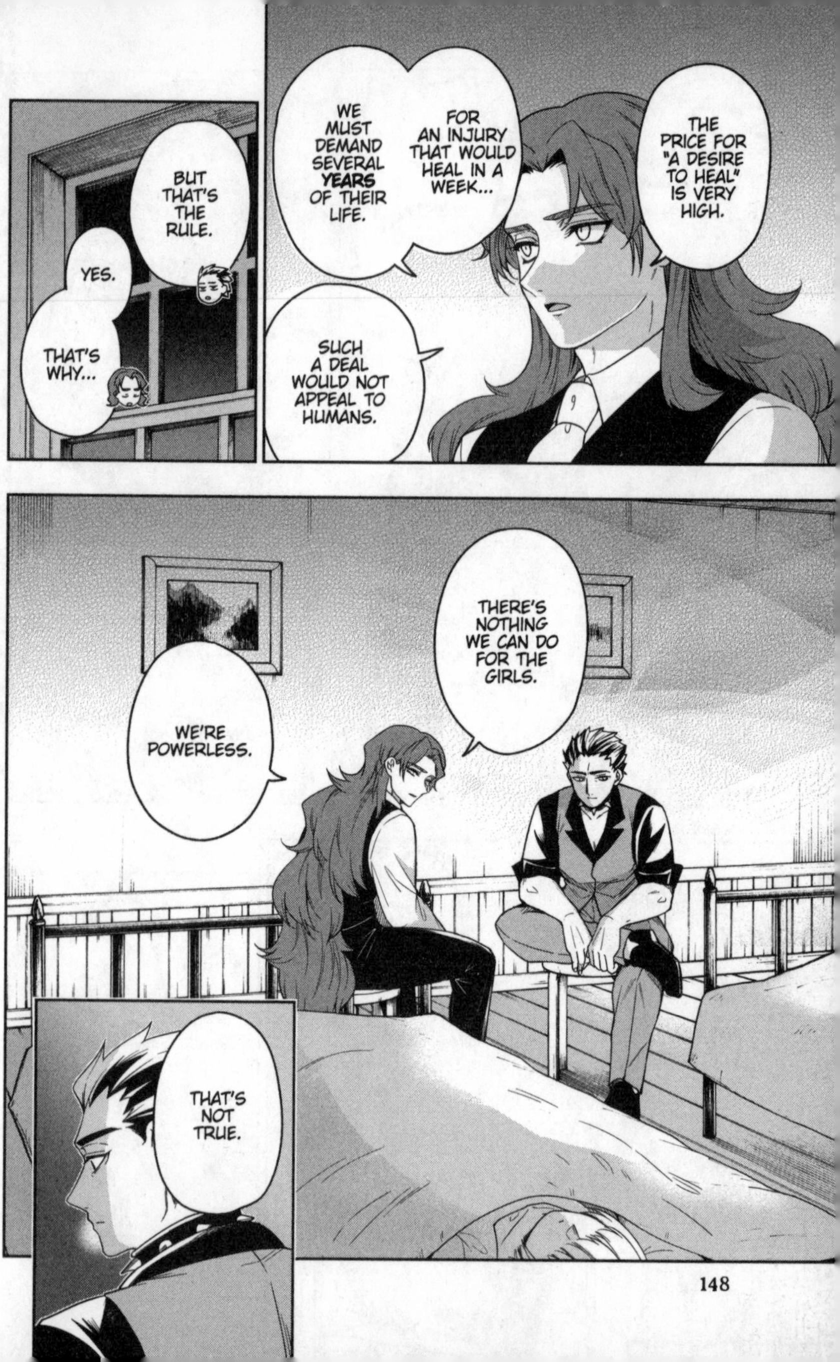
THE PRICE FOR "A DESIRE TO HEAL" IS VERY HIGH.
FOR AN INJURY THAT WOULD HEAL IN A WEEK...
WE MUST DEMAND SEVERAL **YEARS** OF THEIR LIFE.
SUCH A DEAL WOULD NOT APPEAL TO HUMANS.
BUT THAT'S THE RULE.
YES.
THAT'S WHY...
THERE'S NOTHING WE CAN DO FOR THE GIRLS.
WE'RE POWERLESS.
THAT'S NOT TRUE.

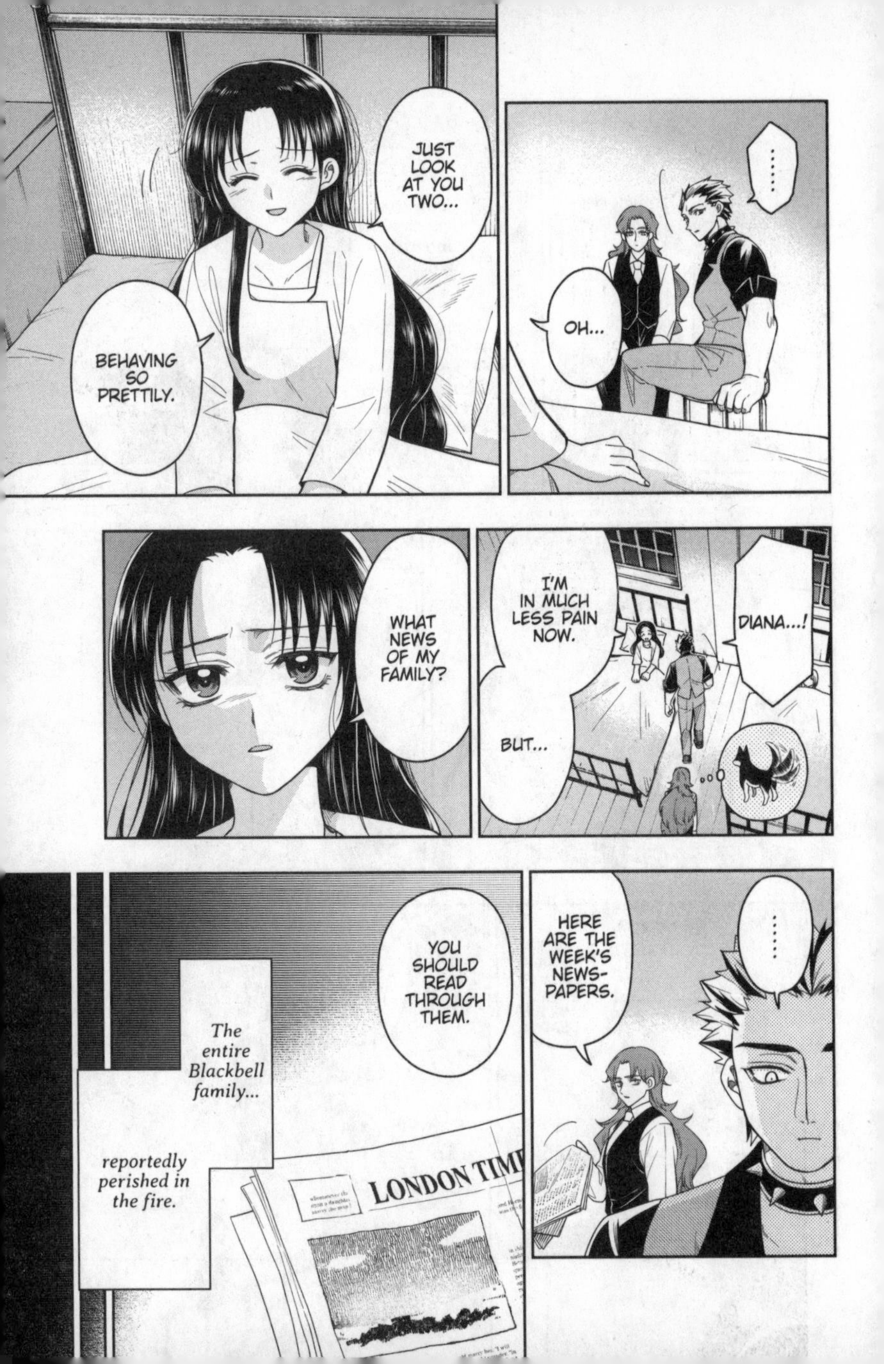
......
OH...
JUST LOOK AT YOU TWO...
BEHAVING SO PRETTILY.
DIANA...!
I'M IN MUCH LESS PAIN NOW.
BUT...
WHAT NEWS OF MY FAMILY?
......
HERE ARE THE WEEK'S NEWS-PAPERS.
YOU SHOULD READ THROUGH THEM.
The entire Blackbell family...
reportedly perished in the fire.
LONDON TIM

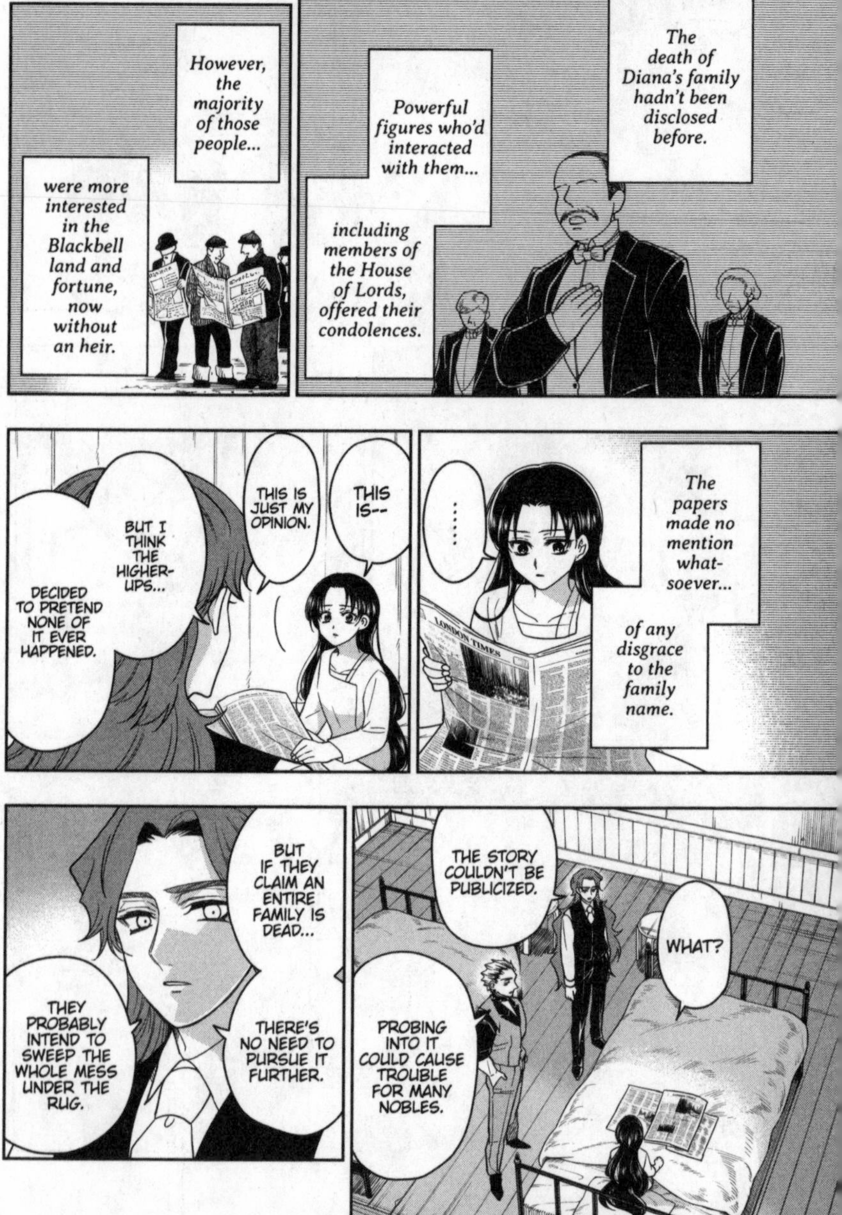
The death of Diana's family hadn't been disclosed before.
Powerful figures who'd interacted with them...
including members of the House of Lords, offered their condolences.
However, the majority of those people...
were more interested in the Blackbell land and fortune, now without an heir.
The papers made no mention whatsoever...
of any disgrace to the family name.
......
LONDON TIMES
THIS IS--
THIS IS JUST MY OPINION.
BUT I THINK THE HIGHER-UPS...
DECIDED TO PRETEND NONE OF IT EVER HAPPENED.
THE STORY COULDN'T BE PUBLICIZED.
WHAT?
PROBING INTO IT COULD CAUSE TROUBLE FOR MANY NOBLES.
BUT IF THEY CLAIM AN ENTIRE FAMILY IS DEAD...
THERE'S NO NEED TO PURSUE IT FURTHER.
THEY PROBABLY INTEND TO SWEEP THE WHOLE MESS UNDER THE RUG.

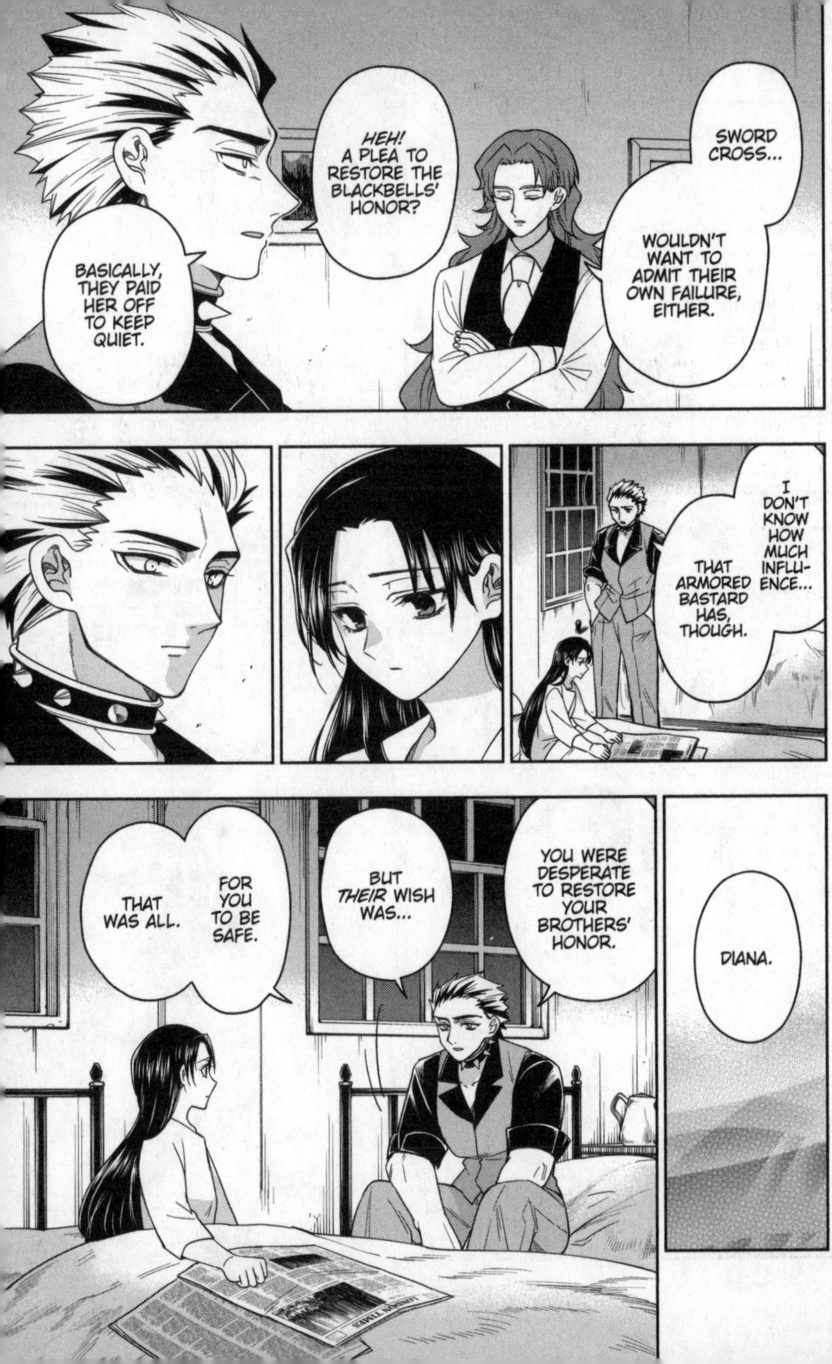
SWORD CROSS...
WOULDN'T WANT TO ADMIT THEIR OWN FAILURE, EITHER.
HEH! A PLEA TO RESTORE THE BLACKBELLS' HONOR?
BASICALLY, THEY PAID HER OFF TO KEEP QUIET.
I DON'T KNOW HOW MUCH INFLU- ENCE...
THAT ARMORED BASTARD HAS, THOUGH.
DIANA.
YOU WERE DESPERATE TO RESTORE YOUR BROTHERS' HONOR.
BUT *THEIR* WISH WAS...
FOR YOU TO BE SAFE.
THAT WAS ALL.

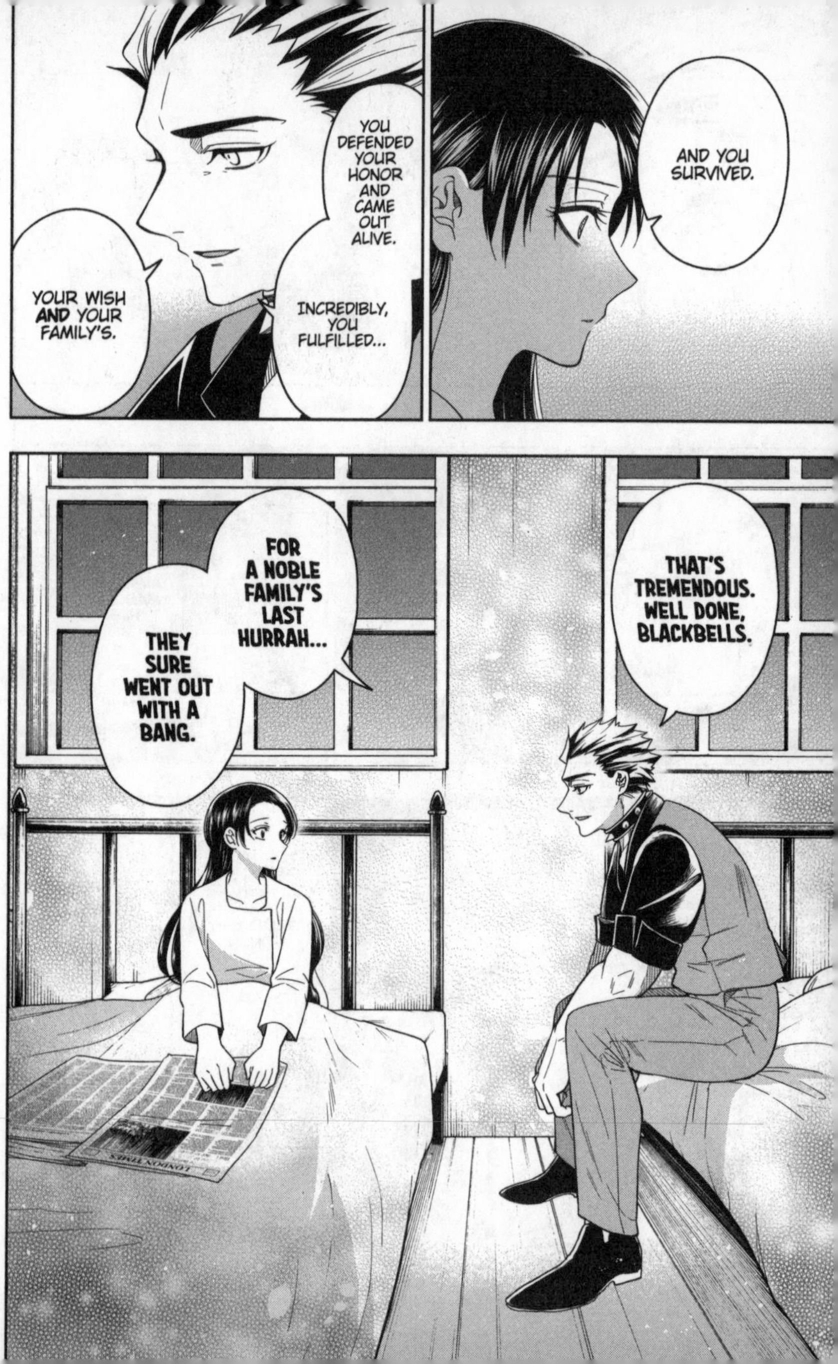
AND YOU SURVIVED.
YOU DEFENDED YOUR HONOR AND CAME OUT ALIVE.
INCREDIBLY, YOU FULFILLED...
YOUR WISH AND YOUR FAMILY'S.
THAT'S TREMENDOUS. WELL DONE, BLACKBELLS.
FOR A NOBLE FAMILY'S LAST HURRAH...
THEY SURE WENT OUT WITH A BANG.

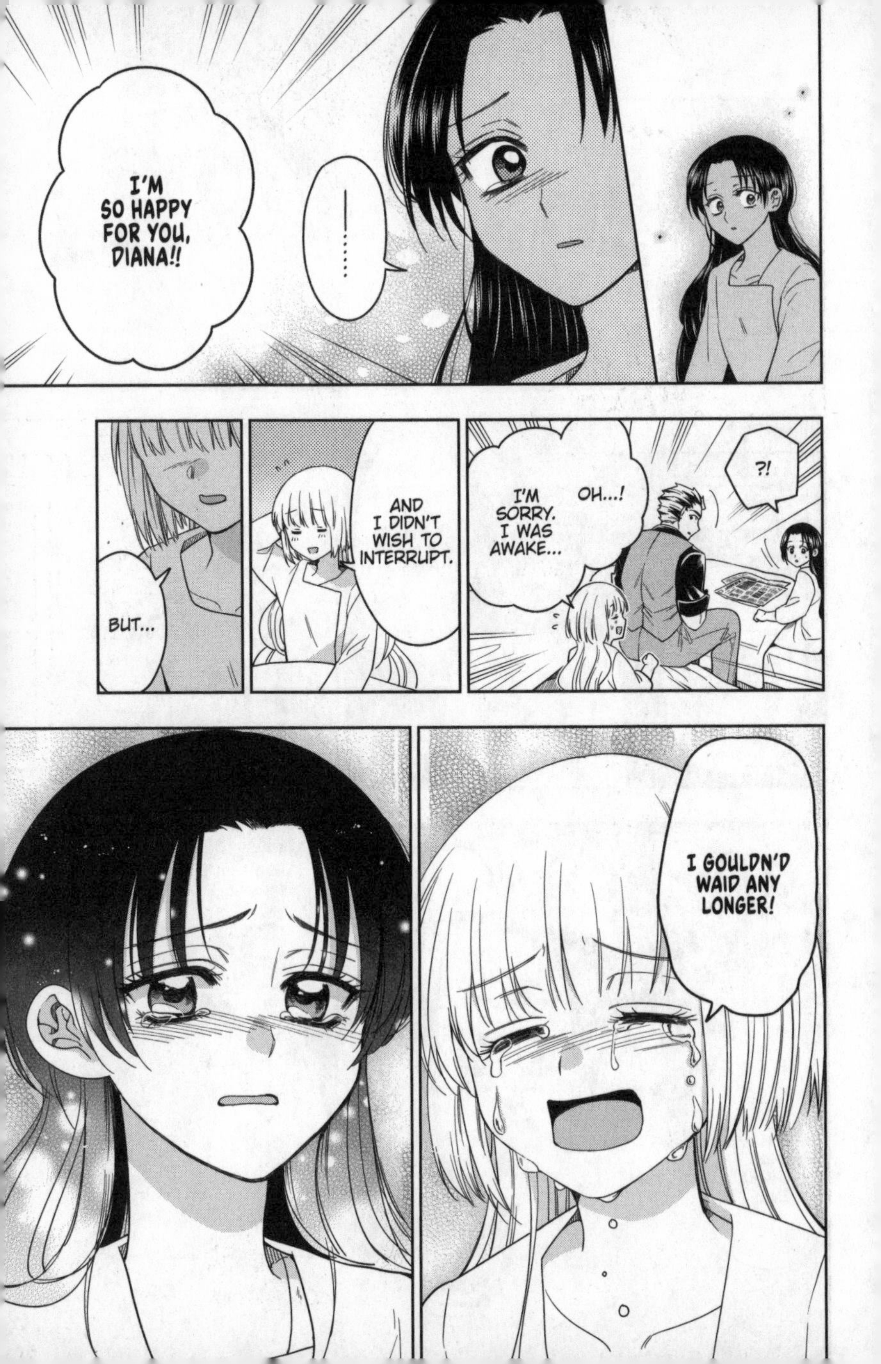

......!
I'M SO HAPPY FOR YOU, DIANA!!
?!
OH...!
I'M SORRY. I WAS AWAKE...
AND I DIDN'T WISH TO INTERRUPT.
BUT...
I GOULDN'D WAID ANY LONGER!

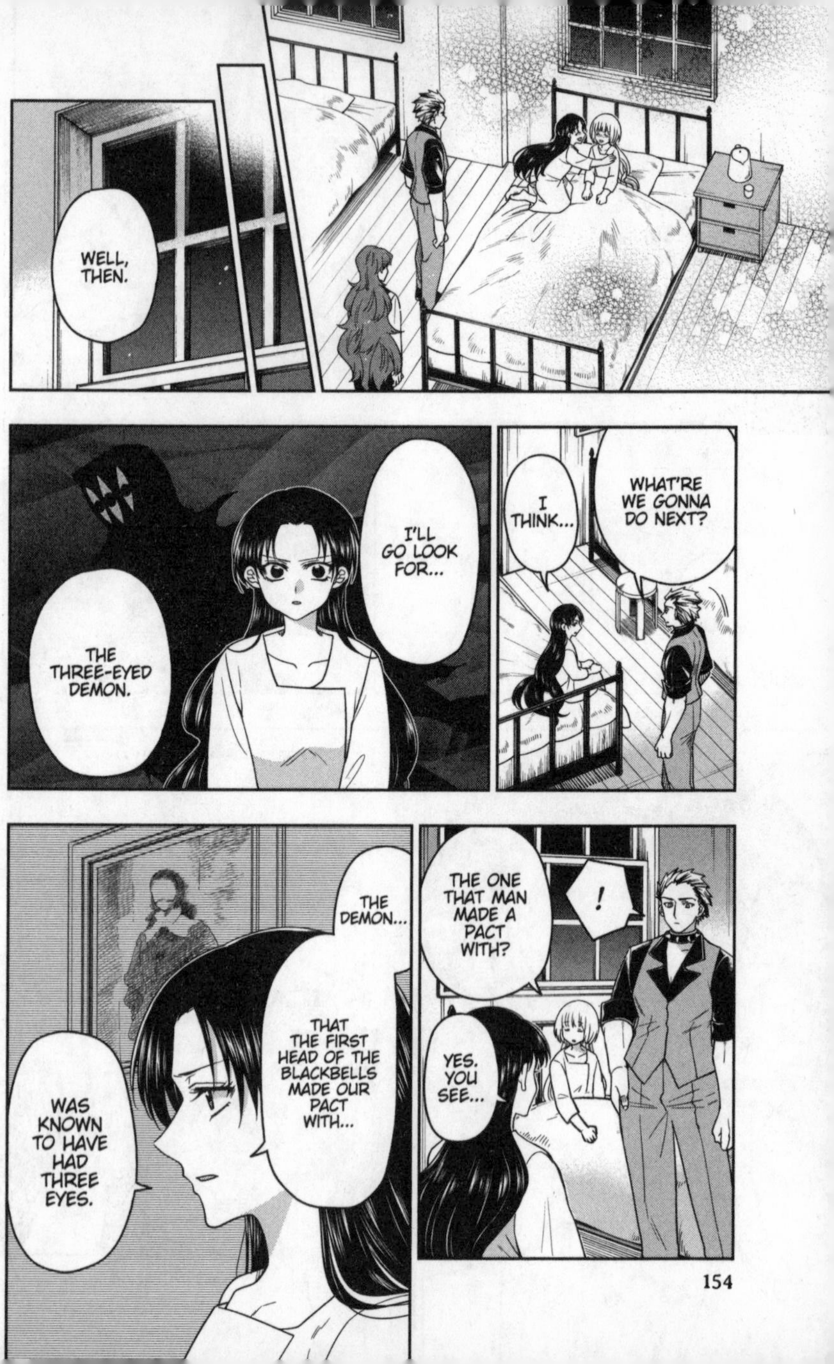
WELL, THEN.
WHAT'RE WE GONNA DO NEXT?
I THINK...
I'LL GO LOOK FOR...
THE THREE-EYED DEMON.
!
THE ONE THAT MAN MADE A PACT WITH?
YES. YOU SEE...
THE DEMON...
THAT THE FIRST HEAD OF THE BLACKBELLS MADE OUR PACT WITH...
WAS KNOWN TO HAVE HAD THREE EYES.

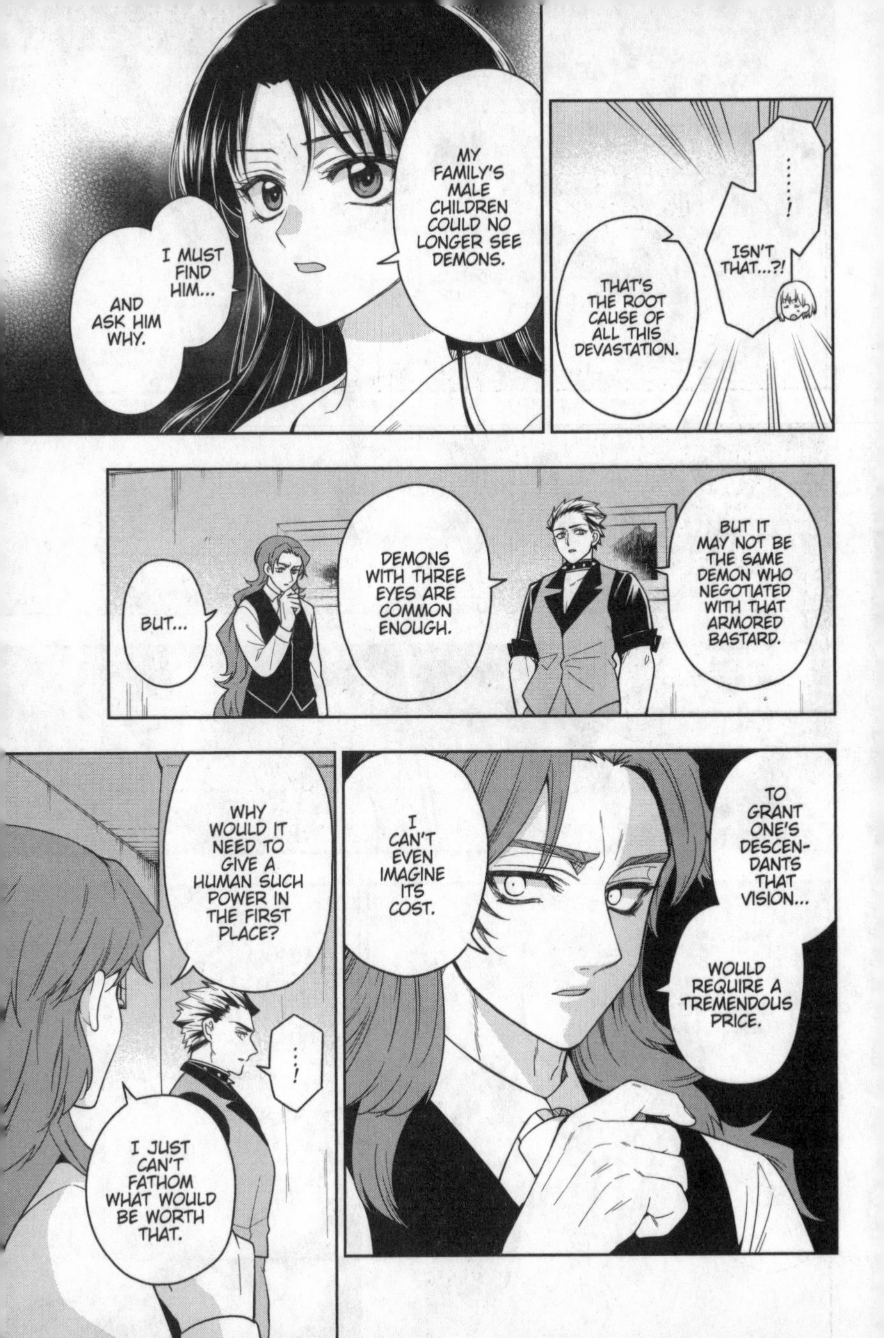
……!
ISN'T THAT...?!
THAT'S THE ROOT CAUSE OF ALL THIS DEVASTATION.
MY FAMILY'S MALE CHILDREN COULD NO LONGER SEE DEMONS.
I MUST FIND HIM...
AND ASK HIM WHY.
BUT IT MAY NOT BE THE SAME DEMON WHO NEGOTIATED WITH THAT ARMORED BASTARD.
DEMONS WITH THREE EYES ARE COMMON ENOUGH.
BUT...
TO GRANT ONE'S DESCEN-DANTS THAT VISION...
WOULD REQUIRE A TREMENDOUS PRICE.
I CAN'T EVEN IMAGINE ITS COST.
WHY WOULD IT NEED TO GIVE A HUMAN SUCH POWER IN THE FIRST PLACE?
…!
I JUST CAN'T FATHOM WHAT WOULD BE WORTH THAT.

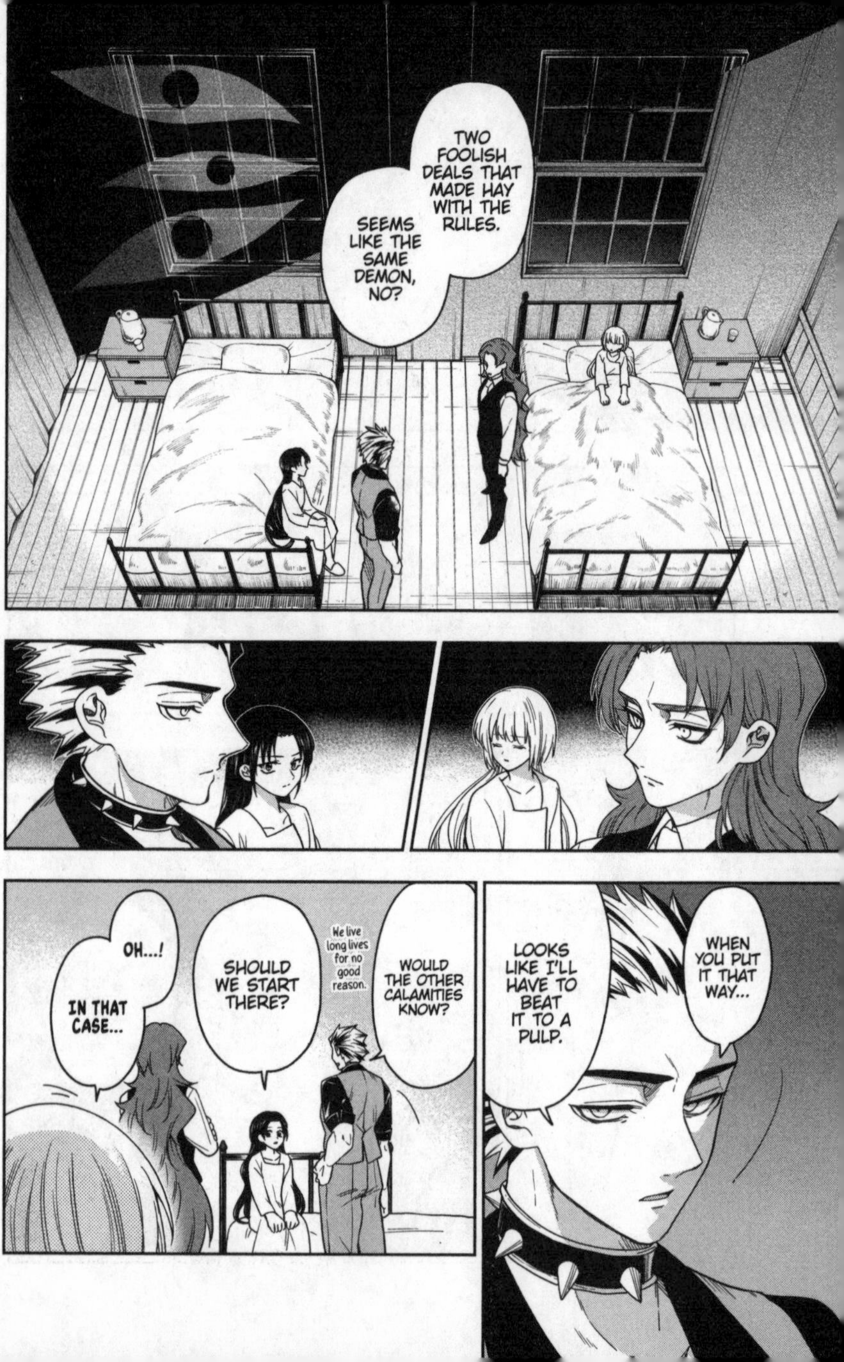
TWO FOOLISH DEALS THAT MADE HAY WITH THE RULES.
SEEMS LIKE THE SAME DEMON, NO?
WHEN YOU PUT IT THAT WAY...
LOOKS LIKE I'LL HAVE TO BEAT IT TO A PULP.
WOULD THE OTHER CALAMITIES KNOW?
We live long lives for no good reason.
SHOULD WE START THERE?
OH...!
IN THAT CASE...

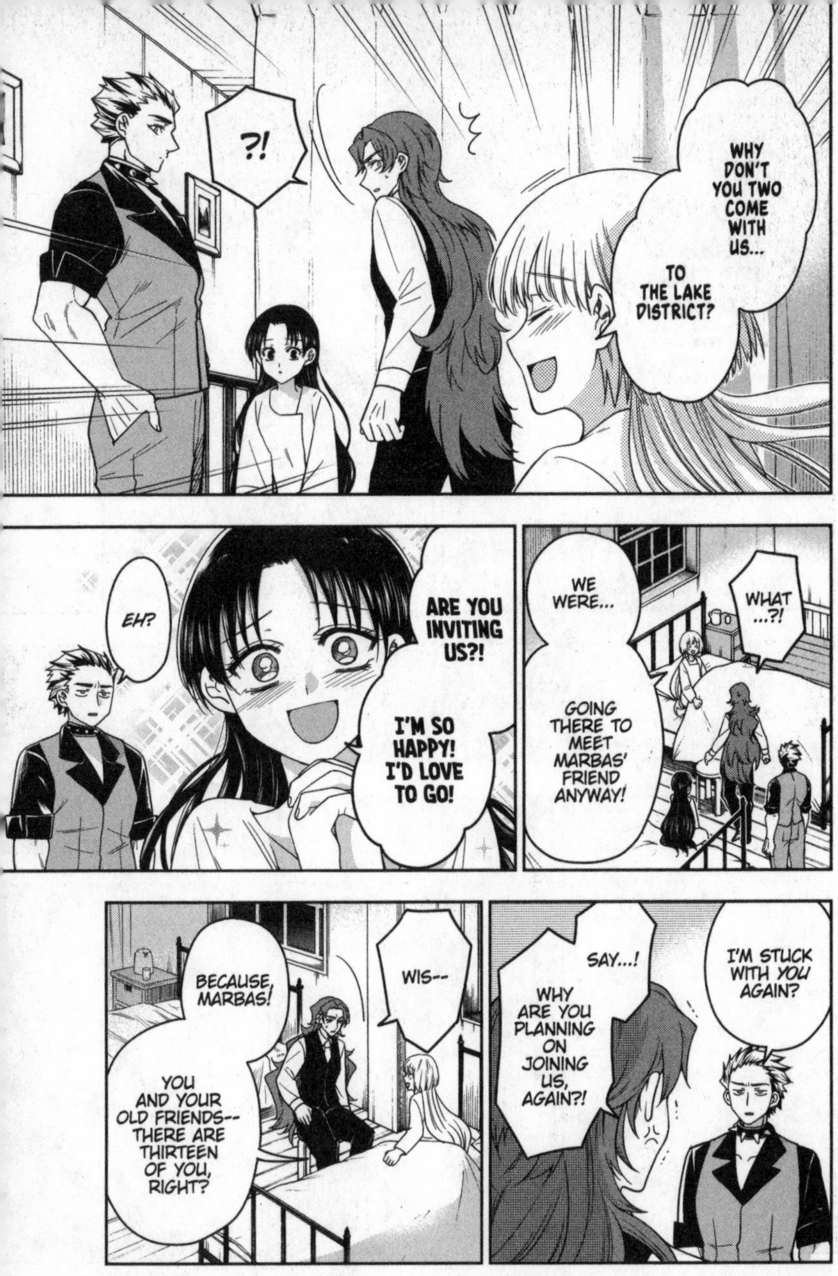
WHY DON'T YOU TWO COME WITH US...
TO THE LAKE DISTRICT?
?!
WHAT ...?!
WE WERE...
GOING THERE TO MEET MARBAS' FRIEND ANYWAY!
ARE YOU INVITING US?!
I'M SO HAPPY! I'D LOVE TO GO!
EH?
I'M STUCK WITH *YOU* AGAIN?
SAY...!
WHY ARE YOU PLANNING ON JOINING US, AGAIN?!
WIS--
BECAUSE, MARBAS!
YOU AND YOUR OLD FRIENDS-- THERE ARE THIRTEEN OF YOU, RIGHT?

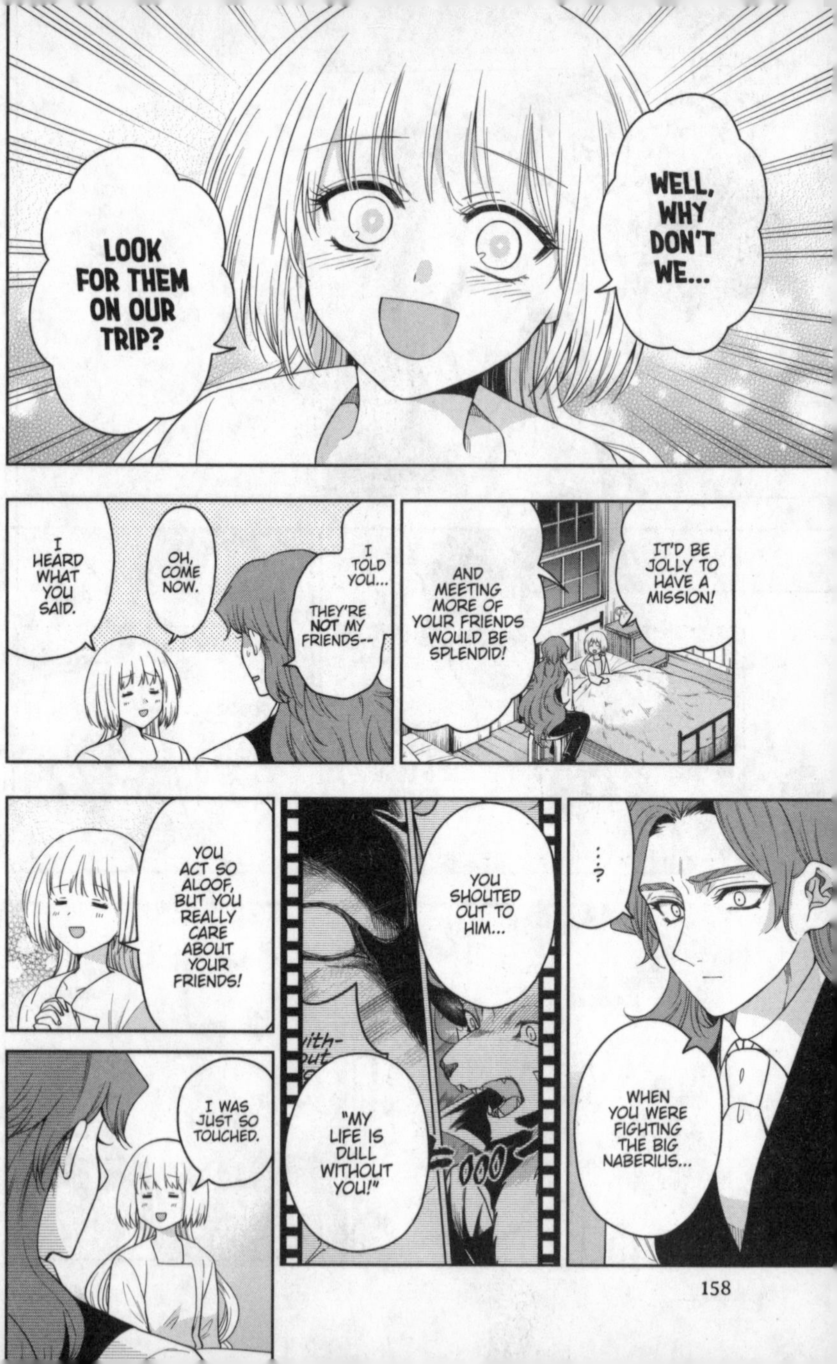
WELL, WHY DON'T WE...
LOOK FOR THEM ON OUR TRIP?
IT'D BE JOLLY TO HAVE A MISSION!
AND MEETING MORE OF YOUR FRIENDS WOULD BE SPLENDID!
I TOLD YOU...
THEY'RE NOT MY FRIENDS--
OH, COME NOW.
I HEARD WHAT YOU SAID.
...?
WHEN YOU WERE FIGHTING THE BIG NABERIUS...
YOU SHOUTED OUT TO HIM...
"MY LIFE IS DULL WITHOUT YOU!"
YOU ACT SO ALOOF, BUT YOU REALLY CARE ABOUT YOUR FRIENDS!
I WAS JUST SO TOUCHED.

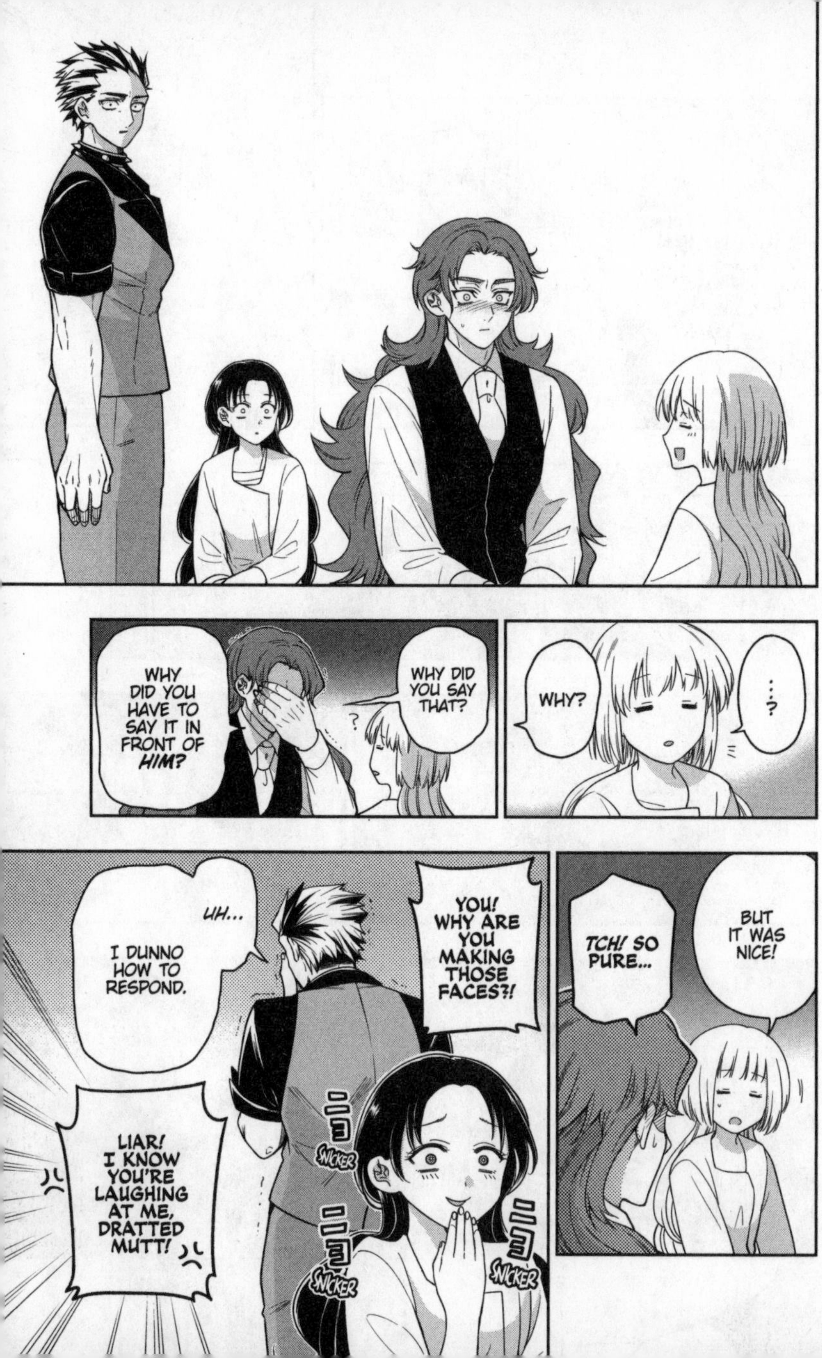
…?
WHY?
WHY DID YOU SAY THAT?
WHY DID YOU HAVE TO SAY IT IN FRONT OF *HIM*?
BUT IT WAS NICE!
TCH! SO PURE...
YOU! WHY ARE YOU MAKING THOSE FACES?!
UH... I DUNNO HOW TO RESPOND.
SNICKER
LIAR! I KNOW YOU'RE LAUGHING AT ME, DRATTED MUTT!
SNICKER
SNICKER

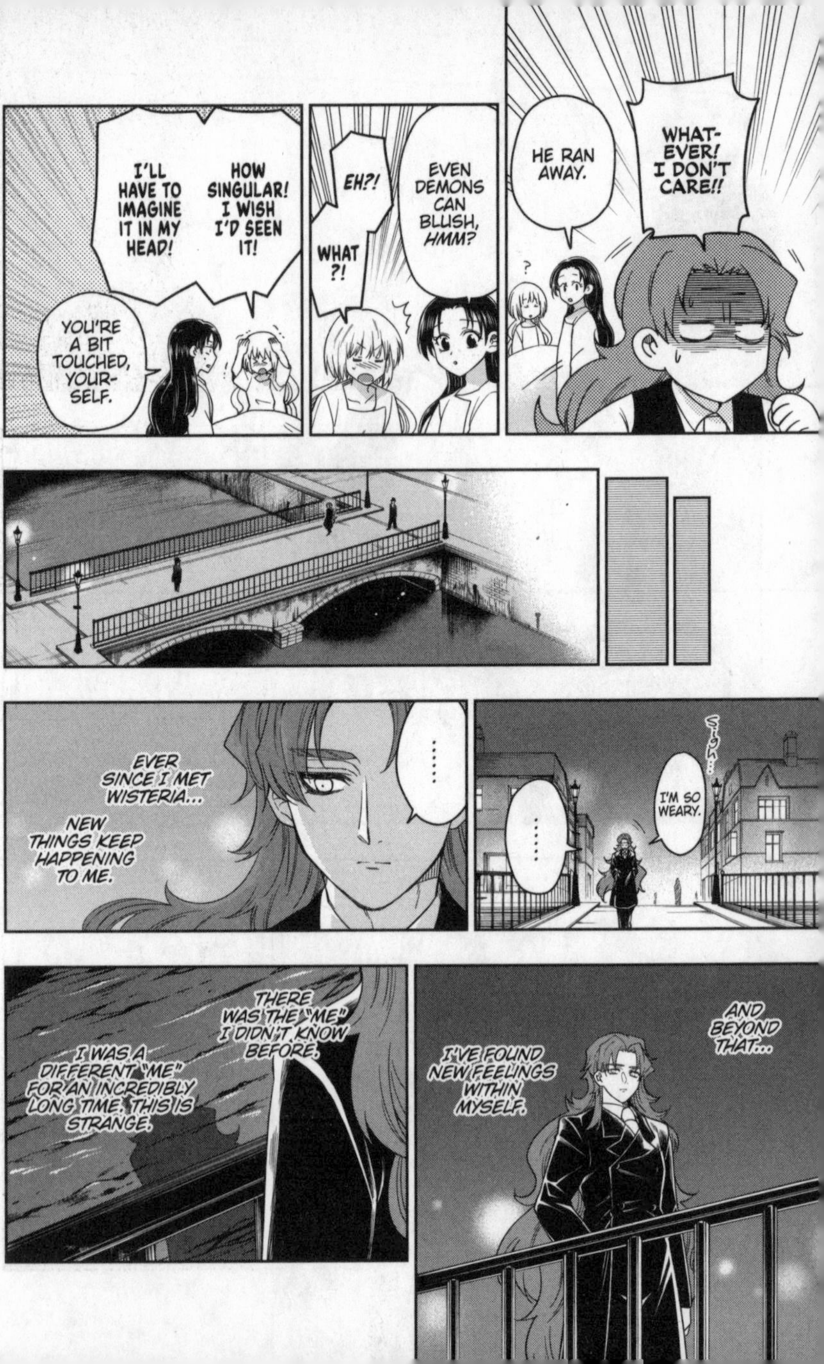

WHAT-EVER! I DON'T CARE!!
HE RAN AWAY.
EVEN DEMONS CAN BLUSH, HMM?
EH?!
WHAT?!
HOW SINGULAR! I WISH I'D SEEN IT!
I'LL HAVE TO IMAGINE IT IN MY HEAD!
YOU'RE A BIT TOUCHED, YOURSELF.
Sigh...
I'M SO WEARY.
......
......
EVER SINCE I MET WISTERIA...
NEW THINGS KEEP HAPPENING TO ME.
AND BEYOND THAT...
I'VE FOUND NEW FEELINGS WITHIN MYSELF.
THERE WAS THE "ME" I DIDN'T KNOW BEFORE.
I WAS A DIFFERENT "ME" FOR AN INCREDIBLY LONG TIME. THIS IS STRANGE.

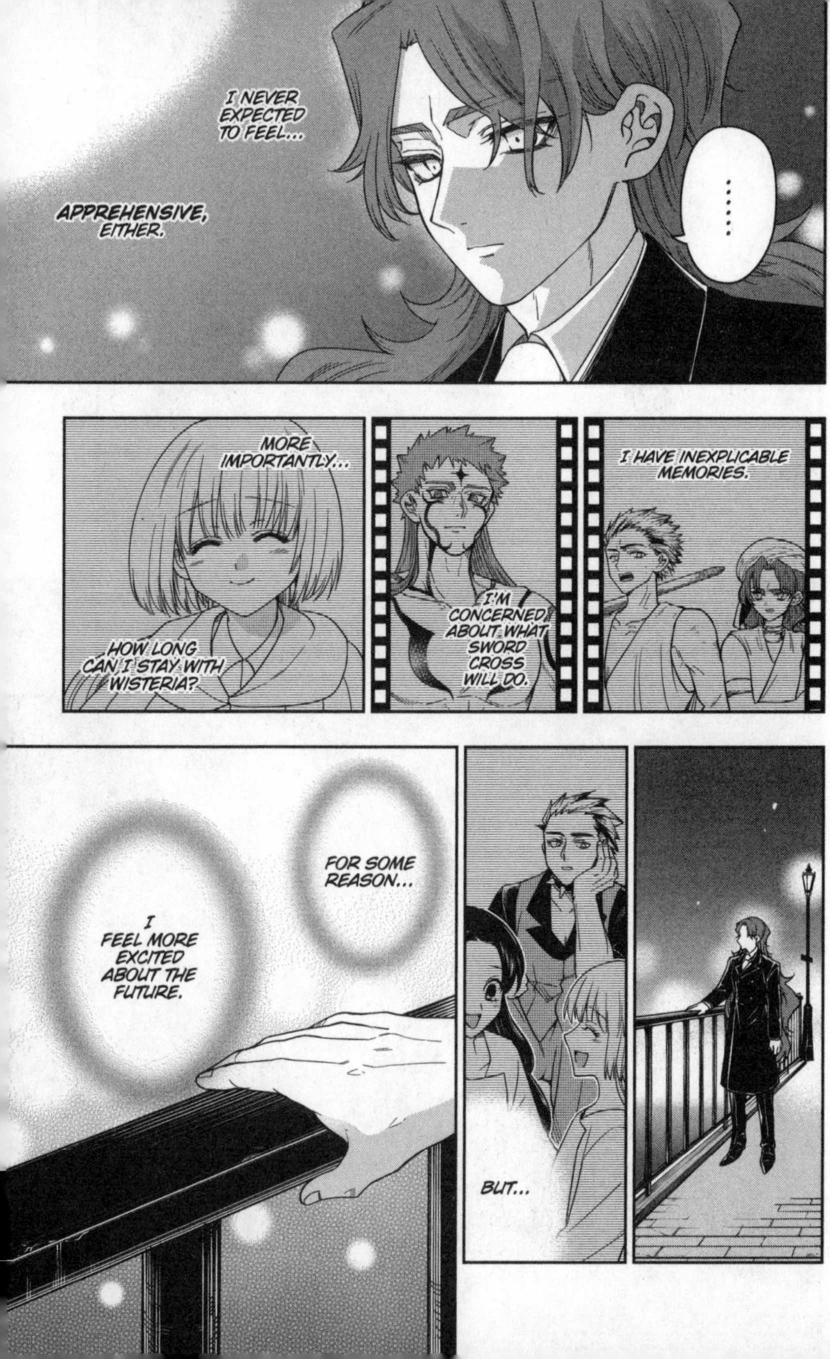
......
I NEVER EXPECTED TO FEEL...
APPREHENSIVE, EITHER.
I HAVE INEXPLICABLE MEMORIES.
I'M CONCERNED ABOUT WHAT SWORD CROSS WILL DO.
MORE IMPORTANTLY...
HOW LONG CAN I STAY WITH WISTERIA?
BUT...
FOR SOME REASON...
I FEEL MORE EXCITED ABOUT THE FUTURE.

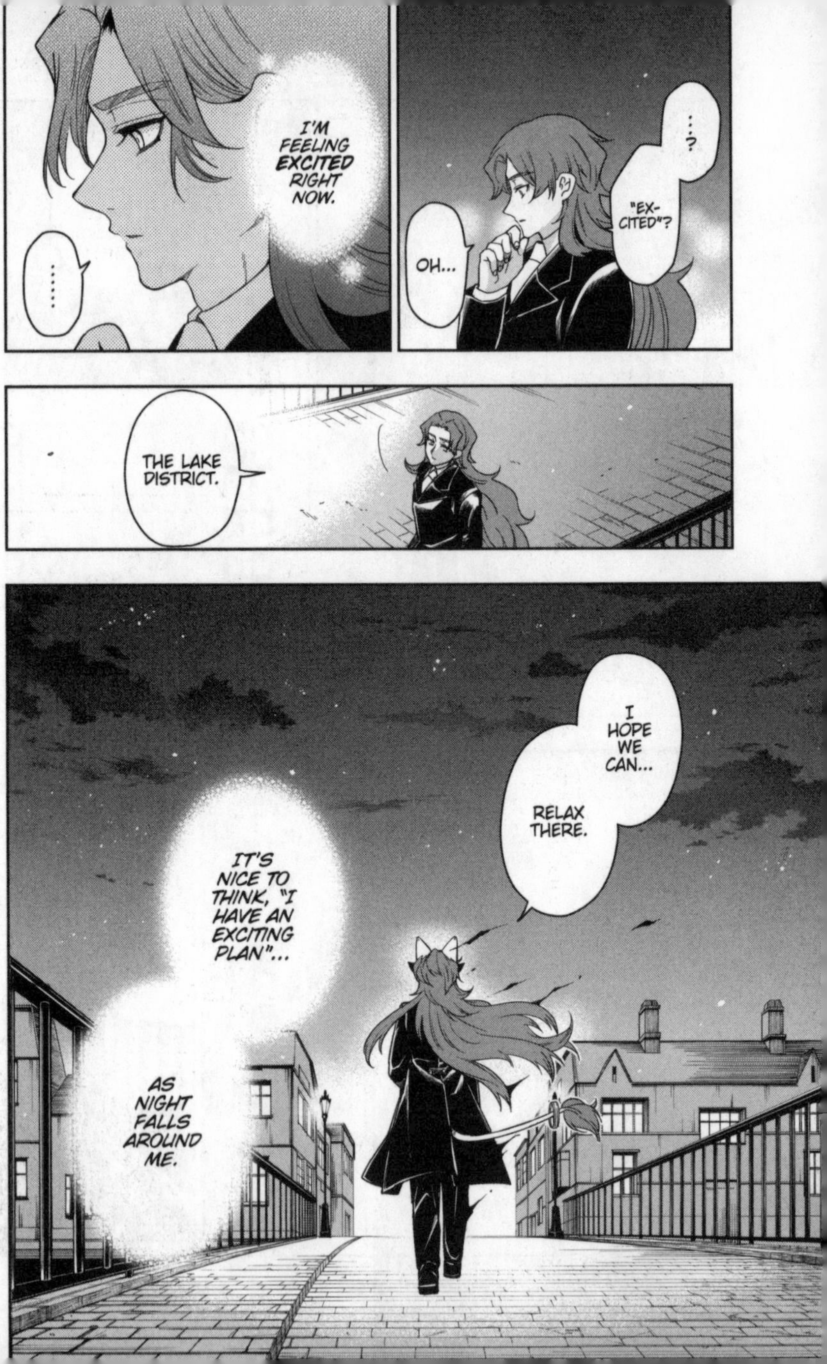
…?
"EX-CITED"?
OH…
I'M FEELING EXCITED RIGHT NOW.
……
THE LAKE DISTRICT.
I HOPE WE CAN…
RELAX THERE.
IT'S NICE TO THINK, "I HAVE AN EXCITING PLAN"…
AS NIGHT FALLS AROUND ME.

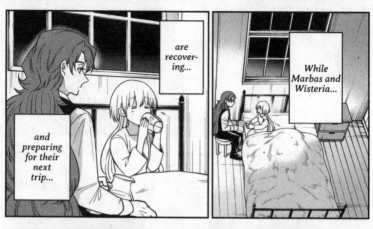

⚜Night 37⚜ The Curtain Rises with a Gunshot from the Past

While Marbas and Wisteria...
are recover-ing...
and preparing for their next trip...
A London suburb.
A cell in the Sword Cross Knights' headquar-ters.
......
WHAT TIME IS IT NOW?
NIGHT-TIME...?
IT'S NIGHT-TIME, ISN'T IT?
I DON'T LIKE THE FEEL OF THIS.
ON NIGHTS LIKE THIS...
I ALWAYS HAVE THAT DREAM.
THE ONE FROM TWO YEARS AGO.
YAAHHHH!!!
BANG BANG
Dam dam

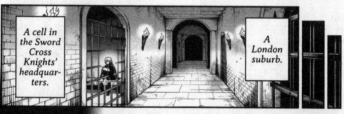

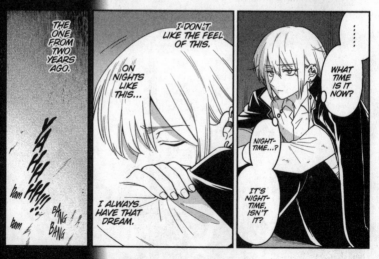

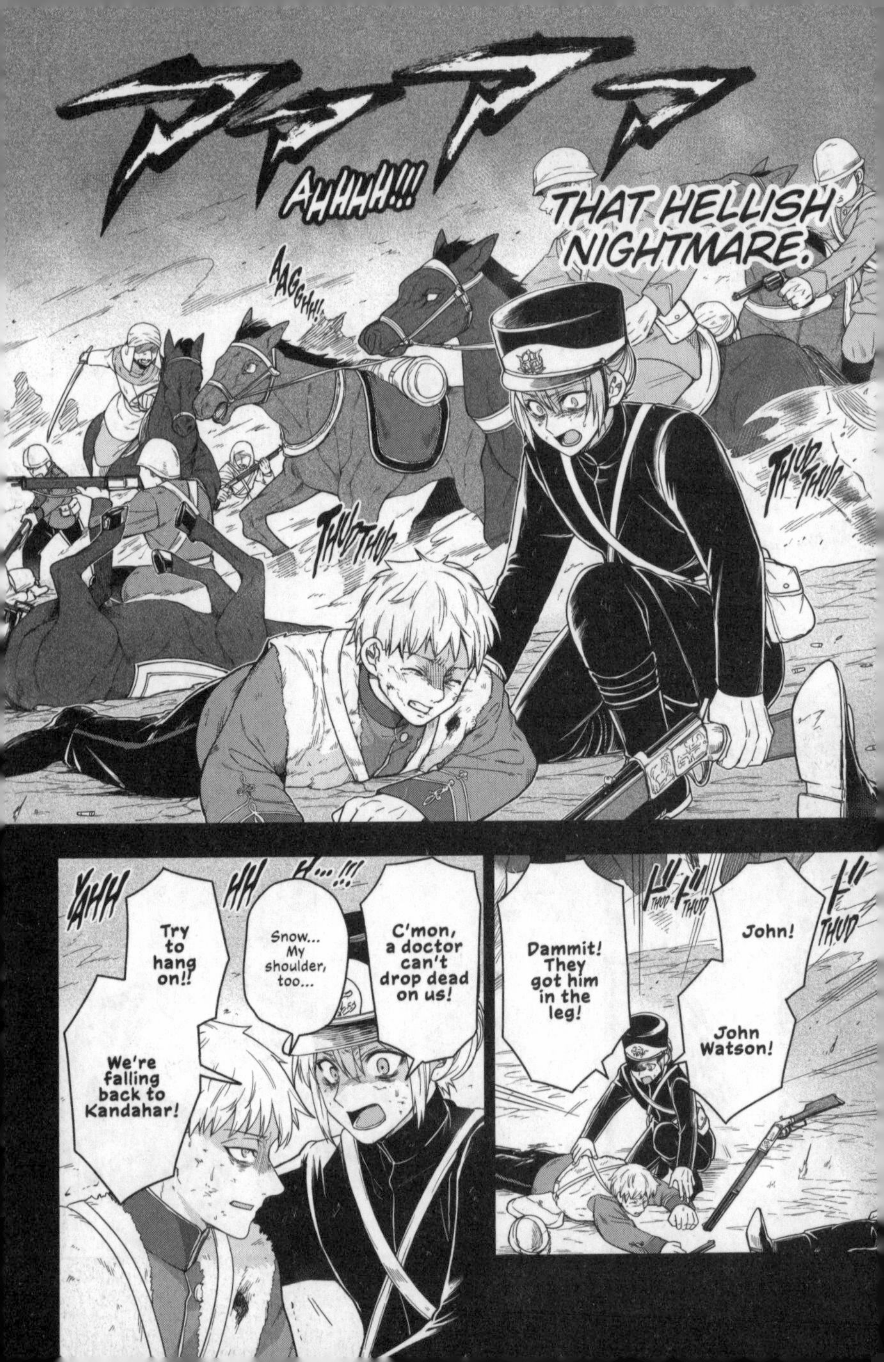
THAT HELLISH NIGHTMARE.
AHHHH!!!
THUD THUD
AAGGHH!!
THUD THUD
THUD
THUD
THUD
John!
John Watson!
Dammit! They got him in the leg!
YAHH HH H...!!!
C'mon, a doctor can't drop dead on us!
Snow... My shoulder, too...
Try to hang on!!
We're falling back to Kandahar!

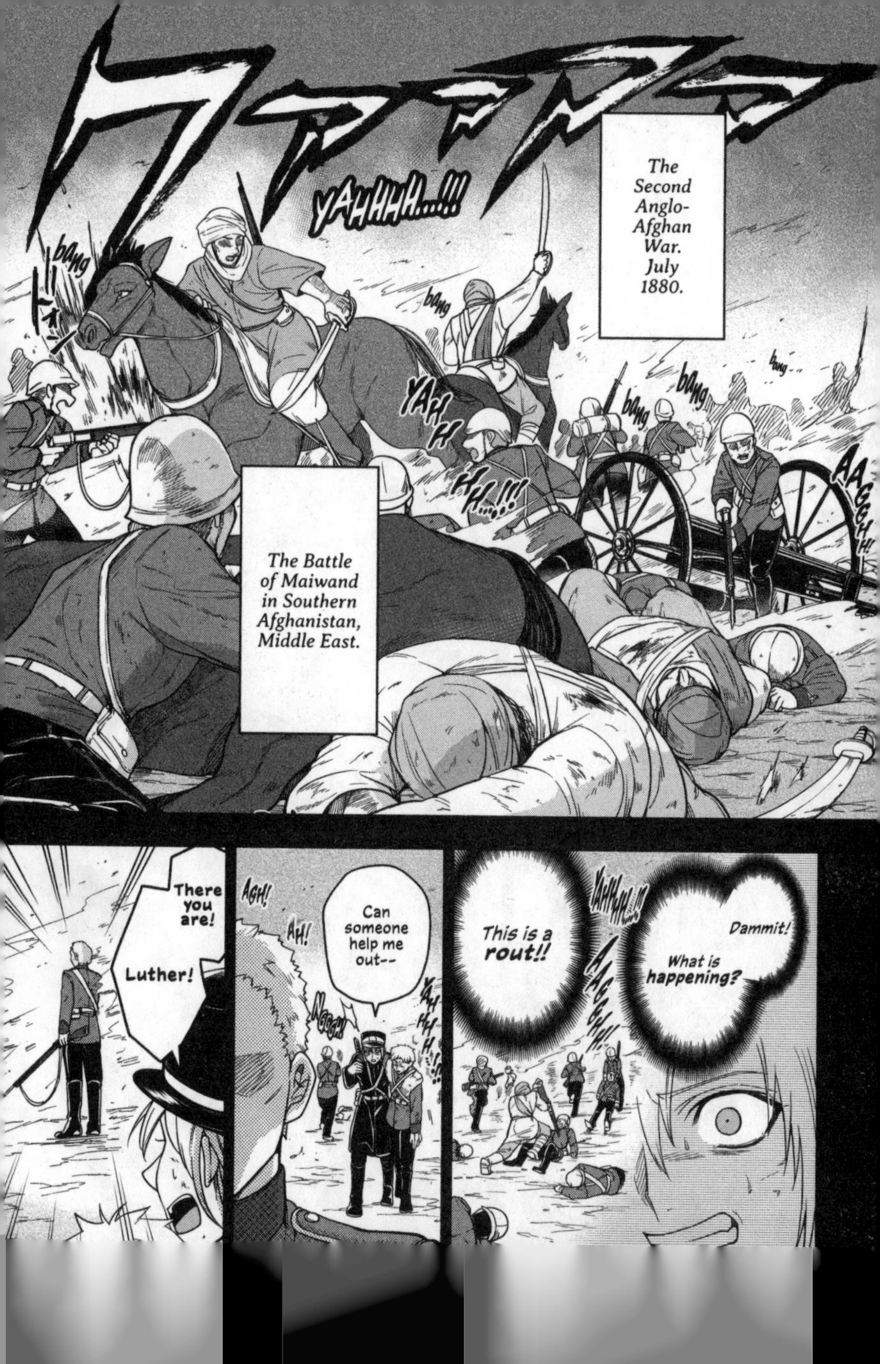
The Second Anglo-Afghan War. July 1880.
YAHHHH...!!!
The Battle of Maiwand in Southern Afghanistan, Middle East.
bang
bang
bang
bang
bang
YAHHH...!!!
AAGGHH!!
Dammit!
What is happening?
YAHHHH...!!!
AAGGHH!!
This is a rout!!
Can someone help me out--
AGH!
AH!
NGGGH!
YAHHHH...!!
There you are!
Luther!

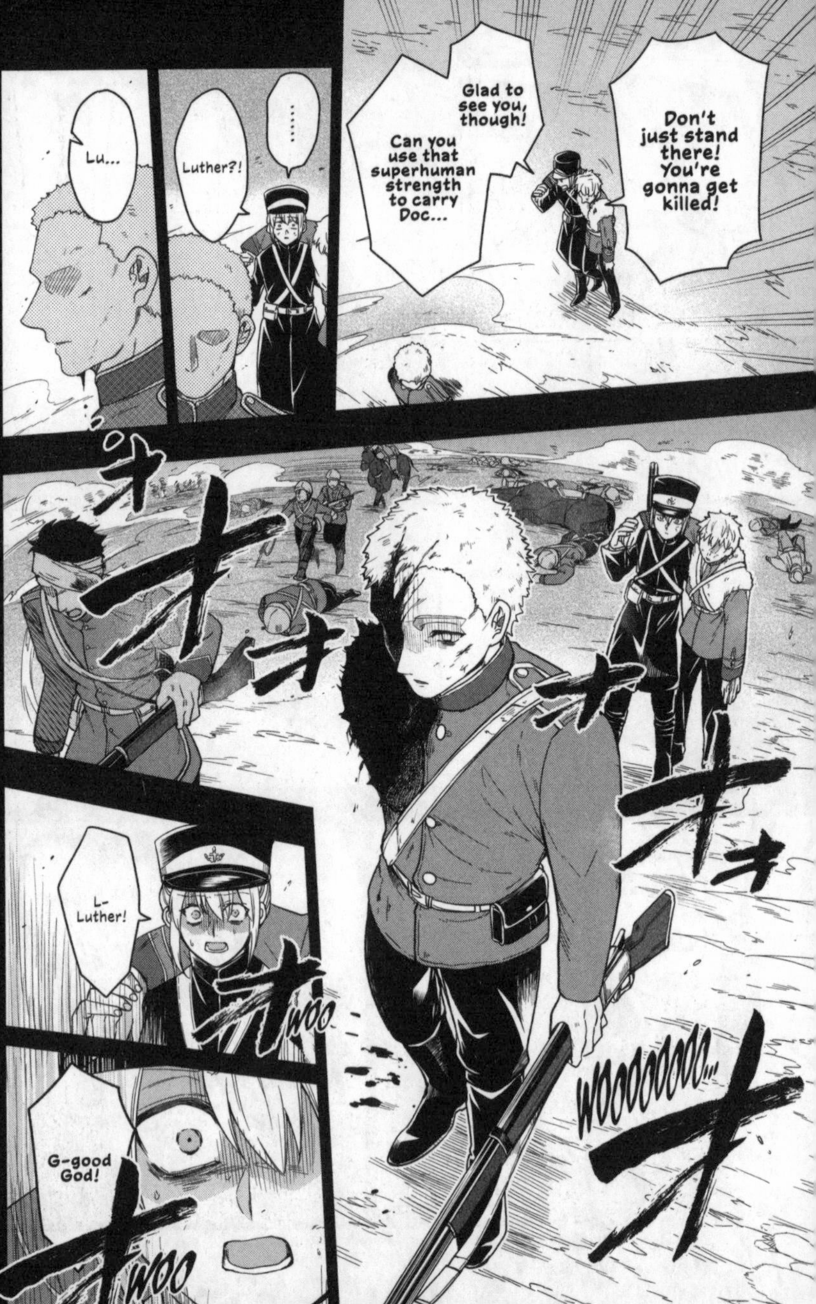

Don't just stand there! You're gonna get killed!
Glad to see you, though!
Can you use that superhuman strength to carry Doc...
......
Luther?!
Lu...
WOOOOOOO...
L-Luther!
WOO
G-good God!
WOO

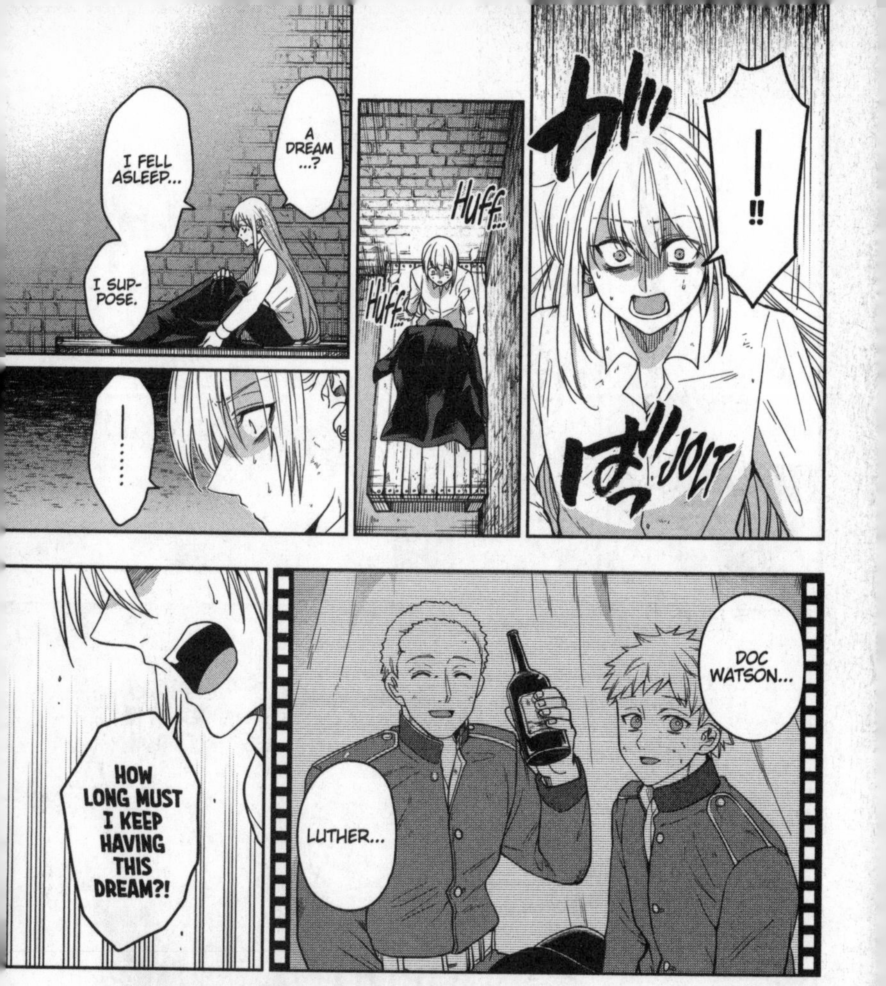
—!!
JOLT
Huff...
Huff...
A DREAM ...?
I FELL ASLEEP...
I SUP-POSE.
—......
DOC WATSON...
LUTHER...
HOW LONG MUST I KEEP HAVING THIS DREAM?!

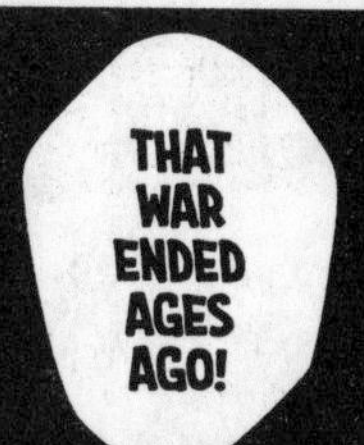
THAT WAR ENDED AGES AGO!

⚜Night 37⚜
The Curtain Rises with a Gunshot from the Past

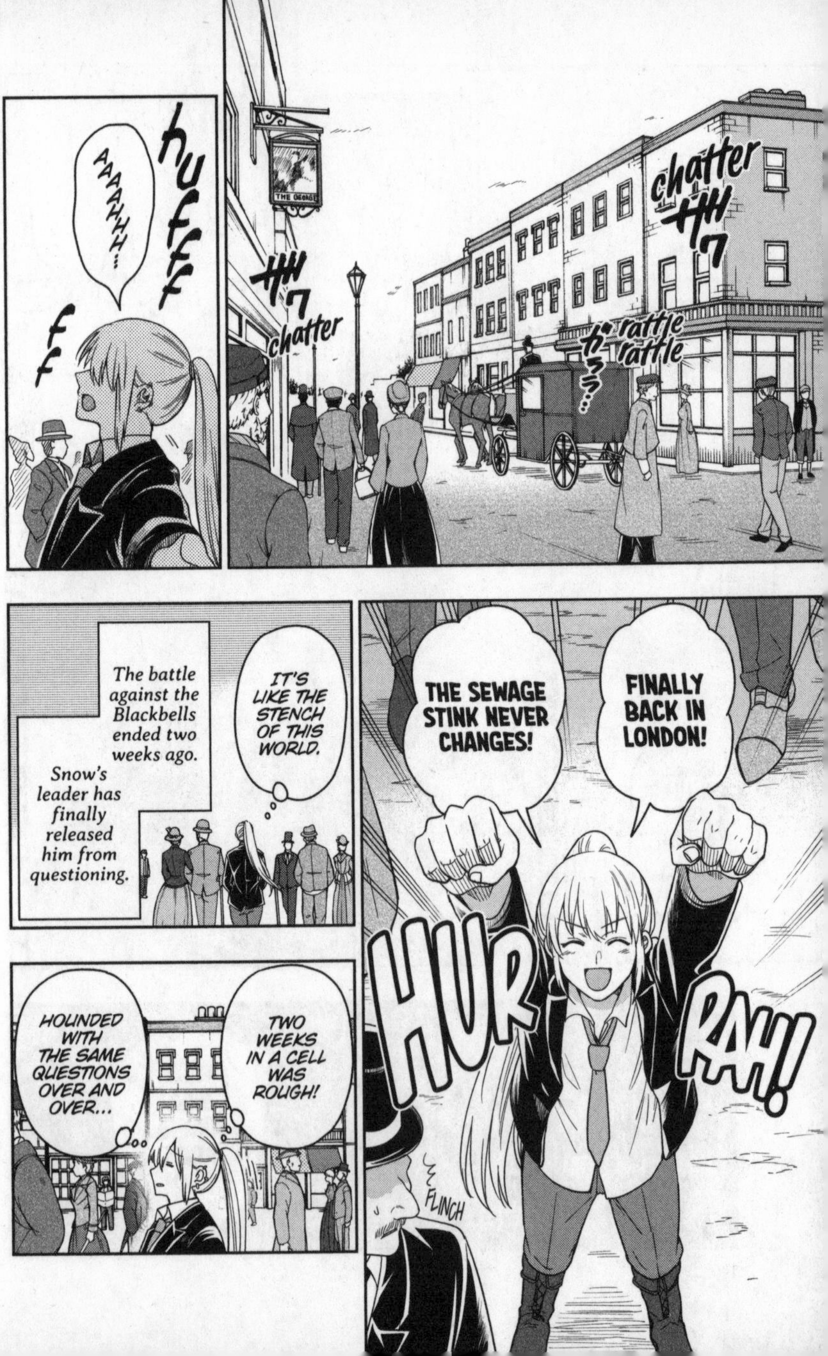
chatter
chatter
rattle rattle
AAAAHHH..!
hufffff
ff
FINALLY BACK IN LONDON!
THE SEWAGE STINK NEVER CHANGES!
HURRAH!
FLINCH
The battle against the Blackbells ended two weeks ago. Snow's leader has finally released him from questioning.
IT'S LIKE THE STENCH OF THIS WORLD.
TWO WEEKS IN A CELL WAS ROUGH!
HOUNDED WITH THE SAME QUESTIONS OVER AND OVER...

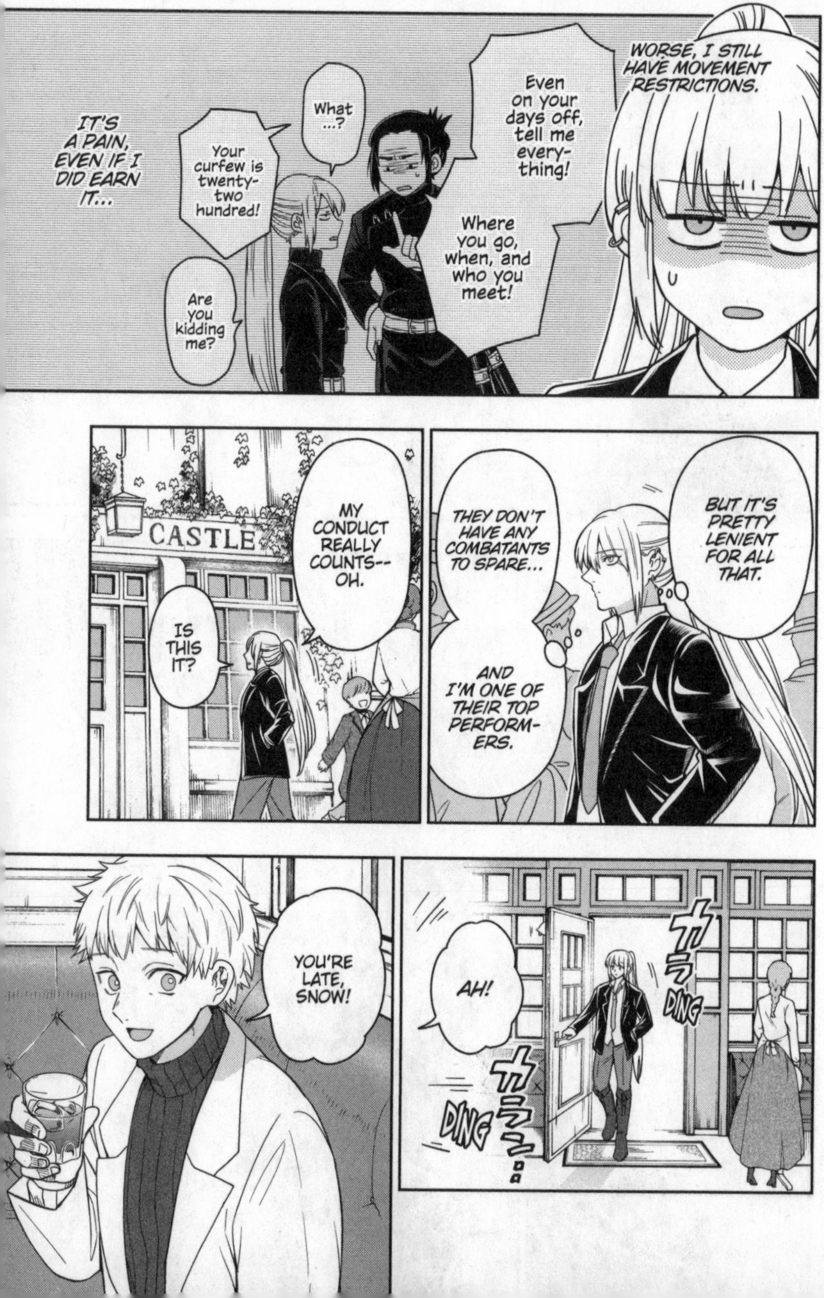
WORSE, I STILL HAVE MOVEMENT RESTRICTIONS.
Even on your days off, tell me every-thing!
Where you go, when, and who you meet!
What ...?
Your curfew is twenty-two hundred!
IT'S A PAIN, EVEN IF I DID EARN IT...
Are you kidding me?
BUT IT'S PRETTY LENIENT FOR ALL THAT.
THEY DON'T HAVE ANY COMBATANTS TO SPARE...
AND I'M ONE OF THEIR TOP PERFORM-ERS.
CASTLE
MY CONDUCT REALLY COUNTS-- OH.
IS THIS IT?
カラ
DING
AH!
カラン
DING
YOU'RE LATE, SNOW!

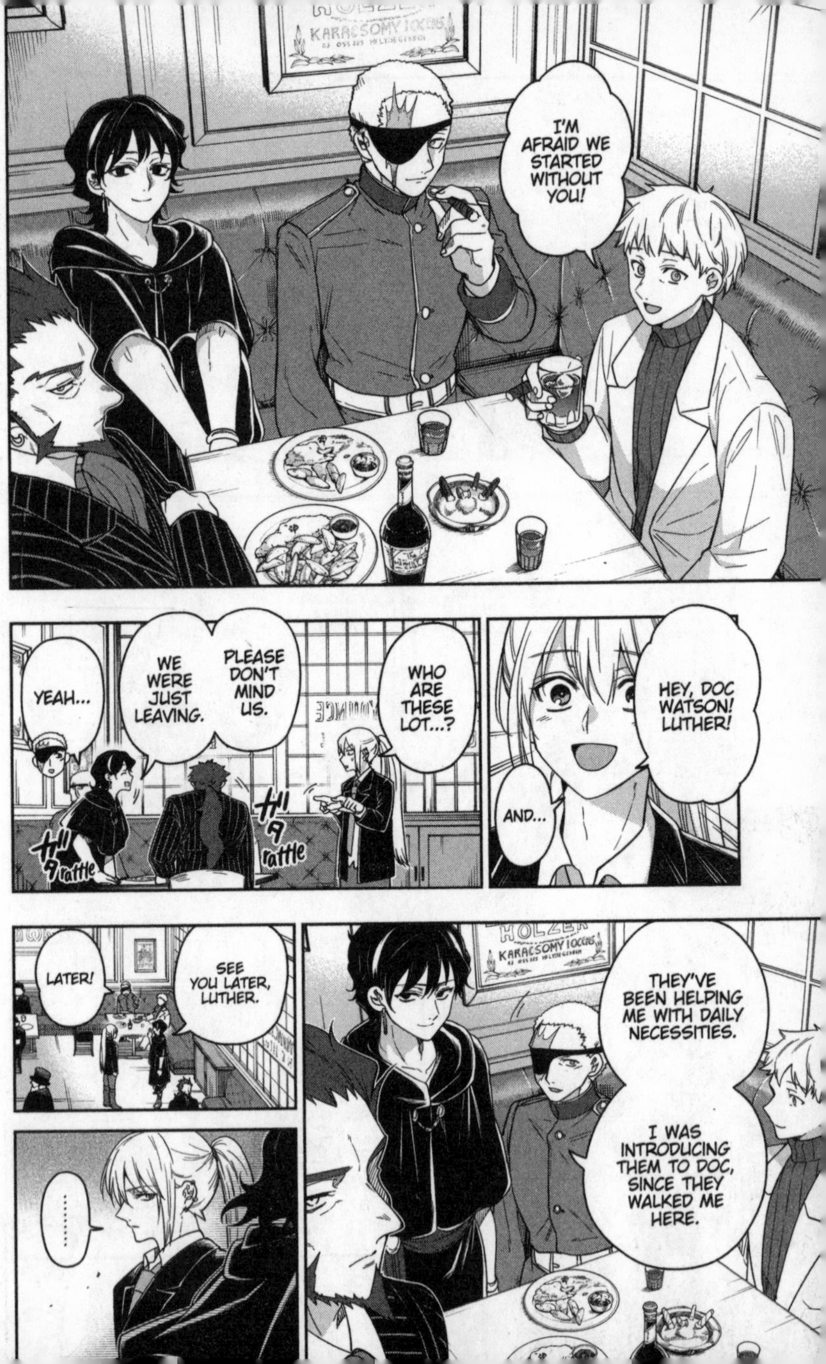
I'M AFRAID WE STARTED WITHOUT YOU!
HEY, DOC WATSON! LUTHER!
AND...
WHO ARE THESE LOT...?
PLEASE DON'T MIND US.
WE WERE JUST LEAVING.
YEAH...
rattle
rattle
THEY'VE BEEN HELPING ME WITH DAILY NECESSITIES.
I WAS INTRODUCING THEM TO DOC, SINCE THEY WALKED ME HERE.
SEE YOU LATER, LUTHER.
LATER!
......

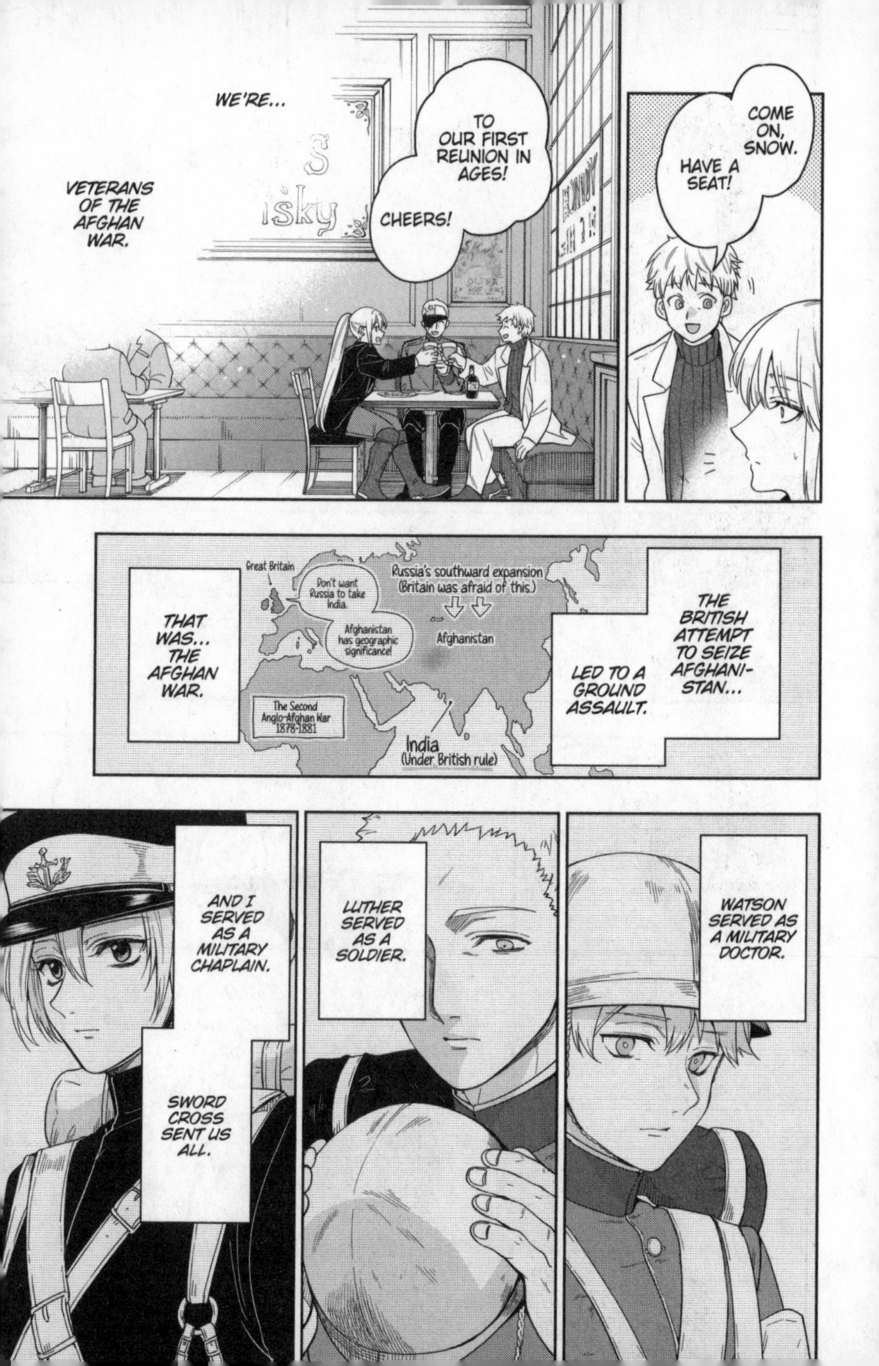
COME ON, SNOW.
HAVE A SEAT!
TO OUR FIRST REUNION IN AGES!
CHEERS!
WE'RE...
VETERANS OF THE AFGHAN WAR.
THE BRITISH ATTEMPT TO SEIZE AFGHANI-STAN...
LED TO A GROUND ASSAULT.
Russia's southward expansion (Britain was afraid of this.)
Afghanistan
India (Under British rule)
Great Britain
Don't want Russia to take India.
Afghanistan has geographic significance!
The Second Anglo-Afghan War 1878-1881
THAT WAS... THE AFGHAN WAR.
WATSON SERVED AS A MILITARY DOCTOR.
LUTHER SERVED AS A SOLDIER.
AND I SERVED AS A MILITARY CHAPLAIN.
SWORD CROSS SENT US ALL.

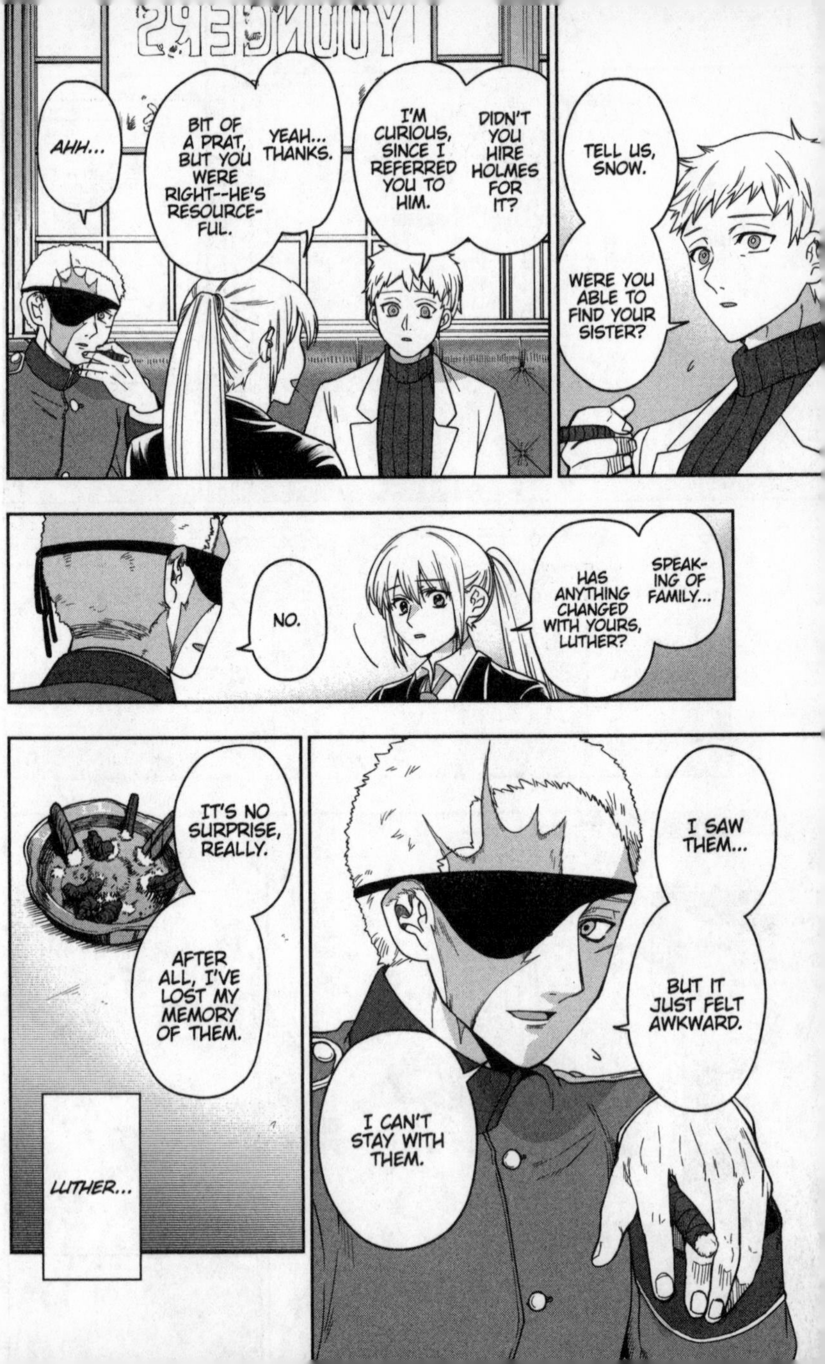
TELL US, SNOW.
WERE YOU ABLE TO FIND YOUR SISTER?
DIDN'T YOU HIRE HOLMES FOR IT?
I'M CURIOUS, SINCE I REFERRED YOU TO HIM.
YEAH... THANKS.
BIT OF A PRAT, BUT YOU WERE RIGHT--HE'S RESOURCE-FUL.
AHH...
SPEAK-ING OF FAMILY...
HAS ANYTHING CHANGED WITH YOURS, LUTHER?
NO.
I SAW THEM...
BUT IT JUST FELT AWKWARD.
I CAN'T STAY WITH THEM.
IT'S NO SURPRISE, REALLY.
AFTER ALL, I'VE LOST MY MEMORY OF THEM.
LUTHER...

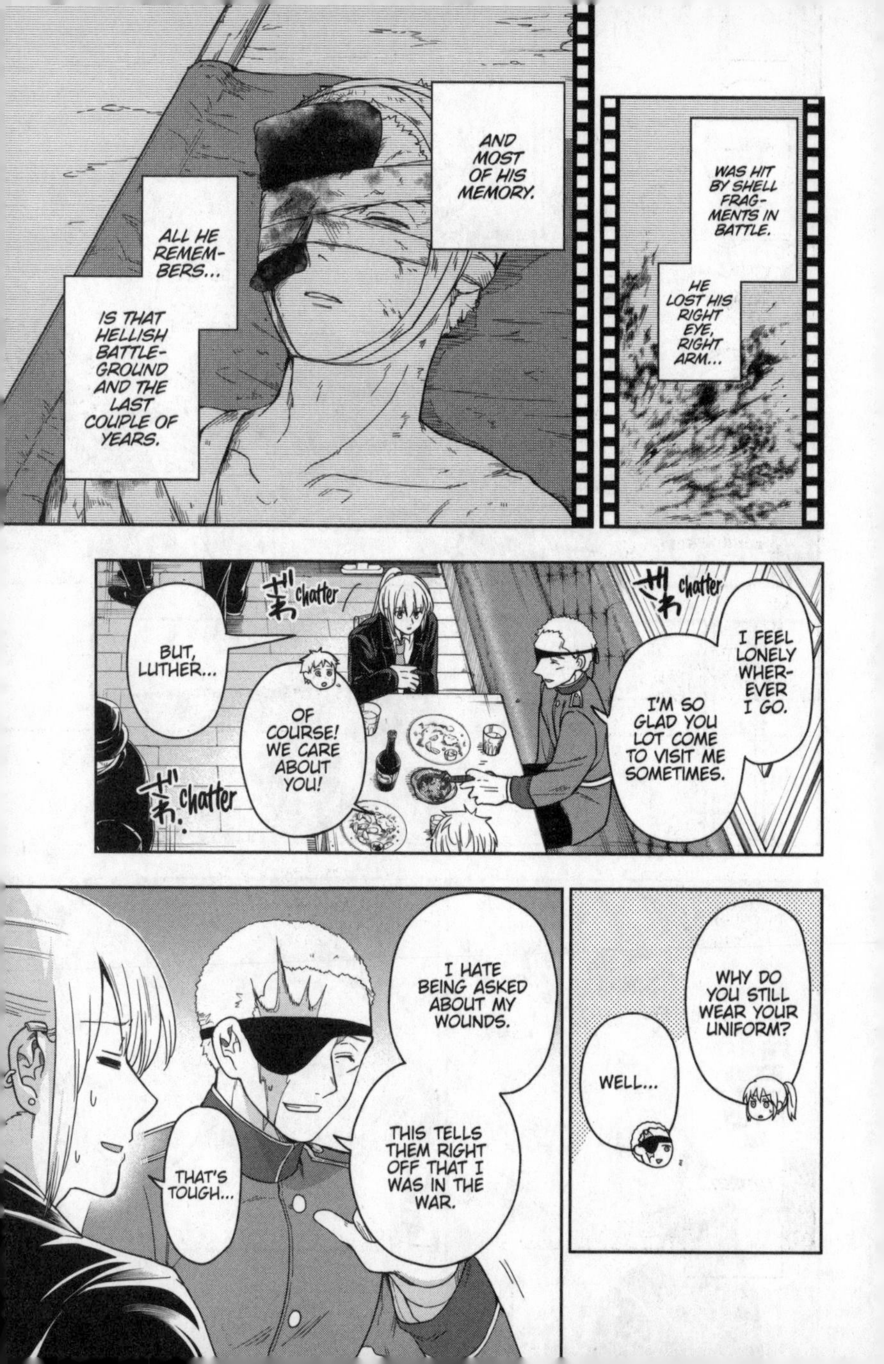
WAS HIT BY SHELL FRAGMENTS IN BATTLE.
HE LOST HIS RIGHT EYE, RIGHT ARM...
AND MOST OF HIS MEMORY.
ALL HE REMEMBERS...
IS THAT HELLISH BATTLEGROUND AND THE LAST COUPLE OF YEARS.
chatter
I FEEL LONELY WHEREVER I GO.
I'M SO GLAD YOU LOT COME TO VISIT ME SOMETIMES.
chatter
OF COURSE! WE CARE ABOUT YOU!
BUT, LUTHER...
chatter
WHY DO YOU STILL WEAR YOUR UNIFORM?
WELL...
I HATE BEING ASKED ABOUT MY WOUNDS.
THIS TELLS THEM RIGHT OFF THAT I WAS IN THE WAR.
THAT'S TOUGH...

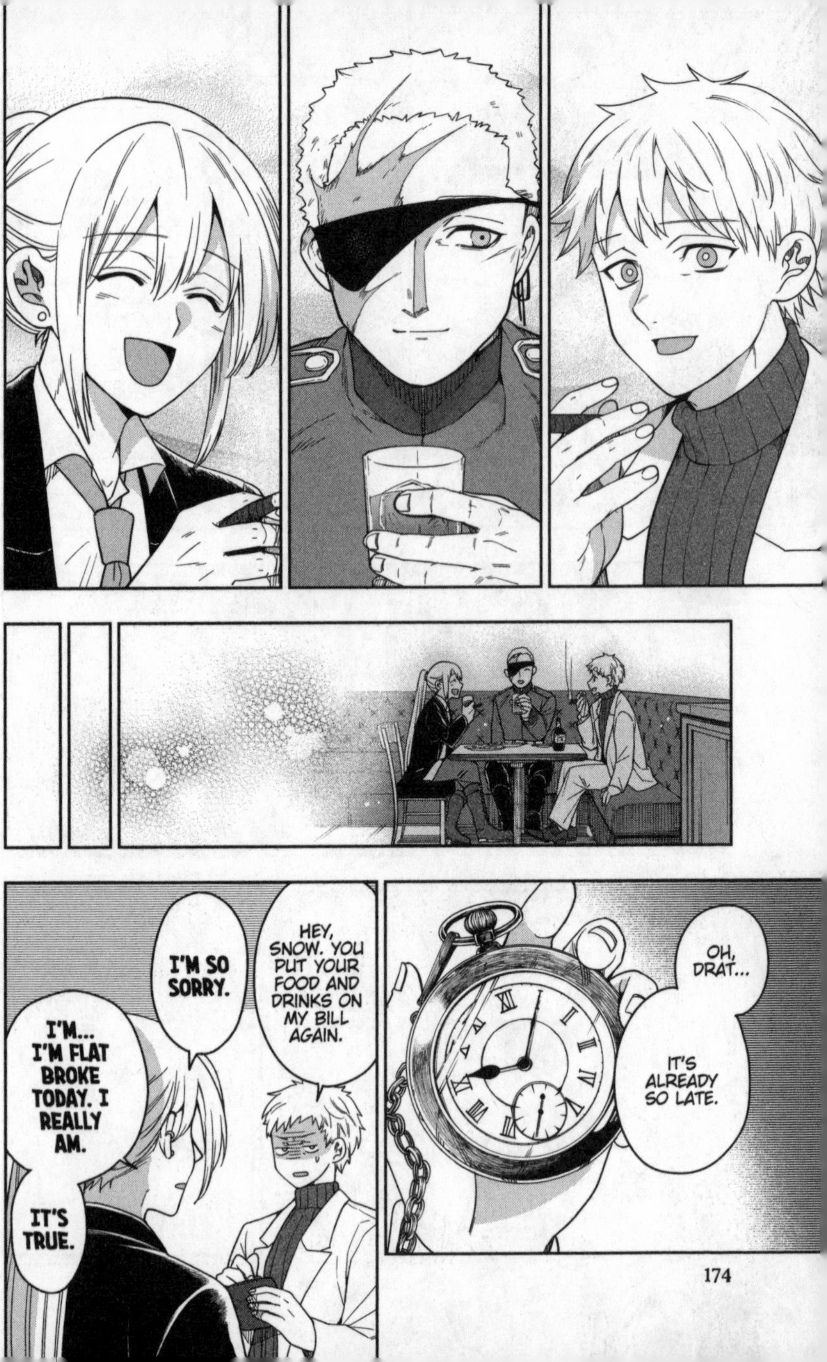
OH, DRAT...
IT'S ALREADY SO LATE.
HEY, SNOW. YOU PUT YOUR FOOD AND DRINKS ON MY BILL AGAIN.
I'M SO SORRY.
I'M... I'M FLAT BROKE TODAY. I REALLY AM.
IT'S TRUE.

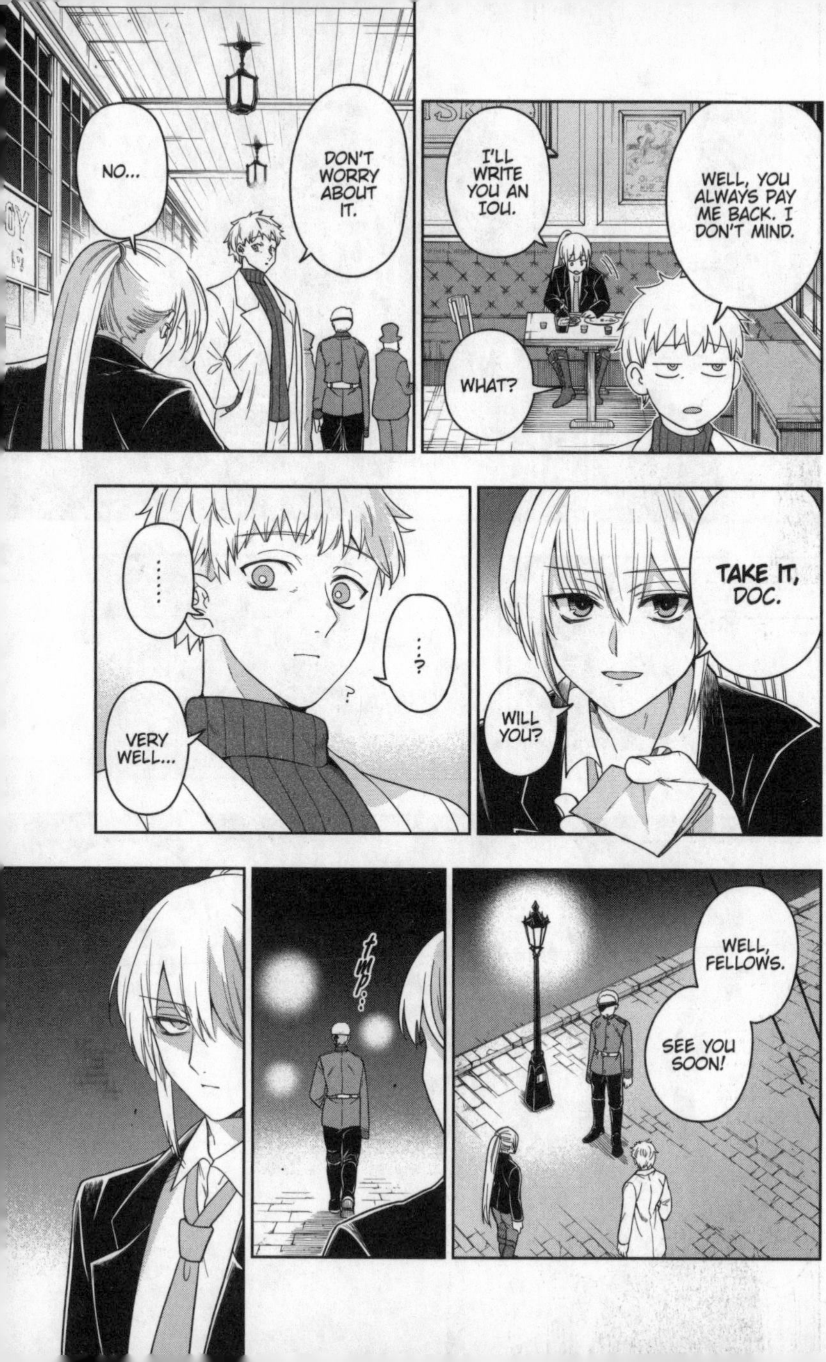
WELL, YOU ALWAYS PAY ME BACK. I DON'T MIND.
I'LL WRITE YOU AN IOU.
WHAT?
DON'T WORRY ABOUT IT.
NO...
TAKE IT, DOC.
WILL YOU?
......
...?
VERY WELL...
WELL, FELLOWS.
SEE YOU SOON!
tmp...

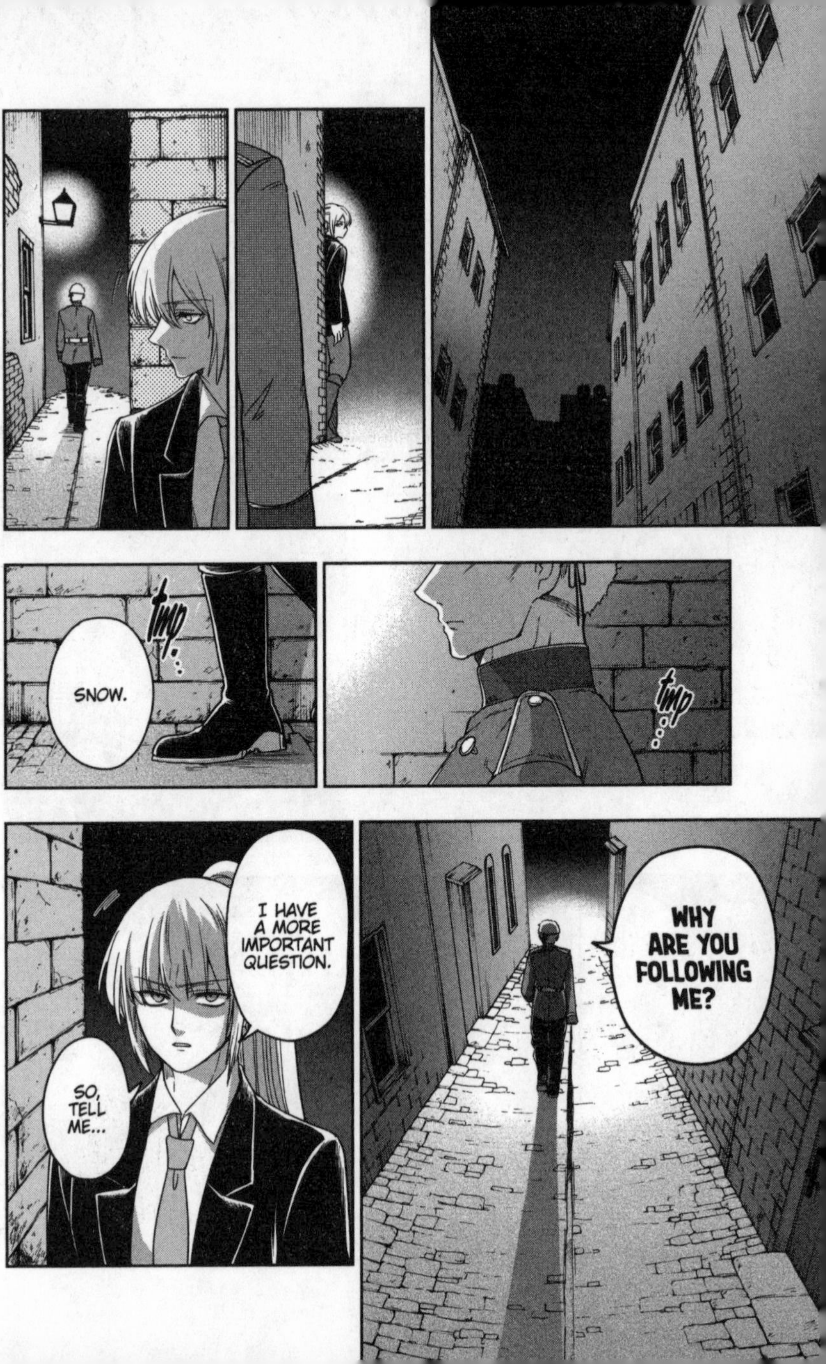
tmp...
tmp...
SNOW.
WHY ARE YOU FOLLOWING ME?
I HAVE A MORE IMPORTANT QUESTION.
SO, TELL ME...

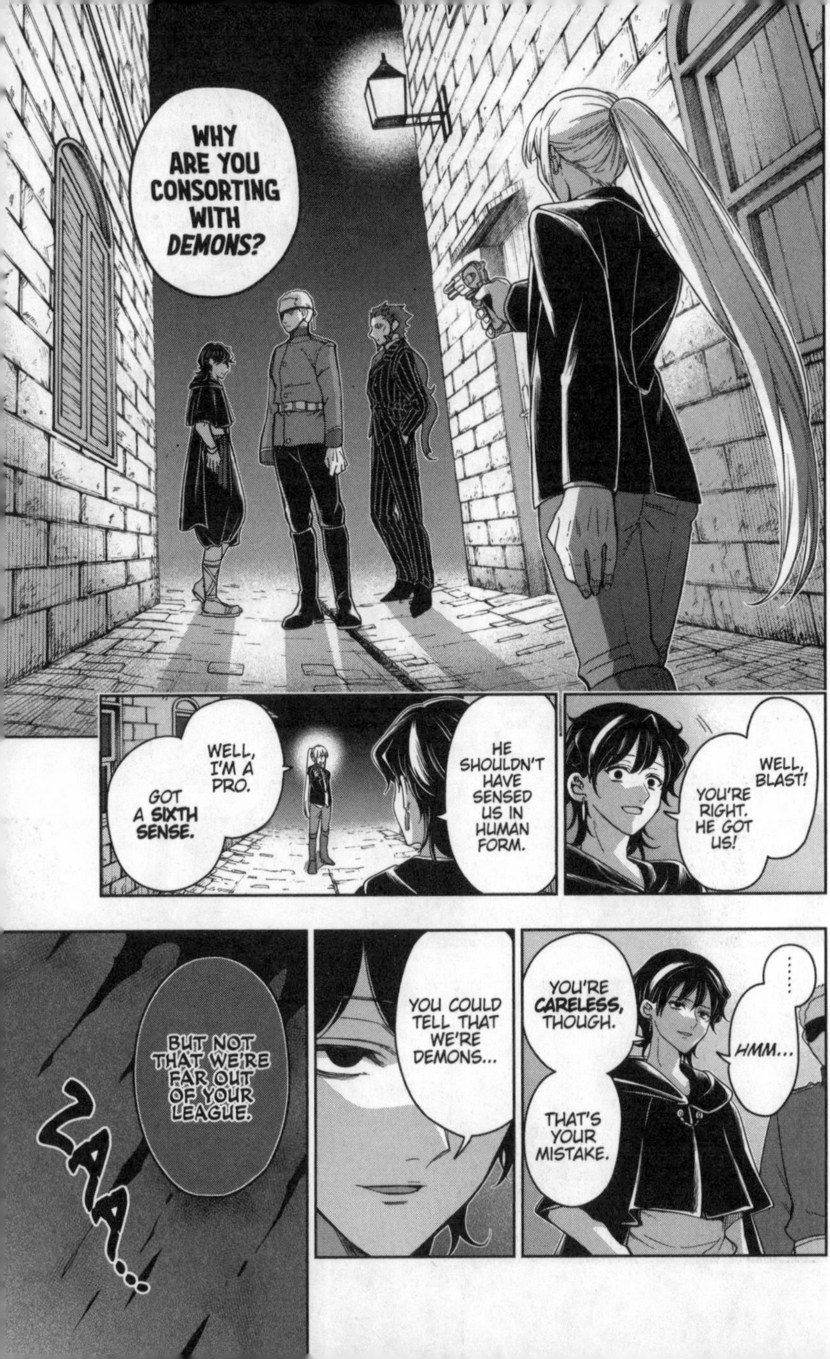
WHY ARE YOU CONSORTING WITH DEMONS?
WELL, BLAST!
YOU'RE RIGHT. HE GOT US!
HE SHOULDN'T HAVE SENSED US IN HUMAN FORM.
WELL, I'M A PRO.
GOT A SIXTH SENSE.
......
HMM...
YOU'RE CARELESS, THOUGH.
THAT'S YOUR MISTAKE.
YOU COULD TELL THAT WE'RE DEMONS...
BUT NOT THAT WE'RE FAR OUT OF YOUR LEAGUE.
ZAA...

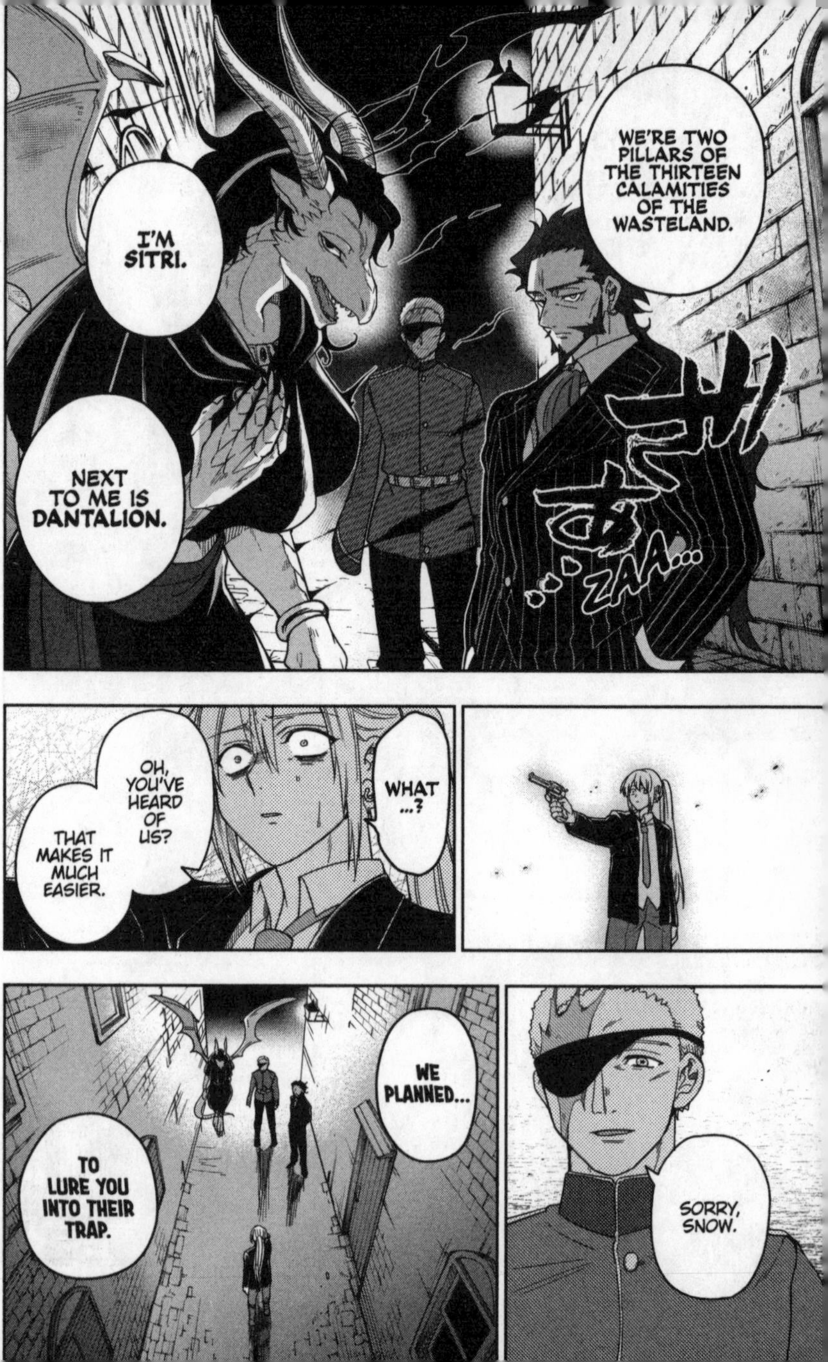
WE'RE TWO PILLARS OF THE THIRTEEN CALAMITIES OF THE WASTELAND.
I'M SITRI.
NEXT TO ME IS DANTALION.
ZAA...
WHAT ...?
OH, YOU'VE HEARD OF US?
THAT MAKES IT MUCH EASIER.
SORRY, SNOW.
WE PLANNED...
TO LURE YOU INTO THEIR TRAP.

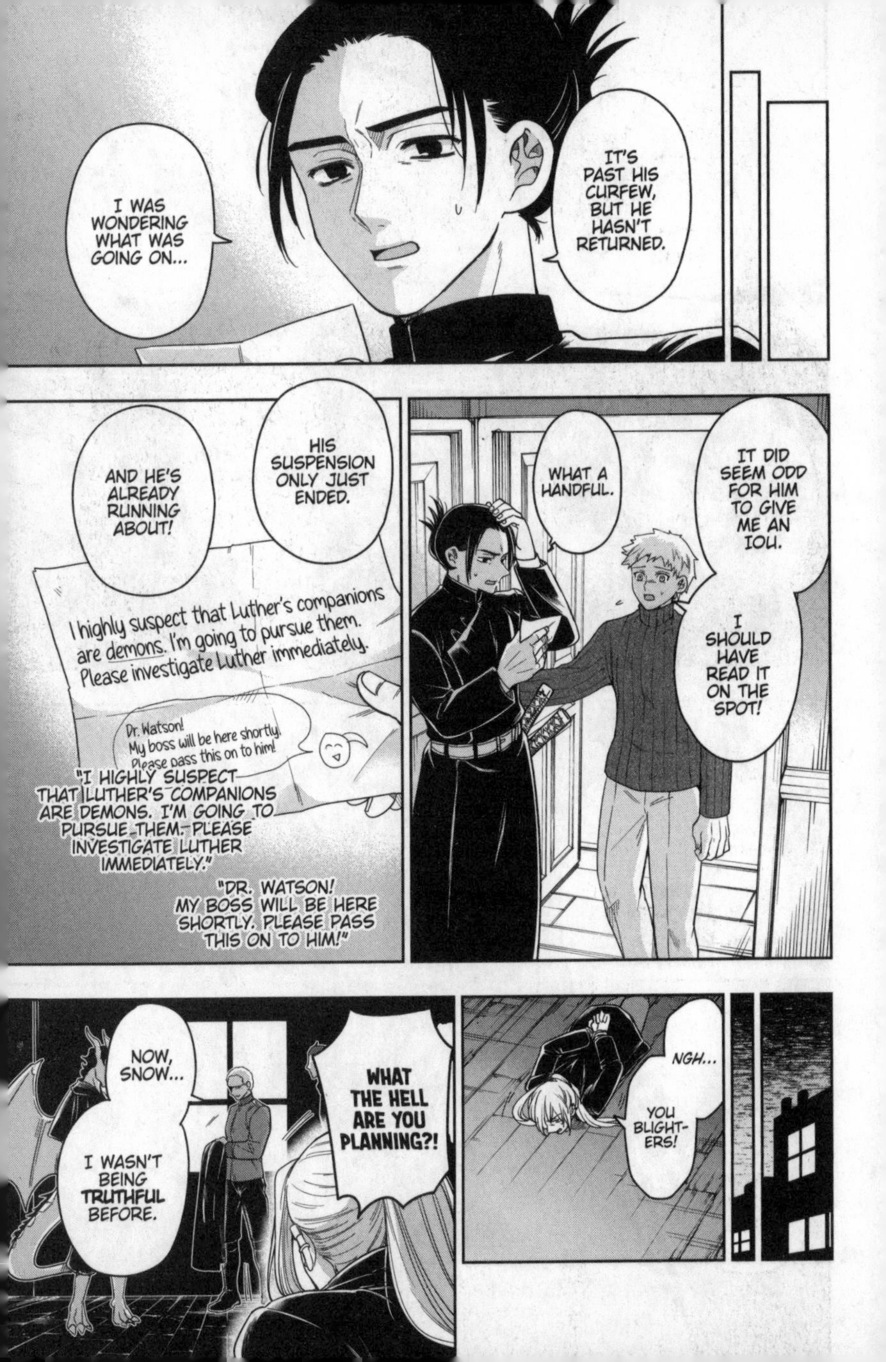
IT'S PAST HIS CURFEW, BUT HE HASN'T RETURNED.
I WAS WONDERING WHAT WAS GOING ON...
IT DID SEEM ODD FOR HIM TO GIVE ME AN IOU.
WHAT A HANDFUL.
I SHOULD HAVE READ IT ON THE SPOT!
HIS SUSPENSION ONLY JUST ENDED.
AND HE'S ALREADY RUNNING ABOUT!
I highly suspect that Luther's companions are demons. I'm going to pursue them. Please investigate Luther immediately.
Dr. Watson! My boss will be here shortly. Please pass this on to him!
"I HIGHLY SUSPECT THAT LUTHER'S COMPANIONS ARE DEMONS. I'M GOING TO PURSUE THEM. PLEASE INVESTIGATE LUTHER IMMEDIATELY."
"DR. WATSON! MY BOSS WILL BE HERE SHORTLY. PLEASE PASS THIS ON TO HIM!"
NGH...
YOU BLIGHTERS!
WHAT THE HELL ARE YOU PLANNING?!
NOW, SNOW...
I WASN'T BEING TRUTHFUL BEFORE.

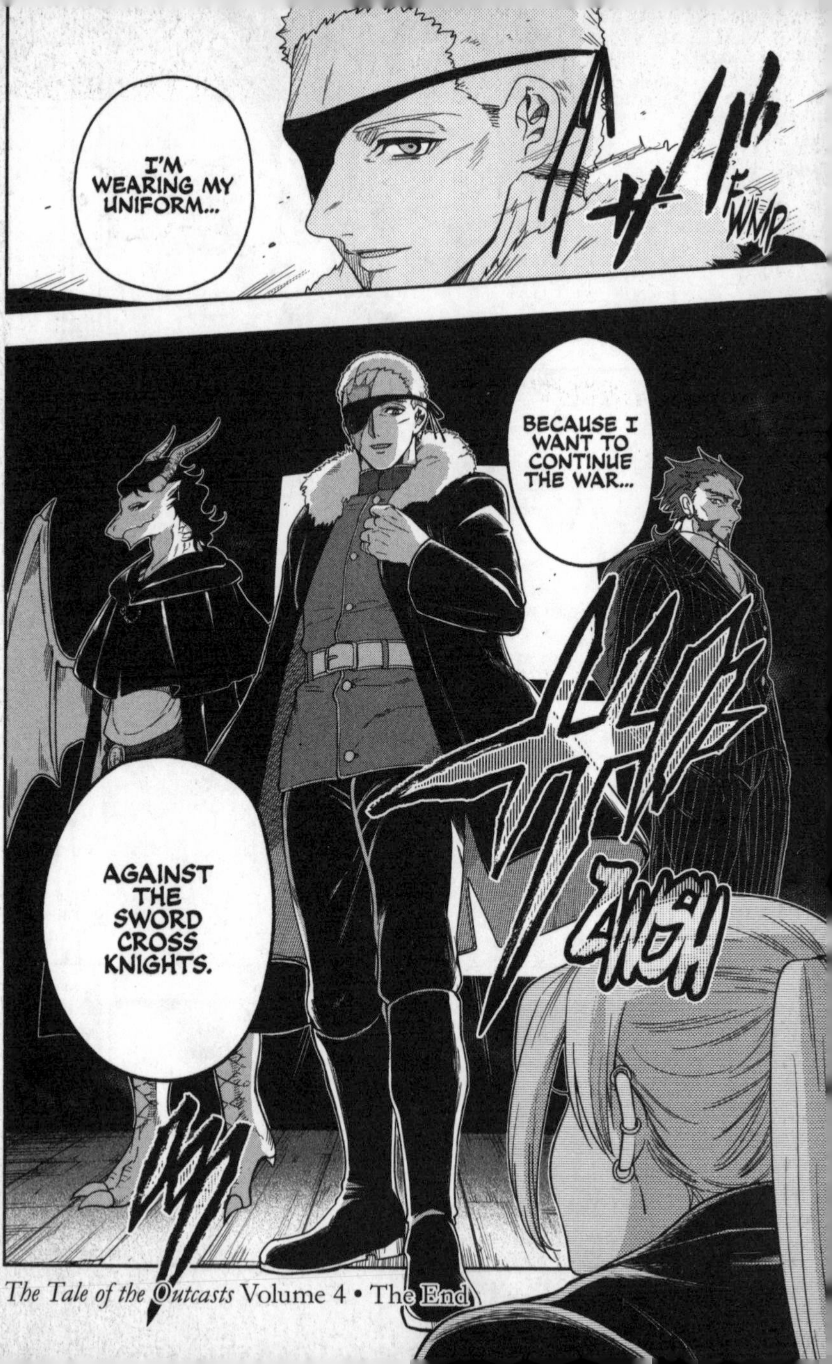
I'M WEARING MY UNIFORM...
FWMP
BECAUSE I WANT TO CONTINUE THE WAR...
ZANGH
AGAINST THE SWORD CROSS KNIGHTS.

The Tale of the Outcasts Volume 4 • The End

Bonus
You'll be punished, of course, but not corporally!
Night 35
But I got punched in the face in Night 26.
He's scary...

The Tale of the Outcasts Volume 4

<Special Thanks>

Chihiro Makiguchi
Akihisa Maki
Sanshi Fujita
Ugebeso Hatsumaru
Hirorin

<Editors>

Shiotani-san
Ogura-san
Hayashi-san

HI! I'M THE CREATOR, HOSHINO.
THANK YOU FOR READING THE TALE OF THE OUTCASTS VOLUME 4!
I HAVE LOTS OF BONUS PAGES FOR YOU THIS TIME.
I DECIDED TO SHOW YOU SOME OF THE MANY PRELIMINARY CHARACTER DESIGNS I DREW BEFORE THE SERIAL-IZATION.
POSTING OLD DRAWINGS IS PRETTY EMBARRASSING FOR A CREATOR.
Stop!
Don't look!!
Embarrassing Stuff
I'M GOING TO DO IT ANYWAY. I HOPE YOU'LL ENJOY THEM!
IT STARTS ON THE NEXT PAGE!

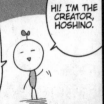

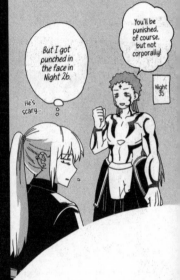

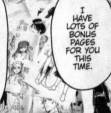

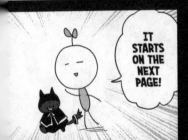

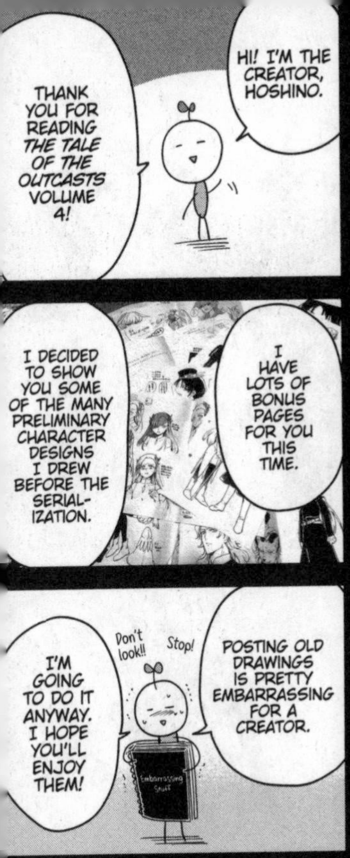

Marbas

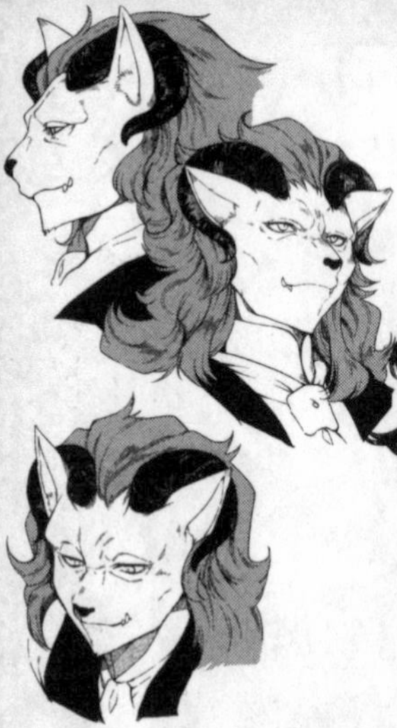

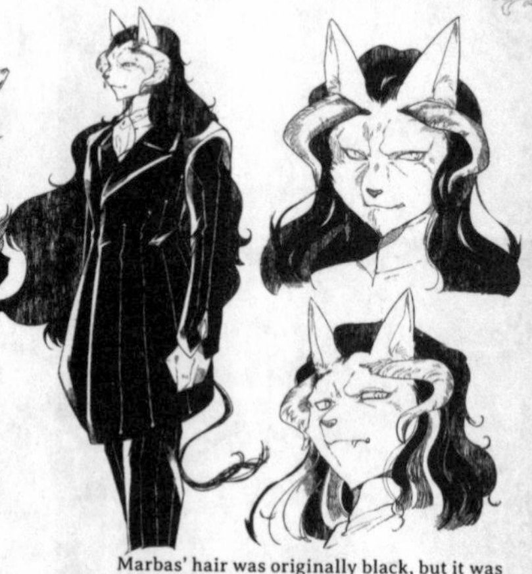

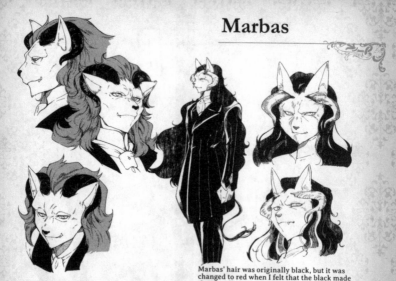

Marbas' hair was originally black, but it was changed to red when I felt that the black made the overall picture look too dark.

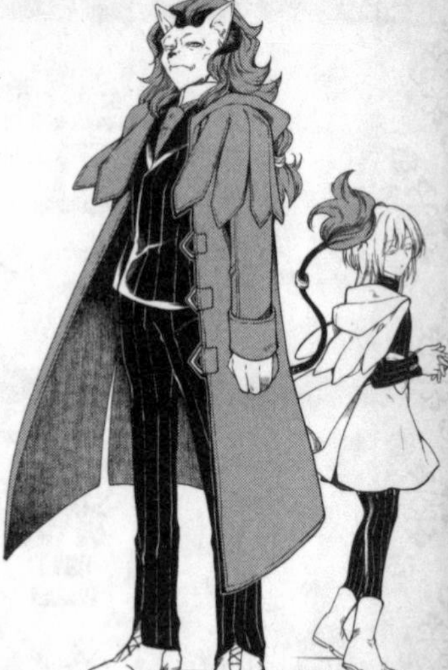

Wh-who the hell is this?!

Ugh... I didn't really want to show this! (laughs) In his initial designs, Marbas looked burly, or like...a middle-aged man.

Actually, I had never drawn any beastmen until I planned out this series. I learned through trial and error.

In the first chapter, I redrew his face twice: once before it was released in a magazine and again before the book came out. I ended up drawing the same face three times over for fifty-nine pages! It was hard labor.

If anyone asks, "Why did you make the protagonist a beastman if you were bad at it?" my response is, "Because I wanted to!"

As hard as it may be, I really have fun drawing Marbas' face.

Wisteria

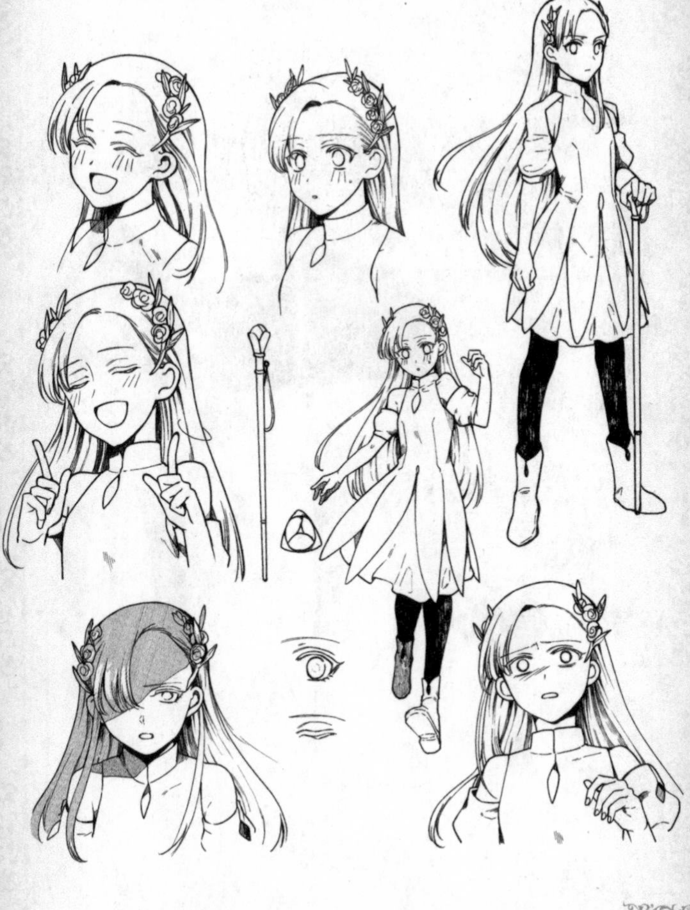

This is Wisteria's "Preliminaria." She is much more feminine and less of a country bumpkin. Her original name was Chris, but it was changed to Wisteria when I realized I had too many characters with similar names. It came from Wakamurasaki from *The Tale of Genji.* It has nothing to do with England!

Wisteria

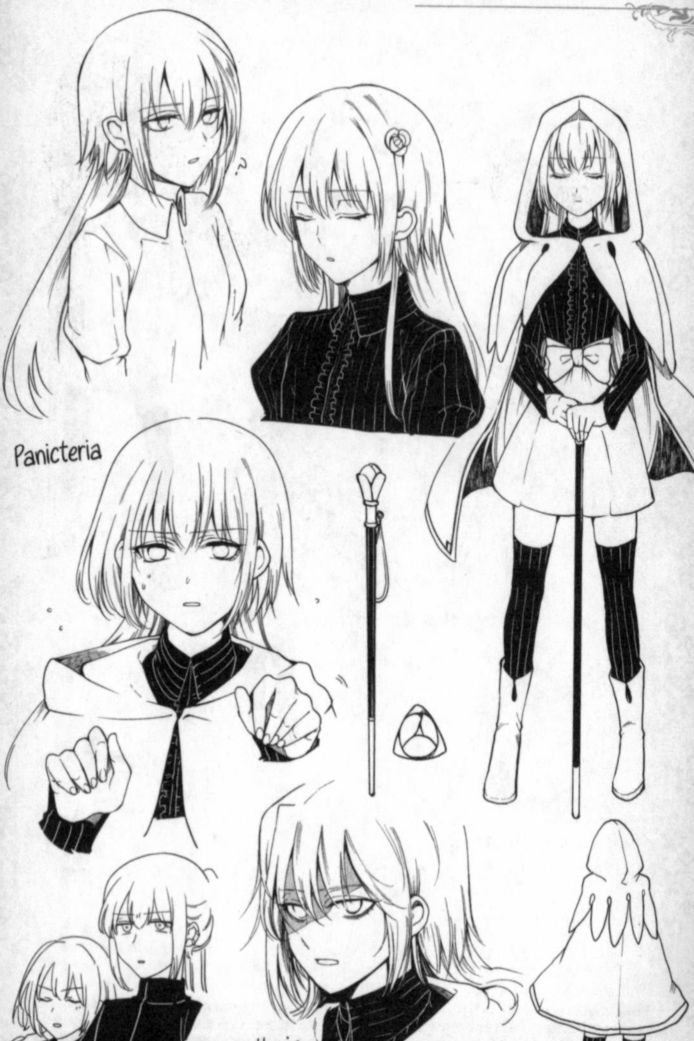

Panicteria
Pissedteria

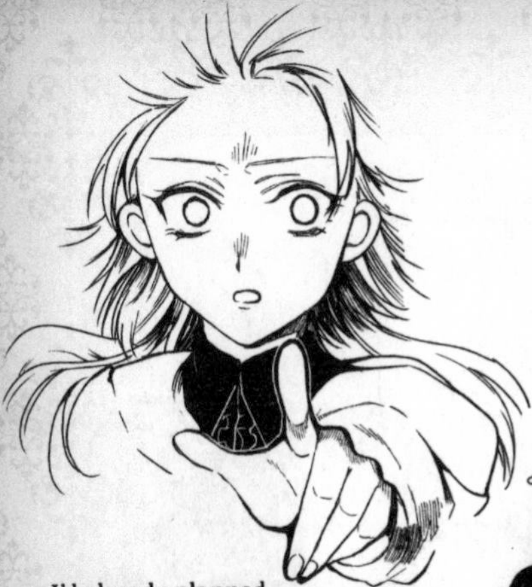

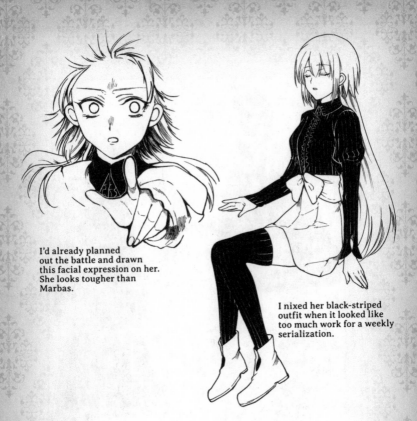

I'd already planned out the battle and drawn this facial expression on her. She looks tougher than Marbas.

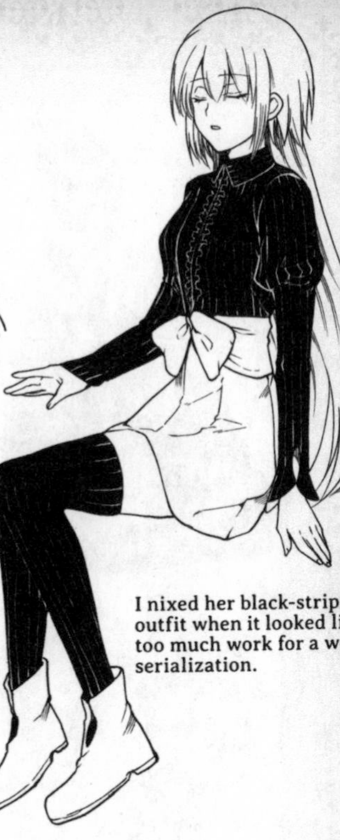

I nixed her black-striped outfit when it looked like too much work for a weekly serialization.

This Wisteria looks much closer to the final version. She had a rather somber look because she wasn't getting along with Marbas in the original storyboard. Can you imagine?

What I originally had in mind was a story of...them building trust in their relationship as they butt heads, but it didn't feel right to me. Neither of them were lovable. (laughs)

After reworking the storyboard a few times, I finally created the current version of Wisteria.

The planning stage of the series was a long, drawn-out struggle with no end in sight, but I feel it was all necessary to meet the true Wisteria.

Snow

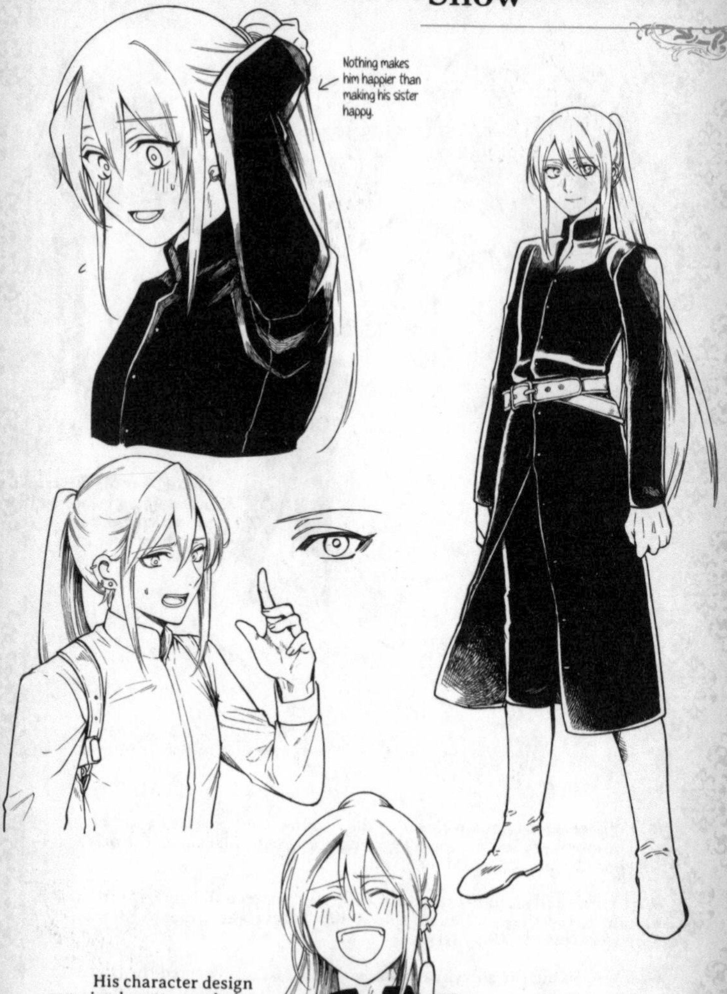
Nothing makes him happier than making his sister happy.

His character design remained pretty much the same, but these drawings look so stiff.

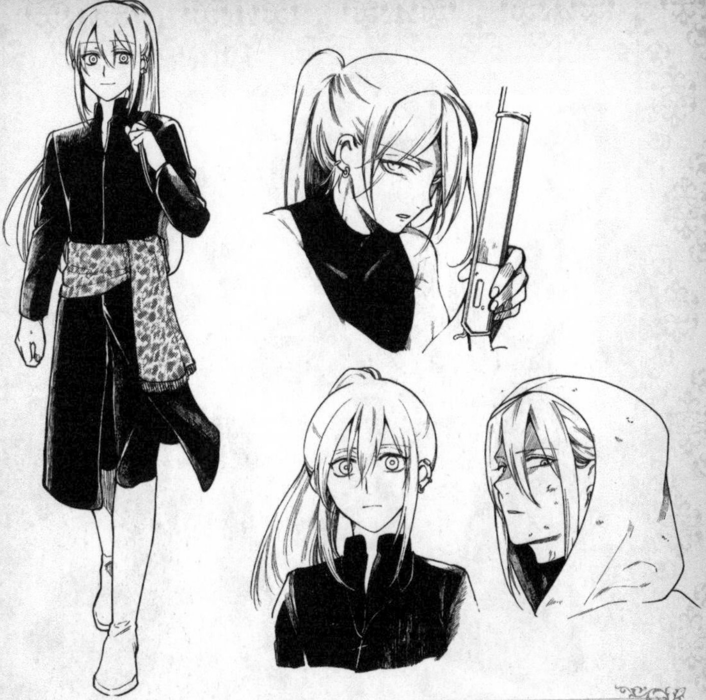

This is Big Brother Snow. I already had a clear image of his character and got my design accepted in one go. He hasn't changed one bit!

I first drew Snow around 2015. He was the hero of a one-shot manga I submitted for a monthly award in *Shonen Sunday* called the New Generation Sunday Award. That's when I decided he'd be a tough chaplain. Of course, he had his ears pierced.

I was personally very bitter that this manga ended up with the Effort Award. However, my editor lauded it highly, which made a huge impact on me.

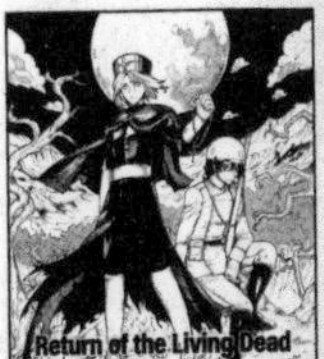
Return of the Living Dead

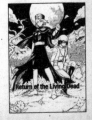

In fact, it influenced me so much that my desire to someday draw Snow in a serialization became instrumental in creating *The Tale of the Outcasts.* That must have impressed me a lot.

You may still be able to find this manga, *Return of the Living Dead,* online!

Diana

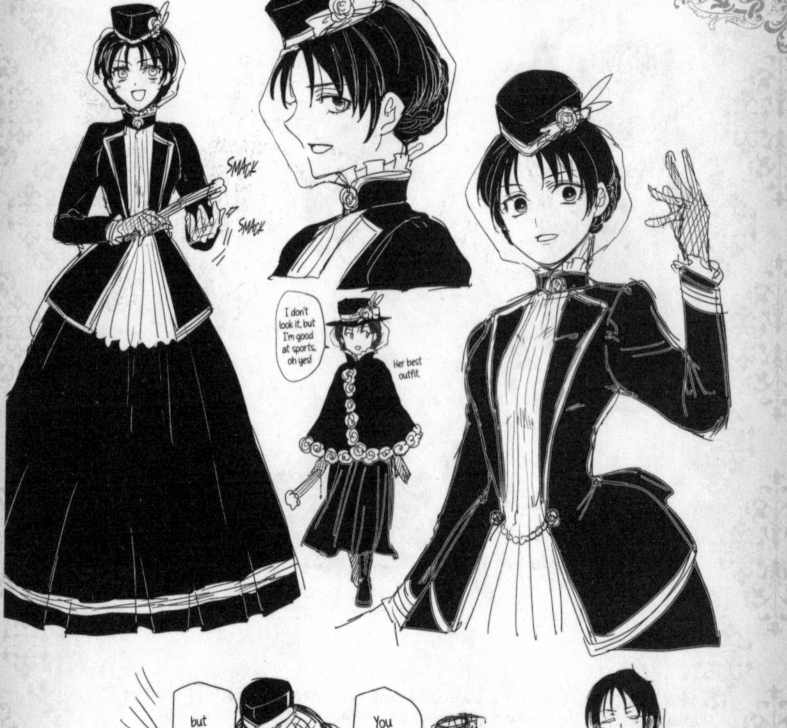
Her best outfit.
I don't look it, but I'm good at sports, oh yes!
SMACK
SMACK

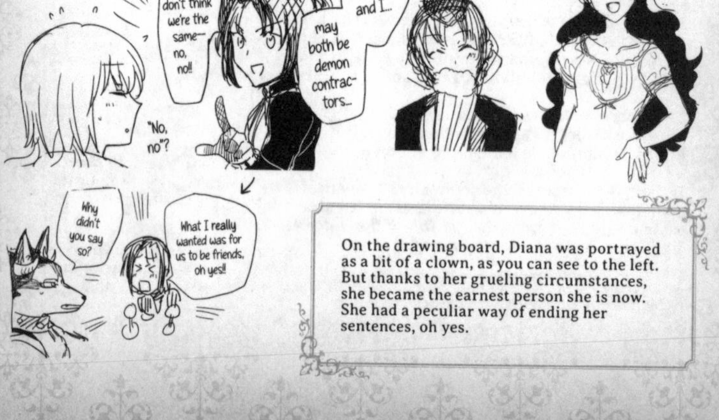
You and I...
may both be demon contractors...
but don't think we're the same—no, no!!
"No, no"?
What I really wanted was for us to be friends, oh yes!!
Why didn't you say so?

On the drawing board, Diana was portrayed as a bit of a clown, as you can see to the left. But thanks to her grueling circumstances, she became the earnest person she is now. She had a peculiar way of ending her sentences, oh yes.

Naberius

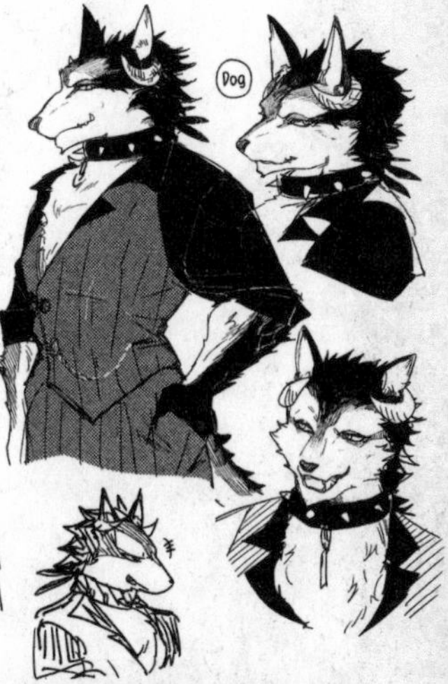
Dog

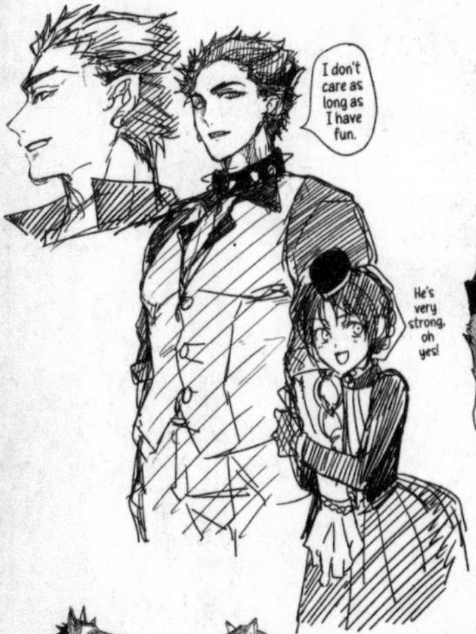
I don't care as long as I have fun.
He's very strong, oh yes!

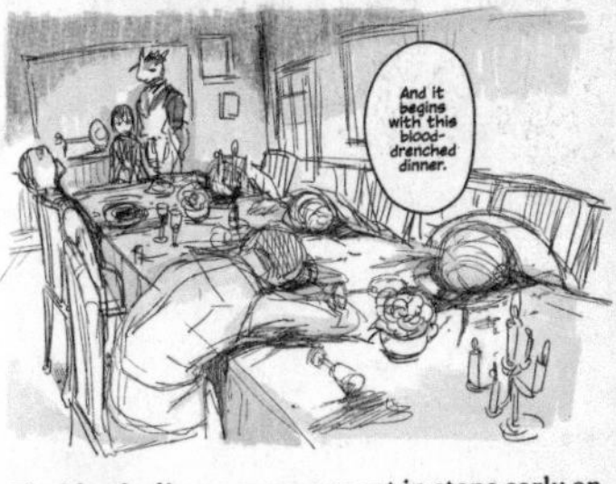
And it begins with this blood-drenched dinner.

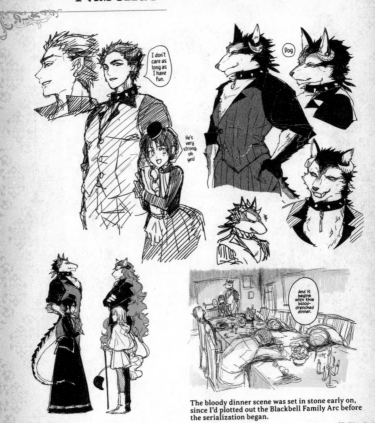

The bloody dinner scene was set in stone early on, since I'd plotted out the Blackbell Family Arc before the serialization began.

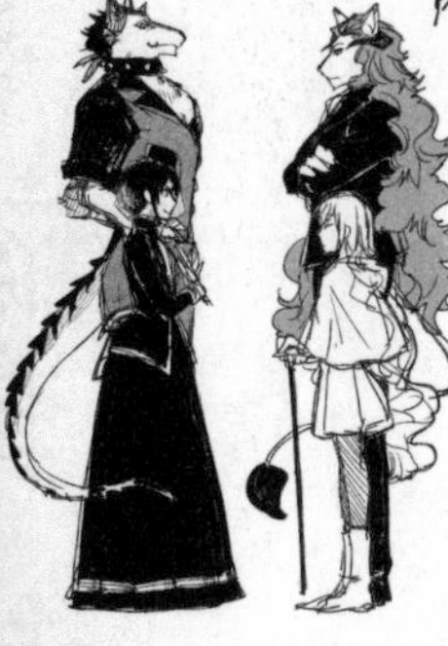

You can tell that I really wasn't used to drawing dogs here. I didn't want to show any of this, either! (laughs) Marbas was difficult enough to draw. I was wondering how I was going to handle drawing another beastman when Naberius first appeared.

For Naberius' collar, I learned that Cerberus, a monstrous dog that is identified as Naberius in demonology, usually wore a spiked dog collar. I drew a similar collar on him, but...it made him look like a dude with questionable taste in clothing.

Sword Cross Knights

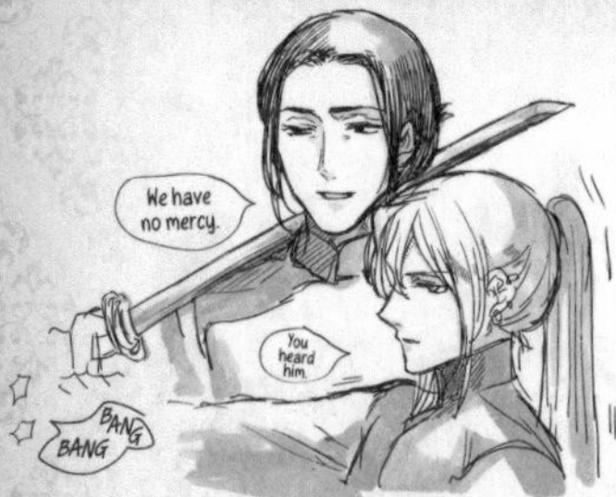
We have no mercy.
You heard him.
BANG
BANG

I did a rough sketch of this scene and kind of liked it. I used it in Night 12.

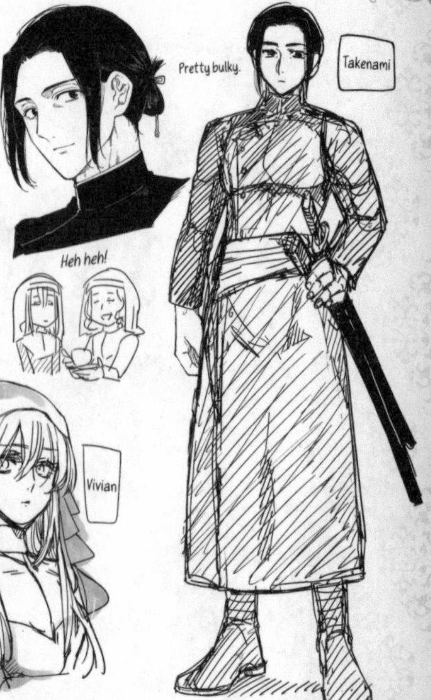
Pretty bulky.
Takenami
Heh heh!

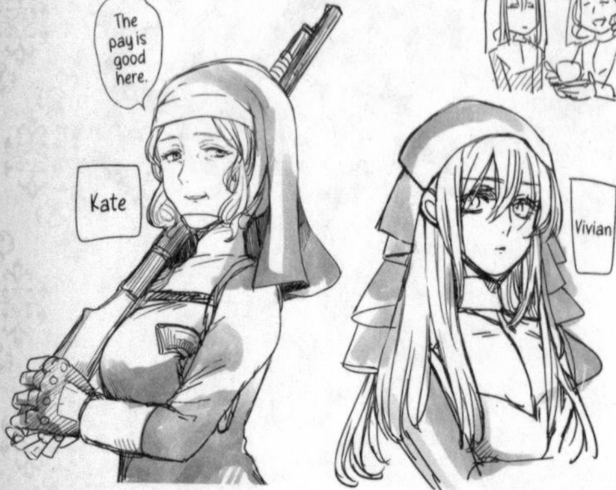
The pay is good here.
Kate
Vivian

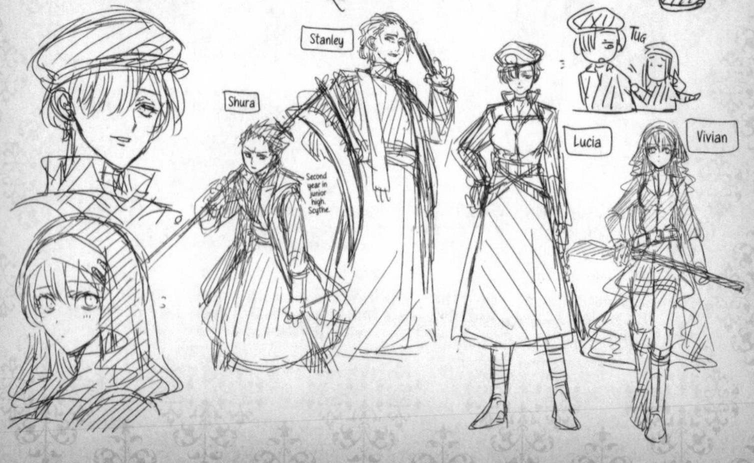
Stanley
Shura
Second year in junior high. Scythe.
TUG
Lucia
Vivian

Preliminary Rough Sketch

Astaroth

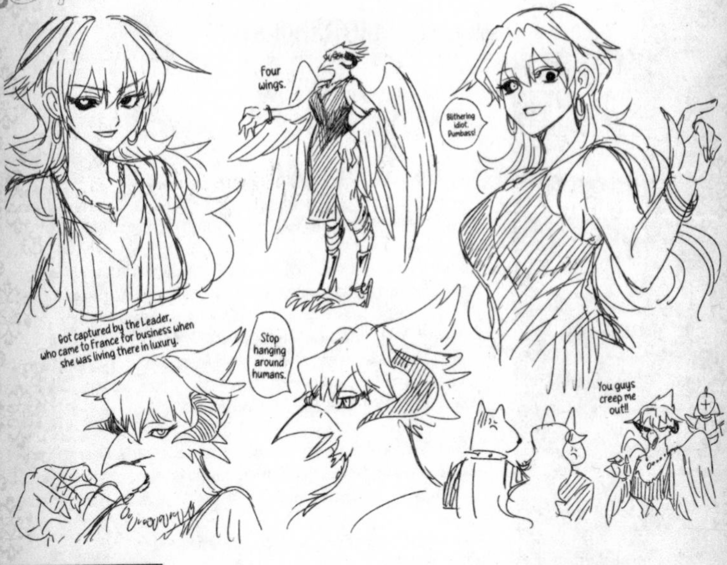

Four wings.
Blithering idiot. Dumbass!
Got captured by the Leader, who came to France for business when she was living there in luxury.
Stop hanging around humans.
You guys creep me out!!

Preliminary Rough Sketch

Marbas with Limited Release

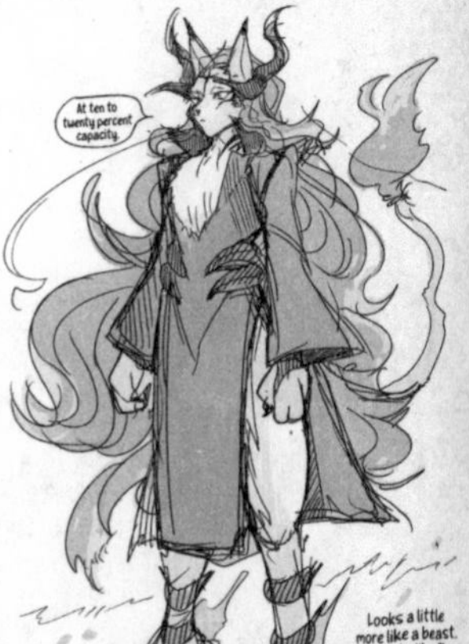

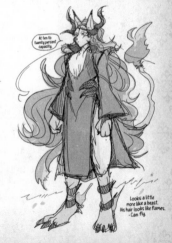

At ten to twenty percent capacity.
Looks a little more like a beast. His hair looks like flames. · Can fly.

I had so many sketches that I didn't know which ones to show at this point. There are plenty that I couldn't include here.

I took great care to be playful when I designed the Sword Cross Knights. Isn't a samurai fighting in England cool? The mom who works part-time and uses a rifle was a fantasy of mine, too. I love middle-aged women.

That's enough of my stories. It wouldn't be right to give away everything. I want my characters to have their chance to shine in this series. Don't miss it!

SEVEN SEAS ENTERTAINMENT PRESENTS

The Tale of the Outcasts

Vol. 4

story and art by MAKOTO HOSHINO

TRANSLATION
Elina Ishikawa

ADAPTATION
Ysabet Reinhardt MacFarlane

LETTERING
Brendon Hull

COVER DESIGN
Hanase Qi

PROOFREADER
Cae Hawksmoor
B. Lillian Martin

EDITOR
Shanti Whitesides

PREPRESS TECHNICIAN
Melanie Ujimori

PRINT MANAGER
annon Rasmussen–Silverstein

PRODUCTION ASSOCIATE
Christa Miesner

PRODUCTION MANAGER
Lissa Pattillo

MANAGING EDITOR
Julie Davis

ASSOCIATE PUBLISHER
Adam Arnold

PUBLISHER
Jason DeAngelis

NOKEMONO-TACHI NO YORU Vol.4
by Makoto HOSHINO
© 2019 Makoto HOSHINO
All rights reserved.
Original Japanese edition published by SHOGAKUKAN.
English translation rights in the United States of America, Canada, and the United
Kingdom arranged with SHOGAKUKAN through Tuttle-Mori Agency, Inc.

Seven Seas press and purchase enquiries can be sent to Marketing Manager Lianne
Sentar at press@gomanga.com. Information regarding the distribution and purchase of
digital editions is available from Digital Manager CK Russell at digital@gomanga.com.

Seven Seas and the Seven Seas logo are trademarks of
Seven Seas Entertainment. All rights reserved.

ISBN: 978-1-64827-580-7
Printed in Canada
First Printing: January 2022
10 9 8 7 6 5 4 3 2 1

//// READING DIRECTIONS ////

This book reads from *right to left*,
Japanese style. If this is your first time
reading manga, you start reading from
the top right panel on each page and
take it from there. If you get lost, just
follow the numbered diagram here.
It may seem backwards at first,
but you'll get the hang of it! Have fun!!

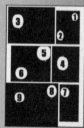

Follow us online: www.SevenSeasEntertainment.com